31

Personal Perspectives

A Guide to Decision Making

Other McGraw-Hill Titles in Home Economics

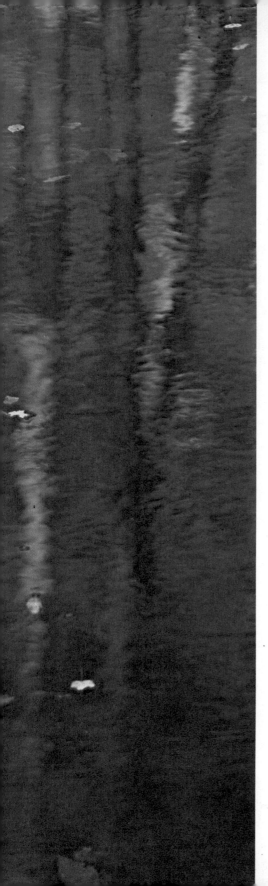

Personal Perspectives

A Guide to Decision Making

Beatrice Paolucci, Ph.D.

Professor and Acting Chairman, Department of
Family Ecology, College of Human Ecology, Michigan
State University

Theodora Faiola, M.A.

Regional Supervisor, Bureau of Homemaking
Education, California State Department of Education

Patricia Thompson, M.A.

Adjunct Lecturer, Department of Family and
Consumer Studies, Herbert H. Lehman College

Janet Kiser, B.S., formerly a senior high
school home economics teacher and 4-H
agent in New Jersey, developed the case
studies and the *Think Back* and *Look
Around* sections of each chapter.

Webster Division   McGraw-Hill Book Company

New York St. Louis San Francisco Dallas Montreal Toronto

Acknowledgments

The authors wish to thank the following people for reviewing portions of the manuscript:

Frank J. Antonini, Project ACTION; Catherine Cowell, Bureau of Nutrition, Department of Health, City of New York; Donna Newberry Creasy, WHAT'S NEW IN HOME ECONOMICS; Marcella Guiney, Dairy Council of Metropolitan New York; Sandra Hagman, Wheat Flour Institute; Evadna Hammersley, American Sheep Producers Council, Inc.; Elizabeth Handy, United States Department of Agriculture; Gloria Hansen, National Canners Association; Pat Hewson, Rice Council; Martha Johnston, American Meat Institute; Mary Bushee Murphy, WHAT'S NEW IN HOME ECONOMICS; Patricia Myles, Poultry and Egg National Board; Dr. Norma Newmark, Department of Family and Consumer Studies, Herbert H. Lehman College; Nathalie D. Preston, Brooklyn Bureau of Community Service; Dr. Sidney Schwartz, Department of Family and Consumer Studies, Herbert H. Lehman College; Reba Staggs, National Live Stock and Meat Board; Gail Steves, National Marine Fisheries Service; Jane Uetz, United Fresh Fruit and Vegetable Association; Ruth Weisheit, Cereal Institute, Inc.

Editorial Development:	Tom Mellers
Illustration Program:	Mary Ann DeMers
Editing and Styling:	Paul Farrell
Design:	Walter Schwarz
Production:	Al Lambiase

Library of Congress Cataloging in Publication Data
Main entry under title:
Personal perspectives.

SUMMARY: A senior high school home economics text which focuses on decision making.

1. Home economics. 2. Decision-making. [1. Home economics. 2. Decision making]
[TX167.P42]   640   72-8842
ISBN 0-07-048437-6

When I was a child,
I spake as a child,
I understood as a child,
I thought as a child:
but when I became a man,
I put away childish things.

I Corinthians, 13:11

Contents

UNIT TWO: **Perspectives on Food**   **101**

Making Decisions

The purpose of *Personal Perspectives* is to help you to sharpen your focus on your own life. It is to help you gain a clearer idea of who you are and how you got that way. It is to help you decide where you want to go and how you best can get there. The purpose is, in other words, to help you gain a measure of control over your future. To do this you have to pay a price: You have to accept responsibility for what you do.

Begin now to accept responsibility. Below are the first *steps* on each of four *paths*.

These *paths* stretch through Unit One. They will help you to apply to your own life what you will learn in the text.

Some *paths* must be traveled alone. One or more classmates may join you on others. Perhaps your teacher can help you choose the most worthwhile *path* for you.

Agree now to take the *steps* at the end of each chapter. Follow your *path* to the end of Unit One.

PATH ONE: Keep a Log

Your log should be a personal record of what you do, think, and feel.

Step 1 Obtain some 3 by 5 index cards. Every day, write about yourself for five minutes. Begin each new thought on a new index card. Try to write a little bit about many different things. Keep your record honestly. Do not dismiss anything as too silly or unimportant. Keep your log up to date throughout this entire unit.

PATH TWO: Write a Skit

Write a ten-minute skit about a family.

Step 1 List your characters. Next to each character's name, write his age and his place in the family. Are one or both parents present? Are there any children? Are there any relatives or friends living with the family? How many family members work? What do they do? How much does each earn? Be specific; if you do not know how much a certain job pays, call an employer or employment agency, or read the "help wanted" column of a local newspaper.

Step 2 Describe the setting. Does this family live in a city? A town? An apartment? A house?

Step 3 Outline your plot. Many successful plays revolve around resolving some kind of conflict. Conflict makes the play exciting. Be sure your plot contains some conflict. (It may arise from a simple disagreement between two family members.)

PATH THREE: Play a Role

Form a "family" with three or four classmates.

Steps 1 and 2 Same as Steps 1 and 2 for Path Two.

Step 3 Have a meeting to discuss which "family member" each of you will play.

Step 4 Each "family member" should then take on a personality to suit his role. Will you be noisy or quiet? Aggressive or shy?

Do not discuss your new personality with other members of your classroom family. Keep them in suspense.

Step 5 Without planning, act out the following scene: The family member who earns the most has been laid off for two weeks. The family must get by on other sources of income. Discuss how.

Tape-record or take notes.

PATH FOUR: Sponsor a Child

Alone or with classmates, form an imaginary social service agency to help young children.

Step 1 Each member of the agency should pretend to assume the responsibility for a child under ten years of age. The child you "sponsor" should be one you know—he may live in your neighborhood. Whoever he is, choose someone who needs help.

Make up a name for this child. Do not tell the child what you are doing. To protect the child, do not tell anyone his real name.

Step 2 In order of importance, list what you feel your child needs. Compare your list with the lists of others in your agency. Overall, what seem to be the most urgent needs?

Step 3 Suppose your community government has given $75 a month to help your child. You cannot give the money directly to the child or his parents. You may only buy things for the child. How will you spend a month's $75? List the items you buy and their cost. Check prices in stores or newspaper ads.

You and Your Life

"Where are you?"

"I am on Liberty Avenue."

"Is there anything you need?"

"I need three dollars to buy a new belt."

The answers to some questions seem so simple. They are not. Yes, you are on Liberty Avenue or Cosgrove Street or Fordham Road. You live in Pittsburgh or Valley City or Quebec. You are a citizen of the United States or Canada. You live on the planet earth.

Those three dollars may seem important at the moment, but *must* you really have them? Certainly, you could stay alive without a new belt. A belt is hardly as vital as food, or sleep, or friendship. When thought of in this broader context, the belt becomes less important.

Here in Chapter 1 we will discuss some of the things that shape your choices. We will discuss your obligations to yourself, to your fellow man, and to your surroundings.

HUMAN LIFE AND HUMAN ECOLOGY

All human beings belong to one species, which we call *homo sapiens,* or man the wise. We call ourselves wise because we have both "brain power" and "muscle power."

Because of brain power, we can use symbols, like words and numbers, which can help us to *reason.* They can, in other words, help us to put things in order in our minds.

Many elements have been added to the environment which did not exist even a few years ago. This continues to happen with such speed that it is sometimes difficult for man to see any order in his surroundings.

They can help us to communicate our thoughts and needs and plans.

Only the human species can record its past and envision a future. Man alone can have hopes and dreams and can act to realize them. He can make choices that are based on reason; he can make *rational* choices.

One Species: One Environment

Your *environment* is made up of all the living and nonliving things around you. The word embraces everything from governments and parades to trees and air. In the broadest sense, your environment is the planet earth. This is the *habitat,* or home, you share with all other living things. The word *environment* also refers to more limited surroundings. One might refer to the environment of a city or a home.

The study of the patterns of relationship between *homo sapiens* and his environment is called *human ecology.* It grew from the science of *ecology,* which is the study of the patterns of relationships between any environment and the organisms which inhabit it.

Our changing environment Our environment is complex. We are surrounded by information from newspapers and television. We are threatened by bombs and saved by medicines. Machines are nearly everywhere. These and other inventions have changed our world. It is changing still.

Your near environment Your *near environment* includes your home and family. This special place is more within your control than is the world at large. At home, you have the opportunity to make choices about things like food, clothing, and shelter. There, you form emotional relationships with other family members. Within your home, you have the opportunity to establish a highly individual style of life.

4

Natural resources have always been limited, but the modern world can exceed those limits. Most people feel that starvation and disease, two natural means of easing the strain on resources, should not occur. We are challenged to maintain the balance of nature in ways we can accept.

The Balance of Nature

Human life is possible because animals, plants, microorganisms, and nonliving things provide us with the means to survive. From them we take our food, our clothing, and our shelter. The plants and animals on which we depend are also dependent upon one another. Plants use sun, water, and soil. Animals eat plants and other animals. Everything in nature is interrelated and balanced. Everything depends on the natural environment and at the same time shapes it. If we are to survive, we must see to it that the living and nonliving things we need survive also. We are challenged to preserve a balance of nature which is favorable to us.

This is a challenge that primitive man, for the most part, did not have to face. His ability to permanently change his world was limited. A few berries that would not grow into new plants or a bison that was caught and killed did not upset the balance of nature. New berries still grew. New bison were still born. Even if primitive man did manage to make his immediate environment unusable, he was able and willing to move to new land.

However, the human population increased. Man developed his technology. The changes he made improved the quality of life, but they did not always maintain the environment. We have scooped out the earth to reach coal and iron ore for factories. Then we have left the earth scarred, its ecological balance unfavorably changed. We use steel to make automobiles and household appliances which ease our lives. But the factories in which this steel is made also cough up smoke which fouls the air we breathe. We are using up irreplaceable natural resources; we are endangering some forms of life. If we are not to become extinct ourselves, we must take steps to preserve the balance of nature. We must make responsible decisions about the use of the earth's limited resources. We must ask ourselves what effects our decisions will have on our total environment. We must ask ourselves what effect they will have on the quality of life that today's and tomorrow's people will enjoy.

IDENTIFYING BASIC HUMAN NEEDS

You have *basic needs* that you must meet if you are to lead a fully satisfying life. It is to meet these needs that you do many of the things you do. Four kinds of basic needs are: physical, psychological, social, and spiritual. These are the same for every human being, although they may be met in any number of different ways.

Basic needs are not to be confused with acquired needs, or *wants*. Wants also influence behavior, but meeting them is not necessary for leading a satisfying life.

Physical Needs

Physical needs are biological requirements. Unless they are met, you cannot stay alive. It is necessary, for example, to have air, water, food, sunshine, and space. You must rid your body of wastes. You must maintain a steady body temperature and protect yourself from exposure to radiation and disease. You help meet these basic needs by your choices of food, clothing, and shelter.

Today, because of population growth, proper food and living space are in short

This strip-mined land represents the effect of a decision made by industry. Yet, as the world population grows, even individual decisions concerning the use of resources can have a tremendous collective effect.

supply in many parts of the world. Even fresh air and water are becoming scarce. In large cities, tall buildings block the sun.

To satisfy our physical needs, we use the earth's resources. Because these are limited, we must work and plan together if we are all to survive.

Psychological Needs

As a human being, you need more than food and shelter. You have a complex brain and nervous system. You have a mind and you have emotions. You have psychological needs.

To be fully human, you must satisfy these needs. You need to love and be loved. You need to know who you are. You need to feel safe and secure. At the same time, you need to feel independent. You also need to make sense of your environment and your experiences.

People feel psychological needs in varying degrees at different times. They meet these needs in different ways. Often they are satisfying psychological needs when they seem to be satisfying physical needs. Food and clothing, for example, are often used to satisfy psychological needs.

The need for love Of all our emotional needs, our need for love is the most basic and ongoing. At different times in life, we experience the need for love in different ways. For the helpless baby, love is felt in response to physical care. Love means being kept dry, fed, and warm. It means being cuddled. As the infant's nervous system develops, he can sort out the many impressions he receives from his environment. He connects the care he receives with the people who provide that care. A gentle touch, reassuring sounds, and firm support while a baby is cleaned, clothed, and fed create a feeling of trust. The baby learns to trust the people who care for him. He learns to trust the world around him. This feeling of basic trust is the cornerstone of all forms of love—both love

The earliest solution to the problem of getting enough food was to increase nature's supply. We learned to ranch and farm rather than to hunt and forage. This man is "checking the crop" on a fish farm in Thailand.

of self and love of others. A person who feels unloved cannot love others.

The need for safety and security All human needs are ongoing needs. They may be stronger or more intense at one time than another, but none are met once and for all. A person needs to feel that physical and psychological needs, once met, will continue to be met. Knowing this, he will feel safe and secure. Learning to make choices that will satisfy present needs and that will put you in a position to satisfy future needs will help you to develop and maintain feelings of security.

The need for independence The more control you gain over yourself and your environment, the more independent you will be.

7

People develop such control gradually, with experience and opportunity. Young children show their independence in small ways: by sitting up, crawling, standing, and walking. They demonstrate their need for independence when they struggle to drink and eat by themselves. Later, children and young adults gain independence by achieving success in meeting tasks beyond the home—at school, at work, and in personal relations.

The need for a personal identity Each human being needs to feel that he is a distinct and separate person. He needs to establish a personality, an individual identity. A sense of personal identity comes through a long and sometimes painful process of growing and developing. As you developed from infancy to young adulthood, you passed into and out of a number of identities. You are now experiencing the need to form a new identity as a young adult. All your previous identities will contribute to your new sense of self.

Your sense of self includes your ideas of who you think you are. It is influenced by what others think of you. It is influenced by what you think they think of you. Successful adjustment involves putting all these selves together into a unified personality.

Your **self-concept** is your feeling of who you are and who you are becoming. It began to form when you were born, when you were physically separated from your mother. For a time, your self-concept was tied to the person who cared for your infant needs—your mother, or a mother substitute. Gradually you became aware of *your* fingers, *your* toes, and other parts of *your* body. As you grew and changed, your self-concept also changed. It was influenced by the way other people

In "An Old Man And His Grandson," Ghirlandaio captured the tenderness, admiration, and love that every human being needs. He recorded every detail of the old man's face. Does this make the painting more effective?

I am a child in these hills
I am away, I am alone
I am a child in these hills
And looking for water
And looking for water.

Who will show me the river
And ask me my name
There's nobody near me to do that
I have to come to these hills
I will come to the river
As I choose to be gone
From the house of my father
I am a child in these hills
I am a child in these hills.

treated you. When they treated you with love, kindness, and understanding, they helped you to develop favorable feelings about yourself. They helped you to feel like a worthwhile person, and helped you to develop a positive self-concept. When they ignored, mistreated, or rejected you, they influenced you to develop unfavorable feelings about yourself. They influenced you to feel like an unworthy person. At such times your self-concept was negative.

No matter how you feel about yourself, you may project another "you" to others. People react to your **public image**. They react to what they see. They react to your appearance and your behavior, rather than to your private thoughts and feelings.

Many of the activities which you perform are defined by society. These activities are known as *roles*. You assume roles as a family member and as a student. You have friends or acquaintances and you may have a job. In time, you may become a marriage partner

It is not necessary that your self-concept, your public image, and your ideal image be identical. If they are too different, however, it may be difficult to establish a continuing sense of personal identity.

and a parent. You behave differently in each of the roles that you assume. Consequently, you may have a number of public images.

You also have an **ideal image**. This is your idea of who you would like to be and who you would like others to think you are.

Your self-concept, your public images, and your ideal image are pieces of the complex puzzle of personality. You can fit these pieces together. You can begin now to create a unified self, or *integrated personality*. To do this involves your seeing yourself objectively—as others see you. It involves making careful choices about the way that you look and the way that you behave.

The need for stimulation and variety You can see and smell and taste and touch and hear. You can use your senses to pick up messages from your rich and complex environment. You can use them to meet your need for stimulation and variety. Through your choice of friends and recreation, you can make your life more varied and exciting. You can learn to select food, clothing, shelter, and activities which help to satisfy this need for stimulation and variety.

Social Needs

You do not usually satisfy your physical and psychological needs by yourself. Other people often provide the means for you to meet them. You, in turn, have opportunities to interact with others and to meet their needs in many ways. People offer each other love. They provide each other with safety and security. They create for one another the social setting in which personality develops.

People also have certain basic needs which are distinctly social. These needs not only can be satisfied through groups; they could not be satisfied without groups. People need, for example, to belong and to be accepted as members of a group. They need recognition and approval from their group. Their group must also provide ways for each group member to feel a sense of accomplishment, either alone or as a part of the group.

The family is the first group to which an individual belongs. Later, this individual comes to depend on other people and groups, as well. One of the largest of these groups is a society.

It is characteristic of groups to generally respond to similar situations in similar ways. These similar forms of behavior are called *customs*. Customary behavior makes social relations easier. A person feels safer and more secure when he has some idea of what others expect of him. Children learn the customs of the group to which they belong early in life.

Some groups have a distinct combination of customs and beliefs. There is a particular pattern to the ways in which their members act and in the kinds of things which they produce. Such groups are said to have a unique *culture*. The members of a cultural group share a common life-style.

Many food, clothing, and shelter customs vary with different cultural groups. Language also frequently differs. You may take some customs—such as eating with a knife and fork—for granted. It is just as natural for other people to eat with their fingers or with chopsticks. Like you, they were taught to do so as children.

People tend to look at the way they are accustomed to doing things as the only way to do them. As their contacts with different cultures increase, they may begin to realize that cultural differences determine the "how" and "why" of much human behavior.

Today, more and more people are aware that customs vary. This is partly because these people receive more information about different cultures. It is also because so many modern societies contain a number of subgroups, each of which has its own subculture. The United States, for example, has some subgroups which have arisen from within. One subgroup, the Indians, predated the coming of the first European. Still others comprise peoples who wish to preserve the cultural traditions of their forefathers from Africa, Europe, Latin America, or Asia. In their own way, each of these subgroups presents a challenge to American society as a whole; each offers some alternate ways of behaving.

CASE STUDY: MARIE

THE SITUATION   *Marie brought a group of younger girls to a Spring Festival sponsored by a local young people's organization. She had been hesitant at first because the girls were shy. They were unknown to most of the people there. Still, she decided to take advantage of this opportunity for them to mix with others their own age.*

Her girls had participated in a few activities during the evening. Now they were engaged in serious conversation with three other girls. The chaperone from the group approached Marie, saying, "My girls said your girls were writing on the mirror and throwing paper cups in the restroom. My girls cleaned up after them."

Marie glared at the chaperone. "Did they actually see my girls do it?"

The chaperone nodded. Marie walked angrily away.

THE INTERVIEW   *Q: Do you think your girls did litter the restroom and mark the mirrors?*
A: They said the other girls did it. They told the girls to stop because they knew they'd be blamed for the mess.
Q: Why is this situation so serious? The room was cleaned. Why not overlook the incident? Your girls are young. Are they really affected by this situation?
A: Have you ever been suspected of doing something you didn't do? How would you feel?
Q: What are you going to do?
A: Nothing. But we'll never come back here.

REACT   *What creates such gaps between groups of people? If you were Marie or the chaperone, how would you handle this situation?*

In a process called socialization, children learn from family and society what their culture expects of them. At mealtime, for example, a child may learn what is considered to be polite behavior. He may also gain an insight into the larger roles of men and women in his culture. How are your customs similar to or different from those of the Hawaiians, Japanese, and Nigerians?

Societies can grow through gradually incorporating different ideas and customs. They can meet their members' needs for safety and security through orderly change—through change that is built on what they have learned from the past. By whatever means, a society should provide some ways to fulfill the basic social needs, as well as the basic physical and psychological needs, which human beings share.

The need to belong   Social groups set rules for belonging. These rules may be based on custom; some are enforced by laws. Those who accept the rules, or *conform*, are "in." They are accepted as group members. Those who do not conform are "out." They may be looked upon as social outcasts. Because different groups have different rules, one group's nonconformist may become another group's ideal member.

Within their families, young people may conform to the rules set down by their parents. Gradually they may learn to act in ways that may entitle them to membership in an outside group. When there is too great a difference between the customs of their family and the customs of their friends, a "generation gap" exists. (Friendly relations can still exist across this gap.)

A person experiences the need to belong in different ways throughout his life. As a child, he needs support, comfort, and security from his family. Later he will seek membership in a team, a club, or a circle of friends. In the teens, he feels a strong need to be accepted by his *peer group*, by the group made up of his age mates. As personality matures, dependence on peer group acceptance decreases. Acceptance by other mature individuals, regardless of age, increases in importance.

The need for recognition and approval Closely related to the need to belong is the need for recognition and approval. You need to be appreciated by some group.

The members of every culture and subculture give rewards for certain kinds of behavior. The kind of reward which is given and the kind of behavior for which it is given depend on the particular group. Some rewards—like money and large houses—are material; other rewards—like power and fame—are impossible to touch. The kind of behavior which merits these rewards may vary. It may be an ability to sing or a skill with numbers. Groups also have punishments for those of whom they disapprove.

The need to achieve   Each person has a need to feel a sense of accomplishment. No one who constantly fails can develop a healthy personality. Some adults make it hard for young people to achieve. They often do this in the belief that they will encourage striving. For those young people who experience failure and defeat instead, this approach may have the opposite effect. Little successes are more likely to stimulate further striving than are failures. Everyone needs to feel that he can succeed at something.

Spiritual Needs

A spiritual need is a need to understand the mysteries of the natural environment and of human existence. Men have always had such needs. Evidence from early times, from the caves and burial places of our distant ancestors, suggests that man has always tried to comprehend these mysteries. Modern man has developed science, art, philosophy, and religion to deepen his understanding of what it means to be human.

In examining the forces of nature, man is constantly reminded of his limitations. He becomes aware that no matter how far science pushes the frontiers of knowledge, something more lies just beyond his grasp. His spiritual needs remain and must be satisfied. We admit to our spiritual needs when we strive to live in harmony with nature and our fellow man.

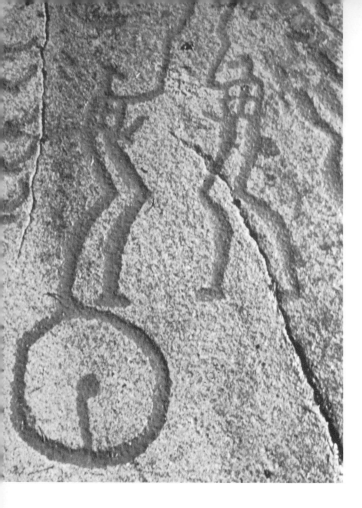

A cave painting in Sweden showing the God Thor on the Wheel of the World is an ancient answer to questions we still ask: How is the universe governed? What is man's place in it? What does it mean to be human?

Overarching Needs

Our basic needs are not separate and distinct from one another. They all exist all the time within us all. The intensity with which you feel any need at any given time is related to how well all your other needs are being met. Two overarching needs, the need for need reduction and the need for self-fulfillment, help us to see how all our needs are interdependent.

The need for need reduction We have a need to reduce needs by satisfying them.

We need to satisfy our most urgent needs first. The psychologist Abraham Maslow has suggested that needs can be ranked by levels of intensity. He calls this ranking the *hierarchy of needs.* He says: "For the man who is extremely and dangerously hungry, no other interest exists but food." In other words, physical needs should generally be met before all others, because they are more urgent. Here, we are considering psychological needs to be more urgent than social needs. We are considering social needs to be more urgent than spiritual needs.

The need for self-fulfillment Each person has a need to realize his own physical, psychological, social, and spiritual potential. He needs to develop his abilities and use his talents. You can make choices that bring you closer to meeting your own need for self-fulfillment. The more you know about yourself, the better able you will be to make these choices.

Men and women have overcome extreme hardships, handicaps, and adversity to make lasting contributions to the betterment of human life and the uplifting of the human spirit. Beethoven created musical masterpieces after he became deaf. Helen Keller overcame blindness, deafness, and muteness to inspire others, with fewer handicaps, to great achievements. George Washington Carver overcame both poverty and prejudice to become an agricultural chemist. His research and experiments have had a widespread influence on soil conservation in the South. The lives of many great men and women reveal that they had serious personal, physical, social, or economic obstacles to overcome on the road to success and self-fulfillment.

SATISFYING BASIC NEEDS

To live a satisfying life, people must have most of their needs met most of the time. If your need for food is not met, you will starve. If your need for water is not met, you will die of thirst. If your psychological and social needs are not met, you may feel tense. Needs need to be satisfied. They are forces within you which push, or *motivate*, you to act.

Sometimes, in striving to satisfy a need, you meet an obstacle. You may seek the acceptance of your peer group, for example, and they may reject you. You may try to win a race and lose. In such cases, it is not surprising to feel *frustration*. Some frustration is to be expected in our daily lives. We have to learn to live with it. There are ways to temporarily reduce some frustration. These may be called *coping strategies*.

When Needs Are Not Met

Frustration, which a person feels when he has not been able to meet his needs, shows itself in several ways. Most often, a frustrated person tends to become angry or frightened.

On the one hand, a person can put this anger and fear to work to help him satisfy the unmet needs which helped cause them. Out of fear, for example, he might run away from a situation that threatens his safety and security. Out of anger, he might fight to keep something which he must have. In both cases, he channels the energy from these emotions toward fulfilling a need.

On the other hand, misdirected anger and fear can add further stress and tension. This is especially true if a person holds these emotions inside him. Unexpressed fear and anger can turn into resentment and hostility. They can leave someone feeling helpless, distrustful, and alone. If these emotions remain unexpressed for a long time, a person may become extemely antisocial.

Sometimes societies fail to provide the climate for whole groups of people to meet their basic needs. In such cases, difficult social problems—even mob violence—may result.

Self-actualization Needs

Self-esteem Needs

Social Needs

Security Needs

Physical Needs

Dr. Abraham Maslow has ranked human needs on five main levels: physical needs, security needs, social needs, self-esteem needs, and self-actualization needs. These levels exist simultaneously, but in a hierarchy of strength. Only when the lower needs have been more or less satisfied do the higher needs become active. How does Maslow's ranking of needs compare with what you have read in this text?

Many people rely on their sense of humor to help them cope with stress. Humor as a coping strategy may become an identifying characteristic; it may be as simple as the laugh that offsets embarrassment.

Coping Strategies

We can use coping strategies to help reduce frustration. We might cope with stress by "letting off steam." We might dance, or play tennis, or simply go for a walk. Such exercise can help us to unwind, to feel more relaxed. We might also cope with stress in the opposite way—by sleeping or by resting. People cope by telling jokes and solving puzzles. They cope by "forgetting" such unpleasant situations as appointments with the dentist.

One common coping strategy is *substitution*. We have already discussed this: it is when a person substitutes wants for basic needs. Another well-known coping strategy is *sublimation*. A person sublimates when he satisfies a higher need instead of an unmet lower need. The Italian artist Michelangelo, for example, was quite unsuccessful at forming close friendships. Yet, he was one of the world's greatest artists.

Many people *rationalize*. If they find themselves in a situation in which they look foolish, they refuse to admit it. They must preserve their self-concept at all costs. They explain circumstances to themselves in such a way that—to themselves, at least—they appear in a good light. A girl who is ignored by her classmates, for example, might deny her wish to be accepted by them. "They are all snobs," she might say. "I wouldn't want to be part of such a group."

Other people admit that needs are unmet. They are unable, however, to accept responsibility for this failure. They put the blame for their failure to meet needs on someone else, on someone called a *scapegoat*. "John kept me from studying. Otherwise, I would have gotten a *B* on that test." In this case, John has been made a scapegoat.

Daydreaming is another way to cope with tensions. A daydreamer imagines he has the cars, clothing, jewels, or love that he wants. This coping strategy can spur people to turn their dreams into reality. It can also lead them to postpone making the decisions that would help them to realize their desires.

From time to time we all use coping strategies of one kind or another. They can be temporarily helpful. They cannot, however, offer anyone the long-term satisfaction he might feel from having met his basic needs.

CHOICE AND CHANGE

Man changes. In the past, we changed slowly. We were able to adapt to the gradual alterations in our environment. Now, with the help of the new tools we have invented, we are able to exert greater control over our surroundings. We have the power to make better use of our world. We also have the power to upset the balance of nature upon which we depend. Given particular knowledge and understanding, everyday events no longer need "just happen." We can influence them. Our destiny, the direction of our future evolution, can be affected by the choices that we make.

CASE STUDY: ALLEN

THE SITUATION   *Allen is nineteen, and for six years has been a member of Rhythm Riders, a large horse-riding club. In spite of the fact that he has a part time job, he participates enthusiastically in almost all activities sponsored by the club. He has gained the reputation for being "full of fun," a "natural-born leader," and a "great guy to have around." Most of his friends were club members, and Allen has scrapbook memories of the things they did together over the years.*

Another person with leadership qualities has recently joined the club. She thinks that younger club members should be encouraged to assume responsibility and voice opinions. She is opposed to the way Al "takes over."

THE INTERVIEW   *Q: Allen, do you think she has judged the situation correctly?*
A: No. Inexperienced kids need a leader.
Q: Can't she guide them?
A: I'm the most experienced person around. I've done everything for this club.
Q: Do your friends think the club will fall apart?
A: They couldn't care less. They are working or going to school now. They've resigned.
Q: Don't your school work and part-time job keep you pretty busy? How do you find time for club work, too?
A: I manage. I'd rather come to these meetings than hang around with the "do-nothings" at school.

THINK BACK

We ought to think about the world beyond the near environment.
Discuss: *Are we each "our brother's keeper"?*

Each person is responsible to others, as well as to himself, for the decisions he makes.
Discuss: *Is it unrealistic to expect a teenager to think of others first?*

Every human being has the same basic needs.
Discuss: *Will knowing this help eliminate unfairness to others in your community?*

The satisfaction of basic needs influences our behavior.
Discuss: *Is the person who does things "just for kicks" being honest?*

Separating wants from needs makes decision making easier.
Discuss: *Who decides what you want and what you need?*

LOOK AROUND

1. What is the most outstanding feature of your own "near" environment? Bring to class an object or the picture of an object that well represents that feature. Explain your selection to class members.

2. Which basic need appears strongest in the children, teenagers, and adults you know? How is that need expressed in each age group?

3. What is a culture? What is a subculture? Which are represented in your high school class?

4. Might a person satisfy the basic needs of others before first satisfying his own basic needs?

5. What are examples of crimes that might occur when an individual's basic needs are not met? As a lawmaker, what penalties would you impose on the offender in each crime?

6. What is a self-concept? How does it develop? What are the characteristics

of people you know who seem to have positive self-concepts?

7. In your opinion, who plays the most important role in the development of each family member's self-concept? Suggest some ways in which you may influence the self-concept of members of your own family.

FOLLOW YOUR PATH

PATH ONE: Keep a Log

Step 2 Separate your log entries into those that refer to met needs and wants, those that refer to unmet needs and wants, and those that do not seem to refer to any needs or wants at all. Separate your met needs and wants into those referring to each basic need (the need to belong, the need for a personal identity, and so on). Some entries may seem to fit in more than one category. Others may not fit easily in any. Place these entries where you think they most belong.

Count the entries for each met need and want. List them. Do the same for the unmet needs.

Step 3 Which two met needs and wants did you refer to most? Which two did you refer to least? What about unmet needs and wants? Explain these results. Refer to the hierarchy of needs chart.

Step 4 The third category of log entries is directly concerned with the environment. List the three kinds of things you most discussed (clothing, people, or whatever). Do these interests reflect the way you meet your needs and wants? Write a short paragraph discussing this point.

PATH TWO: Write a Skit

Step 4 Write a short paragraph on each of your main characters. Describe the wants and needs which most affect each of them.

Step 5 The environment influences what people do. Write a paragraph for each of two main characters. Explain how each might have been different if he had lived in a different place.

Step 6 Which character in your play do you feel is most like you? In what ways? In what ways are you different?

PATH THREE: Play a Role

Step 6 List the needs and wants which you most often expressed in your "family" role. Cross off the needs which are being met.

Step 7 Hold a family meeting. Begin by demanding that your unsatisfied needs be met. Remember that your family is in financial trouble at this time. If what you need costs money, you may have to try to think of other ways to meet your need. Do not talk in general terms. Use specific examples that are appropriate to your family's situation.

Step 8 Write a short theme describing one way in which you and the character you play are alike. Give examples.

PATH FOUR: Sponsor a Child

Step 4 Compare your list from Step 2 and your budget from Step 3 with the hierarchy of needs chart (page 15). Are you trying to satisfy your child's most urgent needs first? Have you put wants before needs? If necessary, revise your planned purchases and the order of the needs you listed.

Step 5 You are a social worker. How do you feel about your work role? Is it in harmony with your other "selves"? Which basic needs does it satisfy? Which does it not satisfy?

Step 6 Suppose someone donated $20 to your committee. He gave the money on the condition that you use it to take the child on a trip somewhere in your community. Describe where you would take the child. Tell which needs you feel this trip would help satisfy. Are they the most urgent?

CHAPTER 2

Becoming a Mature Individual

At one point in a book called *Alice in Wonderland*, Alice meets a caterpillar:

"Who are *you*?" said the Caterpillar.

This was not an encouraging opening for a conversation. Alice replied, rather shyly, "I—I hardly know, Sir, just at present—at least I know who I was when I got up this morning, but I think I must have been changed several times since then."

"What do you mean by that?" said the Caterpillar sternly. "Explain yourself."

"I can't explain *myself*, I'm afraid, Sir," said Alice, "because I'm not myself, you see."

"I don't see," said the Caterpillar.

"I'm afraid I can't put it more clearly," Alice replied, very politely, "for I can't understand it myself, to begin with; and being so many different sizes in a day is very confusing."

Unlike Alice, you have not been many different sizes in a day. All your life, however, you have been growing. Changes have been taking place in your body, your mind, and your emotions. Presently, these changes are occurring more rapidly than at any time since you were a baby. Quite naturally, you may be as confused as Alice. With her, you might wonder who you are. In addition, you might wonder what you will do with your life. You might wonder what place you will occupy in a large and changing world.

Now, you are entering into adulthood. Are you mature enough for the tasks ahead?

ACHIEVING MATURITY

A single fertilized cell becomes a human being. With proper nurture, that human can reach his potential. He can learn to think, feel, choose, and become responsible for his actions. This happens through the process of *maturing*.

We mature both physically and psychologically. Physical maturity is the natural result of physical growth and development. A person is likely to reach it if he eats, sleeps, and clothes himself adequately. The choices he makes about eating, sleeping, and protecting himself from the elements will in part shape his physical development.

Psychological maturity requires a person to make a more deliberate effort. He must develop ways to regulate his own life. To do this, he must understand himself; he must find ways to meet his basic needs. The psychologically mature person can both live with himself as he is, and accept responsibility for what he is becoming.

It takes time for a person to develop such mature-personality traits. He learns what he needs to know in stages. Some things he learns as a baby. Others he learns as a child and as a teenager. At each point in his life he is capable of reaching a certain level of psychological maturity.

Some Traits of the Mature Personality

A mature person is aware of who he is. He respects himself, he has confidence in himself, and he is self-sufficient. He can direct his actions toward goals that he knows will bring him satisfaction. He has a capacity for self-renewal; he can stimulate his further growth and work to reach his potential.

Self-awareness If a person's needs for love and security have been met in the past, he is more likely to meet them in the future. He will have more time to look at the world around him and thus develop self-awareness.

The self-aware person recognizes that he is unique. He has developed a strong and positive self-concept; he has confidence. He is free to see the people and events around him from his own point of view. He is also willing to seek out new people and events; he is not put off by the unknown or unfamiliar. Wherever he is, he tries to treat others with courtesy and consideration, because he wants to and not because he feels he must.

Self-control The self-controlled person thinks before he acts. He asks himself if what he is going to do will help to satisfy his own basic needs or those of others. If the answer is yes, he does it. He understands himself; he acts on his own convictions. He enjoys solitude to think, relax, plan, and do. Among others, too, he is capable of acting on his own beliefs.

He knows that people influence what he does. When he wants to do something, he can estimate the effect of others' influence on this intended action. In this way he can better estimate how much he might be able to accomplish. In other words, he can compromise. He has developed a workable philosophy of life. Rather than have all events

Maturity brings with it a keener sense of individuality. You are mature when you recognize the things that define you. You rely less on others. At the same time, maturity helps you see yourself in relation to others, so that you share common goals with them.

control him, he controls certain events. He is thus in a better position to accept the consequences for what he does. He accepts success, and when he must, failure.

Self-renewal To live and act requires physical and psychological energy. From food comes physical energy, which gives us the *ability* to move and think. The *desire* to move and think comes from psychological energy. This comes from a number of sources.

Maturity and Developmental Stages

No one is born with these mature-personality traits. Each person must develop them over a lifetime. The process of psychological maturing begins with birth. A person then passes through six more *developmental stages*, the last of which is adulthood. At each stage, he becomes capable of maturing further. There are *developmental tasks*, or skills, considered appropriate for different developmental stages. The mastering of a specific developmental task may overlap several developmental stages. In different cultures, the appropriate developmental tasks may differ. Here we will consider the developmental tasks of contemporary, middle-class, Western culture.

There are two reasons why certain developmental tasks are related to certain developmental stages. First, a person's body must physically mature to the point where he is capable of performing a certain developmental task. Second, one developmental task is usually "built" upon another. Successfully accomplishing one developmental task paves the way for successfully accomplishing future tasks.

In each developmental stage, then, a person can become somewhat self-regulating. We may speak of a mature infant, even though that infant has not learned to walk.

Infancy   Infancy is the first developmental stage. The baby naturally trusts those around him. This feeling of trust needs to be encouraged by mothers, fathers, and others. Unless a person has learned to trust others, he can not learn to trust himself. He will not be able to develop a positive self-concept. He will not be able to develop self-respect.

Early childhood   By early childhood, muscles and nerves have begun to mature. The toddler can learn to control his body functions. He can, for example, be toilet-trained. At this stage, the child makes significant moves away from his mother. He begins to express his need for independence. As he masters this developmental task, he lays the foundation for self-confidence in his mature personality.

Later childhood   The child's main task in later childhood is to find out who he can be. He should be given opportunities to develop a sense of initiative and purpose. One way for

him to do this is to watch the people around him. He can then act out many different roles and thus begin to form an identity separate from that of his parents.

During this time the child should have learned basic communications skills. He needs to learn both visual and verbal symbols.

The preteens   In the preteen years the child is expected to master some of the "tools" of his environment. The preteen may learn, for example, to use hammers or knitting needles, thus satisfying the need to achieve and at the same time developing a sense of industry. Failure to achieve may result in feelings of inferiority. Further progress may then be difficult. If a child does not feel that he can ever master a skill, he may stop trying.

At this time the child must also learn to cooperate. He must learn to plan and share with others. In school and among his friends, he needs opportunities to satisfy his need for recognition and approval by a group.

Adolescence   Changes take place in the adolescent's body. A new energy fills him. He reaches sexual maturity, and thus begins to move out of the world of childhood. Psychologically, however, he is not yet ready for adult society. The developmental tasks he has so far mastered worked well in earlier developmental stages. Now, he must adjust them to his present level of physical maturity. This is the first developmental task of adolescence. It is a confusing one. The second developmental task is to reduce some of this confusion: The maturing adolescent must put together, like the pieces of a puzzle, all the developmental tasks which he is adapting. From them, he must form a single identity.

Why must the teenager **adapt earlier tasks**? Consider the development of a sense of trust. An infant's trust may not work for an adolescent. A baby simply trusts; if he is fortunate, someone cares for him and his sense of trust is strengthened. A teen must actively express this sense of trust. Generally, he does this

As his identity emerges during adolescence, the teenager becomes less sensitive and more self-confident. He begins to realize his adult potential. He may be unsure of himself until he has tested this newfound identity in unfamiliar situations.

by looking for people and ideas to believe in. He does not, however, wish others to see him as overtrusting or weak. He does not wish to surrender his independence, either. Therefore, he may mask his true feelings. Outwardly he may show cynicism or contempt.

In early childhood, the maturing adolescent first expressed self-will. He will now seek to do what he wants to do without being told what to do. He will try to act without restraint. At the same time he may avoid situations that might reveal his self-doubts. He is sensitive to teasing and ridicule, especially from those his own age. He may react with silence or with emotional outbursts.

The teenager must also take another look at the roles he began to assume in later childhood and at the practical skills he started to learn as a preteen. Through adapting and re-learning these tasks, he may gain an awareness of what he might become. He gains a better understanding of his own potential.

In the process of all this changing, the adolescent may be confused. He will begin to wonder who he is. He must **form a new identity**. The difficulty of this task is recognized by Erik Erikson, an authority on human development. He describes adolescence as a period of *identity crisis*.

The teenager's new identity emerges from his past. The maturing adolescent, like everyone else, needs to maintain a feeling of continuity. He needs to feel that the events of his life are somehow linked together. He needs to feel that, although he is changing, he is also still the same person.

Young adulthood Just as the adolescent matures physically, the young adult matures

The intellectual maturity that you achieve in young adulthood helps you to make decisions that launch adult life. You are able to assess your development, your previous roles and relationships, your interests and abilities, and to relate them to decisions you make for your future.

mentally. He becomes better able to look at the world around him and to make sense of what he sees. He develops an improved ability to *conceptualize*. This means two things. First, it means that he is better able to make *generalizations*: after looking at many people or events, he can more easily determine what kinds of things these people or events have in common. Second, he can better *think abstractly*: he is more capable of developing ideas of his own. In his mind, he can manipulate these ideas and he can manipulate generalizations. He can put them together in different ways. He can also draw conclusions: on the basis of what he knows, he can try to figure out what might happen in the future.

The young adult needs this intellectual maturity if he is to master the developmental task of this stage. This task involves planning; it involves making decisions. It leads the young adult to search the adult world for people and institutions with which he can link himself. These new people and institutions must be more or less in harmony with the identity he formed in adolescence.

Mastering this developmental task involves the young adult in learning many different kinds of skills. He needs to learn how to form lasting personal relationships. He needs to learn how to mingle confidently with members of both sexes. He needs to choose a career that is "right" for him. To become financially self-supporting, he must master the occupational skills which that career requires. He also needs to develop a system of values and a personal philosophy of life.

Adulthood The mature adult has developed the traits of the mature personality. He can regulate his own behavior; he knows how to meet his basic needs through work and play. Being self-aware, he accepts a part in maintaining a livable environment. Having self-control, he finds ways to extend his interests into the neighborhood, the community, and the world. He may assume the responsibilities of marriage and parenthood.

The developmental task of later adulthood is to adjust to the reality of growing older and dying. If he has successfully met earlier tasks, the mature person will be better able to make his retirement as meaningful as possible.

CAUSES OF INDIVIDUAL DIFFERENCES

A quick look around your classroom will tell you that, while you and your fellow students may be nearly the same age, not all of you are at the same level of maturity. Physically and psychologically, individuals mature at different rates. Some reach a certain level and never go beyond.

Why are you growing and developing so uniquely? Part of the answer is that you were born with very particular characteristics and possibilities. You *inherited* them. A baby does not become a red-headed boy by chance. He, like you, has genes and chromosomes that determine the color of his hair. Similarly, you have hormones that influence your rate of growth.

The answer also has a second part: No one else has experienced the precise combi-

---

CASE STUDY: BEATRICE

THE SITUATION *Thirteen-year-old Beatrice joined a club for girls that was organized specifically for city children. She was learning to sew and met with the other girls once a week in a nearby church community room. As garments neared completion, the group decided to plan a fashion show for their parents. They chose to hold the show at the home economics department of the Community College. Everyone but Beatrice seemed enthusiastic about the location. "Why the frown, Beatrice?" asked the club leader. "You and your parents are within walking distance and can easily get to the fashion show."*

"I know," replied Beatrice. "But my mother

says there's no use for me to even look at that college! I'll never get in there."

THE INTERVIEW *Q: Do you believe your mother when she tells you things like that? A: Sure. I figure she knows more than I do. Q: But don't you get good grades in school? And you like to read, too, don't you? A: That's right. But I've got so many brothers and sisters that I'll have to go to work as soon as I'm old enough. There won't be time for school. No use trying for what you can't get.*

REACT *What do you think of the mother's attitude? If Beatrice were your friend, or you were her teacher, what would you say to her?*

nation of events which you have. No one else has had exactly the same opportunities. Your environment and your experiences have influenced the kind of person you have become. They have influenced the level of maturity which you have reached. You, in turn, can influence them. You can change the things you do; you may be able to change the environment in which you do them. To this extent, you can control your development toward full maturity.

The Influence of Heredity

When a builder builds a house, he usually starts with a plan, or a blueprint. This blueprint shows the size of the future house. It shows building materials and floor plans.

In a way, we can say that a human being, too, is built according to a blueprint—a biological blueprint. Your blueprint was passed to you by your parents when you were conceived. From that moment, the plan of your body was set. The detailed instructions for building every one of your cells were "written down" in a chemical code. Your sex was determined. Your size, shape, and color were indicated, as was something of the nature of your intelligence and temper.

The biological blueprint contains the directions not only for much of *what* a person becomes but also for *when* he becomes it. This blueprint contains a timetable, which instructs a person's body about the rate at which it is to grow and develop.

You can think of this timetable as a kind of *biological clock*. Imagine that the numbers on the face of the clock are the years of a person's life. Beside each number are certain instructions; these are the kinds of growth and development that can take place at that time. When the hands of the clock reach certain "hours"—when a person has lived a certain amount of time—certain changes may take place in his body. The biological clock suggests the time when a child's bones will be hard enough for him to learn to walk. It

suggests when puberty will occur. It suggests if and when his hair will turn grey in later life. A person's biological blueprint and biological clock do not entirely determine how and at what rate he will develop physically. This is also influenced to some extent by his environment. By not eating the right foods, for example, a person may slow the speed at which he physically matures.

A person's biological blueprint and biological clock only partly determine how and at what rate he will develop. His development is also influenced by the food and medicine he consumes, the amount of sleep he gets, and the amount of stress he undergoes from day to day.

The Influence of Environment

A builder builds a house from a blueprint; then the owner furnishes the house. In the same way, while much of a person's character is influenced by his biological blueprint, his life must still be "furnished" with experiences. The people and things around him influence his growth and development. Without this exposure, he cannot reach psychological maturity.

The most important environmental influence on any individual is his family. There he should learn how to meet his needs. There he passes through the vital early developmental stages. There, in adolescence, his identity may be formed and tested.

People have different families, different near environments. This is one reason why most people differ. Of course, even within the same family no two people are alike. Each member views the family in a distinct way. Each is influenced by his own unique experiences outside the family. Friends, schools, and clubs—just to name a few

Your biological clock influences when you become physically mature. Your biological blueprint influences how. The chart shows that the potential shape of the body and age of full maturity differ with individuals.

26

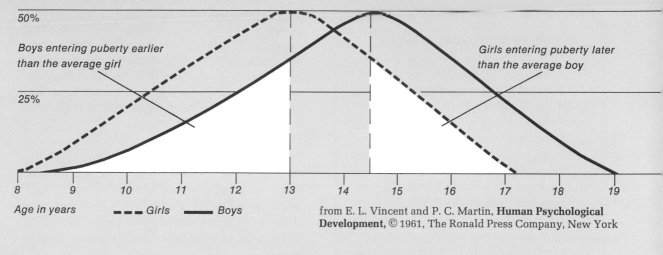

50%

Boys entering puberty earlier than the average girl

25%

Girls entering puberty later than the average boy

8   9   10   11   12   13   14   15   16   17   18   19

Age in years   — — — Girls   ——— Boys

from E. L. Vincent and P. C. Martin, **Human Psychological Development,** © 1961, The Ronald Press Company, New York

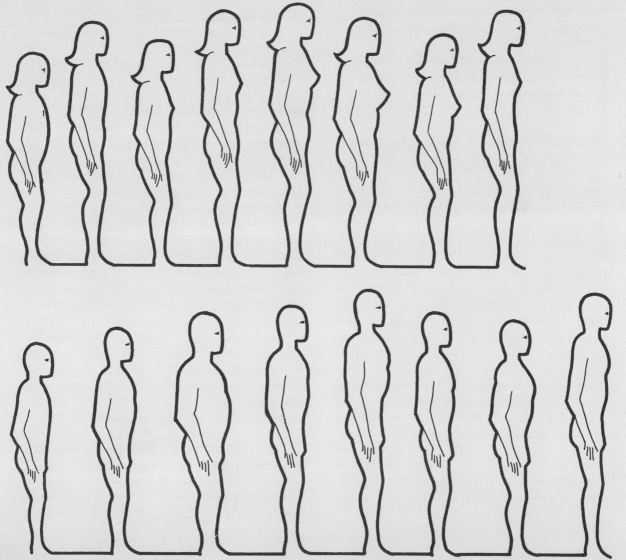

THE INTENTIONAL FAMILY

In its broadest sense, the *family* can be defined as a group of people living together who share resources and care for each other. This definition includes not only the nuclear family and the extended family, but the intentional family, as well. An *intentional family* is a group of people, not necessarily related by birth or marriage, who live together. A familiar form of intentional family is a religious community of "brothers" or "sisters." There are and have been a variety of nonreligious intentional families, also.

Some intentional families do not survive for long. Others, notably some religious communities, have endured for centuries.

"pieces" of the environment—all contribute to making each person a very particular individual.

The family The family is the essential unit of all societies. Two basic kinds are the nuclear family and the extended family. The *nuclear family* is made up of parents and their children. The *extended family* includes other relatives. Both types may include foster or adopted children, friends, or household help. Both types change as members are born, grow old and die, marry, remarry, separate, divorce, and leave home.

For a number of reasons, no two families are exactly alike. Some families, for example, occupy distinctive positions within the community; some have little prestige. Some families last many years; some last only a short time. Some are relaxed; some are tense.

Some are large; some are small. Some are virtually ruled by one person; some consider everyone's opinion before making a decision. All these factors contribute to the growing child's idea of what the world is like. They all contribute to his early notions of how he should react to the people and things that surround him.

A typical family might last forty years. During this time the parents age and the children grow and learn. Eventually—at least in nuclear families—the children leave and begin families of their own. Together, all these events are called the *family life cycle*. This cycle can be described in seven **family stages.**

The life cycle of the average family can more simply be described in three stages. The first, the *beginning stage*, refers to the time when the family is starting. When the first child is born, the family has entered the *expanding stage*. As children mature and leave, the *contracting stage* is reached.

At various family stages, different family members are at different levels of maturity and have different interests. Consequently, the family environment in the expanding stage, for example, is different from the family environment in the contracting stage.

All families are constantly changing. At the same time, they are all to some extent the same. They have some degree of **family stability**. Their members feel that one stage of family experience has something in common with the next; they feel that their lives are continuous.

A family is stable when all its members are together and when they feel that they are likely to stay together. This unity can be eroded by illness, death, separation, and divorce.

Every family makes decisions; different families make them in different ways. In this they are influenced by their **family authority patterns**. In some families one parent is boss. That parent makes all the major decisions. Others may have a loose pattern of authority,

2 5 Yrs. 20-25 Yrs.   20-25 Yrs.   1-8 Yrs.

Newlywed Stage

Crowded Stage

Teenage Stage

Launching Stage

One Member Stage

GROWING FAMILY

Beginning Family Stage

Empty Nest Stage

In some families, the seven stages of the family life cycle overlap. In others, the family is in two separate stages at the same time. What reasons could there be for this? Compare the average time spans for the various stages. What conclusions can you draw?

with each member permitted to more or less go his own way. Family activities, including shared meals, may be kept to a minimum. A third pattern is found in the democratic family, where the group as a unit shares in making decisions.

Some members of a family—because of the roles they assume in the work world—are seen as more important or less important than others. The individual learns about status in his family; he learns how to view others in the world. Learn to answer the question "Who is my brother?"

Every family creates its own **family climate**. It creates a certain feeling which affects all its members. Some families are relaxed, comfortable, and accepting. Others may be tense,

strained, and critical. In between these two extremes, there is a whole range of possible family climates.

The atmosphere of a family is not unrelated to the other factors we have been considering. Illness or death, for example, may darken a previously happy family atmosphere. Disputes over who is at the helm of family affairs can create very strong tensions in a household.

Society The family does not exist in isolation. It is a part of a community. The community, in turn, is part of a society. Many family habits reflect the customs of the society. Many family interests are the result of the size and location of the community.

*L*et me tell you about the very rich.
They are different from you and me.
They possess and enjoy early, and it
does something to them, makes them
soft where we are hard, and cynical
where we are trustful, in a way that,
unless you were born rich, it is very
difficult to understand.

from "The Rich Boy" (F. Scott Fitzgerald)

Families in an agricultural community may be more likely to be interested in the effect of rain on crops than would families in a city.

Regardless of the kind of community, family members associate themselves with local institutions. The family may attend religious services. The children will go to school. If the mother has a job, younger children may spend her working hours in a day-care center. These and other exposures to the world beyond the family influence each family member.

KINDS OF INDIVIDUAL DIFFERENCES

Individuals differ physically and psychologically. These differences are caused by heredity and environment. Most physical differences are the result of heredity. Some scientists say that heredity is the more important influence on psychological differences. Others say that the environment is more important. Most agree that both factors play a part in the shaping of an individual personality.

To understand the effects of environment and heredity on personality, scientists have studied identical twins. Identical twins are those who have the same biological blueprints; they look very much alike. Most are raised in the same family, but some are not.

In cases where identical twins have been raised in different families in different communities, mental and emotional differences have been observed.

Physical Differences

A person's biological blueprint contains instructions for his physical makeup. It influences everything from his height and the size of his bones to the shape of his nose. It influences the color of his skin, eyes, and hair. It even influences whether he will be nearsighted, farsighted, or color-blind.

Environment also influences the way a person looks. While heredity, for example, influences the tendency to be overweight or underweight, such a tendency is also influenced by the kind and amount of food a person eats. Eating habits, in turn, are acquired at home. Also, these habits depend on the kind of food available in the environment.

A person's energy level is related to both heredity and environment. From birth, some children are stronger and more lively than others. Without the proper diet, however, they are not likely to maintain this advantage.

Some diseases are inherited; others are acquired. One inherited disease is *hemophilia*, in which a person cannot stop bleeding after he has been bruised or cut. Measles and mumps, on the other hand, are acquired diseases. Scientists are not agreed whether certain other illnesses, like allergies or diabetes, are caused by heredity or environment.

Psychological Differences

Some mental and emotional tendencies are inherited. These tendencies are so greatly influenced by the environment, however, that it is difficult to tell how much—psychologically—someone is born with.

A person's degree of intelligence, for example, is inherited. It must, however, through his experiences, be developed. A person is also to some extent born with his temperament. Again, the role of environment is quite influential. Certainly, no matter how much of a child's temperament comes from his biological blueprint, he would benefit from a stable family climate in which he was accepted. In an atmosphere where he was constantly being criticized, a child might be afraid to master such early developmental tasks as learning to trust. The authority pattern of the home shapes a child's attitude toward authority. If the home is ruled by a single person, the child might expect a similar authority pattern to exist elsewhere.

A child is also affected by his family's status. A high-status family might contribute to his self-confidence. It might also be destructive; a child might not feel he can "live up to" what is expected of him. Being raised in a low-status family might leave him feeling powerless. In either case there are many exceptions. The community and school, for example, have important modifying effects.

Some children are brain-damaged at birth. Today it is believed that proper treatment for any mental or emotional difficulty can help to offset its handicaps.

Maleness and Femaleness

Besides the physical differences between men and women, there are behavioral differences. Every society has its own idea of what is appropriate male and female behavior.

Gender identity A person's sex is probably the most physically significant characteristic which he inherits. The essential

---

CASE STUDY: PENNY

THE SITUATION *Penny, her husband, and three children live in a two-bedroom garden apartment near a large metropolitan area. The oldest child, David, is six years old. Mary Anne is four and Cindy is three. Penny spends many of her summer afternoons with the three at the swimming pool, while her husband works. Usually, the children are well-behaved and quiet. But today, Cindy has been sulking and staying so close to her mother that Penny has paid very little attention to the two other children. Finally, as Cindy tucks herself well back into a roomy beach chair, Mary Anne approaches her mother. "What's wrong with Cindy?" she asks.*

"I guess she's not feeling on top of the world today. That happens sometimes, you know," replies Penny.

Mary Anne patted Cindy gently.

THE INTERVIEW *Q: Penny, why did you answer Mary Anne that way?*
A: Because it's true. And Mary Anne has felt the same way herself sometimes. She knew what I was talking about.
Q: It seems that you are trying to teach your children respect for one another.
A: Yes. I think it's best for us to try to understand each other in this family.
Q: Were you raised that way?
A: Not exactly. But I've thought a lot about it and decided it was important. In fact, I decided that it was so important that I will really work on it when I become a mother myself.

REACT *Are most mothers like Penny? How important is the idea of respect for each other in family living?*

The Suffragettes demanded the vote for women. In World War II, women succeeded in traditionally "male" jobs. Today, opportunities for self-realization are less likely to be limited by culturally determined sex roles.

physical difference between men and women is that they have different sex organs. They have different sex glands inside and different genitals outside. These are the organs directly concerned with reproduction, with the creation of new human life. We refer to these organs as *primary sex traits*. Men and women also differ in their other sex traits. These include the differences in the distribution of body fat and muscles. The male's beard and the female's generally higher voice are the result of differing kinds and amounts of hormones.

Physically, girls tend to mature more quickly than boys in the early years. Teenage girls, on the average, are taller and more fully developed than boys the same age. By the end of the teens, such differences usually have leveled off.

Sexuality Different societies have had different ideas of what it meant to be male or female. Some of these ideas have little to do with the distinct biological functions of each sex. They are culturally determined.

At one time, masculine and feminine behavior was defined in terms of work roles. The woman's role was in the family. The man's role was in the world outside the home. This was changed by the industrial revolution: women and children left their homes to work in factories. The distinction between male and female roles became harder to define.

As further technical advances were made, many people were released from some forms of time-consuming physical work. Hence, many men and women had some freedom to pursue new interests. They had more time to seek opportunities for self-expression. In seeking these opportunities, some men and women were freed from traditional "stronger" and "weaker" sex roles; there were machines to do much of the heavy work.

Today, not every woman feels that marriage and motherhood are the only ways in which she can meet her need for self-fulfillment. Today, many men wish to spend more time at home with their children. Individuals have greater freedom concerning the expression of their sexuality. Work and family roles are becoming increasingly flexible.

CONTROLLING CHANGE THROUGH CHOICE

Every human being must be prepared to live in a world of change. Some changes occur as a result of natural biological events. The biological clock ticks on for every person. Some change comes about through the actions of others in our environment. Natural forces, many aided by man, also change the environment. The mature person must find in himself the secure center from which to cope with change.

Until adolescence, much of what had happened to shape your personality was outside your control. From adolescence on, you have had to find ways to develop your own personality, to stimulate your own growth. You can direct your own growth through the choices you make. Your future choices, therefore, are more important to your long-range satisfactions than most events of your past.

We each live our lives against a different background. We each face different opportunities and different obstacles. As you are launched into life as a young adult, you must learn to take control of the events with which you are confronted. That control can come only through learning to make rational, satisfying decisions.

THINK BACK

A mature person accepts responsibility for his own growth and behavior.
Discuss: *Answer the person who says, "It's not my fault that I act the way I do."*

Becoming mature is a lifelong process.
Discuss: *What are the characteristics of a person who "acts his age"?*

Growth in maturity is influenced by both heredity and environment.
Discuss: *"I can't help it, I was born that way."*

Family life is an important environmental influence on our growth and development.
Discuss: *Why is it that children in some families are considered complete opposites of each other?*

LOOK AROUND

1. Which traits of the mature personality do you consider most difficult to develop? Which do you consider easiest? Give reasons for your answers.

2. How can a parent or a "substitute" parent provide the care and attention a child needs to develop a feeling of basic trust?

3. What are the major environmental influences on your life today? Show photographs or drawings of each.

4. Look through a family picture album. What common physical hereditary characteristics are most noticeable among the family members?

5. Do you like the definition of family given on page 28? To which of the three types of family would you enjoy belonging?

6. What kinds of changes could occur in family authority patterns when families grow? Why? How do changes of maturity affect families?

7. As a young adult, how do your views of family life differ from those of your parents? Where do similarities in thinking occur?

8. Who decides what is acceptable masculine or feminine behavior? What are the major influences on *your* ideas about masculinity and femininity?

FOLLOW YOUR PATH

PATH ONE: Keep a Log

Step 5 Sort through all your log cards. Take out those that refer, however indirectly, to the three traits of the mature personality. Which trait do you feel closest to mastering? Which seems most difficult?

Step 6 Refer back to your lists of met and unmet needs and wants. What clues do your met needs and wants give about your stronger mature-personality traits? What clues do your unmet needs and wants give about those traits you have developed least?

Step 7 People mature at different rates. Regardless of your age, and purely on the basis of your log cards, in what areas do you consider yourself mature? Give examples. What is the next developmental task confronting you? How might you go about meeting this task?

Step 8 Which person inside your family do you refer to most in your cards? Which person outside your family do you refer to most? (Give the age of this person and his relationship to you). Judging just from the cards, tell how each of these people has influenced your development.

Step 9 Take out the ten cards which seem most important to you. Without giving yourself reasons, rank them by importance.

PATH TWO: Write a Skit

Step 7 At what developmental stage is each of your characters? Discuss the conflict in your skit in terms of the developmental tasks facing each character.

Step 8 Briefly discuss the authority pattern, status, and climate of the family about which you are writing. Do any of these change as the skit progresses?

Step 9 Begin to write your skit.

PATH THREE: Play a Role

Step 9 Step out of your role. In front of the whole class, discuss the climate and authority pattern of your family. Ask the class to comment.

Step 10 Prepare a scrapbook or bulletin board that shows the preferences and interests of the family member that you played. Use magazine pictures, movie ticket stubs, advertisements, or anything else that you feel is suitable.

PATH FOUR: Sponsor a Child

Step 7 What is your child's level of maturity? Is he ahead of his age level in some respects and behind in others? Will your plan help your child to master his next developmental task? Can it? Discuss.

Step 8 What is the next developmental task facing your child? Is there anything in his heredity or environment that holds him back? Discuss.

Step 9 Plan how you will spend your $75 for next month. Include something that will help the child master a developmental task. Discuss *what* you want to do and *how* you want to do it with your teacher or a social worker. Revise your plan.

CHAPTER 3

Framework for Decision Making

Heraclitus, a Greek philosopher, pointed out some similarities between a person and a river. From one day to the next, he said, you might recognize a river as being the same. Yet, at no two times is the water in the river the same, for the water flows downstream and away. A person remains recognizably the same over a period of time. Nevertheless, information from the environment is constantly flowing through him. The water in a river slowly changes the course of the river. At one place it might erode the river bank; at another it might build up the bank. Information from the environment has a similar effect on a person. It alters the course of his life. It builds up certain interests; it directs him away from other pursuits.

At this point, our comparison between a person and a river ends. A river must flow in a riverbed. There is no single path a person must follow in life.

He has the ability to exert some influence over the things that he does. He has the ability to make choices.

Making a choice means picking from among a number of alternatives. Choosing is basic to decision making, which involves realizing you have a choice, making a choice, acting on it, and thinking about what you have done. Here, we will examine the framework within which decisions are made.

DECISIONS ARE BASED ON VALUES

A *value* is a belief or feeling that something is worthwhile. You might value an idea or a course of action. You might value a person, a place, or a thing. Three kinds of values are material values, moral values, and esthetic values. When you attach *material value* to something, you believe it to be of some practical importance to you. You find it useful. When you place a *moral value* on something, you believe that it is good or bad. When you place an *esthetic value* on something, you feel that it is beautiful or tasteful, ugly or untasteful.

Clarifying your values will help you to weigh one course of action against another. It will help you to understand the "why" of what you are doing. A rational decision reflects the values of the person or the group making it. Before undertaking a study of decision making, you will want to examine and understand your values. You will want to know where they came from and why they mean so much to you. Some values could almost be said to be shared by all men. These are called universal values. The most significant universally held value is the belief that the human race must survive. At least some individuals must live long enough to produce others of our species. Beliefs in some sort of family life and in some sort of larger society are two other widely held values.

You acquire many values from your family and your community or culture. As you grow up, your values are influenced by those around you. In many cultures, there is a prevailing belief that individual human life is important: Everyone has a certain amount of potential which he ought to be allowed to realize. In the United States and Canada today, most people value youth and physical attractiveness. Other cultures value age.

The social and political values which you hold have also been strongly influenced by your family and your society. Many people in the Western world value representative democracy. Most feel that schools and courts of law are worthwhile institutions. Of course, you experience your world in your own unique way. Your values may not be exactly those of other members of your family or society.

Whatever the kind of value and whatever its source, you should remember that some values have importance because they can be traced back to basic needs.

Material value can be attached to ideas and attitudes as well as to things. The drive for status has material value to those who find it useful in satisfying their need for recognition.

THE DAMONS LIVE HERE JUST ACROSS THE FREEWAY FROM JOHN WAYNE

What is beauty? A child's answer is expressed in his painting of his environment. Your answer to this question is probably different today from the answer you would have given at six. Although your definition of beauty may change as you mature, you form esthetic values early in life.

Material Values

Is it useful? If it is, it has material value for you. Clearly, the things which have the greatest material value are the things—like food and water—which are necessary for survival.

You place material value not only on material objects. You might also consider an idea or an attitude to have use. Some people, for example, feel that self-discipline is of great practical use. The possession of such a quality, they believe, enables people to acquire things they want.

Nearly everyone places material value on other people. Without them they could not satisfy their psychological and social needs.

Esthetic Values

You experience your environment through your senses of sight, hearing, taste, touch, and smell. You look, for example, at a long, yellow fruit and you see that it has a certain shape and color. You touch it and you find that the skin has a soft, smooth feel to it. You peel back the skin and detect a distinctive smell. From your past experiences, you know that you are holding a banana and that this banana is food. Then you eat it. You have used your senses to stay alive.

A monkey could do exactly the same thing.

As a human being, you are capable of using your senses in a much more refined way.

This is because you have *esthetic values.* Certain shapes and certain combinations of colors give you pleasure. To you they are beautiful. You can take pleasure in hearing certain sounds: you can enjoy the melodies and harmonies of music. You can prefer the fragrance of certain flowers or perfumes. You can be partial to the way a certain cloth feels against your skin.

Esthetic values deepen our understanding of the world and our fellow human beings. Without esthetic values, we could not create beauty from the materials of our environment. We would not enjoy painting, sculpture, music, poetry, literature, and architecture. We could not very well appreciate the beauty in the everyday: clothing, home furnishings, snowflakes, and sunrise.

Moral Values

Our moral values reflect our feelings for what is right, good, and just. In the Western world, many of the more commonly held moral values can be traced to three religions: Judaism, Christianity, and Islam. These religions share a belief in one God. They also share the whole body of moral values contained in the Old Testament. (Each has other written sources, as well.) All three subscribe to some form of what has been called the Golden Rule: "Do unto others as you would have others do unto you."

Many people who do not subscribe to any formal religions have very clear moral values. Without attending religious services, one can believe that loyalty to one's friend is good. One can believe that it is right that each human being be treated in a dignified way.

CLARIFY YOUR VALUES

You can clarify your values by asking yourself what and how much of anything you would be willing to give up for something. You have heard people say, "I'd give any-*thing* to have that car!" But you know they would not give up their freedom by going out and stealing it. They value their freedom more than the mere possession of a car. Have you heard someone say, "What I wouldn't give to be on the team!" But the person saying it would not give up the time or the energy to work for such an honor. He values other things more than hard work.

Many people say they value the natural environment. How many of these people would be willing to give up air-polluting cars? How many use returnable bottles? You truly value something only when you are willing to pay the price. You cannot value all things equally. Your *scale of values* reveals the order of importance of what you value.

Few decisions involve such clear-cut consequences as life or death. At such crucial times, most people see their values very clearly. Everyday situations may be less critical, but they require awareness of values if satisfaction is to be achieved.

The words "should," or "ought," or "supposed" are clues to you that a statement or idea is value-based. Such statements as "The government *should* provide social security," or "She *ought* to be nicer to her sister," or "The school is *supposed* to teach good citizenship," are called *value judgments.* They take certain values for granted. Your own values are reflected in your conscience, which serves as your personal guide to what is worthwhile and acceptable behavior for you.

GOALS DIRECT YOUR DECISIONS

You set *goals* to gain something of importance, something that has value, for you. Thus, if you value knowledge, your goals will include education. When a goal is achieved, you have realized something of value in your life. Your actions have produced satisfying results. While values are the

Things that have material value may also have esthetic and moral value. You may get a great deal of satisfaction from recognizing more than one kind of value in the things that you acquire, in the things that you do, and in the relationships you have with others.

inner guides that shape your decisions, goals are the aims you wish to reach.

For most mature people, values remain fairly constant over time. Goals, on the other hand, will shift and change as wants and needs are satisfied. Thus we tend to think of goals in terms of the time periods involved in reaching them. There are long-range, short-range, and intermediate goals.

Long-range Goals

Most of us dream of what we would like to do or be someday. Such goals may take weeks, months, or even years to achieve. Such long-range goals often reflect our highest values. We are willing to give the most of ourselves—our time, energy, and other resources—to achieve them. They are likely to take patience, effort, and endurance to reach. For example, the goal of preparation for a special career may, as in the case of a high school student who wants to become a doctor, stretch out over twelve or more years. On the other hand, the goal of becoming a medical technician might be reached in two years after high school. Both of these career objectives are long-range goals.

CASE STUDY: MIKE

THE SITUATION *Mike and other art students in class were enthusiastic about a new project they had developed for some children from the city. Each Saturday, a busload of preteen city children would travel the short distance from the city to Mike's school to participate in a special art workshop. The idea was to have the children use inexpensive "found" materials as the basis for art projects. The art students collected clay from the river, wooden sticks, paint, aluminum, and sponges for the first day's class. When the children and adult chaperones arrived, they were introduced to the various art activities and spent the morning making the projects of their choice.*

By the fourth week, it was time to evaluate the art workshop. Mike was surprised and upset to learn that the parents and chaperones viewed the past few weeks as "a waste of time." They saw no "art" in any of the projects done by the children. They felt it was "about time the children took lessons in how to draw trees and paint real pictures." If their ideas were not accepted, the parents would withdraw their children.

THE INTERVIEW *Q: Well, Mike, what are you going to do about this situation?*
A: I don't know. If you ask me, these people are pretty uninformed about what art is.
Q: Did anyone talk with them about the workshop before inviting them to participate?
A: Not that I know of. I don't see why that's necessary. After all, it's our workshop.
Q: People apparently view art in different ways. Perhaps your participants need to be "educated" about this new approach.
A: You mean teach them about art?
Q: Why not? How can you succeed if people don't know what you are talking about?
A: I guess none of us thought of it that way before. Is it too late to talk about it now?
Q: Why don't you try it and see?
A: I guess we'd better. We really want this workshop to succeed. I'll talk to the other class members and we'll set up another meeting for everyone.

REACT *Do you think the adults' views reflected the children's view of the workshop? What is the "value" in this kind of art experience?*

Short-range Goals

If you want to realize a long-range goal like losing twenty pounds, you may have to cut down on food intake at every meal for a period of months. If you want to purchase a new suit, you may have to set aside money from your weekly paycheck or allowance. Short-range goals may be stepping stones on the way to reaching long-range goals. Such short-range goals may seem insignificant and easy to reach; but they are essential to attaining many long-range goals.

Intermediate Goals

You may have certain checkpoints along the way to meeting long-range goals. Such checkpoints are intermediate goals. Reaching them brings you some satisfaction, while motivating you to work toward your more distant goal. For example, if your goal is to win in a national spelling tournament, reaching the semifinals brings you the satisfaction of knowing that you have surpassed some of your competition. It also reinforces your goal of success in the finals.

IDENTIFY YOUR GOALS

If you have started to think about your life—your experiences of the past and present, and your hopes for the future—you have also started to think about your goals. Setting realistic goals for yourself will take into account your interests, abilities, and opportunities. Think about the goals you have set in the past. How did you establish them? How well did you reach them? How much closer have they brought you to reaching other goals?

Most young adults have many goals. They want to feel at ease with themselves and to establish their independence. They want to form secure friendships and to find rewarding work. They want to develop and enrich themselves through their leisure activities. Later in this text we will offer suggestions as to how you may achieve such goals.

STANDARDS GUIDE DECISIONS

You may have heard of "standard tests," "standard procedures," or "standard sizes." A *standard* is an agreed-upon measure of quantity, quality, performance, or achievement.

Standards are guidelines for measuring success in reaching goals and working toward values. They help you to know whether you have done what you set out to do (your goal) as well as you had hoped to do it (your value). Thus, a standard becomes a point of reference, or a baseline, that tells you whether you have gone beyond or fallen below what you expected. Some standards are fairly subjective; they are based on your personal values. Others are more objective because they have previously been agreed upon by large groups of people.

A short-range goal, such as the pursuit of a hobby, may help identify a long-range goal, such as a career. You can. then set intermediate goals that will bring the long-range objective within reach.

H e's a real Nowhere Man
    sitting in his Nowhere Land
    making all his Nowhere plans for
        nobody.
    Doesn't have a point of view,
    knows not where he's going to,
    isn't he a bit like you and me?
    Nowhere Man please listen,
    you don't know what you're missing,
    Nowhere Man, the world is at your
        command.
    He's as blind as he can be,
    just sees what he wants to see,
    Nowhere Man can you see me at all?

from "Nowhere Man" (Lennon and McCartney)

Standards of Quantity

A *standard of quantity* measures the amount or the number of something. There are standards of quantity to measure time, distance, weight, volume, and energy. You are probably familiar with many of them. Distance can be measured in meters or feet. A clock divides time into seconds, minutes, and hours. A calendar measures larger units of time: days, months, and years. Familiar measures of weight include grams, ounces, pounds, and tons. A teaspoon and a bushel are both measures of volume. A calorie and a horsepower are two measures of energy. With the space age we have new standards of quantity, like the light-year and the "g".

The U. S. Bureau of Standards sets standards for many weights and measures.

Standards of Quality

A *standard of quality* measures the degree or level of something. How many threads per square inch must there be for sheeting to be classified as "first quality percale"? How many units of vitamin D are in "enriched

bread"? What proportion of chicken to rice is in a can marked "chicken with rice"? How much less chicken is in a can marked "rice with chicken"? Such specifications are carefully stated to insure standards of quality.

Standards of Achievement

Standards of achievement are objective measures of something we have done. One example would be the number of pushups or knee bends that establish a standard of physical fitness. We all take standard achievement tests of one kind or another during our school careers. From these we gain some idea of how our achievements measure up against those of other students. Your academic or general high school diploma reflects a standard of achievement, as do college degrees with honors or with high or highest honors.

Standards of Performance

Among the most important standards are those you set for your own performance. Your standards of performance ask how *well* you did something. Are you satisfied that you have done a good job of dishwashing if there is a speck of dried egg on the back of a dish? Are you satisfied if the car you are cleaning is shiny on the outside but dusty inside? Are you satisfied if you miss one note on the scale, or do you keep trying until you play the scale perfectly? Will you rip out a seam if it is crooked? The satisfaction you gain from how a job is done reflects your standard of performance.

SET YOUR STANDARDS

Life will offer you many occasions to set your own standards. At such times you will have to carefully consider both your values and your goals. You may decide to bring your goals in line with your values; you may decide to apply different values to your goals.

Take the example of a young married couple without children. They have a high standard of living. They value material comforts. Their goals are to eat in restaurants, to send their laundry out to a service, and to travel as much as possible. Then a baby is born, and they have to review their standard of living. Because the baby's health and welfare are important to them, they alter their goals. They eat in their apartment. They buy a washing machine. They save their "travel money" in order to buy a home.

This couple's values, goals, and standards all fit together. When circumstances changed, they adjusted their standards.

RESOURCES HELP YOU REACH GOALS

A resource is anything you can call upon to help you reach a goal. If your goal is to make music, your resource might be a trumpet. It might be another instrument—a guitar or a kazoo. If you are handy, your resource might be a piece of bamboo which you can make into a flute. In this last case, your skill in making the instrument is also a resource. Tools, also, are resources. There is an additional resource involved in all these examples: a musical aptitude.

Resources are human and environmental. Your human resources are what you have and develop, physically and psychologically. They include your intelligence, aptitudes, and skills. Environmental resources might include a house, a tree, an employment agency, a book, a lump of coal, or a friend.

For any resource to help you reach a goal, you must be aware of it. You must know how to use it.

Human Resources

The list of your human resources would include everything from your teeth and fingers to your determination to get something done.

Competition is evaluated by standards of achievement and performance. Success is sometimes measured by the highest standard of achievement. Often, meeting the standard of performance is equally important.

To make such a list would take nearly forever. Moreover, such a list would contain resources which most people never use.

The human resources which we consider here are fairly common to everyone. These are mental abilities, skills, and personal qualities.

Mental abilities A person's potential mental abilities are perhaps his greatest untapped resource. Even the most accomplished people use only a fraction of their intelligence, creativity, aptitudes, and talents.

The human mind is the most complex, versatile instrument known to man. It is the reservoir of all human potential.

The ability to learn from experience is called **intelligence**. It is the ability to put

43

things in order in your mind. In its higher forms, it is the ability to think abstractly and to make generalizations. (We discussed these terms in Chapter 2.) It is a resource which different individuals possess in differing degrees. Certainly everyone has more intelligence than he uses. Nearly everyone has enough to solve the problems and to perform the tasks involved in most everyday situations. Nearly everyone, for example, has learned that a red traffic light means that cars will not stop to allow you to cross the street. Nearly everyone is capable of thinking abstractly enough to do basic addition and subtraction.

No matter how much or how little you are achieving now, there are still fresh and untried areas of your mind that can be stimulated through reading, study, thought, conversation, and exploration of your environment. School performance is the single most important factor in revealing mental ability for certain tasks.

The person who has **creativity** is one who can make ideas and things that have never been made before. Someone can be original and innovative in his approach to painting or writing, needlework or woodworking. He can be innovative in the way he solves everyday problems and in the way he relates to other people. Were it not for creativity, people would do the same things in the same ways, year after year.

In a world where so much is mass-produced, creativity is to some people an increasingly valuable resource: man still has his basic need for stimulation and variety. Creativity can add interest and excitement to life. It can make the near environment more satisfying in many ways.

An **aptitude** is an inborn capacity to perform well in certain areas. An aptitude might be mathematical, mechanical, artistic, musical, athletic, or verbal. Aptitudes usually become evident when a person has had a chance to try a number of different activities. There are tests to help you identify whatever

aptitudes you possess. If an aptitude is present, make an effort to develop it.

A special aptitude in a narrow area is considered a **talent**. Within an area of musical aptitude, for example, a person may have a talent for singing, performing on an instrument, or composing music. In mathematics, one person may have a talent for theoretical mathematics while another may have a talent for the applied mathematics used in business and accounting.

Personal qualities Certain personal qualities can help you overcome a serious lack of other resources. Courage and fortitude can help you overcome illness, injury, physical and emotional handicaps, frustration, loneliness, hardship, and failure to reach a goal. Faith and belief in yourself can help you to persevere when goals seem unlikely to be reached or impossibly distant. For those who believe in a higher power, the strength to withstand severe trials and stress in the attainment of goals comes with spiritual faith.

Our feelings about ourselves and other people can become resources in reaching goals. Count among the plus factors in your personality such resources as emotional stability and sensitivity to the needs and wishes of other people. Adult living is made easier if you have developed a feeling of inner stability. Such a stable personality is possessed by those who have had most of their basic needs reasonably well met. As you mature, it is possible for you to make up for lacks that may have been present in your early life. With positive attitudes, it is possible to move forward, to investigate and explore the opportunities that open up to you each day.

Skills When you develop a skill, you create a human resource. Many different skills can be helpful for modern living. These range from driving a car and taking shorthand to preparing food and using power tools. To make use of some of these skills, certain

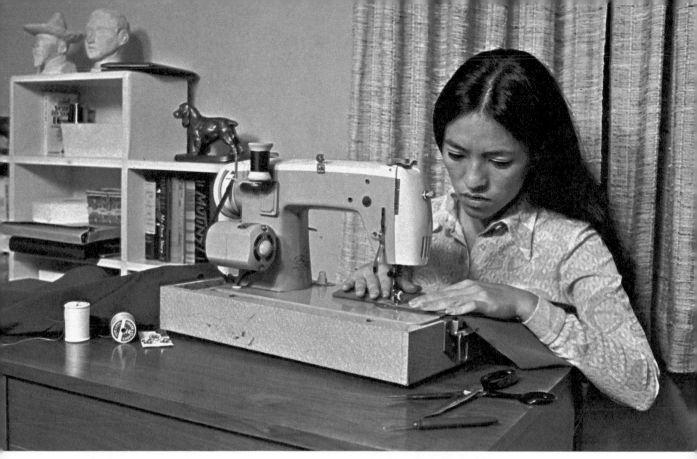

Some resources, such as creativity, increase with use. You can "spend" these resources to create new ones, as you do when you use your mental abilities and aptitudes to develop a skill. As you add to your fund of resources, you will have more alternative ways to reach goals.

physical resources—like strength and stamina—are required.

Another fundamental skill is the ability to communicate. We communicate in many ways. Most obvious are our language skills: speaking, reading, and writing. In reading and writing, we usually have longer to consider the impact of a message. In speaking, however, our message may be communicated before we have fully grasped its impact on our listener. In communicating, we must be aware of the importance of listening as well as the importance of getting our own message across.

We also communicate nonverbally through body language—through the way we move and through our facial expressions. Body language may be communicated without your being aware of it.

Environmental Resources

Anything in the world around you that helps you to reach a goal can be an environmental resource. For our purposes, we will consider four categories. The material resources include what are usually called natural resources, as well as houses, chairs, and other potentially useful items. Technical resources refer to tools. Relationships and social institutions are two other categories of environmental resources.

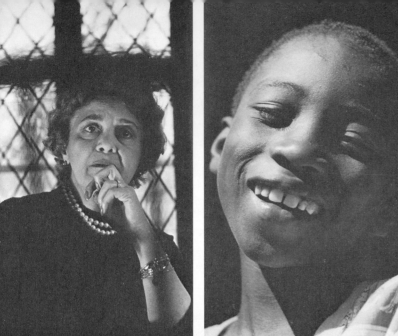

Nonverbal communication signals often say more than words. Learning to be aware of these signals and to interpret them are important in developing good communication skills. If you had to talk with these people, would you approach each of them in the same way?

Material resources Each person finds himself in a special environmental situation. Each environment offers different material resources in the way of money, housing, and possessions. The space and privacy afforded by housing can be considered among your material resources. Without them it is difficult, if not impossible, to pursue such goals as self-improvement and recreation.

Technical resources Modern science has created technical resources that may be called upon to reach goals. Any tool or device that extends your capability beyond your own skills in performing certain tasks is a technical resource. In the form of household appliances, they become important resources in the near environment. A coin-operated laundry and an automatic car wash are two such technical resources.

Relationships Most people who truly value other people may reject the notion of "using" them to reach goals. Human relationships, however, are important resources because of the help and support they offer. From family relationships, for example, you can gain self-confidence. From friendships your

---

CASE STUDY: BILL

THE SITUATION *"I'm tired of being unable to afford what I want," Bill said to his brother. He had been thinking of dating more often, but found, with his job as shipping clerk, that he just "couldn't swing it." He had opened a savings account several months before, specifically to save money toward the purchase of an expensive dog. He wanted the dog and hesitated to withdraw the money for any other purpose.*

"The only way you can have both the dog and more dates is to get a better job," replied his brother. Bill knew his brother's suggestion was a good one, but he considered it "boring" to job-hunt. He had found his present job in one day, and took it without looking further. He liked it because he didn't have to "work hard" at it, and he had plenty of leisure time for other activities. Besides, the job was close to home. Any better job would require commuting twenty miles every day.

"Don't tell me your money troubles," continued his brother. "With the brains and know-how you have, you don't deserve my sympathy.

THE INTERVIEW *Q: Did the conversation with your brother solve any of your problems, Bill?*
A: Not exactly. He didn't have any good ideas to offer.
Q: What about his suggestion that you look for a better job?
A: He always suggests something like that. He thinks I don't make best use of my abilities, but I'm not really interested in doing that.
Q: Why not? Some people find it a very satisfying experience.
A: Oh? Who needs it? I'll find a better way to get what I want. I'm young. I have a lot of time yet.
Q: Have you decided, then, that you are not interested in dating more often?
A: No, I haven't decided that. I still want to date often.

REACT *What are Bill's priorities? What could be better than reaching goals with "natural" human resources that Bill already possesses?*

Social institutions may provide resources that would otherwise be unavailable for the achievement of group goals. In a workshop associated with the New York City Department of Cultural Affairs, neighborhood teenagers designed and executed a mural for their community.

spirits can be lifted. From relationships with teachers and counselors you can gain sound advice and constructive criticism. All these relationships can provide the kind of support needed to help you reach goals.

Social institutions Many social institutions, including marriage and the family, are resources for the achievement of goals. Beyond the family, social resources exist in the neighborhood and the community. Many institutions exist for the achievement of individual and group goals. Many offer important services to individuals and to families. Hospitals and clinics offer medical, dental, and mental health services. Agencies exist for the treatment of drug and alcohol addiction. Libraries, schools, museums, art galleries, and training institutes are resources, as are banks, day-care centers, police departments, employment agencies—the list is endless.

ESTABLISH YOUR PRIORITIES

In a given amount of time, with a given set of resources, you can only accomplish so much. Therefore, you may wish to rank your values and goals in order of importance. You may wish to establish your priorities. On occasion, this may lead you to put off certain goals until you have reached others.

You will rank goals in a different order of importance at different times in your life. Your priorities will change. What may have had first importance to you in your younger years may give way to other goals as you mature. A person who as a teen thought only of popularity may grow into an adult who ranks his family's health and security first.

By establishing your priorities, by deciding which goal comes first and why, you stand a better chance of reaching several goals without sacrificing your values.

FREEDOM TO CHOOSE

No one has unlimited choices. Choices can be limited by lack of resources or by our own lack of experience and education. We can overcome the latter limitations. We can increase our choices as we live and learn. Knowledge and past experience become resources in helping us reach goals.

No one has perfect freedom. People who are too hungry, frightened, angry, or insecure are not really free to choose. Consequently, they have little control over their own lives. Freedom to choose can exist only in a society that values such freedom and can satisfy certain basic needs. Nevertheless, each society must restrict some freedom. Unchecked freedom results in chaos and in lawlessness. Such conditions threaten men's safety and security. Thus, real freedom to choose cannot exist without some form of law and order.

No choice is really "free." Every choice has a cost. The cost is measured in resources used to reach a goal. The very act of making a choice limits your other choices. When you choose one goal, you may be closing the door on other goals. Yet, choose we must. People who do not make choices are allowing things to happen to them by default. They fail to act in ways that will bring them satisfaction. As you mature, more and more opportunities lead to real choice. By learning to make decisions, you can expand your freedom for future choices.

THINK BACK

The values we hold influence the decisions we make.
Discuss: *How will the values you now hold change as you mature?*

Society helps establish our system of values.
Discuss: *"Today's young people have lost their sense of values."*

Actions are a clue to values.
Discuss: *"Actions speak louder than words."*

Setting goals makes decision making easier.
Discuss: *How do you begin helping the person who "just can't make up his mind"?*

Standards we set "measure" progress towards reaching goals.
Discuss: *What is meant by the phrase, "His standards are low"?*

Selecting and using resources wisely helps us reach goals.
Discuss: *What are your best resources for reaching goals?*

LOOK AROUND

1. What are the values stressed in society now? Which are primarily material? Which are primarily moral? Which are primarily esthetic?
2. Illustrate your feeling about these values by making a bulletin board.
3. Discuss your system of values with your classmates. How do yours differ from theirs?
4. Discuss your system of values with an adult at home. How do yours differ from theirs?
5. In what ways has the Women's Liberation Movement reflected a change in men's and women's values? Are any of these changes appealing to you? Which ones?
6. Develop a "Commitment Corner" bulletin board to describe your more important long-range, intermediate, and short-range goals. Describe also the standards that you will apply in order to determine whether or not you have reached these goals.

7. Develop a "Commitment Corner" bulletin board that you imagine might apply to an adult whom you admire.

8. What changes in values and goals would be necessary to plan and carry out solutions to environmental problems in your community? Do you support these?

9. Develop a project chart, indicating goals you have set for yourself in this study unit. At the end of the unit, decide if you have accomplished what you set out to do. What "rating" would you give to your achievements?

10. Identify what you feel are the major resources available in your community. Give a use for each.

11. Suppose you are planning a children's party. What would your values, goals, and standards be? What human and environmental resources do you have at your disposal?

FOLLOW YOUR PATH

PATH ONE: Keep a Log

Step 10 Copy the line below on a blank piece of paper.

| 0 | 10 | 20 | 30 | 40 | 50 | 60 | 70 | + |

This line represents your life line. Sort through your log cards for goals you have set. Mark the points on the life line where you feel your goals will be accomplished. Are all your goals achievable? Explain how your goals reflect your values.

Step 11 What human resources do you discuss most often in your log? List several that you might use in the future, but haven't yet gotten to. As you reach higher developmental stages, what human resources do you think might increase in value to you? What new ones might you begin to use? Answer by using words, your own drawings, photos, or magazine pictures, or a combination of the three.

Step 12 Repeat Step 11 for environmental resources.

PATH TWO: Write a Skit

Step 10 Continue to write your skit. Plan to have it finished by the time you have read Chapter 4. Make sure the important values, goals, standards, and resources of the principal characters are mentioned.

PATH THREE: Play a Role

Step 11 Act again the same scene you acted in Step 5. This time, consider beforehand the values, goals, standards, and resources of the character you will play.

Step 12 Play the tape recording made in Step 5.

Step 13 In front of the class, compare the two scenes. Invite the class to make comments. Did it help you to think about your situation in terms of the framework for decision making? Did it help your family? In what ways? Were resources better used?

PATH FOUR: Sponsor a Child

Step 10 Determine some of the values held by your sponsored child. Which can you see in his family? Which do you think he might have developed elsewhere?

Step 11 Compare the child's values and goals with your own. Are they different? Why? How do values and goals change? Why?

Step 12 Plan three activities which will help your sponsored child to extend his own resources. Make sure the resources and the level of the activity is suitable to the child's developmental stage. Discuss your planned activities with others.

CHAPTER 4

Learning to Make Decisions

Imagine that, as you read this book, the day is sunny and you are sitting beneath a shade tree. Suddenly you feel a little uncomfortable. You put aside your book and lean back and gaze up at the maze of branches. Why not climb the tree? You pull yourself up to where the trunk divides into three strong branches. You look along each branch, deciding which is strongest and which provides a comfortable place in which to sit. You choose one and climb out. Your perch is not quite as comfortable as you thought it would be, but you accept that. You will stay awhile and enjoy the view of the country and the warmth of the sun.

As in this imaginary episode, soon you will be putting *Personal Perspectives*— as well as all your other schoolbooks—aside. Some of you will be leaving home. You will be entering a larger world. You will be entering a world in which you

will have the opportunity to make more choices than a tree has branches. This is not to say that you can make a choice in every situation. There are always some things over which you have little or no control. If, for example, you are short, it will do you no good to choose to be tall. Also, there are time limits on some choices. You have only until December 25 to give a Christmas present on time.

To what kinds of situations can the decision-making process be applied? What must you know before you can really make decisions? How might you go about "mapping out" a plan to reach a goal? Before discussing some answers to these questions, let us find out under what circumstances someone wants to make decisions in the first place.

SITUATIONS THAT DEMAND DECISIONS

As time passes, our values and goals change. We meet different people; we find ourselves in different situations. Such changes sometimes leave us with values or goals that clash, or with values and goals that do not suit our circumstances. When this happens, tensions and conflicts are created. These conflicts can, on occasion, spark us to make decisions. As a result of making these decisions, we may be able to reduce tensions.

Conflicts in Values and Goals

The natural processes of human growth and development, of maturing and aging, bring about changes in values and goals. Such changes can cause conflicts within the individual and among family members, friends, and groups. Some conflicts involve a whole society.

You may already have experienced conflicts between two such values as loyalty to your family and loyalty to your friends. You

have encountered a conflict between loyalty and honesty if you have asked yourself whether you should tell a friend a painful truth.

A conflict in goals would occur if you had a limited amount of money, and wanted to choose between buying a typewriter to improve your schoolwork and buying a record player to enrich your leisure time. A family may feel conflicts between such goals as buying new curtains, pots, and pans, investing in a vacation for the whole family, or sponsoring a year of graduate study for one child.

Sometimes individuals and groups challenge the values that are held by the society as a whole. Such confrontations occur at times when people see a difference between things as they are and things as they think they ought to be.

If conflicts are not to result in a breakdown of relationships at many levels, decisions must be made. Conflicts produce constructive results when they push decision makers to well-thought-out choices among alternatives.

Role Conflicts

Our complex society demands that we play many roles. When these roles make opposing demands on us, we have a *role conflict*. The person who undertakes the dual role of homemaker and worker outside the home may face conflicts between marriage and career, marriage and education, and parenthood and a career. Those whose jobs demand late hours or frequent absences from home may experience conflict with family members who expect more of their interest, time, and attention. Resolving role conflicts involves decisions concerning the values and goals of each member of the family. It may also involve redefining roles, readjusting relationships, and redirecting energies if the family unit is to thrive.

Through rallies and demonstrations, groups of people express social values and pursue social goals that conflict with the goals of institutions or society as a whole. When there is a conflict in economic values, a group may boycott a business, refusing to buy certain products.

53

THE PROCESS
OF DECISION MAKING

Decision making has no formula. It has no set rules. There are no magic steps which one can follow through every conflict situation. There is no single approach with which one can solve every problem he confronts.

Decision making is an activity which begins when a person recognizes that he is faced with a situation in which there is a conflict and several possible ways of resolving it. The process continues until the person has resolved the conflict to the best of his ability. In between, the decision maker must consciously and deliberately choose what he will do.

CASE STUDY: BOB AND HIS FATHER

THE SITUATION   *Bob and his father were in the living room, listening to a debate between political candidates for a state government office. Bob had decided earlier that since he would soon be able to vote, he would pay more attention to election issues this year. He also wanted to participate more actively in political conversations with his father and friends. He was a little disturbed because his father seemed to be ignoring much of what was being said. In fact, Dad was playing with the family's dog and had his back turned to the television program.*

"Aren't you interested?" asked Bob.

Dad did not answer the question and Bob repeated it a second time. "I've heard what they have to say every year. They never say anything new," replied Dad.

"Elections don't occur every year."

"Son, you just can't believe everything you hear. These people are very careful about what they say. They want to be elected, yet once they are in office, they usually have to do what any other person in the same position would do. In governing, they don't have the choices they tell us they have."

Bob was angry. He disliked his father's habit of stereotyping people. He liked even less his father's know-it-all attitude, particularly about issues as important as those of politics. Sometimes he wondered if it was worth trying to carry on a conversation with someone as narrow-minded as his father. Bob watched the program in silence.*

THE INTERVIEW   *Q: Your son is very quiet. Is that the end of the conversation about this political campaign?*
A: Probably not. I'm sure it will come up again at the dinner table. In fact, there is probably a very interesting conversation going on right now in Bob's imagination. You know how teenagers feel about parents.
Q: How do they feel about parents?
A: Teenagers think we don't care about the world around us. They think we're old and stuffy and unimaginative.
Q: Are you?
A: Let me put it this way. I figure that there is not much that hasn't been done before. Maybe I should be a little more patient with Bob, but I have already experienced everything he's going through right now. I don't feel like reliving the problems of the teenage years again.
Q: Do you mean that each generation is much like the last?
A: Yes. Ideas don't change much from father to son. Someday he will be in my position, and will think the same things I now think.

REACT   *In future years, will Bob think as his father thinks? Whose "side" do you take in this situation?*

City planning boards make social decisions to control changes and developments in the community. In reviewing proposed projects, they should take into account the needs, values, and goals of various groups, so that changes will be beneficial to the community as a whole.

Decision making is required in many situations. The nature of the problem determines the type of decision. A single problem may involve one or more social, economic, or technical decisions. *Social decisions* involve understanding the likenesses and differences among the goals and values held by the people involved in making a group decision. Such decisions might involve your parents, peers, or fellow workers. *Economic decisions* help you to focus on allocating a scarce resource. They require you to see the relationship of your goals to available resources. They help you to weigh the practicality of achieving a goal. *Technical decisions* focus on the task or procedure required to carry out a decision. Technical decisions often follow from having made social or economic decisions.

Social Decisions

Social decisions are necessary if any group is to function effectively. Social decision making must take into account the wants and needs, values and goals, and resources and standards of many people. These must be taken into account for every member of the group. In order to be effective at social decision making, one ought to be sensitive to the human factors involved.

In making a social decision, it is not enough to identify a want, a need, a goal, a value, or a standard. Social decision making must harmonize opposing or conflicting wants, needs, goals, values, and standards. It is concerned with bringing such conflicts within tolerable limits. Thus, social decision making is a process that involves adjusting many interrelated factors.

This can be done in three different ways. The first way is through consensus. When people reach a *consensus*, they reconcile their differences. They come to a general agreement about what should be done. The second form of social decision making is compromise. When people *compromise*, they agree to something, even though certain

When values are strongly held and when differences are great, people who cannot compromise can still succeed in making social decisions by putting aside, or compartmentalizing, the area of conflict.

Economic Decisions

You make an economic decision when there are competing uses for the same resource, of whatever kind. Economic decisions determine whether you consume, produce, or conserve resources.

Any resource can be the object of economic decision making if you have more than one use for it. For example, let us say that you want to improve your personal appearance, but you have only so much time, money, energy, and skill to use in reaching your goal. You are making economic decisions when you must choose among such alternatives as spending money to buy a garment instead of a record album, using time and money to construct a garment instead of a storage unit for your bedroom, or using time and energy to alter or remodel a garment instead of cleaning your room.

In some situations, your goal is to get the maximum return from the minimum outlay of resources. Such an economic decision can be called a "mini-max." You make a "mini-max" economic decision when, after checking the prices of identical items in different stores, you buy the least expensive.

Technical Decisions

A simple "how-to-do-it" decision is called a *technical decision* or implementing decision. A technical decision leads you to find the "best" (which usually means the "most direct") way to get something done. Changing a tire, washing dishes, or hemming a dress involve finding the most efficient way to carry out a decision. Whether you want a workable car, clean dishes, or a straight hem, you will need certain skills to implement technical decisions.

Technical decisions can be built into routines. Once routinized, such technical tasks as washing and vacuuming can be accomplished without the need for further decision making.

parts of that agreement may not please them. Each person accepts some part of the opposing view in order to gain something that he wants. Sometimes differences are too serious to permit compromise. In those cases, it may be necessary to *compartmentalize* the conflicting factors. To compartmentalize means to act as if the conflicting elements do not exist. In many cases, decision makers may find it necessary to compartmentalize or compromise. At a later time, they may reach consensus.

Like any other group, a family is composed of people who do not all share the same values, goals, and standards. A decision concerning the family budget, a family vacation, or a home-improvement project could well involve all three types of social decision making.

READINESS
FOR DECISION MAKING

Decision making requires a certain level of maturity. You must have first mastered certain developmental tasks. When you learned earlier skills, you may not have known that they were necessary for decision making.

Five basic skills reinforce your ability to make decisions: You need to know how to measure and use time. You need to have learned that some events cause other events to happen. You need to be aware that you yourself can cause events, and you need to be able to judge which events you want to make happen. Also, you often need to be willing to postpone immediate gratification of some wants and needs and to accept responsibility for whatever you do.

Developing a Time Sense

As an infant, you were only aware of the present. As you grew older, you came to understand "yesterday" and "tomorrow"; you learned to recall past events and to anticipate the future. You learned to measure time.

Without a well-developed time sense, you cannot appreciate that what you did yesterday has influenced the way you are today, and what you do today will influence what you become tomorrow. A developed time sense is necessary if you are to control your actions and make rational decisions.

Whatever the job to be done, the use of appropriate tools will increase the likelihood of satisfactory results. This couple made sound technical decisions when they elected to paint flat areas with a roller, to use a small brush for the woodwork, and to protect the floor with papers.

In cities, space is a limited resource that can be put to many good uses. Allocating such a resource requires an economic decision. Often, economic decisions are also social decisions.

Observing Cause and Effect

Every day you observe many things: airplanes flying, dogs barking, people crossing streets. If you are to become a decision maker, you must do something with these observations; you must *process* this information. In other words, you must organize this information so that it has some meaning to you. You can do this by determining cause and effect relationships. In a cause and effect relationship, one event (the cause) makes another event (the effect) happen. If you let go of an egg, for example, it will fall to the floor and break. "Letting go" is the cause; "dropping and breaking" is the effect. Understanding what cause and effect relationships are depends on the ability to conceptualize, which usually peaks in the young adult years.

By understanding what causes what, you have taken a step toward causing things yourself—toward gaining control of your environment.

Exercising Judgment

When we exercise judgment, we consider all the information we have at our disposal, and we weigh each factor against the others. To do this takes time. In making a spur-of-the-moment choice, we seldom consider the effects of what we want to do. When making a judgment, however, we always examine cause and effect relationships, and assign values to some of them. Judgment helps us to establish the probability of success or failure in a particular situation. You know, for example, the likelihood of your passing a quiz if you study for it. You also know you will be less likely to pass if you trust only your luck.

Postponing Gratification

Many instant satisfactions may produce long-range problems. Children act to gratify needs immediately. A mature person is able to postpone the gratification of one need to satisfy another. He can, for example, put off a social engagement to study for a test. He can turn down a snack before dinner, no matter how hungry he feels, to better appreciate the meal to come. He knows that many goals worth reaching are worth working and waiting for.

Accepting Responsibility

When you say "I don't blame anyone but myself for what happened," you show willingness to accept responsibility for the outcome of your behavior. You have learned that you can cause certain things to take place. Of course, the unexpected can happen. If you plan a picnic and it rains, you are certainly not to blame. If, however, you decide to skip classes in favor of some other activity, you—not your parents, friends, or teachers—are responsible if you fail the course and have to repeat it.

PREPARATION
FOR DECISION MAKING

A person becomes prepared to make decisions as he matures physically and psychologically, as he masters certain essential developmental tasks. Parents help create the family climate in which this growth takes place. Through sensitive guidance, parents can help children to learn about decision making. They can give their children opportunities to make simple choices. Parents guide children in such "decisions." They give them the freedom to choose, and they show them the possible effects of different courses of action.

It is sometimes hard for a parent to find situations in which the alternatives are clear enough for his children to follow. All the child's possible choices must be acceptable to the parent. Of course, none of these choices should be potentially harmful.

When I was one-and-twenty
    I heard a wise man say,
'Give crowns and pounds and
        guineas
    But not your heart away;
Give pearls away and rubies
    But keep your fancy free.'
But I was one-and-twenty,
    No use to talk to me.

When I was one-and-twenty
    I heard him say again,
'The heart out of the bosom
    was never given in vain;
'Tis paid with sighs a plenty
    And sold for endless rue.'
And I am two-and-twenty,
    And oh, 'tis true, 'tis true.

from *A Shropshire Lad* (A. E. Housman)

With understanding parents, and in the right situation, a child will be fortunate enough to gain some early, direct preparation for decision making.

DECISION-MAKING STRATEGIES

A *strategy* is a plan of action. The strategies listed here are suggested plans of action. In making decisions, you may find it helpful to consider them. In some circumstances, some plans might not apply. Some might seem to overlap. This is to be expected, since they are intended only as general guidelines. These strategies are to:

1. Analyze the choice situation and all its parts. Is there a choice?
2. Identify your goal.
3. Check what you need to make your goals possible. What resources do you have or could you make available?

CASE STUDY: PAMELA

THE SITUATION *"I guess I'd better call Mom."*

Pamela had thought for quite a while before coming to this conclusion. She and two of her girlfriends were in the lobby of a small rooming house in Florida. They had driven south during the University's spring weekend, as had thousands of other students. There was just one problem: No one in Pamela's family knew where she was. No one even knew she had been thinking of going to Florida. She had no money to do so, no transportation, and no friends there. This was a spur-of-the-moment idea, as were many others she had had.

Pamela listened as someone picked up the telephone receiver at home. It was Mother.

"Hi, Mom! How are you?"

"Hello, Honey. I'm fine. You sound very far away. Where are you?"

Pamela hesitated before answering. *"I'm in Florida. We just arrived this evening. I want to know if there is anyone here you would like me to say 'hello' to."*

There was a long silence, and then her father's voice, on the extension: *"How did you get there?"*

"I came with some friends. We're in a rooming house. Don't worry."

"Where did you get the money?"

"I borrowed some from a friend and some from the bank at school. I'll pay it back."

"You certainly will, young lady! And with no help at all from either your mother or me, understand? Now you get yourself into that car and back to this house by tomorrow night, if you don't want to find yourself locked out for good."

THE INTERVIEW Q: *It sounds as though you might have made the wrong choice, doesn't it? How are you going to get home by tomorrow night?*
A: *I won't. I don't have a ride because no one is going back until tomorrow night.*
Q: *Did you think your parents would be this upset about what you did?*
A: *I really didn't think too much about it. I wanted to come to Florida so I packed up and drove down.*
Q: *Can you pay back the money?*
A: *Yes, but it will take a while. I only have a part-time job.*
Q: *Your mother was very quiet. Why didn't she talk with you?*
A: *She was probably crying.*

REACT *Did Pamela's decision to go to Florida show careful consideration? How can she solve the problems that have resulted?*

4. Discover what alternatives are really possible for reaching the goal. How many alternatives do you have?
5. Weigh the consequences of each alternative. What is the cost of each?
6. Narrow your alternatives. Select the alternative that seems most likely to bring the most satisfaction with the best use of available resources.
7. Determine what procedures need to be followed to reach your goal.
8. Activate the choice.
9. Adjust the procedure for carrying out the choice as needed, *if* needed.
10. Take responsibility for your actions and for any unexpected consequences.

We will look at Lee's problem as an example of one person's making a decision.

Analyzing a Choice Situation

Lee is a sixteen-year-old high school sophomore. By the time he is seventeen, he wants to have a car available to him, and he wants to be able to drive it.

His parents cannot afford to give him a car. They cannot afford the additional insurance coverage for a teenage driver, either. If Lee wants to drive the family car, he must pay the additional insurance himself. Even then, the car will not always be available to him. His father drives it to work; his mother and sister use it on prearranged occasions.

Lee's parents have no objection to his opening a savings account for a car of his own. However, if he is to buy his own car, his father would like to see him complete a course in driver's education first.

There are many facets to Lee's choice situation. Should he buy his own car? What about insurance? What about driver's education? However Lee goes about gaining access to a car, it will cost him money. If he does decide to act, where will this money come from?

Lee feels that having his own car will give him greater independence. Even if he is only to drive the family car, he must save to reach a goal that is a year away.

It is said that "to see a problem as a whole is to see part of the solution." Can you see how this applies to Lee's situation?

Identifying Goals

The solution to Lee's problem involves reaching several goals. He must (1) be prepared to drive well enough to get a license, so he must pass the driver's education course by the time he (2) has saved the money to buy a car that will (3) pass his state's stiff inspection laws; and (4) he must have the money to pay the insurance premium for his age group. Thus, Lee's wish to have a car, or even to drive his parents' car, involves several intermediate and long-range goals. To overlook any part of this total problem could make the final goal unattainable. It is clear that Lee's goals will take careful planning to be reached. He must arrange to take the driver's education course and find a way to pay for a car, auto insurance, and operating expenses. Then he must find a car—one that will pass inspection—at a price within his means.

Checking Available Resources

Lee's resources are limited. He has $68 which he has saved from gifts and odd jobs. There is a summer session driver's education course for $25. There is also a free course he can take after school in the fall. This course is not really "free," however. The time he spends in the class will reduce the time he has available for work. The cost of a car is another potential expense for Lee. He finds that the ones he considers suitable are about $300.

Insurance would cost another $150. The state in which Lee lives has a special registration fee of $100. License plates and his driver's license would be additional expenses. Job-hunting appears to be Lee's top priority; this will involve time, energy, and some money. In other words, Lee must use some available resources to acquire different and additional resources. He will then be in a better position to reach his goal.

Discovering Alternatives

Lee begins to survey the job market. One job, delivering for a local store, pays the minimum wage plus tips. Another job pays a higher hourly wage, but without tips. Lee recalls that several neighbors have asked him to mow their lawns. He checks out the going fee for this service. He estimates that if he has

his own power mower, he will earn a higher hourly income than with a regular job.

Weighing the Consequences

If Lee takes the first job, delivering for a store, he may have high and low points of income with no risk. If he takes the other job, he will have a dependable income and a steadily growing savings account. If he buys the mower and goes into business for himself, he may make more money, but he also runs the risk of losing his investment if anything unforeseen happens to his mower.

Making the Choice Workable

Lee discusses the alternatives with his parents and his sister. His sister is in favor of the second job. "What will you do," she asks, "if you don't get enough lawns to mow?" His father observes that working with the mower could teach him some mechanical principles that would be useful if he owned a car. His mother thinks it is safer to leave his money in the bank and to continue saving. The decision is left to Lee. A friend tells him about a shop that sells rebuilt mowers. Lee investigates. He decides to invest his savings in one. This means he cannot afford the summer driver's education course. He will take the free course in the fall. Lee seems to have taken a step sideways in order to move toward his goal. What factors do you think he considered in making his choice?

Determining How to Proceed

Lee makes practice runs on his parents' and one neighbor's lawns. He masters the efficient use of the mower. He is pleased to see that with each try he improves his performance. When he has trouble with the mower, he learns to take it apart and repair it. He thus learns, with help from his father, some of the basic principles of how a gasoline engine works. He is also improving his mechanical

skills. By carrying out his short-range goals, Lee is gaining the satisfaction of knowing that he is moving closer to his long-range goal.

Activating the Choice

Lee surveys the neighborhood for potential customers. He lists the names and addresses of homes that he thinks might use his services. His sister volunteers to make a mimeographed flyer to advertise his service. He leaves one in the mailbox of each house that he considers to be a good prospect. He checks back. He has only a couple of leads. He stays with his plan, however, keeping a close tab on the time and expenses incurred for the mower. He gains customers as news of his good work and dependability spreads by word of mouth through the neighborhood.

Adjusting the Procedure

Lee finds that he is not averaging the same hourly income that he would have earned had he taken the second job. A long dry summer is bad for business. He decides to take a weekend job delivering for the store and to mow lawns during the week. He is then able to save the planned amount. Because he lives in a state with cold winters, Lee decides to add snow shoveling as a winter service for his established clients. This way, he is working harder than he expected, but he is getting closer to his goal.

Accepting the Consequences

By the following summer, Lee has learned a great deal from his experience. He has found that he had not correctly estimated the cost of replacement parts for the mower. He had not counted on the cost of gas and oil, either. He sometimes found it hard to get out of bed early to shovel snow and to give up some summer activities to work.

All in all, however, Lee feels his plan was a good one. He has bought his car. He has learned that he likes working out-of-doors and being his own boss. From these experiences, he begins to investigate careers in landscaping, in which he plans to take a two-year course after graduating.

Some decisions, once made, eliminate other alternatives and opportunities from your life. One value of rational decision making is the chance to weigh, in advance, the possible effects of your commitments.

THE VALUE OF DECISION MAKING

Decision making involves so many complex activities. Why bother? Why not take life as it comes? Why not react spontaneously to everything? Committing yourself to decision making does mean that you will often have to stop and reflect. It does mean that you cannot always act spontaneously, without considering the consequences. Rather, it provides a method through which you may find satisfaction by an effective use of your resources and with a considered degree of risk. You may become, up to a point, the designer of your life. Impulsive action may, on occasion, result in immediate gratification, but it does not always provide long-range satisfaction.

In Separating Needs From Wants

In making decisions, you must identify your goals and set your priorities. Your goals will reflect your needs and wants. In establishing your priorities, you should think carefully. Satisfaction means that needs are met, and satisfaction is the purpose of decision making.

In Resolving Conflicts

Needs are not always clearcut. They are felt in different degrees at different moments. They are felt in different ways at different times of your life. Even if you know what your needs are, the direct fulfillment of them may clash with the needs of others. All this means that you have conflicts—both role conflicts and conflicts in values and goals. Only through careful reflection can you develop plans that will help you to resolve these conflicts.

In Reducing Risk

There is some risk involved in everything you do. No one can control a situation so perfectly or so completely that there is never any element of risk. However, rational decision making can help to reduce the risks in many situations. By thinking of possible consequences of different courses of action *before* you act, you can avoid those that might be dangerous or fruitless.

In Conserving Resources

The world has a limited supply of natural resources. Human resources such as intelligence, creativity, and compassion also appear to be in short supply. Increasing demands are being made upon both natural and human resources as the world's population increases and as people's expectations rise. In establishing priorities, decision making promotes wise management in the use of all resources. This means reducing waste. You can do this by taking positive steps, wherever possible, to recycle or re-use material resources. It may also mean using less of scarce resources such as energy. If, by doing so, we support the environment, then we can be assured that the environment will continue to support us.

THE COURAGE TO CHOOSE

To make a decision you have to commit yourself to something. You have to take a stand. This requires courage and considerable maturity. Courage and maturity will give you the ability to manage your future.

It is not always possible to have all the facts in a particular situation. Still, we must try to predict what will most likely happen if we pursue a certain course of action. Decision making makes it possible to estimate the likelihood of success; the more experience we gain in making decisions, the better our chances for satisfaction. When you know what has happened in the past, what is happening in the present, and why, you are growing closer to understanding what might happen in the future. You are in a better position to act than had you merely taken guesses or made wishes. Since we must live with the results of what we do—and of what other people and events do to us—we might do well to exercise both control and cooperation.

In a larger sense—in the sense of what happens not only to you, but to your brother and sister human beings and to your environment—decision making is also of vital significance. The sum total of all the actions—or failures to act—of everyone goes a long way in determining our future and the future of our world. Ours is the opportunity to decide our future rather than to leave it to chance.

THINK BACK

Conflicts can best be resolved by rational decision making.
Discuss: *"Everything is just perfect. I needn't do a thing."*

Knowing how to make decisions gives us control over much of our lives.
Discuss: *"I don't care what it is. If I want to do it, I can."*

We can make rational decisions only after we have learned the necessary background skills.
Discuss: *"I don't know how I'll reach that goal. Nobody ever taught me how."*

Decision making involves accepting responsibility for one's actions.
Discuss: *"Don't look at me! I didn't know that was going to happen."*

LOOK AROUND

1. Clip four examples of conflicts from your daily newspaper. Tell how each of these might be resolved by social, technical, or economic decision making, or by some combination of these three.
2. Identify a choice situation you might face today. List some alternatives and potential resources.
3. Make a poster with suggestions for solving, through consensus, compromise, or compartmentalizing, an existing problem in your school.
4. How do young children indicate their "readiness" to make decisions? What types of "decisions" can be made by young children?
5. What kind of goals do young children seem to have? What are examples of ways by which they reach their goals? How will maturing change their method?

6. Which of the decision-making strategies seems easiest to do? What does this tell you about your developmental stage?
7. Make collages illustrating each of three decision-making strategies.
8. Name one kind of conflict in a family with young children that might be resolved by decision making. With teenagers. With grandparents.

FOLLOW YOUR PATH

PATH ONE: Keep a Log

Step 13   From your cards, select the one long-range goal that seems most important to you. What conflict or conflicts are involved? Tell how you think this goal might be reached. Identify the decision-making strategies you think you might use.

Step 14   How many times in your cards do you discuss each of the skills necessary for decision making? Do you feel you have developed any of the skills that you do not discuss? Which skills do you feel you must still acquire? Make a collage or a bulletin board to illustrate the one skill you feel you have mastered least.

Step 15   From your cards, select one choice you made by not making a choice at all. If you had used the decision-making process, do you think the results would have been the same? Explain.

PATH TWO: Write a Skit

Step 11   Create an advertisement for your play. You might wish to prepare a drawing, a cartoon, or a collage. The advertisement should suggest the main conflict situation.

Step 12   In your play, identify each decision-making strategy that is used in working out the conflict. Are some strategies used that are not mentioned in the text? Which unused strategies might have offered additional help in resolving the conflict?

Step 13   List the key characters and the necessary decision-making skills which each has not mastered. If you were to rewrite your play to make the conflict situation easier, which one unlearned skill would you have which character master? Why?

PATH THREE: Play a Role

Step 14   Listen to both tapes again. Make lists of the decision-making strategies used each time. Discuss the differences in the two lists. Decide which situation involved more of a rational decision-making process.

Step 15   What choices has your role-played character made in each of the two situations? Explain the relationship between these choices and his values. Discuss the character you acted out in terms of resources. Which resources could your character have further developed? Outline a plan for your character to extend his resources.

Step 16   Which decision-making skill has your character not mastered? At what point in the second situation might mastery of this skill have helped your character?

PATH FOUR: Sponsor a Child

Step 13   Review 12. Can you see any conflicts that might have arisen between yourself and your sponsored child in your attempt to activate your choices for him?

Step 14   Analyze your sponsored child's opportunities to make simple "decisions." Plan an activity that will allow the child to make a "decision." For example, the decision may be choosing among buying an ice cream cone, buying a book, and buying a toy. How would you explain each choice to the child? Consider the decision-making skills someone his age would have mastered.

Step 15   Review all the plans you have made for your sponsored child. Give examples of each of the decision-making strategies you employed. Could you have used others? How and when?

Managing Your Resources

Once you choose to do something, there are often a variety of ways in which you can do it. Some of these ways might take more natural and personal resources than others. If these resources were unlimited, there would be no reason to be concerned about how many were used up. As it is, many feel a responsibility to help preserve their environment. Many people also question whether they are being fair to themselves if they use much time, for instance, to attain a single goal, thus reducing the amount they have left to use for reaching other goals.

The purpose of Chapter 5 is to suggest strategies you might use to *manage*—to make wise use of—your resources. These strategies may help you to reach present goals quickly and efficiently. They may help you to conserve resources for other times and other goals.

OVERARCHING RESOURCES

Three of the most important resources are time, energy, and money. We use time and energy in every phase of everything we do. We use energy even when sleeping, for then the body is at work rebuilding itself. Money is not quite so integral a part of our lives: there are things—like sitting on a log—that we can do without it. We do, however, live in a world where money is in constant use. We use it to reach many of our goals.

We might call these three fundamental resources overarching resources. We generally use them as we use our other resources. In asking whether we have made the wisest use of what we have, we are frequently asking if we could have better used our time, energy, and money.

Consider, for example, a young man who has finally realized his dream to become a tennis champion. He evaluates what he has accomplished. Could he have reached his goal more easily? He recalls the long afternoons spent in hard practice. Certainly he spent a lot of time and used a lot of energy playing tennis. He used hundreds of tennis balls. On occasion he replaced his racket. Rackets, balls, and the use of the courts cost money.

Was the result worth the effort? Did the tennis player make the wisest use of his resources? Only he can really say. The point here is that there are convenient standards for measuring these overarching resources.

If the player wishes, he can record the minutes, hours, and days he spends on some activity. We have conventional measures of time. The same is true of money. In the United States and Canada, there are dollars and cents. Other countries have different units of exchange which serve the same purpose.

There are also precise measures of energy, like calories and BTU's. These can be mea-

Time, energy, and money can be combined in different proportions to reach a goal. You can compensate for the lack of one by spending more of another.

■ Time   ■ Money   ■ Energy

Time is one resource that cannot be increased or reserved. When we speak of "buying time" or "saving time," we are really talking about using the time that is available. Ideally, the goals and activities most important to you will be reflected in the way you spend your time.

sured with delicate instruments. The average tennis player, of course, does not have such an instrument on the court. His standards are more approximate: he judges how tired he feels after the match is over.

Because time, energy, and money are "behind" so much of what we do, we might consider them in more detail.

Just as important as a person's biological clock is his sense of time. This is his idea of what time is; it is his awareness that things happen in time. To a large extent, this sense of time is culturally determined. Some languages, for example, have no future tense; they have no word for "tomorrow." Other cultures are future-oriented; they emphasize what is to come. Still other cultures are present-oriented.

Within cultures, individuals vary in their sense of time. In the Western world, individual attitudes toward time often vary with age, background, and experience. Young people sometimes feel they have all the time in the world to make a decision. Yet each person lives within the restrictions of a twenty-four hour day. Attitudes toward work and leisure influence a person's attitude toward time. For example, many young adults place a higher value on Saturday nights than on time spent in school or at work.

Time

Everyone has a biological clock ticking inside him. He has, barring accident or disease, a more-or-less set amount of time to live. This time is one of his most precious human resources. Perhaps, if he lives very carefully, he might lengthen his life some small amount. Essentially, though, his time resources are limited. Whether he acts or does not act, they are constantly being used up. He can only try to achieve what he wants to achieve in the time he has available.

Energy

We need energy to function. We cannot make this energy ourselves. We must take it, in the form of food, from the environment. Energy, then, is both a human and an environmental resource.

Both our physical and our psychological activities require energy. The physical energy we need comes from food. Mental and emotional energy is far more difficult to describe. In a sense, it is the same as physical energy: all our energy originates in what we eat. We usually find it harder to solve a problem or to feel certain emotions on an empty stomach. At the same time, we do not necessarily feel psychologically excited just because we have eaten a full meal. We might almost say that psychological energy is generated by a person himself and by the people and events he encounters.

Human energy can be defined as the ability to stay alive, to act, to think, and to feel. Clearly, without energy, there would be no other resources.

While a person's supply of time is always decreasing, his supply of energy can be constantly renewed. It can be renewed, that is, as long as the balance of nature is such that plants and animals can survive to support us. The energy in nature is in limited supply. It must be properly managed if we are going to survive.

Money

Money is a standard of economic value. Frequently the answer to the question "How much is it worth?" can be given in dollars and cents. By itself, however, a dollar bill is worthless. It is just a piece of paper. It has value because everyone agrees that it has value. People are willing to say that a banana is worth five cents and that a refrigerator is worth $200. The person who sells the banana is willing to accept five cents as a payment. The buyer is willing to pay that much.

One reason the seller is willing to accept money for something of more immediate value is that he can keep the money. He can spend it later for something which he wants. Money, then, is not only a measure of value, it is a store of value. It can be kept for future needs. As you must know, a person's money resources can either increase or be depleted.

PRICE: THE STANDARD OF THE MARKETPLACE

Money is not only a measure of value—of how much you are willing to pay for something. It is also a measure of price—of how much something costs. This monetary price is determined by a number of factors. One of the more important of these is availability. If there are only one or two of an item, it will cost more than if there are seven thousand. The price also depends on how much an item costs to make. If a house costs $10,000 to build, you will probably not be able to buy it for $6,000. The price also includes taxes and the costs of advertising and transporting materials to the building site.

Supply and Demand

Suppose 1,000 people want to buy fountain pens. (There is a *demand* for 1,000 pens.) Suppose also that there are three stationery stores, and that each of these stores has 2,000

CASE STUDY: SAM AND BRENDA

THE SITUATION *Christmas shopping time again! The Christmas lights were pretty, the decorations attractive, the streets crowded, and the prices high! Sam stood in line with his sister Brenda, waiting to pay for his purchases. Every year he vowed that he would not wait until the last minute to buy gifts. The best thing to do would be to keep his eyes open for suitable presents throughout the year and pay reasonable, rather than absurd, prices for his selections. But so far, he had failed to live up to his resolve. His mind was usually occupied with "more important" matters.*

"I want one of those jackets," said Brenda. "Come tell me which looks best."

"You want to buy one today?" Sam asked. "Look how expensive they are! After Christmas they'll be on sale and a much better buy than they are right now. I think you should wait. You have a coat you can wear.

"Don't tell me how to spend my money, Sam," retorted Brenda. "If I wait, the selection will not be as good as it is now.

"But you have other gifts to buy yet," said Sam. "If you buy the jacket you won't have money for anything else."

"I'll put the coat on layaway," answered his sister. "That way, I'll pay only a small sum for the coat now and have money left over for the other gifts. I can pay the balance on the jacket after Christmas, when I'll have earned some more money. I'll meet you at the car in thirty minutes."

THE INTERVIEW *Q: It sounds as though Brenda is determined to buy a jacket. She had her money situation all figured out.*
A: Yes, but she still won't be able to pick the coat up until she has paid for it after Christmas. It makes more sense to wait and buy it then. She'll probably be sorry she was so impulsive when she sees the sale price of the jacket then.
Q: Why is Brenda so willing to pay the higher price for the jacket?
A: Because having the jacket is important to her, I guess. She's more interested in personal appearance than she is in saving money.
Q: Is she any different from the rest of us?
A: No. Look how many of us are in the same boat. The people who are shopping here today are not as concerned about wise use of their dollar as they are about other things. We all waste our money by being influenced by holiday atmosphere or "tradition" or advertising. We all need to exert a little more self-discipline in spending money.

REACT *Is it "right" for stores to raise prices at holiday time? Why are people not more concerned about how they spend money?*

---

pens. (There is a *supply* of 6,000 pens.) The storeowners, anxious to sell their pens, will lower their prices. Now, suppose the three stores each have only 200 pens. The owners, sure they will sell their stock, will raise their prices. These two examples illustrate the *law of supply and demand:* Oversupply drives prices down; scarcity drives prices up.

Natural events can cause fluctuations in supply. An early frost in Florida will reduce supplies of oranges. Supplies of items might also be deliberately limited by manufacturers who wish to raise their products' prices. Demand can vary, too. As autumn begins in cool climates, interest in summer clothing lessens. Consequently, prices drop.

You may have resources that go unused because you do not recognize them. If you have not discovered your own creativity, for example, you are not likely to call upon it to reach goals, even when you can.

Merchandising and Distribution

A merchant's *overhead* is the amount of money it costs him to run his store. It includes everything from rent and electricity to special display cases. When he sets a price on his merchandise, he includes his overhead.

If his store is in a high rent district, if he offers exceptionally high-quality or brand-name merchandise, his overhead will be high. If, in addition, he offers "free" delivery, his overhead will be even higher.

Understanding the cost of overhead will help you understand why the same product costs more in some stores than in others.

Advertising and Promotion

Those who make products advertise to tell you what they have made and what it will do. Advertising costs money; the cost is passed along to the consumer in the price of the product. This explains why many nationally advertised products cost more than their unadvertised counterparts.

Sometimes, those who make products pay movie, television, and sports stars to endorse their products. You can sometimes find the names of such popular personalities on clothing labels and bread wrappers. Products are also promoted through colorful, attractive, appealing packaging. The cost of endorsements and packaging are passed along in a product's selling price.

Other Factors

People are paid to make products, to distribute them, and to sell them. Their wages and salaries must be included in the cost to the consumer. Higher wages in a certain industry, then, often cause higher prices. A pay raise in the steel industry might result in higher prices, not just for steel, but for toasters and refrigerators, too.

Also included are the costs of transporting a product from the place where it is made to the place where it is to be sold.

Another increasingly important element in the price of goods and services is taxes. A tax is a charge which a government places on goods, services, and income. In the United States, federal, state, and local governments impose taxes.

MANAGING YOUR RESOURCES

You use what you have to get what you want. If you wanted only one thing in life—if you had only one goal—you could use all your resources to attain that goal. You would not have to worry about saving anything for the future. You would not have to manage your resources. You *manage* your resources when, to reach a goal, you use them in the most effective way. Resources are closely intertwined. They are all part of you or of your environment. Sometimes, in using less of one resource, you use more of another. (You might spend money to save time.) Sometimes you use one resource to acquire another. (You might spend money to go to college to acquire knowledge. You might use your food preparation skills to prepare a dish quickly, and thus save time.) Some resources increase with use. (Skills and other human resources are good examples. With practice a person usually becomes better at sports.) Other resources decrease and can never be recovered. (Energy is the most significant example.) Other resources, like money, decrease and increase.

What does it mean, then, to get more for less? How do you decide which resources to conserve and which to spend? Part of the answer lies in the place which any given resource occupies on your scale of values. Part lies in how much you know about your goals. You might use less of those resources which are most important to you. You economize on those resources which will help you to reach future goals—on those resources which will be vital for implementing future decisions.

Also, the way a person manages his resources depends on what resources he has. There are obviously wide differences in the kinds and amounts of resources available to different individuals and families. Many people reach their goals not because they have many resources, but because they make the best use of what they have.

Many everyday tasks and errands, such as going to the laundromat or to the dentist, require us to spend time waiting. But since most of these time traps can be anticipated, they need not be fruitless or boring.

There are two parts, then, to successful resource management: You need to know what your resources are and how to use them effectively. In both these steps, it is helpful to be able to measure your resources. To aid in measurement, we turn to the three resources for which there are standard measures.

Assessing Time Use

What does time mean to you? How are you using your time now? Have you set goals in terms of time? What demands are being made on your time? How much time do you unintentionally let slip by?

Your uses for time have certainly changed in the past years. Can you predict how they will change further in the years ahead? What new undertakings, interests, and responsibilities will make new and different demands on your time? Going to school, working, and dating set one pattern of time use. Parenthood will make new and different demands. Each new responsibility and goal can change your attitudes toward using time.

Keep a record of your use of time for a week or longer. You will then have a basis for evaluating your present use of time. Examine the decisions you have already made concerning time use. What do they tell you? Is your time being used to good purpose? Do you use it to satisfy wants and needs and to reach goals? Your record should show you how much time you set aside to meet basic physical needs. Those needs include sleep, rest, food, grooming, and personal hygiene. It should also show you how much time is needed to meet psychological needs. These include safety and security needs met through sharing family responsibilities. How much time is required to meet your social need for companionship? How much time do you spend in meeting spiritual and esthetic needs? And finally, how much time do you set aside for pursuing studies and hobbies that meet your need for self-fulfillment?

If you find that you are spending far too little on the things you really value and not enough on reaching goals, you might want to find ways to better allocate your time.

Assessing Energy Use

When do you feel most energetic? When do you do the most strenuous things you have to do? Do you enjoy dancing or sports? Are you involved in other physical activities? What are your eating habits? Do you eat the kinds of food which give you the energy to do the things you like to do? How often do you use electrical appliances? When do you walk instead of taking a bus or driving a car?

Efficient performance of tasks is closely related to your energy use. When you choose to replace human energy with mechanical energy, you must keep in mind that you are using up scarce energy resources. To be effective, you need to learn to better use human energy. You will want to match your tasks to the amount of energy you have available. Some people say they are "night people." Most of us can be called "day people" because we have more energy available to us in the morning, after a full night's sleep and a nutritious breakfast.

The quality of school performance is, in many cases, related to how well a program meshes with a student's energy level.

Physiological fatigue Physical activity creates physiological fatigue. Physical exertion speeds up the body's chemical factory. Much as with a factory working overtime, waste products build up during periods of high energy use. A buildup of waste products in muscles and tissues lowers physical efficiency. You feel this as aches and weakness.

Psychological fatigue Psychological fatigue is not related to energy levels, but to mental and emotional factors. You may experience psychological fatigue as a result of conflict or frustration, which may be due to your inability to perform a task because you lack the necessary skill or information. It also occurs when you find a task boring and unchallenging. You overcome psychological fatigue by changing your activity or acquiring the skill you need. Time saved without purpose hangs heavy and is a sure route to boredom. Time filled to no purpose in "busy work" creates boredom and frustration, too.

Improving Time and Energy Use

Both time and energy are put to efficient use when good work habits are formed. Once a simple way of doing a task is found, why not

CASE STUDY: MIRIAM AND VAL

THE SITUATION *"I'm so tired when I come home from work. And look at all the things I have to do at home in the evenings!"* Miriam looked at the dishes in the sink, the dust on the furniture, the soiled clothes to be washed, and her empty refrigerator. There was so much housework to be done that she became tired just thinking about it!

"I keep telling you to set up a routine, a schedule that you follow for doing the housework," replied her sister Val. *"You would be surprised how quickly work gets done when you fix specific times to do it. And then your routine becomes habit, and you begin to have extra time for activities that you really enjoy. Having a routine helps you become much more relaxed!"*

"Your life is different from mine. What works for you won't work for me." Miriam had heard all this before. She was a hard one to convince.

"Of course our schedules would not be identical," responded Val. *"But each of us would still be following a routine. Let's set up a possible plan for you. What are all the jobs you want to do here at home?"*

Reluctantly, Miriam began listing daily and weekly jobs as Val quickly wrote them down. After listing everything she could think of, she separated the daily tasks from the weekly ones. As Val observed, there were many daily tasks that had already become routine with Miriam. After all, if she were to continue getting to work on time, she had to automatically and as quickly as possible dress, wash, put on makeup, eat, and drive to her job.

"Next, you should decide the days on which you would prefer to do these other things, and think about the time required for each job. In some cases, you might be able to do several things on one day. For instance, I usually shop for groceries and do my laundry Friday evening. If something special is happening Friday, though, I'll switch those jobs to another time spot. I try not to let my routine become too rigid." Val's suggestions were again followed and a weekly routine for Miriam developed.

"This is going to take a little effort," commented Miriam.

"Of course it is," answered Val. *"You just have to make a decision to follow your schedule. After one week, make changes where needed. Your routine should be comfortable to follow and should make sense to you."*

THE INTERVIEW *Q: It didn't seem to take long to set up Miriam's routine.*
A: It doesn't take long. It just requires that you become more organized in your way of doing things. And for some people, that's the real effort!
Q: Why should people be organized?
A: Because life is too short not to be organized. At some point in your life you have to take a firm hold and guide it in the direction you think best for you. Establishing routines that become habits leaves your mind free to explore what really interests you. You're freer to develop your potential as much as possible. You're not bogged down in "busy work."

REACT Do you agree that routines are an important part of managing your life? What kinds of routines should you develop?

Businesses, schools, and other institutions use computers to handle both routine tasks and complex problems. Home computers, which can save time and energy spent paying bills and planning menus, are presently on the market. In the future, they may be commonplace in the home.

make it a part of your regular routine? Practicing good techniques so that they become virtually automatic is also a good way to improve your use of time and energy. A "stitch in time" is an excellent idea to keep in mind for managing time and energy efficiently. For example, wiping up as you go will spare time and energy spent in heavy scouring and cleaning. Using the proper product for the job you are doing makes work easier, too. Labels, hangtags, and appliance manuals offer suggestions for using articles and products efficiently.

Simplifying work You can analyze each task to see how many steps you are using to do it.

Ask yourself which steps are superfluous. Try to cut down on extra steps so that you simplify the job. Favor your *handing* where possible: if you are left-handed, look for left-handed appliances or tools. Try to arrange work areas so that they suit your needs. Keep items at the place where they are most often used. Learning to use both hands for such tasks as washing windows might be another way to conserve time and energy.

Establishing routines A good routine is one that eliminates time spent making decisions about jobs that come up regularly. Once a good work habit is formed, further choice may not be necessary. Fixed routines cut down on the time and energy spent in doing daily, weekly, and seasonal tasks. After all, who would want to spend time making decisions each time he brushed his teeth? You can easily routinize certain tasks.

Avoiding strain When you strain yourself physically you overexert yourself in some way. You may even hurt yourself—perhaps "pull" a muscle. Some activities—like running the hundred yard dash—may necessarily involve some strain. If you are to be a resource manager, you must ask yourself how little you need strain yourself to accomplish a certain goal. You ought to form habits which will help rather than hinder the efficient use of your body. If you wish to pick something up from the floor, for example, you can either bend at the waist or at the knees. Bending at the knees involves less strain on any one part of the body. This is because you use leg and stomach muscles as well as arm and back muscles. To perform a physical task, use as many parts of your body as you can. If possible, make relaxed, sweeping movements, rather than tight, tense ones. Wear appropriate clothing and well-fitted shoes. If available, use the right furniture, tools, and appliances.

Dovetailing tasks Each goal you set need not be reached by separate procedures that might just as well be performed together. You can learn to *dovetail* tasks. When you do this, you fit two routines into the same time span. If you have ever dried your hair while reading a homework assignment or worked on a hobby while watching TV, you have already had experience in dovetailing tasks. In dovetailing tasks you create a resource; you make time available.

Being punctual Making and keeping appointments is an important means of improving your own and other people's use of time and energy. To be punctual is to show that you value time for the human purposes it serves. Busy professional people have a right to charge you for missed appointments. Chronic lateness in meeting appointments may suggest poor organization, a lack of concern for others, and a weak self-concept.

Alternating tasks People vary in their susceptibility to monotony. To avoid the psychological fatigue associated with boredom, plan your work to alternate dull with interesting jobs. Motivate yourself by holding out the interesting jobs as rewards for getting the tedious ones out of the way.

The ability to cope with psychological fatigue requires involvement in tasks that bring satisfaction and fulfillment. Every schedule ought to include tasks you enjoy. The tired mind is ill-equipped to stick to problem solving and decision making. It may give in to impulse, on the theory that *any* change is better than *no* change at all.

Homemaking is one of those complex careers in which many things have to be done in a limited space of time. The homemaker who can devise ways to dovetail tasks can make the most efficient use of time and energy.

Credit bureaus maintain credit records of individual consumers and furnish reports to credit granters. The Fair Credit Reporting Act guarantees certain protections to the consumer, among them his right to review his credit file on request and to correct any errors in it.

Assessing
Financial Resources

What does money mean to you? Your attitudes toward money influence the way you use it. Money is needed to provide food, clothing, shelter, health care, and other basic necessities. For those who can afford it, money can be used for nonessential items, or *luxuries*. Apart from direct material benefits, money can buy opportunities in the form of education, travel, and recreation. As a means of acquiring goods and services, it can confer feelings of safety and security. Money may also become a symbol for satisfying unmet psychological needs. Some people try to use it to buy love and recognition. Some think money can give them "instant identity." In the hope that others will think better of them, they buy showy, costly, consumer goods.

The years after high school present new opportunities and challenges for the management of financial resources. For many, the young adult years will involve new problems of money management. You yourself may be contemplating leaving home for the first time to attend school, take a job, join the armed forces, or embark on marriage. Review now your past experience in managing your financial resources. Have you saved to pay your own expenses for a class trip, to buy your own clothes, books, or hobby equipment? If you have already begun to earn, save, and spend, you have probably established some habits of money management.

As a family member, you have been a "built-in" part of your family's financial planning; you have shared in the financial resources available to them. As long as your parents are responsible for you, you continue to figure into their overall planning. An awareness of the expenses faced by your family should help you keep your financial expectations within reason. For a time, you may continue to receive financial help from your family, even after leaving home. Such help, in the form of gifts or an allowance, may be your basic financial resource. Some young adults receive funds from Social Security or from an insurance policy. You may win a scholarship or receive some other form of stipend for your education. But first and foremost among adult financial resources is earning power. Earning power is, therefore, closely related to your level of education and your occupational choice.

Allocating Financial Resources

Keep a record of your spending for a week or more. Your record will show your current uses for money. What are your average weekly spending needs? What expenses do you regularly incur? Have you been getting the return in satisfaction that you expected from your money outlay? As you assume your responsibilities as a young adult, you will begin to allocate your financial resources differently from the way you had at earlier stages and the way you will at later stages

of the life cycle. (Young adults are apt to spend more money on snacks, clothing, and leisure activities than young married couples do, for example.) Here we will focus on the wise use of cash and credit in meeting needs in the near environment.

Planning your money use A spending plan, or *budget*, is a means to help you control your outlay of money. Its purpose is to bring you greater satisfaction for what you spend. From your record of past expenditures, you can make a fairly close estimate of what you will have to spend in the future. You will find you have certain *fixed expenses*—expenses which occur in every budget period. When you assume financial responsibility for yourself, these necessary expenses might include rent, transportation (perhaps car ownership), food, and living overhead (utilities, telephone, and certain items such as laundry). Your fluctuating expenses are those expenses which occur from time to time. These will include clothing, clothing upkeep, grooming and grooming aids (including hair styling and haircuts). You may also include recreation (including newspapers, books,

"Truth in Lending" laws require all lenders to give the terms and cost of credit granted. This information appears on monthly statements. If the balance of this account had not been paid before the closing date, it would have increased by $0.53, the finance charge for one month.

DATE	STORE	REFERENCE NO.	DEPT. NO.	TRANSACTION DESCRIPTION	CHARGES	PAYMENTS AND CREDITS
03/17		622983		PAYMENT REC'D-THANK YOU		35.03

CLOSING DATE	PREVIOUS BALANCE +	FINANCE CHARGE +	CHARGES -	PAYMENTS & CREDITS =	NEW BALANCE	AMOUNT PAST DUE	MINIMUM MONTHLY PAYMENT
04/07/72	35 03	00	00	35 03	00	00	00

For Option accounts. Your **FINANCE CHARGE** is based on a monthly periodic rate of 1·50 % on balances up to $500 and 1 % on any excess over $500 which correspond to **ANNUAL PERCENTAGE RATES** of 18 % and 12 % respectively, applied to the Previous Balance without deducting payments and credits therefrom and without adding charges thereto. **FINANCE CHARGE** is avoided if full payment of the New Balance is received within 30 days of closing date on each statement.

Credit is a convenience to consumers. Like most conveniences, it can be expensive if it is abused. One pitfall is that you are able to spend more than you can actually afford. Another is that you may not do comparison shopping when it is easier to buy where you have an account.

and magazines), gifts and entertainment, and contributions to charity. A wise spending plan might also include a regular plan of savings. Keeping income and outlay in a desired balance takes practice and self-discipline. Try to avoid unplanned "extras."

Using credit wisely A department store gives you credit when it allows you to purchase something and agrees to let you pay later. A bank extends credit when it lends you money.

These and other credit arrangements involve trust. The people in an institution will not advance someone money or goods unless they believe that they will be paid back. They are more likely to extend credit to someone who maintains a steady income and has paid his debts promptly in the past.

The advantage of credit is that it allows someone to enjoy something before he has paid for it. The disadvantage is that some people forget that eventually they must pay for what they buy. They pile up huge debts; they end up in financial trouble.

Institutions do not offer credit free; they charge for it. This charge is called *interest*. The interest varies with the source and type of credit. Generally, if you pay a department store bill within thirty days, you do not have to pay interest. After that month, a certain amount is added on to your bill. This interest is usually a percentage of what you owe. If, for example, your bill after one month is $100 and the interest is 1 percent, your new bill will be $101. Banks also charge interest on their loans. An important part of money management involves examining just how much it costs to borrow money. You will be aided in such examinations by "Truth in Lending" laws. These laws require lenders to state the full terms of credit costs in dollars or percentages or both. When full disclosure is made in this way, you will see not only the percentage cost of credit, but the dollar cost as well. This will help you avoid the irresponsible and costly use of certain forms of credit.

An important form of credit for many young adults is credit to ease the burden of educational costs. The government and certain lending institutions make such credit available for education beyond high school. If education is your goal, sound financial planning might require you to investigate such sources.

THE RESOURCE OF RESOURCEFULNESS

It is seldom that there is only one resource that can be used to satisfy a goal. Usually there are many. The decision maker must decide among them. Can I use this resource instead of that? Can I make a new resource — a resource I do not yet have — which will help me accomplish my goal? Resource management is an important part of the decision-making process. Knowing how to substitute and create resources is an important part of managing resources. To manage resources, in other words, it helps to be resourceful.

This resourcefulness need not always appear in the form of great new ideas. Time, for example, is a resource which one "creates" by saving it; one might save time by developing some routine.

The "do-it-yourselfer" who can make or refinish furniture, repair or remodel clothing, put down a tile floor, paint and hang wallpaper, or apply plastic wall covering is substituting his own skills for the services of others. Think of other suggestions concerning the creation of resources.

THINK BACK

Time and energy are precious human resources that must be used wisely.
Discuss: *Is any activity ever a complete waste of time?*

Efficient methods of working increase the amount of time and energy at our disposal.
Discuss: *How does one learn to become efficient?*

Financial resources must be used wisely in reaching certain goals.
Discuss: *What attitude is reflected in the phrase, "It's only money"?*

The price for which an item sells reflects a great many different kinds of conditions which exist in the marketplace.
Discuss: *"The more something costs, the less I want to buy it.*

LOOK AROUND

1. How can a person avoid feeling that he does not have time to do what he wants to do?
2. List some of the school and household tasks you perform. On which of these do you feel you could improve your time and energy use? Explain how.

3. What is the difference between physical and psychological fatigue? Which do you think is more difficult to remedy?
4. Name five routines you now follow.
5. What two tasks that you usually perform could you conveniently alternate? Do you feel this would actually save time for you personally? Explain.
6. What is money? What are some of the reasons for the price of an item going up?
7. What is credit? How old do you feel a person should be before he is allowed to have credit?
8. How can you *manage* your resources? Assume that two people working toward the same goal manage their resources differently. Can both be equally resourceful? Explain.
9. What is a budget? In making up·a budget, what decision-making strategies do you employ?

FOLLOW YOUR PATH

PATH ONE: Keep a Log

Step 16 Sort out those cards which make a specific reference to time, energy, and money. Make a collage or bulletin board about each of these, summarizing your attitudes.

Step 17 Pretend you have a weekly income of $20. Make up a budget along the lines of the one in this chapter.

Step 18 In the spare time you have available to you, how might you earn that $20? Consider only jobs that are available in your community.

PATH TWO: Write a Skit

Step 14 Which character in your play makes the most economical use of his time and energy? The least economical? Refer to passages in the play.

Step 15 Refer back to Step 1. Make up a budget for the family in your skit. Model it after the budget in this chapter. Consider the wants and needs of every family member.

Step 16 Prepare to stage your skit for the class. Consider the use of hand puppets to act out the dialogue.

PATH THREE: Play a Role

Step 17 Suppose the member of the family who lost his job has found new employment. He will be earning $35 more a month in salary. Without showing anyone else what you are doing, plan a family budget. Carefully consider your own time and energy and how you would like to save or use them.

Step 18 With several classmates, play the roles of a family meeting to discuss the different budgets, arriving at a final spending plan. Recall the kinds of social decisions and the ways to improve time and energy use. Try to convince the family to adopt your budget; try also to make the meeting go as smoothly as possible.

Step 19 Discuss the session before the class. Ask them what they thought of the family budget that was adopted. Ask them what they thought of the way in which the family made its final choice.

PATH FOUR: Sponsor a Child

Step 16 Review the budgets you have made up for your child. Rewrite them along the lines of the budget given in this chapter.

Step 17 Presume you had the same $75 a month to spend on yourself. Make a budget showing how you would spend it.

Step 18 Contrast the two budgets. How does your budget suggest you would spend your time and energy? How does the budget suggest how the child will spend his time and energy? Explain the difference.

Step 19 Plan an activity which would involve the child in dovetailing two tasks.

CHAPTER 6

Finding a Place in the Modern World

We have talked about who you are and about what you can become. We have gone to some length in describing how you might develop as fully as possible. Now open your eyes a little wider. See the millions of people around you. Some have more control over their destinies than others, but all are in basically the same situation as yourself. All either make decisions or do not. All either choose actively or by default.

They do all their choosing, or not choosing, in a social environment. This social environment—this society—affects the natural environment. It also affects you. It provides you with roles which you can assume.

There are more roles than there are kinds of hats. In this chapter we are concerned with two basic types of roles: that of producer and that of consumer.

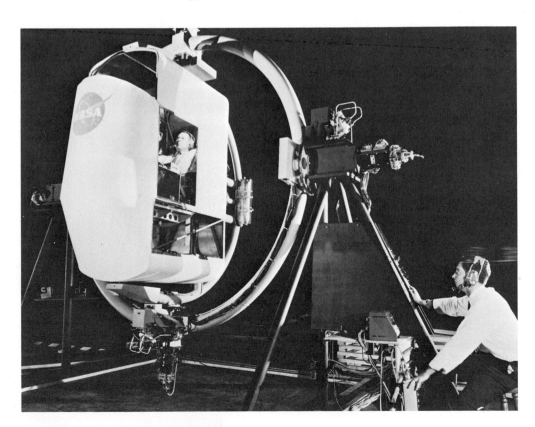

In other words, we make and we take. We work and we buy. Within each of these two general categories of roles, of course, there are many smaller roles. Man has devised many ways to go about making things. He has devised just as many ways to use them up. Here we will discuss what these two types of roles can mean to you. We begin by discussing how you will find a place in the world around you.

YOUR ROLE AS A CONSUMER

At one time, each family could grow or make most of the things it needed. Today, few people possess all the skills or materials required to provide their own necessities. Instead, they exchange the goods and services they have for the ones they need and want. For many of these transactions, money or credit has become the means of exchange. Because money is usually earned in one way or another, a person's role as a consumer and as a worker are closely tied together.

Personality and Consumer Choice

A *consumer* is one who uses resources. You became a consumer with your first breath of air, and you will be a consumer as long as you live.

We are all consumers, but consumers are not all alike. Your particular needs and wants influence what you consume and what you seek to consume. As you grow older, you will find different ways to meet your needs and wants. Your habits as a consumer will probably change accordingly.

Unmet basic needs Much buying is motivated by a desire to satisfy unmet needs. Have you ever been convinced to buy something because you thought it might make you more self-assured, popular, attractive, or lovable? Advertisers try to appeal to unmet needs in their slogans, commercials, and advertising messages. Radio, TV, and the printed media make many appeals to the consumer's unmet psychological needs.

The consumer's self-concept The way you feel about yourself influences your decisions in the marketplace. The person with a weak self-concept may try to build up his "image" with what he buys. He may have to own the "biggest" or the "best" car, house, or wardrobe to make himself feel important. If you see yourself realistically, choices are likely to bring you greater satisfaction than if you do not.

The consumer's changing needs Each stage of the life cycle brings with it new needs and new problems. New wants may be acquired at any time. Often they are linked to increased levels of expectation or a higher standard of living. Young adults have new and different wants from those they had as teenagers and as infants. Their new wants make an impact on family spending. They are major consumers of recreation, transportation, clothing, grooming products, and snack foods. Young marrieds are the major consumers of housing and home furnishings. Older citizens are the major users of health services.

Social Factors in Consumer Choice

A consumer's behavior is influenced by the values and standards of the group to which he belongs. The group says he ought to have certain things. This social pressure influences a group member's choice of what to buy. For example, our national standard of living includes indoor plumbing, hot and cold running water, and gas or electricity. These conveniences were once regarded as luxuries. Today, they are considered basic.

Consumer goals and values In our society, two values are increasingly involved in consumer decision making. They are concerned with the quality of living for individuals and concern with the protection of the environment for all. Sometimes these values conflict. Can mass needs for certain goods and services be met without destroying irreplaceable resources? Consider the convenience offered to millions of city and town dwellers by sewage-disposal systems. Yet some of the sewage from these systems is poured into—and pollutes—streams, rivers, and lakes. We, as a society, must find ways to resolve this and similar conflicts.

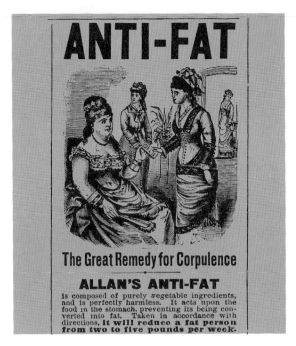

Advertising often appeals to the consumer's desire to satisfy unmet needs. Today, advertisers are restricted from making false claims and promises. This was not so in 1878, when this advertisement was published.

Because the treatment and disposal of trash has become a major environmental problem, many consumers are beginning to return containers for recycling. They value the protection of the environment.

All fads are shortlived, but consumers can enjoy some of them without making a large investment. Others require the purchase of expensive items that may never be used after the "craze" has passed.

The damaging cumulative effect on the environment of certain individual consumer decisions is becoming widely known and generally understood. New social goals may challenge the long-range desirability of certain goods and services.

Fad and fashion Among the most unpredictable social phenomena are the fads, fashions, and "crazes" that sweep the country from time to time. They are surely related both to the need for variety and the need to belong. In the food industry we have periodic food fads, often in the form of ill-conceived diets or wonder foods. In the clothing industry, hemlines and colors have their day. In home decoration we have Mediterranean decor at one time and next we have Scandinavian. Each year designers and manufacturers look for something new to catch the public's fickle fancy and pocketbook. The buyer who has developed a discerning eye for good value and good design will appreciate some of the enduring styles, or *classics*. Classics outlast shortlived fashion trends that are soon "old-fashioned."

SOME STRATEGIES FOR CONSUMER DECISION MAKING

A wide range of choices is open to the American consumer. Variations in cost, quality, style, and serviceability are a constant challenge to decision making. The well-informed, observant consumer can find his way through the confusing array of look-alikes. He can find the product that meets his needs in terms of his values, goals, and resources.

The goods and services that suit one person or one family may not suit another. Not every consumer has all the options he might need to make the wisest choice. At different times, the consumer may give cost, appearance, serviceability, or even status highest priority. Most smart shoppers take pride in

UNSOLICITED MERCHANDISE

Sellers often deliver unsolicited merchandise to unwary customers. No one is obliged to accept or pay for unordered merchandise. If he so wishes, the recipient may, on the one hand, keep the goods without payment. He may ignore strong sounding letters that demand payment and threaten legal action. He is under no obligation to pay. On the other hand, he may return the merchandise to the sender at the sender's expense.

getting the best value for their outlay. To achieve this goal, they identify their needs, learn what is available, and make a choice based on their own standards. They then evaluate what they have bought. They ask themselves if their purchase serves the purpose for which it was intended. The consumer may also consider alternatives to buying—such as do-it-yourself projects.

Shopping:
Discovering Alternatives

Shopping often begins at home. It is there that television, magazine, and newspaper advertisements proclaim the wonders of many goods and services. There the consumer becomes aware of the variety of products that might help satisfy his needs. He may also find that advertisements create some wants that did not exist before. The process of discovering alternative products continues in the store. If the consumer is clear about what he wants, he will have less trouble resisting high-pressure salesmen and deceptive selling practices.

Keeping informed There are many reliable sources of consumer information. Among them are federal, state, and local government agencies. At the federal level, there are the Department of Agriculture, the Federal Trade Commission, and the National Bureau of Standards. Many government agencies are charged with protecting the consumer by enforcing laws, regulations, and industry controls. Some publish pamphlets which are available to you free or at low cost. Private agencies test products and then publish the results. Television, radio, magazines, and newspapers carry much consumer-oriented information. They are probably the best source of day-to-day information about such things as sales. All forms of advertising— which should be viewed critically—can provide the consumer with information about the availability and use of new products.

High-pressure sales pitches are aimed at getting you to make a decision before you can assess your needs and, sometimes, your ability to pay. Consumers may regret purchases made under such pressure.

Comparison shopping The wise consumer has learned to compare quality and cost by shopping in more than one place. He observes details carefully. In his head or on paper he keeps a record of prices and manufacturers of the items he plans to buy. He studies price tags and reads labels carefully, to be sure that the items he is comparing are really similar in quality. He compares, for example, nationally advertised and less famous products. A brand name is sometimes an assurance of quality and value. The wise consumer decides how much he is willing to pay for this assurance. He must consider whether he might not make better choices if he applied his own standards to lesser-known brands. The good comparison shopper stays alert about prices.

Considering guarantees Many major manufacturers provide the consumer with guarantees and warranties for their products.

Independent laboratories test goods and appliances. They "name names" when they publish results. Because most large businesses want to make their brand name a symbol of quality and performance, they also subject their products to testing in their own laboratories.

Both are assurances on the part of the seller that something being sold will be replaced or repaired if it does not meet specifications. In certain cases, the warranty also assures the buyer that the seller is in fact the owner of the goods he is selling. Both guarantees and warranties are intended to inspire the buyer's confidence. The prospective buyer should read them carefully, especially for the length of time the article, its parts, or replacement parts can be obtained without extra charge. If the manufacturer requires it, guarantees should be filed with him at the time of purchase. The consumer can then demand satisfaction if the purchase does not live up to the manufacturer's claims or promises.

Resisting pressure selling Some salesmen have a positive talent for spotting the consumer who can't say "No!" when he does not want to buy. The opportunity to shop creates no obligation to buy. Inexperienced shoppers may give in to flattery or to "hard sell" tactics. If you have made a plan in advance to shop for items you know you need and want, you will find it easier to resist pressure tactics in selling.

Watching for deceptive practices Many alluring advertisements bring customers into stores and showrooms with promises of bargain furnishings or appliances. The customer can demand to see the article advertised and should check the claims made about the item that is being offered. The customer has a right to buy merchandise as advertised. Should the salesman try to switch to a more costly line of merchandise, the consumer has a legitimate complaint. Beware of this deceptive practice, which is commonly known as *bait and switch*. A ruling of the Federal Trade Commission now penalizes food chains and grocery stores if they advertise sale items without stocking quantities to meet "reasonably anticipated demands." The wise consumer is also conscious of loss leaders. A *loss leader* is an article sold at less than cost. Its function is to draw customers into the store.

Buying and Paying:
Activating the Choice

If and when you have selected the particular product you want, the next step is to buy it. The product may have only one price tag on it. There are, nevertheless, several different amounts which you might pay for it. If you pay cash and you pay at once, you will pay no more than the listed amount. If you buy in quantity, you might receive a discount. Many items, especially foods, are "cheaper by the dozen," or even cheaper by the pair. Buying on credit is a different story.

When you buy on credit, you pay for the privilege of using other people's money. Interest rates are regulated by law, but charges for the use of money fluctuate. Interest charges also vary from seller to seller. The consumer is protected by "Truth in Lending" laws which require full disclosure of credit rates and charges. Still, he must learn to read the credit contract carefully and understand fully the cost of the credit he is arranging for. The consumer should be aware of the total dollar cost of credit.

When you arrange for credit, you do so by contract. A contract is a binding legal agreement that obliges you to pay the stated amounts at the specified times. A consumer should read installment contracts carefully before he signs.

Using and Evaluating
the Purchase

The thoughtful consumer buys something so that he can use and enjoy it. To be sure that he gets the most satisfaction out of his purchase, he should observe whatever instructions came with the product.

Suppose that, having done all this, the consumer has ended up with a faulty product. What might he do then? In earlier times, the consumer dealt directly with the producer. If his purchase broke or fell apart, he could go straight to the maker and complain. Some sort of adjustment might be worked out on the spot. Today, the producer may be far removed from the purchaser. The consumer must protect himself in other ways.

Reading labels Responsible manufacturers try to reach the consumer with information printed on labels, packages, hangtags, and in booklets packed with products. These pieces usually give you the information you need for the use and care of your purchases. Follow their instructions—especially for

SHOPPING FOR SALES CREDIT

	List Price	Monthly Payment	Total Price	Dollar Finance	Annual Rate
A	$328	$31.49	$377.88	$49.88	27%
B	342	30.87	370.44	28.44	15%
C	357	31.72	380.64	23.64	12%

In shopping for sales credit, remember that both the price of the merchandise and the cost of credit may vary. Stores A, B, and C sell identical TV sets at three different list prices and on credit plans with three different finance charges. All three stores have a repayment plan of twelve months. Store A offers the best buy only if you can pay cash. If you use credit, the high finance charge offsets the low list price. Store C has the lowest finance charge, but it is the most expensive of the three stores. When you buy on credit, the lowest total price is the best buy.

CASE STUDY: LARRY

THE SITUATION *The decision to sell his small foreign car had been a difficult one for Larry to make. He knew very little about engines and when the knocking sound had developed, he went immediately to the foreign car dealer who usually serviced his car. The mechanic was very pessimistic, stating that the engine should be replaced, a procedure costing several hundred dollars. Larry had bought the car secondhand from his parents several years ago with money he had earned as a supermarket stock clerk. The car had worked well until now, and though he hesitated to give it up, Larry did not consider the car worth the money needed to repair it. He asked the mechanic if the agency would buy the car from him. The low price offered him was unacceptable, and he decided to sell the car, with its problems, to someone who would enjoy trying to fix it.*

Later, Larry spoke with the new owner. He asked about the engine problem.

"Oh, that?" replied the new owner. "Something I got fixed for $50. The car is running beautifully now. Whoever told you it would be expensive to fix must not have looked at the problem carefully enough."

Imagine Larry's surprise and anger! He immediately wrote a letter of complaint to the manager of the car agency, vowing to tell everyone he knew of his dissatisfaction with the agency.

THE INTERVIEW *Q: Have you ever before written a letter of complaint to a company or agency?*
A: No, this is the first one. And I think I have a perfect right to complain.
Q: What action do you expect them to take?
A: I hope they talk with me about my complaint. It takes years to build up a good reputation, but only a few letters like mine to destroy that image.
Q: You have been satisfied with their service before this incident, haven't you?
A: For the most part, but this is too expensive a mistake for me to ignore. They acted incompetently and dishonestly, and somebody should know about it. They owe me an explanation.

REACT *In a similar situation, would you have written a consumer complaint letter? How effective will Larry's letter be?*

---

handling textiles. Much merchandise returned as defective may actually have been damaged by uninformed consumers. Many service calls could have been avoided if the instruction book had been read.

Registering complaints If the consumer is dissatisfied, he must voice his complaint. He may do so to the producer or to the retail seller. He may contact consumer protection agencies at every level of government. He may contact the Better Business Bureau (a private organization) in his area. He may also join with other consumers in public information and letter-writing campaigns. Class actions (group lawsuits) may be permitted.

Returning unsatisfactory merchandise Examine all "no return" articles closely before purchasing them. Such items are rarely subject to exchange or refund. These include many items that are on sale. By law, certain articles for personal use may not be returned. Most articles are sold subject to satisfactory performance. They should be returned if defects are discovered after purchase.

YOUR ROLE
AS A WORKER

Some of the things which we consume we have to make. We have to work to *produce* many of the things we need and want.

Our complex society cannot function without the contributions of workers in many areas operating at many different levels. The trained worker has a wide variety of jobs to choose from.

Towards acquiring which kind of job should you direct your time, skills, energy, and intelligence? That depends, first, on who you are and on what you expect from life. Second, it depends on which of your expectations you feel you could realize in the world of work. A job need not merely be something you do to earn money. It can also be an experience which aids you on your path to self-fulfillment.

Levels of Jobs

There are more unskilled workers than there are jobs for them. Consequently, in many areas, unskilled workers are easily hired and easily fired. Many entry-level jobs in the unskilled category require physical energy, strength, and stamina. An unskilled worker becomes semiskilled by mastering more advanced tasks. When he does, his value in the job market often increases. The skilled trades usually involve a period of training and apprenticeship. Some people who master such skills may later start their own businesses and become self-employed.

A new category of worker, *the paraprofessional,* has developed. Paraprofessionals work alongside highly trained personnel in many fields, and work under direct professional supervision. Another occupational category includes the independent technicians and semiprofessionals engaged in small businesses of their own. Workers who supervise the work of others and who function at a middle level of responsibility fall into the *professional* and *managerial* category of employment. Those who bear full responsibility for their own work, as well as for the work of others who report to them, fall into the category of professional and top management personnel. Creative workers often fall outside this general classification of the world of work, unless their creative responsibilities also involve working in a shop, a laboratory, an office, or a business.

Opportunities to advance, in terms of rewards and responsibilities, are described as *career ladders.* Starting at the bottom and reaching the top has been a strong work value in our society. Opportunities to move *laterally,* or sideways, from one job to a similar one in a different, but related, field are called *career lattices.* Career lattices represent opportunities to transfer skills

TAXES

The first time you see a deduction for taxes on a paycheck may be your introduction to your financial responsibility to the community in which you live. Yet you have been the beneficiary of other people's tax dollars in many ways for many years. Taxes provide schools, highways, social services, and recreation facilities to the public.

Taxes contribute to maintaining economic stability for the unemployed, the widowed, and the orphaned. Taxes provide help for the sick and the aged. In time, taxes may also provide an income "floor" to help each family maintain an adequate standard of living. Thus, taxes form a link between the producing and consuming functions of society.

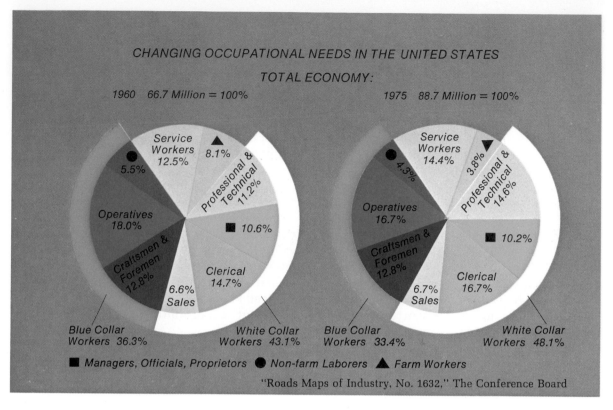

CHANGING OCCUPATIONAL NEEDS IN THE UNITED STATES

TOTAL ECONOMY:

1960   66.7 Million = 100%   1975   88.7 Million = 100%

Service Workers 12.5%
Professional & Technical 11.2%
5.5%
8.1%
10.6%
Operatives 18.0%
Craftsmen & Foremen 12.8%
Clerical 14.7%
6.6% Sales
Blue Collar Workers 36.3%
White Collar Workers 43.1%

Service Workers 14.4%
Professional & Technical 14.6%
4.3%
3.8%
10.2%
Operatives 16.7%
Craftsmen & Foremen 12.8%
Clerical 16.7%
6.7% Sales
Blue Collar Workers 33.4%
White Collar Workers 48.1%

■ Managers, Officials, Proprietors   ● Non-farm Laborers   ▲ Farm Workers

"Roads Maps of Industry, No. 1632," The Conference Board

The graphs compare employment by occupational groups in 1960 with what is expected to be the occupational distribution in 1975. As you explore career possibilities, consider how advances in technology and changing social conditions affect the demand for different kinds of jobs.

from one area of work to another. This might happen to a nurse's aide in a hospital who goes to work in a nursing home.

Personality and Career Choice

Many factors enter into a person's choice of career. Work helps you to become who you are through what you do. Your career choice is not just an "outside" choice about something you are going to *do*. It is an "inside" choice concerning something you are going to *be*.

Work and basic needs   Work isn't only a means of exchanging time and energy for money to buy goods and services. It is more

than that. It has value for the development of human potential.

Work can offer you opportunities to meet your needs for independence, personal identity, and for stimulation and variety. Work can offer ways to meet your need to belong, your need to achieve, your need for recognition and approval, and your need for self-fulfillment.

Your established habits of meeting basic human needs influence your entire life, including your attitudes toward work. The right kind of work offers you ways to meet your basic needs in a satisfying manner.

Work and your identity   Your ideas about what a certain kind of work involves for the worker forms your *role expectation* for that occupation. You form your ideas of work roles from many sources. You gain some ideas from observing people when they are at work. Some you gain from reading about jobs. Still others you gain from your own work experience.

It helps to be able to "see" yourself in a line of work before you move into it. A satisfying career choice allows you to be the person you know yourself to be or know yourself capable of becoming. Your level of aspiration, that is, your ambition in a job and other activities, also reflects your self-concept and ideal image. How you think and feel about yourself molds your attitudes toward achievement, toward success and failure. A strong self-concept can withstand failure. A weak one may be damaged by even a minor setback.

Work-related goals and values Your final choice of an occupation might bring together many goals and values. Among these you might consider personal growth, service to others, and sufficient income to maintain a home and family. Have you ever thought about your values in relation to work? What would you like a job to offer? Income? Challenge? Glamour? Status? Public service? Do you want a job that interests you? What would make it interesting? Do you want a job that you can do easily and hold with little effort? Or do you want a job that presents challenges and offers you the satisfaction that comes from overcoming obstacles? Do you rate the money income as more important than the psychological income gained from enjoyment, independence, involvement with people, and creativity? Would you be interested in a job that offered you security without a chance to grow? Would you want the person you married to accept a job that provided you with security, at the expense of his or her self-fulfillment? All your answers will reflect your values and goals in terms of work.

The working environment The employed worker spends much of his waking life in his place of employment. Each working environment has a different climate for self-expression and for self-fulfillment. The environment that provides the greatest number of opportunities for doing things in ways that you prefer is the one most likely to offer you satisfaction in your work.

Sex Role and Work Roles

At one time women expected to express their total personalities through their home-centered roles as wives and mothers. The work of homemaking was a lifelong, full-time occupation. Today women live longer. They have time- and energy-saving devices in the home. Many receive an education equivalent to that of men. Consequently, many modern women wish to develop and use their personal potential through activities outside the home.

They are aided in this desire by the neutralization of many jobs, jobs that are no longer thought to be exclusively man's or woman's work. Passage of fair employment

But yield who will to their
    separation,
My object in living is to unite
My avocation and my vocation
As my two eyes make one in sight.
Only where love and need are one,
And the work is play for mortal
    stakes,
Is the deed ever really done
For Heaven and the future's
    sakes.

from "Two Tramps in Mud Time" (Robert Frost)

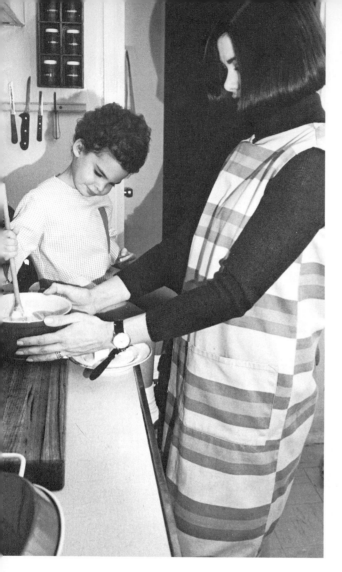

Many women choose homemaking as a full-time career. Those who do not may pursue jobs in areas formerly not open to women and entirely unrelated to homemaking functions. Fulfilling a dual role requires the ability to resolve conflicts that arise from being part of two different worlds.

laws, which prohibit discrimination in the employment of women, have also done much to equalize work roles.

Men have also been affected by job neutralization. They, too, see broader channels for reaching their full potential.

Today, then, both sexes have a growing freedom in their choice of work. They need not take for granted who is to be the major wage earner in a family. A married couple

may, for a time, choose to have the wife work to support her husband through a course of vocational preparation. Couples may even decide to reverse roles. For example, the wife might be engaged in a profession outside the home, while the husband might do his work in the home.

More and more, women today expect to fulfill *dual roles*. They expect to work both at home and in the outside world. They may do this before their children are born, when children are in school, or after children leave home to establish homes of their own. For women, this is a major area of decision making. When they marry, the decision becomes a joint concern of husband and wife. Thus, an occupational choice can help shape the entire life-style of men and women.

SOME STRATEGIES FOR CAREER DECISION MAKING

It can be baffling to make a career choice. The alternatives and consequences are not always clear. Rational decision making may unravel some of this confusion. Decision-making strategies may help one make the

---

CASE STUDY: JILL

THE SITUATION *Jill was speaking with her aunt about her husband Jim's offer of a sales position on the West Coast. "We have to decide by tomorrow whether to accept."*

"Why are you so hesitant?" asked her aunt. "The salary and hours are good, the moving arrangements easy, and living conditions are reasonable. Go ahead and say 'yes'."

But it's not that easy, thought Jill. During the five years of their marriage, her husband had been a telephone order clerk and sales trainee. The major source of income during those years had been Jill's income from her jobs, first as a teacher, then as a business woman. Now she was employed in work which not only provided a substantial salary increase over her other two jobs, but which afforded her great personal satisfaction. So far, it had all the elements of work she would enjoy doing for the next five or ten years. She was distressed to think of resigning. For her, life was just beginning. She was meeting people who enjoyed and respected each other. She had freedom to come and go as she pleased. Her work hours were very flexible, and she could try new ideas.

"Well, it is the kind of job Jim is looking for," answered Jill. "He dislikes the high cost of living here and the crowded conditions everywhere we go. He's tired of locking doors at night and having no safe places for walking or riding a bicycle. He is anxious to

begin working, and this job is exactly what he wants to do for several years. The job market is tight now.

"Encourage him to take the job, Jill," said her aunt. "It's time for you to settle down. You can start to think about buying a home and having children now."

THE INTERVIEW *Q: Are you going to follow your aunt's advice and take the job?*
A: She grew up during an age when women spent married life raising children and following in their husband's footsteps. I don't think her advice can apply to the way young people want to live today.
Q: What alternatives do you have?
A: Not many. I can go with Jim. I can try to convince him to put up with this area of the country for a few more years. Or I can refuse to go, and he will have to make the decision about his job all by himself.
Q: The last alternative is a drastic one. If he took the job, you would be on the East Coast and he would be in the West.
A: As you see, this job situation is a serious problem. I feel I have as much right to a satisfying job experience as he does. And right now I could not ask for a better situation.

REACT *What is your recommendation about Jim's job offer? Must each married couple "settle down and have children"?*

Summer camps that give instruction in particular occupations may provide practical experience in the world of work. This Youth Conservation Corps camp gave this young woman instruction in forestry.

best use of time and energy in making career choices.

The real basis for making an occupational decision is for a person to know who he is and what, in general, he wants from life. Only then can he fruitfully examine various job possibilities to see what they might offer.

Discovering Job Alternatives

Which job is for you? To answer this question you might first gain a better idea of what jobs there are. You might investigate the world of work. Factual information is all around you. There are a variety of people who can advise you. The mass media can also be of help. Part-time and summertime work can also provide valuable experience.

Gathering information You can get occupational information in many forms: printed, filmed, recorded, and directly from well-informed people. You may refer to textbooks (including this one), government pamphlets, or booklets prepared by trade or professional associations or trade unions. You may attend an educational forum or film. You may talk to people already actively involved in the kind of work that interests you.

You may hear a lecturer at school or meet a person socially who brings new information concerning work to your attention. You get further ideas from reading newspaper stories, biographies, and magazines. Television sends a constant flow of occupational information your way. The way work is shown in drama and fiction can also influence your role expectation. So, too, can television news programs, talk shows, and specials that explore a particular occupational field in depth.

Working part-time Some part-time or summer jobs may not seem glamorous or exciting. Their low pay may seem unappealing. Still, such jobs can offer chances to become oriented to the world of work. They can provide chances to see many different types of work. They can give opportunities to evaluate first-hand those areas of work and levels of jobs that seem to offer possibilities for you.

Activating Career Choices

A few single-minded people make an occupational choice fairly early in life and then stick to it. Others must accumulate various types of experience before they can make up their minds. Some try one career, find they do not like it, and then try another. The sooner a person learns that a certain line of work does not bring him the satisfaction he expects, the better off he is. It takes time to put oneself on a different occupational track. It takes time to meet the educational standards necessary to succeed in a new career.

To apply for some jobs you might need only to show interest and availability. For others, you may have to complete application forms or take aptitude tests. For still others, you may need to prepare a résumé or portfolio and know how to conduct yourself in an interview.

It takes time to find another job—one more in keeping with one's personal objectives.

Furthering your education   In our complex technological world, one often requires special education to reach his occupational goal. Learn all you can about educational offerings in your field. Where is the outstanding school? Which is the best program in your community? Can you begin now to study or work to reach your goal sooner? Check on two-year and four-year programs.

If your occupational goal requires some specialized training, as it would if you wanted to become an airline steward or stewardess, check on the schools recommended by prospective employers. If you want to enter a skilled trade, check with the appropriate trade union. You may find that you have to work as an apprentice for a specified period. You may choose to prepare yourself for other careers through a work-study program. In such a program you alternately attend classes and work. The work situations are usually set up to familiarize people with a particular occupational field.

Finding a job   Entry-level jobs are often gained by applying directly to an employer. An unskilled worker may also be directed to entry-level jobs by community manpower development agencies. The person with some training or experience might also use the services of an employment agency. He may refer to the "help wanted" ads.

Placement in any job involves some contact with the people hiring you. A discussion of the job usually occurs in an interview.

An employer is almost always interested in finding out what you can do to improve the quality or efficiency of his business. In such situations you may sell yourself. You may present the prospective employer with a *résumé*, describing your education, experience, and career objectives. Also, the employer may have an application form.

When coming in contact with prospective employers, appearance, communication skills, and general behavior make a strong impression. When you feel and look your best, you are more likely to communicate a positive impression to others. You increase your chances of getting the job you want.

FACING THE FUTURE

The philosopher Jean-Paul Sartre considers a career choice the key decision that determines adult personality. Another writer in the field of vocational guidance has said,

"At the time an individual chooses a career, he . . . decides 'to become' or to frustrate his basic tendencies toward fulfillment."

Early in life, each of us has many "futures." The future closes in as one option after another is taken or rejected. Your choice of a vocation is the result of a long chain of decision making. Your final career choice becomes a central decision because it influences so many other decisions. The sum total of these decisions shapes your entire life-style and the quality of life made possible for others in your family and your community.

You cannot change the past. You cannot change the time into which you were born. But you can change the times into which your children are born. You cannot change the parents you had. But you can change the kind of parent you become. You cannot change your past experiences, even if you want to. You can, however, through your consumer and occupational choices, make your future happen.

THINK BACK

Satisfaction of wants and needs is the major force behind most consumer decisions.
Discuss: *Do advertisers "take advantage of" consumers?*

The cornerstone of effective consumer protection is the informed, concerned consumer.
Discuss: *Why are some people more interested than others in consumer protection?*

Choosing the "right" job involves knowing who you are and what you want.
Discuss: *How does one know when a job is "right" for him?*

Work should provide both men and women with opportunities for self-fulfillment.
Discuss: *Do women have "equal opportunity" with men in today's job market?*

LOOK AROUND

1. Develop a "Consumer Conscious" bulletin board on which the best buys among teenage consumer goods are displayed and analyzed.
2. List ten of your most recent purchases. Which do you consider a "waste of money"? What accounts for the differences between them and the ones with which you are satisfied?
3. Analyze several of your favorite advertisements for consumer goods. How does the advertiser encourage you to buy his product? What would influence you to buy it?
4. How would you promote a not-so-popular teenage consumer item? Consider such factors as originality, artistic merit, and effectiveness of the presentation.

5. When you buy goods, how are you influenced by your own wants and needs? How are you influenced by opinions of others? Which influence is stronger in your consumer decisions?

6. Develop a "Do You Pay the Price?" display of high-priced teen consumer items. Indicate whether or not each item is worth the price.

7. Bring to class for auction little-used, almost-new items. What accounts for the difference between the final auction price and the original price of each item? Which price more nearly represents the item's true value?

8. Why are unskilled workers "easily hired and easily fired"? What obstacles must be overcome if an unskilled worker is to become skilled?

9. What is "destiny"? What part does it play in aiding or preventing a person from reaching self-fulfillment?

10. What financial expenses are common to a high school graduate employed in his first full-time job? Estimate the amount of money involved. How much must he earn to live comfortably?

FOLLOW YOUR PATH

PATH ONE: Keep a Log

Step 19 Now you are aware of the wants, needs, values, goals, and resources which most readily come into your mind. On the basis of this, make up a description of the kind of things you would like to find in a job.

Step 20 Make an appointment with your school guidance counselor. Bring your description with you and discuss it with him. Find out what jobs might interest you.

Step 21 Find ten advertisements for items you want that appeal to your unmet needs. Which items would actually help you to meet those needs?

PATH TWO: Write a Skit

Step 17 From what you know about your main character, do you think he had the job for which he was best suited? Make up a description of the kinds of things you think he might look for in a job.

Step 18 In magazines, find several advertisements which appeal to the unmet needs of each of the characters in your skit. Which items would actually help them meet those needs?

Step 19 Perform your skit. Ask the class to comment on each character's recognition of values and goals and use of resources.

PATH THREE: Play a Role

Step 20 What was the job that the main character found? Find out from your school guidance counselor what sort of tasks this job involves. Do you think this is the job for which your main character is best suited? Make up a description of the kinds of things you think he ought to look for in a job.

Step 21 In magazines, find ten advertisements that appeal to the unmet needs of the character you played. Which items would actually help him meet those needs?

PATH FOUR: Sponsor a Child

Step 20 Interview at least one person who is professionally occupied in an agency which serves others. Find out what that person does. Find out why he selected his occupation.

Step 21 From this and from your own "experience," tell whether you might be interested in pursuing this line of work. Why? If you are not interested, explain why you chose this path in the first place. What made you change your mind?

Step 22 In magazines, find ten advertisements that appeal to the unmet needs of the character you played. Which items would actually help him meet those needs?

Perspectives on food

Food means life. It gives us our continued ability to stretch and grow, to reach and change.

Food means acceptance and security. We use food to help satisfy our higher needs. The smallest morsel offered to a guest is a gesture of welcome. We make the offering because we want the guest to feel at ease.

Food means variety. It means colors and shapes, textures and tastes.

Food means jobs. The plants and animals from which our food comes pass through many hands on their way to us.

To make wise food choices, we should know what is behind food. We should know how foods became available to us. We should know what different foods will do to us once they are inside our bodies.

With what you know presently about who you are and what you like, choose, with the help of your teacher, one of the paths below. As you progress along your path, you will learn about the value and complexity of the world of food.

All the paths involve making technical and economic decisions. Those paths in which several people work together also involve making social decisions (see pages 55–56).

PATH ONE: Design an Advertising Campaign

Work with others to form an advertising agency. Your agency will plan ads for Vitalveg, Inc., a company that sells a variety of canned and frozen fruits and vegetables. This path involves examining ads on TV and in print, discussing and evaluating these ads, creating at least one magazine ad and one TV commercial, and performing a TV commercial.

Step 1 Each member of the agency should select from magazines ten vegetable advertisements which he feels are "good."

Step 2 Meet with other members of your agency. Agree on the five best ads. Create a campaign for one vegetable.

Step 3 Independently of the other members of your agency, think up a slogan or an idea that you feel will work well in magazines and on TV.

PATH TWO: Feed an Intentional Family

With several of your classmates, form an intentional family (see page 28). This path involves making food plans which will suit every family member. It involves making charts, some of which may benefit from a small amount of outside research.

Step 1 Each member should list five foods he likes most and the five foods he likes least.

Step 2 Meet to discuss these lists. Form master lists of "liked" and "disliked" foods.

Step 3 From the foods on the "liked" list, each member of the family should privately plan one meal. Consult cookbooks if you wish.

PATH THREE: Operate a Restaurant

This path may be followed alone or with others. It involves looking around in your community, interviewing people, planning menus, and figuring costs.

Step 1 Your restaurant may be anything from a luncheonette or cafe to a fancy restaurant. The only requirement is that it must serve full meals. Scout around until you find a specific street where you feel your restaurant would succeed.

Step 2 To go into business, you will have to borrow money from a bank. Before a bank will lend you money, you must convince them that you will make enough profit to repay the loan. With this in mind, write a statement telling why you feel your restaurant will succeed where you wish to open it.

Will the people who live or work in the neighborhood patronize your restaurant?

PATH FOUR: Study Your Food Habits

This path involves listing and evaluating what you eat, discovering influences on your food choices, planning improvements in your diet, and planning menus.

Step 1 For each day of the next week, keep an hour-by-hour list of the principal activities that you perform. (If you spend forty minutes between ten o'clock and eleven o'clock reading a magazine, write in ten o'clock, and beside it write "reading.")

Step 2 For each day of the next week, keep a list of the foods you eat, and when and where you eat them. Include snacks and beverages.

CHAPTER 7

Background for Food Decisions

Every Sunday morning the family goes to church. Afterwards, they return home to a large meal, usually of beef or pork. On special days they have turkey. These meals are always noisy occasions; everyone talks at once. The grandmother recalls the time before the roads were filled with cars, and the twins talk about their kindergarten teacher. The mother complains about the new gas station that might be built on the corner. The father teases his daughter about her new boyfriend; she insists she really does not like him. Halfway through the meal, someone becomes aware of how good the food tastes. Everyone compliments the mother on the meal.

On this and on many similar occasions, food meets needs on many levels. The people involved may later remember the particular kind of food—its tastes, colors, smells, and shapes—and associate the food with the event.

Attitudes toward food are influenced by culture, family, and resources. To make rational food decisions, a person must take his background into consideration.

FOOD AND HUMAN ECOLOGY

You are part of your environment; your environment is part of you. Food is one of the links between you and the world. "You are what you eat," is an old expression.

The food you swallow is *digested*. It dissolves inside you. It changes into particles which travel to various parts of your body. There, some of them change again. They can become skin, kidney, muscle, or bone. Many complex processes are involved; different foods play different parts in these processes. Through the science of nutrition, we are learning how different foods contribute to good health.

Knowing what the "right" foods are, however, is not enough. These foods must be adequately supplied by the environment. The quality of our environment affects the quality of our food. Polluted air and water can keep food from growing. Soil which has been incorrectly farmed will not yield nourishing food. It is within our power to develop or destroy nutritious food resources.

Food and the Environment

Through a process called *photosynthesis,* green plants can change the sun's energy into stored chemical energy. When animals eat plants, they consume this stored energy. They convert it to energy for their physical activities. The energy they do not use is stored in their bodies. Most human beings take their food—and their energy—from both plants and animals.

New energy for life comes from the sun. Only plants can convert this energy into a form that men and animals can use. Thus, plants are our most basic food resource.

The Science of Nutrition

Nutrition deals with the materials your body needs to function. It is concerned with what men do eat, should eat, and why. It borrows from natural sciences like biology and physiology, and social sciences like anthropology and economics. The immediate concern of nutrition is with *nutrients*, the materials the body needs to operate. We will discuss their particular functions in Chapter 8.

FOOD AND BASIC NEEDS

Food supplies the means for satisfying some basic physical needs. Food helps you grow and maintain yourself. It helps regulate bodily functions. Food also helps you meet psychological and social needs. In many cultures, for example, food occupies an essential place in wedding celebrations. Food can also play a role in meeting spiritual needs: it is used as a symbol in religious ceremonies.

By choosing to eat foods that meet wants instead of needs, a person can develop unsound eating practices. This can happen if you eat more than you need and grow overweight, or if you eat food that is low in nutrients. Rational food decisions cannot be made purely on the basis of your likes.

Some people would "rather starve" than eat a certain food. Some will not eat steak, or milk, or ham, or orange juice. If that surprises you, ask yourself how you would feel if you were offered insects or whale blubber. The idea of such foods may not appeal to some, but in other cultures these foods are considered delicacies. Many food preferences reflect the food customs of a person's family and culture.

This detail from "The Harvesters," by Bruegel the Elder, shows agriculture in the fourteenth century. Today's methods must still ensure the health of the plants and animals that become our food.

The number of calories that you expend and that you need to maintain your ideal weight is determined by your individual basal metabolism rate and by your day-to-day level of activity.

Physical Needs

When you feel hunger, your body is signaling you that it needs food. When you eat, you begin a process of breaking down food and releasing energy to build up and maintain your body. This process is known as *metabolism*. Metabolism is related to your body's energy level.

S omewhere—the place it matters
    not—somewhere
I saw a child, hungry and thin
    of face—
Eyes in whose pools life's joys
    no longer stirred,
Lips that were dead to laughter's
    eager kiss,
Yet parted fiercely to a crust
    of bread.

from "Prayer for Children" (Francis Cardinal Spellman)

You might think of your body as a biochemical factory. The hunger bell rings and you take in food, the raw materials, from which your body manufactures living tissue.

Hunger The feeling of hunger is triggered by a drop in your blood-sugar level. This sends a message to your brain. Your brain then signals your stomach muscles to contract, or shrink. Your awareness of these contractions is the feeling of hunger.

Alcoholics and drug addicts seldom feel hungry. Their blood composition is altered. Consequently, their hunger signals are distorted. Other biochemical imbalances may also upset the ability to distinguish between food wants and food needs.

Basal metabolism rate (BMR) Your basal metabolism rate is the measure of your particular energy needs when resting. It helps to measure your energy needs. Not everyone has the same BMR. A person's age, sex, weight, and level of health are all influencing factors. In general, however, young people have higher BMRs—and hence need more food—than older people. Thin people generally have higher BMRs than heavy people. Men's BMRs are usually higher than women's, though women's may be higher during pregnancy.

When certain glands produce more or less of a hormone, a person's BMR may change radically. In such cases, a doctor may prescribe a special diet or medication.

Calories Food energy is measured in standard units called calories. A calorie could raise the temperature of one quart of water approximately two degrees Fahrenheit. When we say that a piece of cake contains one hundred calories, we mean that it contains enough potential heat to raise the temperature of a quart of water from freezing to boiling. The number of calories you need is determined mainly by your basal metabolism rate and by your level of physical activity.

Psychological Needs

Eating habits are complex forms of behavior. You know this if you have ever eaten—or failed to eat—because of emotional stress.

Food is important to mental and emotional health. It meets your needs for love, safety, and security in many ways. Food "like mother used to make" is more than a sentimental reminder of food preferences. It is tied to the fact that from birth, food is offered to children in an emotional climate; it involves deep emotional overtones for all of us. Even the simplest, least expensive food, when offered with love and concern, provides a child with more than the most elaborate and expensive food offered mechanically and indifferently. If food is early associated with love and rewards for approved behavior, people may later eat to fill emotional, rather than physical, needs. A mother who rewards her child with snacks of fresh fruit or raw vegetable sticks, instead of candy or soft drinks, helps him to form sound eating habits.

An infant stands a better chance of being born healthy if his mother received the proper nutrients not only during pregnancy but *before*. Without proper nutrition from before birth through early childhood, a child's mental capacities may fail to develop. Some

Whether it is a birthday cake for a child or a "surprise" on an invalid's tray, food that is specially prepared can satisfy psychological needs. The extra effort adds a flavor of its own.

nutritional deficiencies may even cause mental retardation. An early understanding of each child's nutritional needs is essential for building physical and psychological health.

While hunger is an indicator of a physical need for food, your appetite expresses your wants, or food preferences. Appetite is a combination of physical and psychological factors. Taste and smell influence your appetite, but early experiences shape your feelings about which smells and tastes appeal to you.

Preparing, selecting, and serving appetizing food offers outlets for your imagination and creativity. In their wide varieties of color, flavor, and texture, foods meet your need for stimulation and variety. Learning to prepare foods in new and unusual ways also meets this need.

Food is the basis for many social gatherings. The food you offer provides an opportunity to extend a very basic form of hospitality. It can make a statement about you and your life-style or it can afford a chance to explore the life-styles of other regions or cultures.

Social Needs

In every society, eating is a social occasion. It is an opportunity for people to satisfy their need to belong. This is done in different ways. For special occasions there are special foods. There are also special ways of behaving — special forms of hospitality and customary manners. Being served formally in an expensive restaurant, for example, is a way some people use food to achieve status. Other people might realize their need for recognition by having a weiner roast, or by serving casual snacks to friends.

Preparing food, as well as eating it, can be a means of satisfying social needs. A skilled chef can meet his need for achievement as he creates special dishes. A cook who prepares a meal for others to enjoy is on his way to satisfying his need for recognition and approval.

Social behavior surrounding food differs from culture to culture. In some cultures, men and women are never guests at the same social functions. In others, they do not even eat together at home. In modern Western societies, of course, men and women usually eat together.

As a sign of respect, people can observe the customs of another culture when eating

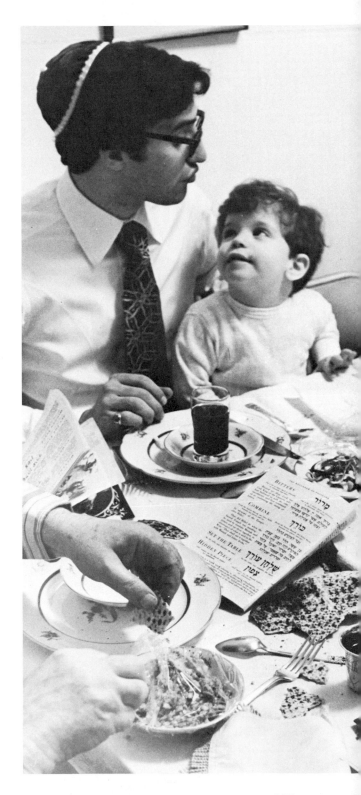

In some religions, foods are symbols of a heritage. For example, matzo is served at a Passover seder because, during their flight from Egypt in biblical times, the Jews had no time to leaven bread.

the food of that culture. If you have not already done so, you might try eating Chinese food with chopsticks, or Hawaiian food with your fingers.

Spiritual Needs

Rituals associated with food and drink form an important part of many religious traditions. Food may be central to religious and spiritual experience in feasting and in fasting. In many religions, fasting at specified periods allows the individual to reflect on the higher matters of the spirit.

The relation of food to the human spirit has been captured in the term "soul food." Because food joins people in a feeling of kinship of a special kind, each culture has its own form of "soul food." Sharing meals with people from different cultures, therefore, can create bridges of human understanding.

INFLUENCES ON YOUR FOOD CHOICES

Many factors have shaped your food values. These values influence your food choices. Attitudes toward food can be traced back to early experiences in the home. This home life has probably been influenced by the foods of a cultural tradition. Your friends can also influence your food preferences. Education and advertising have some influence on food choices; so do many nutritionally unsound food fads that sweep the nation from time to time. Your food preferences are also influenced by those foods which are readily available, such as crops that might be grown locally.

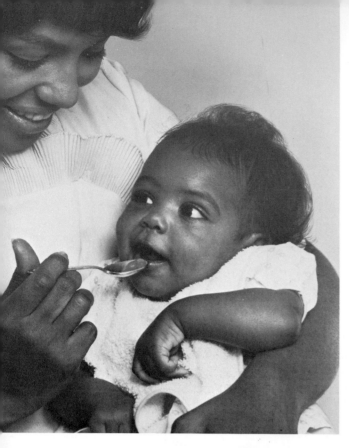

Most people have deep-seated food preferences. Some of these preferences keep them from eating certain foods. Consequently, although nutritious foods are available, in many parts of the world people have nutritionally inadequate diets. It is unfortunate that nutritional knowledge usually comes *after* food habits have been formed. If such food preferences did not exist, it would be easier to meet the nutritional needs of the world's population.

Family Differences

Once a rich man stayed at a fine hotel. He ordered prunes for breakfast, and returned them three times for not being "right." Each time the waiter sent back to the kitchen for fatter, juicier, sweeter prunes. Finally, the annoyed waiter grabbed a plate of hard, dry, wrinkled prunes and took them to the customer. The rich man smiled. "Now that's what I call good prunes!" he said. These simple fruits reminded him of the prunes he had eaten at home in his childhood. He genuinely preferred them.

Like this rich man, we form our food habits and preferences in our families. There, we eat certain types of meals and certain amounts and varieties of food. We eat at certain times of the day, and when we eat, a certain social atmosphere often prevails.

Cultural Meal Patterns

The term *cultural meal patterns* refers to what foods are eaten in a particular culture, to how these foods are prepared, and to when they are eaten.

Climate partly explains people's preferences in foods and methods of food preparation. Climate determines which foods

*C*eremony was but devis'd at
  first
To set a gloss on faint deeds,
  hollow welcomes . . .
But where there is true friendship,
  there needs none.

from *Timon of Athens* (William Shakespeare)

can be grown in an area; people choose the foods they like from among these available foods. Some cultures which are located in hot climates prepare their food with spices, which preserve the food. These cultures favor vegetables over meat because meat spoils quickly. Heartier fare is common in colder regions.

The effect of climate on meal patterns is modified by a culture's level of technical progress. The introduction of modern sanitation, refrigeration, and transportation has expanded the types and quality of food available in most parts of the world.

In most cultures, the times when meals are eaten are geared to the working day. If the working day is interrupted by a midday break, like a *siesta,* the evening meal usually comes late in the evening. In Spain, for example, people generally eat the heaviest meal of the day at eleven o'clock. In Germany, the heaviest meal is eaten at noon.

A familiar pattern in the United States is to eat three meals a day. The timing and composition of these meals may vary. The heaviest meal of the day is called dinner. Breakfast, the morning meal, may be followed by either lunch or dinner. The evening meal may be either dinner or supper. Combining breakfast and lunch as a midday meal, called brunch, is popular with many people.

Snacks are also a part of our meal patterns. America's many ethnic strains have contributed a rich variety of foods. Anglo-Saxons,

The kind of job a person has may influence his meal patterns. If a truck driver has to stay alert to drive long distances, he may prefer to have several snacks or light meals rather than a large, heavy one.

Latins, Germans, Frenchmen, Slavs, Orientals, Scandinavians, Africans, East Indians, and West Indians all brought to this country their traditional preferences in foods and methods of preparation. In addition, Americans have developed many dishes around such native foods as turkey, corn, and pumpkin. Thus, Americans have a rich and enormously varied group of dishes from which to choose.

Economic Differences

A few people have unrestricted financial resources to spend on food; but most do not. Working on a limited food budget is a challenge when the goal is to meet individual and family nutritional needs.

CASE STUDY: HELEN

THE SITUATION *Helen and Dick were planning a dinner for the McCarthys.*

"I'd like to prepare something fancy and delicious," said Helen. "Any suggestions?"

"I wouldn't get too fancy if I were you," replied Dick. "You know what a fussy eater Hank is. Perhaps you should plan just a good, solid 'meat and potatoes' dinner."

Helen had expected this kind of practical suggestion. In the four years of friendship with the McCarthys, she had become acquainted with many of Hank's food "prejudices." Sometimes she had questioned him about his food preferences, but he seemed unable to give exact reasons for liking or disliking particular foods. After such conversations, she felt there were more foods he disliked than liked. She was relieved that she did not have to cook for him on a daily basis.

"This is a special occasion, though," she said. "They're moving into a new home and we probably won't see them for a long time. Besides, I'd like them to know how much we have enjoyed their company. Everyday food just doesn't say what I want to say."

"I think a good hostess considers the food preferences of her guests," reminded Dick. "You should probably cook what the McCarthys will enjoy if you want the evening to be successful."

"I want the dinner to be successful, but I think we should think about Mary, too. She loves to try new foods. Besides, the food I prepare is good. There's nothing wrong with it. I think I'll just serve what I want to, and forget about Hank. He'll either have to eat what I prepare or go without."

THE INTERVIEW *Q: Dick, do you agree with Helen's decision about planning the dinner for Mary and Hank?*
A: Not entirely. I think she should be more concerned about the guests.
Q: Is this her usual way of solving the problem of a special dinner?
A: No, because our other guests enjoy food and like whatever Helen prepares. Hank is the only "problem eater" we know.
Q: Is it fair to the hostess for a guest to require as much time and consideration as Hank apparently does? Putting Hank's preferences first might make extra work.
A: That's true. Helen might become very concerned about pleasing Hank and may not enjoy the evening at all. Maybe we are pampering Hank by trying to please him. Perhaps Helen's solution isn't so undesirable.

REACT *What solution to Helen's problem do you suggest? What mealtime behavior should be expected of guests?*

Both the family budget and the national economy have a bearing on a family's food choices. Food prices fluctuate according to economic conditions, including supply and demand. A careful food shopper can take advantage of the "good buys" in the food market without sacrificing good nutrition. Planning to make creative use of leftovers also adds alternatives to your mealtime decision making.

When a family can produce some or most of its food, it has a strong economic advantage in the face of fluctuating food prices. In this respect, do-it-yourself skills in freezing, canning, or drying foods can make a significant contribution to the family food budget. While you are saving money, however, you are spending time. You should learn to use these two resources in ways that will best help you reach your food goals.

Wise use of government-donated foods and the use of food stamps, where available, can help an eligible low-income family or individual to be better nourished without having to spend large amounts of money. In the long run, the decision of what to eat—and the personal and economic responsibility for that decision—is in the hands of each consumer.

Informational Resources

Besides your family, cultural, and economic background, your food choices depend on your informational resources—on what you know about food and on what you can find out. In modern Western societies, much essential information for making food decisions is available. Unfortunately, incorrect and unimportant information is also available. It is up to you to find out what you need to know. It is also up to you to apply this knowledge.

Education, in school and out You receive much of your food education at home and in school. Courses in home economics and in related areas are designed to offer you a basic knowledge of nutrition and food preparation. Such information is also available from books and magazines, which need not be read only in connection with school.

Such information may also be obtained from radio, television, and newspapers. These media can offer you new recipes. They can tell you what foods are plentiful or seasonal, and therefore less expensive. They can inform you about what foods are not considered safe to eat. Continuing food education is essential because our environment is so complex and because it is continually changing.

Advertising Manufacturers advertise to inform you about their products. Their main purpose is to make you want to buy what they are selling. They are prohibited by law from deliberately misleading you. If you read advertising carefully and critically, you will find much information concerning new products to be helpful in planning nutritious meals. Most major food manufacturers have professional home economists on their staffs. Home economists work in test kitchens with the advertising department. They work in other aspects of product development, as well.

Food fads and fallacies Much misinformation about food is circulated and believed. From time to time, a particular food is

Food stamps enable families to buy more food for their money. The stamps cannot be used to buy beer, cigarettes, or other nonfood items, but all food and nutrition decisions are left to the individual.

Following food fads and neglecting food education can lead to inadequate nourishment and high prices. For the consumer who has a sound knowledge of nutrition, every supermarket is a "health food" store.

promoted as a cure-all for human ills. Some people believe that a single food can make you stronger, smarter, and more attractive. No such food exists.

Sometimes nutritionally valuable foods are disregarded. The tomato, for example, was for centuries considered a poisonous fruit. Some food fallacies are preserved in traditions. Some are left over from a time when food preservation methods were unscientific; food that spoiled quickly was avoided.

Food fads come about for a number of reasons. The desire to control weight is one of the most common. Beware of diets based on a single food. No one food contains the balance of nutrients you need.

FOOD GOALS

Many people operate at a level of performance lower than the level they would expect from a car. They would overhaul the car immediately if it functioned improperly. Yet, they accept their own poor health, appearance, and sagging personality. Such "shortcomings" may be caused by poor nutrition. If they are, a person need not rely on coping strategies like compensation to avoid facing them. With rational food choices, one may achieve good health and better appearance.

Not all food goals relate so directly to nutrition. Food preparation can provide the means for satisfying another goal: creativity.

Many young adults include losing weight among their food goals. Fad and crash diets usually result in a loss of temper and energy, but no permanent loss of weight.

CASE STUDY: CARL

THE SITUATION   *Richard and Carl had not seen each other for several months. Both had graduated together from the high school of the rural community in which they lived. After graduation, Richard had become an apprentice in a machine shop, rising quickly to the position of foreman of the division. He had married Carl's sister and, as a result, spent much time visiting with his parents-in-law at their farm.*

Though separated for months at a time, Richard and Carl had no difficulty renewing their friendship during the times when Carl returned home for a visit. Carl talked about his job experiences in the city and of the places he had visited as a company representative. In turn, Richard asked and answered questions, and discussed his work with Carl.

This evening, the two men were engaged in conversation about "old times" when called to the dinner table. As Mother began pouring coffee to accompany the meal, Carl said, "No coffee for me, Mom. I'll have mine later, with dessert."

Richard grinned, winking his eye at Carl. "Well! You go off to the Big City and come back with city-slicker ways. You used to have coffee with dinner, as the rest of us still do, and now you wait until dessert. What else is different since you left us?"

Carl laughed as he sat down to dinner. He said nothing, waiting for a new conversation to begin.

THE INTERVIEW   Q: *Wasn't that an interesting comment Richard made about the coffee?*
A: *Yes, it was. To me, changing my coffee-drinking habits seems like an unimportant matter.*
Q: *Did Richard consider it important?*
A: *Apparently. That change must have stood out as a big example of the way our life-styles differ.*
Q: *Why do you have coffee with dessert, rather than with dinner?*
A: *Because the people I work with do so. I've just gotten into the habit, I guess. In the city, most restaurants serve it after, rather than with, the meal. There are probably other changes in my mealtime habits, too, that also show the influence of the city. I wonder what else Richard has noticed.*

REACT   *What mealtime habits might reflect Richard's life-style? What mealtime habits might be easier than others to change?*

Health

Each year many people shorten their lives and reduce their efficiency by eating too much of the wrong foods. Foods that relieve hunger or satisfy appetite but that lack the nutrients essential for health are sometimes referred to as "empty calories."

Being underweight or overweight are two signs that your nutrition might be inappropriate to your needs. Tiredness, listlessness, or irritability for extended periods of time can also suggest inadequate nutrition; so does susceptibility to certain infections.

We know that poor nutrition before and during pregnancy can seriously affect both the physical and mental health of the unborn child.

Food preparation offers an opportunity to express creativity and imagination. Whether you have made one food your "specialty," or whether you aspire to the general title of "great cook," your need for recognition will be met when others acknowledge your abilities.

Appearance

Skin, teeth, hair, muscles, and nails are all composed of cells. These cells are nourished by the food you eat. Poor nutrition can contribute to poor muscle tone, poor posture, and a poor complexion. It can result in weakened gums and decayed teeth. It can make nails brittle. It can leave hair dull and thin.

Personality

Your self-concept is influenced by the way you feel and look, and by the way other people react to the way you feel and look. Proper nutrition, together with regular exercise and sufficient sleep, makes you feel physically fit. It helps you look your best. The person who is plagued by problems like being underweight or having a poor complexion may feel unacceptable to others. He may lack self-confidence and self-respect.

Creativity

Each choice you make concerning food offers you an opportunity to satisfy your esthetic sense and to express creativity. The shape and color of foods can be a joy to behold. Flavor, aroma, texture, and temperature appeal to your taste. Tantalizing aromas and subtle flavors can make a simple meal a memorable event.

People master different food-preparation skills. The degree of skill achieved, together with the satisfaction gained from performing the task, influences food choices. One person may master the art of making salads, another the art of making omelets. Some people take pride in baking pastry; others have a way with spaghetti or meatloaf.

The person who finds food preparation creative and satisfying will probably have a wider range of choice in foods than the person who looks upon food preparation and meal service as a chore. The *cordon bleu*, or "blue ribbon" cook, is a cook who takes pride in preparing fine meals, and who has gained recognition for mastering this skill.

FOCUS ON FOOD CHOICES

Food connects human beings to the natural environment. It also connects them, through social customs, to one another. The quality of life is closely tied to the quantity and quality of food available for human consumption. Any contaminant—whether DDT, radioactive fallout, or human or chemical wastes—can endanger our food supplies.

As consumers of food, we are faced with long-range choices that will affect worldwide food availability. People who live close to nature and in harmony with it do not waste food. They use what they take from nature. They would ask: "Why shoot a deer if you don't know how to use it all?" They would tan the hide and use the leather. They would use the last bone, hoof, and antler. We must learn to take a similar view.

To waste food is a luxury not many can afford. Much waste is indirectly caused by the food products we select. The metal, paper, glass, and plastic containers and wrappings in which food is sold cannot all be directly reabsorbed by the environment. Man must find ways to recycle these materials so that the balance of nature is not upset.

THINK BACK

Concern with environmental problems must include wise use and preservation of our food supply.
Discuss: *How might people be encouraged to become concerned with the world's food problem?*

Food is used to satisfy basic physical, psychological, and social needs.
Discuss: *What needs might account for the food habits of the "picky" eater?*

Food attitudes and habits reflect strong cultural, regional, and economic influences.
Discuss: *What food habits are influenced by the area of the country in which you live?*

Nutrition education is one step towards overcoming poor eating habits.

Discuss: *Why do teenagers qualify as the worst-fed group of people in the United States?*

Sound nutrition is closely associated with good physical and mental health.
Discuss: *What is the best way to promote sound nutrition in your community?*

LOOK AROUND

1. Why are plants our most basic source of energy? Trace the two basic ways we get energy from them.
2. What is hunger? When can "hunger" be "all in the head"?
3. Define basal metabolism rate. What physical harm occurs when energy intake does not meet an individual's BMR?

4. Cut out pictures from magazines and make a collage showing, in as accurate detail as possible, how you use food to satisfy social needs.

5. Are you a "good" eater or a "poor" eater? What are the influences on your particular attitudes towards food?

6. Interview a member of your family to learn why he dislikes certain foods. Do his reasons make sense? What might make these foods more palatable to him?

7. Ask around among your classmates. What seems to be the favorite food? Why do you think this is so?

8. Make an advertisement for your favorite food. What need does it appeal to?

9. Which of the four food goals discussed here is most important to you? Why?

FOLLOW YOUR PATH

PATH ONE: Design an Advertising Campaign

Step 4 Meet with the other members of your agency. Discuss each of the slogans and ideas, and ask yourselves which basic needs and wants they appeal to. Are they for people of one economic level rather than another? One sex? Do you think any refer to any one region or cultural group? Remember, you are planning a *national* campaign.

Step 5 Select a magazine in which to advertise. Who do you think reads this magazine? Justify your selection.

PATH TWO: Feed an Intentional Family

Step 4 Do the foods you put on your personal "liked" list reflect any cultural preferences? What about the meal you planned? Can any of the conflicts you faced in Step 2 be traced to cultural or economic differences? Which ones?

Step 5 Find out who will be home and when. When is it worthwhile to serve meals? Plan family menus for an entire week. Consider the "liked" list and the menus each member planned. Consult several cookbooks, if you wish.

PATH THREE: Operate a Restaurant

Step 3 Discover the food preferences of your potential customers. Devise a questionnaire or interview technique that will help you get the information.

Step 4 Use this technique on some of your potential customers. List their preferences in order of popularity.

Step 5 Plan a full menu. How much do your own food preferences, as opposed to those of your potential customers, influence your menu selections? Consult cookbooks if you wish.

PATH FOUR: Study Your Food Habits

Step 3 Consult your list from Step 2. In what three places did you most often eat? Show, in words or pictures, the principal influences on your food choices in each of these places. Be as specific as possible in showing cultural influences.

Step 4 Consult your lists from Step 1. At what time of day do they show you were usually most physically active? Are these times different on different days? These are the times at which you need the most energy.

Step 5 Look at the food advertisements in several magazines. Cut out five ads for foods you eat. Cut out five for foods you do not eat. Paste each ad up on a piece of paper. Circle and comment upon those parts of each ad which most strike your eye. Ask such questions as: Are there people in the ad? How old are they and how do they dress? Does the ad appeal to an unmet need? Which one?

CHAPTER 8

Food for Health and Fitness

Food serves many functions. It contributes to satisfying many needs. Of course, there is one need that food alone can satisfy: the basic physical need for nourishment.

To be sure that your body is properly nourished, you must know certain facts about food. You must know, for example, which foods your body must have to grow. You must know which kinds of food are sources of energy.

There are many people who spend a great deal of money on foods that are not nourishing. There are others who eat constantly—but the wrong things. Whether you eat at home, at school, or in restaurants, you can learn to select tasty, nourishing foods at a price you can afford.

PRINCIPLES OF SOUND NUTRITION

Different nutrients contribute to your life and health in different ways. Most nutrients perform more than one job, although each is usually noted only for its most important function. The primary function of proteins, for example, is growth and repair of the body. Carbohydrates and fats supply energy. Minerals and vitamins help begin and regulate certain body processes. Although water and roughage are not nutrients, they also play vital roles in maintaining body functions.

Our present understanding of nutrition is not complete. More is constantly being learned. It is known that there is no single perfect food. To stay alive and healthy, you need a balanced diet of many foods. Do not overload your system with any one food.

Water and Roughage

Water and roughage are supplied by foods and certain beverages. *Roughage* is the part of fruits, vegetables, grains, and meats that you cannot digest. It has no nutritive value, but it does aid in digestion and the elimination of wastes.

The average adult requires the equivalent of six to eight glasses of water daily. You might live without food for weeks, but you could survive only a few days without water.

Water is distributed throughout your body; it makes up between 50 and 60 percent of your total weight. It forms an essential part of your cells, tissues, and body fluids.

All your body's chemical transformations require water. You need it for digestion. It aids in the distribution of nutrients throughout your body. You need it to remove body wastes. You even need water to keep your temperature constant.

Carbohydrates: Food as Fuel

We have already discussed that physical energy—measured in calories—is an important human resource. We know that this resource comes from food. Not all foods, however, are equally valuable as sources of energy. Carbohydrates are among the most important.

Sugar, found in syrups, candies, and jellies, is a carbohydrate. The starches in all kinds of breads, cakes, and cereals also are carbohydrates, as are the starches in such vegetables as potatoes, corn, and lima beans.

Sugars contain more quick energy than starches. If you feel physically exhausted, sugar can provide a fast "pick-up." Sugars also help bacteria to grow; people who eat a lot of sugar may be prone to tooth decay.

Before starches can be used by the body, they must be converted to sugars. This takes time; the energy from starches is only gradually released to the body. Also, the foods which contain starches may contain other important nutrients, as well. Many of these nutrients are absent from sugar-rich foods.

Protein: Food for Growth and Repair

The cells of your body are constantly being built up and torn down. *Proteins* are a necessary part of this process, and are hence called the "building blocks" of life. Growth and repair are their two essential functions.

Proteins are made up of chemical units called *amino acids*. Scientists have identified over twenty amino acids which your body uses. Some of these amino acids must be present in the food you eat. These are called

We can get much of the water we need from foods and other beverages. People in dry regions have learned that, if necessary, they can survive by drinking the juices of plants. This Moroccan boy is walking by one source of water on his way to another—the village well.

essential amino acids. There are eight essential amino acids for adults, and nine or ten for growing children. From the essential amino acids, the remaining, or nonessential amino acids, can be manufactured by the body.

Proteins which contain enough of the essential amino acids to help maintain life and support growth are called complete proteins. Animals manufacture complete proteins from the plants they eat. Therefore, lean meat, fish, poultry, milk, cheese, and eggs are important sources of complete proteins. Soybeans, for example, are another good source of complete proteins.

Partially complete proteins lack or have an inadequate amount of one or more essential amino acids. They will maintain life, but will not support growth. Partially complete proteins are adequate for physically inactive adults. Dried beans (other than soybeans), nuts, and whole-grain cereals are good sources.

Totally incomplete proteins cannot maintain life or support growth. Most fruits and vegetables fall into this category.

It is possible to provide nutritionally adequate meals by carefully combining complete and incomplete proteins. You can do this by combining beans and a fairly small amount of ground meat, or by combining enriched macaroni with cheese. It is also possible to satisfy your protein requirements by combining various incomplete proteins. A great deal of nutritional knowledge is required if one is to do this effectively.

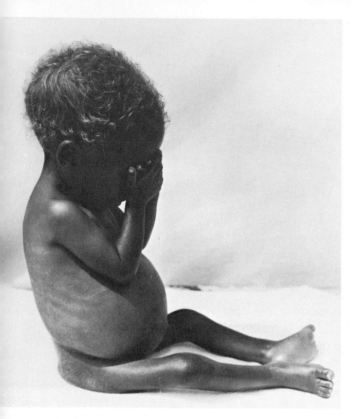

This baby is suffering from Kwashiorkor, a protein deficiency disease. Protein is essential to proper physical and mental development. Prolonged lack of protein results in mental retardation.

Fats and Oils: Sustaining Sources of Energy

Ounce for ounce, fats contain more than twice as much energy as carbohydrates and proteins. Their energy, however, cannot be used by the body as quickly as the energy from carbohydrates. Fats provide a more sustaining kind of energy, which the body can store for future needs.

Physically active people need more fats than inactive people. Because the stored energy in fats can be converted into heat, people who live in cold climates eat fats to keep warm.

Traditionally, fatty foods have been associated with luxury. This is because most of them are expensive, juicy, and succulent. It is also because most are quite satisfying—they remain in the stomach for a long time.

Fats are found in both plant and animal foods. The two are different. Plant fats, or *oils*, are liquid at room temperature. Animal fats are solid at room temperature. (Fish oil is an exception to these generalizations.) Animal fats contain *cholesterol*.

Cholesterol We take in cholesterol from foods; we also manufacture it in our livers. Cholesterol is present throughout our bodies, especially in our brains and nervous tissue. Scientists believe that cholesterol performs certain basic functions in the body, although the nature of these functions is not well understood. Excess cholesterol in the bloodstream can cling to blood vessels and block them up. It can cause heart attacks. In consideration of this, some people limit the fats they eat. Egg yolk, liver, kidney, and fish eggs have a high cholesterol content. Milk products and meat contain smaller amounts.

Fats Fats contain fatty acids. These fatty acids are divided into three categories: saturated, monounsaturated, and polyunsaturated. There is evidence to suggest that polyunsaturated fatty acids may help reduce the possibility of heart and circulatory disorders. Saturated fatty acids may increase the possibility of such disorders. In response to these possibilities, some people have adopted diets low in saturated fatty acids and fairly high in polyunsaturated fatty acids.

As a general rule, plant fats, which are oils, are high in polyunsaturated fatty acids. (Two exceptions are olive oil and coconut oil.) Animal fats contain a higher percentage of saturated fatty acids than do oils.

One reason for the traditional popularity of fats over oils is the fact that fats are solid. In recent decades, scientists have discovered how to make oils solid. They do this through a process called *hydrogenation*. (Margarine has hydrogenated vegetable oil.)

Minerals: Your Diet's Mighty Mites

Ninety-six percent of your body weight is carbon, hydrogen, oxygen, and nitrogen. The elements which compose the other four percent are called *minerals*. Like proteins, minerals aid in tissue growth and repair. They also help begin and regulate certain body processes.

Minerals can be classified as *macronutrients* and *micronutrients*. (In Greek, "macro" means "large" and "micro" means "small.") You need more macronutrients than micronutrients, although you do not need much of either. A teaspoon could easily hold your daily mineral requirement. While your mineral needs are small, they are still extremely important. You must take in the necessary minerals in appropriate amounts for your body to function properly.

Macronutrients include calcium, phosphorus, potassium, sulfur, sodium, chlorine, and magnesium. Micronutrients, or *trace elements*, include iron, copper, manganese, iodine, and fluorine.

Macronutrients Calcium is the most abundant mineral in your body. Phosphorus is next. By themselves they are soft. They combine, however, to build strong bones and teeth. Without calcium, cuts could not form scabs. Nerves could not carry impulses, or messages, to your brain and to other parts of your body. Calcium also helps muscles to contract, or shorten; you need it to

Seaweed has been eaten in the Orient for centuries. High in protein, its primary use in the West has been as a colloid agent in both food and nonfood items. Today, much research is devoted to making seaweed foods and additives that are acceptable to the Western palate.

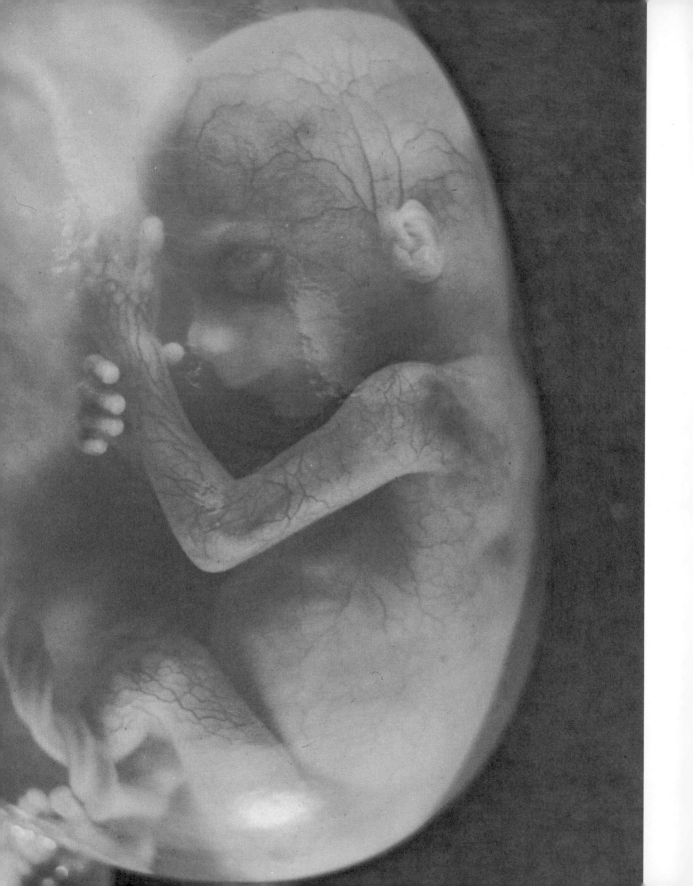

If a woman waits until she is pregnant to start eating "right," she endangers her baby's health. The human fetus develops rapidly. At about twelve weeks, major systems are already formed.

make a fist or bend your arm. The regular beating of your heart, another muscle, also depends partly on calcium. Phosphorus is important for the digestion of fats and carbohydrates.

Milk is the best single source of calcium. Cheddar cheese is also an excellent source. Other good sources—when eaten frequently—are other cheeses, salmon, turnip greens, collards, and kale. Shrimp and clams, rich in protein, are also rich in calcium. Many foods which contain protein or calcium also contain phosphorus.

Not everyone needs the same amount of calcium. Children—whose bones and teeth are developing—need more than adults.

Common table salt, or *sodium chloride,* is composed of sodium and chlorine. These two minerals help you to maintain the balance between the amount of water in your blood and the amount of water in your tissues. You lose salt when you perspire, urinate, cry, or bleed. You replace it when you eat salted foods. For medical reasons, doctors sometimes restrict salt intake.

Potassium, magnesium, and sulfur are three other macronutrients. Protein-rich foods supply your daily needs of these minerals.

Micronutrients Your blood carries oxygen to every part of your body. Copper and iron, two trace elements, take part in this process. Copper plays an indirect role. It must be present if hemoglobin is to be formed. *Hemoglobin,* an iron-rich substance, then carries the oxygen through the blood.

Your body constantly reuses its copper and iron; your need to consume them is not usually great. If you should lose blood, however, your supply of these micronutrients is

Iron is an important requirement for maintaining a person's energy and vitality. Its highest concentration is in hemoglobin, the red protein part of the blood, which carries oxygen to the body.

diminished. Once menstrual periods begin, for example, young women have an increased need for iron-rich foods. For them, an iron supplement may be advisable.

Liver and other organ meats, like heart and kidney, are rich in iron. Egg yolk, lean meat, fish, oysters, and leafy green vegetables are also good sources. Molasses, apricots, dried fruit, and whole-grain cereals contain both iron and copper.

Iodine, another micronutrient, is essential for the proper functioning of the thyroid

125

Through your food choices, you can help control how you look and feel. Health, energy, personality, weight, and the condition of hair and skin are affected by diet, even after growth is complete.

gland, which helps to regulate the basal metabolism rate. As a result, iodine influences body weight. Children need iodine for physical growth and mental development. Too much iodine may cause skin irritation.

The ocean is rich in iodine. Consequently, plants which grow near salt water are good sources. Many inland regions lack a natural supply. Today, *iodized* table salt—salt to which iodine has been added—can satisfy the average person's need for iodine.

The trace element fluorine is found in bones and teeth. In proper amounts it seems to offset excessive tooth decay. For this reason, some communities *fluoridate* the public water supply. They add to it a chemical compound which contains fluorine.

The body also needs minute amounts of manganese, zinc, cobalt, and molybdenum.

Vitamins: Foods That Regulate Your Body

Vitamins do not supply materials for energy and growth. They must be present in the body, however, if other nutrients are to do their jobs. Without vitamins, you would suffer from a number of diseases and your body would not be able to regulate itself.

Some vitamins dissolve in fats; the rest dissolve in water.

Fat-soluble vitamins   Vitamins A, D, E, and K are fat-soluble. They do not dissolve in water. Oily foods, like fish and nuts, are good sources; so are dairy products and green and yellow vegetables.

Moist tissues surround your eyes, mouth, stomach, intestines, and lungs. Your skin must also be kept moist. **Vitamin A** keeps all these tissues from drying and cracking. It keeps them healthy and able to resist certain infections. Frequent colds and fever blisters may indicate a lack of vitamin A. A lack of this vitamin also causes *night blindness*, poor vision in dim light.

Animals and fish store vitamin A in their livers and kidneys. Hence, these foods are good direct sources. Others are whole milk and whole-milk cheeses, Cheddar cheese, butter, egg yolks, and fortified margarine.

Our bodies can manufacture their own vitamin A if given the right raw material. This is *carotene*, which is found in green and yellow vegetables. Rich sources are carrots, kale, mustard and turnip greens, spinach, peaches, yams, and winter squash.

The vitamin which must be present in your body so that calcium and phosphorus can play their part in building strong bones and teeth is **vitamin D**. Without adequate vitamin D, bones and teeth would be soft and weak. This vitamin is most important for pregnant women and growing children.

There are two basic ways to receive vitamin D. The first is to eat plant and animal fats. These contain substances which are

CASE STUDY: LINDA

THE SITUATION   *Arriving home from work, Linda saw Jeri and Gloria on the front steps. The two girls were roommates in Linda's apartment building. Linda now ate dinner with them several times a week.*

"It's your turn to cook tonight, Linda."

Linda smiled. She liked to eat, but she had not been particularly interested in cooking for herself. During the first few months in her new apartment, she found that eating snacks was an easy way to take care of "dinner." She actually became unconcerned about preparing dinner. There were times when milk or juice was the only food in the refrigerator because she was too busy to shop or because she arrived home after grocery stores had closed. She was single and had neither a roommate nor anyone else for whom to cook.

Jeri and Gloria first suggested the idea of the Single Service Club several weeks ago. They wanted to organize a small group of people who wished to eat together several times a week. Each person would take a turn preparing the meal. Everyone who participated would be assured of eating four or five good dinners a week. Though it had taken a little effort to get into the routine of preparing and eating food regularly, Linda was now one of the strongest supporters of the Single Service Club. She talked enthusiastically about the club when asked, and encouraged others to begin similar plans.

THE INTERVIEW   *Q: Why are you so interested in this club?*
A: Because it's an easy way for me to eat well and stay healthy. I just wasn't interested in taking care of myself before Jeri suggested the club. I was tired and gaining weight because I didn't cook and I was always eating "snack" foods.
Q: Were you excited about the club at first?
A: Not when Jeri first suggested the idea. I thought it would be extra work and responsibility for me. I like to feel free to come in and go out whenever I wish. However, Jeri and Gloria kept "badgering" me until I finally accepted a dinner invitation with the group. There wasn't as much involved in club participation as I expected, so here I am.
Q: Would this idea interest others?
A: It would interest some others, I think. There are many single people living in apartments these days. They probably find it as unenjoyable as I did to cook for themselves. And it's expensive to eat in restaurants. Those with roommates might keep such different schedules so that even they would be eating alone. I'd recommend testing the idea, at least for a little while. People might want to begin with a two- or three-day-a-week plan.

REACT   *Would the idea of a Single Service Club interest you? Can you suggest other solutions to Linda's problem?*

---

digested and some of which are then transported, through complex chemical processes, to the skin. When the skin is exposed to particular kinds of rays from the sun—called ultraviolet rays—these substances are changed into vitamin D. This is why vitamin D is called the "sunshine vitamin." We are likely to need more vitamin D than we can produce in this way. We cannot rely on the sun as a source. Window glass, dust, fog, and air pollution filter out many of the sun's rays before they reach our skin.

The second way to receive vitamin D is to take it in directly. The best natural sources are fish liver oils. Cod liver oil is a well-known example. Less adequate sources are fish, liver, and egg yolks. Vitamin D may also be artificially added to food. In the United States, much milk is *fortified* with this vitamin; such milk is one of the best sources.

An excess of vitamin D taken over a long period can cause loss of appetite, fatigue, headaches, and nausea. If this excessive intake continues, serious damage to body organs (especially kidneys and nerves) may result.

Little is known concerning the **vitamin E** requirement for human beings. This vitamin, however, is widely distributed in foods. It protects vitamin A from being destroyed by oxygen in the body, and it prevents harmful changes in heart and skeletal muscles. In animals, a lack of vitamin E causes *sterility*—the inability to reproduce. The requirement for vitamin E, among men in particular, seems to be related to the amount of unsaturated fats in the diet.

Wheat-germ oil, vegetable oils, nuts, peas, beans, and green leafy vegetables are the best sources of vitamin E. It is also found in whole-grain cereals, vegetable greens, egg yolk, and meat. There are small quantities in milk, as well.

Blood clotting is the body's way of preventing excessive blood loss from cuts or other injuries. **Vitamin K** helps the blood to clot. It is often administered in large doses to prevent massive bleeding during surgery. Green leafy vegetables—such as cabbage and spinach—and liver are the best sources.

The water-soluble vitamins The vitamin B which scientists first discovered was later found to be made up of a number of similar vitamins. Each vitamin in this *B-complex* group plays a distinct role. All B vitamins are water-soluble, as is vitamin C.

Foods rich in water-soluble vitamins lose much of their nutritive value if the liquid in which they are cooked is thrown away. It is

Students and working people may find their food choices limited at lunch if restaurants and institutions do not offer an adequate assortment of foods that are both nutritious and inexpensive. Lunches brought from home may allow more variety for less money.

wise to prepare foods containing the B-complex vitamins or vitamin C by either cooking them in very little water or by steaming them. The water in which such vitamin-rich foods are cooked can be used in gravies and sauces. In this way, much of the full vitamin value of the foods is kept in the diet. Eating such foods raw is even better.

The existence of a vitamin B_1, or **thiamine**, deficiency disease was dramatically shown in a cure found for an ancient disease known in the Orient. For centuries men there had suffered from *beriberi*. This painful nervous disorder is characterized by weakness, loss of appetite, swollen body tissue, and heart failure. Seventy-five years ago, an alert doctor observed that there was a difference between the diets of those who were healthy and of those stricken with beriberi. The afflicted ate polished rice; those unaffected ate the whole grain. The outer covering of the rice appeared to contain a substance that prevented beriberi. This substance was later identified as vitamin B. It was eventually isolated from other closely related vitamins and called vitamin B_1.

Thiamine helps the body to break down and use carbohydrates and fats. Wheat germ, whole-grain breads and cereals, yeast, pork, liver, and other organ meats are the best sources of thiamine. Peanuts, soybeans, legumes, and corn are good vegetable sources. Some thiamine is found in milk. Heat can destroy thiamine; toasting or prolonged cooking should be avoided if the thiamine content of foods is to be preserved.

A second vitamin of the B complex is **riboflavin**, or vitamin B_2. This vitamin is essential to the metabolism of proteins and carbohydrates. Lack of riboflavin can cause cracking at the corners of the mouth. The eyes may itch and burn.

The best sources of riboflavin are dried yeast, milk, kidney, heart, and liver. It is also found in eggs, meat, and green leafy vegetables. Some products are enriched by the addition of riboflavin.

If you snack between meals, get good nutrition "value" for the calories you consume. Fruits, vegetables, and cheeses are some likely choices. Many prepared snack foods are loaded with "empty calories."

Another of the B-complex vitamins is **niacin**, known also as nicotinic acid. Niacin deficiency can cause *pellagra*. This disease is characterized by red sores on the skin and by inflammation of the digestive tract. In its final stages, pellagra causes mental problems. If not caught in time, it causes death.

Fish (especially canned salmon), lean meat, poultry, soybeans, peanuts, wheat germ, liver, vegetable greens, and yeast are rich sources of niacin. Corn contains substances that destroy niacin, and a person living on a diet of corn and fatty meat may develop pellagra. Any food rich in complete proteins will contain sufficient niacin.

Any foods which are labeled *enriched* and which are sold in interstate commerce have had thiamine, riboflavin, and niacin added to them. The Food and Drug Administration requires this.

Ascorbic acid, or **vitamin C**, aids in the manufacture of the "cement" which holds cell walls together. It performs a vital function in healing cuts and bruises. It keeps the walls of blood vessels strong and it helps the body to resist infection.

A lack of vitamin C results in improper bone formation and development and weakened blood vessel walls. It leads to a disease called *scurvy*. Scurvy is characterized by swollen, aching joints and bleeding gums. A person who suffers from this disease tends to bruise easily. After a while, he may become too weak to walk.

Good sources of vitamin C are all citrus fruits, West Indian cherries, and strawberries. Fair sources are honeydew, asparagus tips, brussels sprouts, raw cabbage, leafy green vegetables, tomatoes, and potatoes.

A FOOD-SELECTION GUIDE

Foods have been classified in four basic groups. These are: meat, milk and milk products, fruits and vegetables, and breads and cereals. Nutritionists feel that adequate amounts of foods from each of these groups will supply your body with enough of each of the nutrients needed to maintain good health. Many nutritionists suggest that you include something from each group in each of your meals. Such a meal is called a *well-balanced meal*.

Sugar and fats, although also important to your daily diet, are not included in these *Basic Four*. It is believed that in the United States and Canada, sugar and fats are in ample supply when adequate amounts of the Basic Four are eaten.

The Meat Group

The Meat Group foods include meat and meat substitutes. These foods provide the major portion of protein in the diet. They also contain a significant amount of fats. Additional important nutrients from this group are vitamin B_1 (thiamine) and iron. Beef, lamb, veal, pork, liver, heart, kidney, poultry and eggs, and fish and shellfish are the major foods in the Meat Group. Meat alternates include dried beans, peas, lentils, nuts, and peanut butter. Recommended daily are two or more servings of lean meat, poultry, fish, liver, or eggs. An average serving is two or three cooked ounces, without bones or waste. For dried beans, peas, or lentils, a serving is one cup, cooked.

The Milk Group

Milk and dairy products make up the Milk Group. Milk may be whole, evaporated, skim, dry, buttermilk, chocolate milk, or chocolate dairy drink. Cheese may be soft like cottage cheese, semisoft like Muenster, or hard like Cheddar or Swiss. It may be fresh, aged, or processed.

Milk contains relatively large amounts of calcium, high-quality protein, and riboflavin. It also supplies vitamin A, thiamin, and niacin to the diet.

Servings from the Milk Group depend on age and other factors. The daily recommended servings for children are three or more eight-ounce glasses of milk; for some younger children under eight, smaller (six-ounce) glasses may be sufficient; for teenagers, four or more glasses; and for adults, two or more glasses. Pregnant women need three or more glasses of milk. Nursing mothers need four or more glasses. Some dairy

Whatever your cultural food preferences, this food-selection guide will help you to choose, from your own food background, adequate amounts of the kinds of foods you need for a balanced diet.

CASE STUDY: EMMA

THE SITUATION Emma had just finished studying nutrition in her foods course. Though she could not remember every detail of the material she had read, she was now aware of the importance of good nutrition. She had begun giving more thought to her choice of foods from the school cafeteria.

At home, things were a little different. Dinner was usually rushed, the same foods appeared again and again on the weekly menu, and several key nutrients were lacking. Aunt Fern's reasoning was that she "didn't have time to plan 'fancy' meals." She also felt that her meals "had plenty of nutrition if everyone ate something from each dish that was served." By the time Emma arrived home, Aunt Fern had already decided the evening's menu. Emma's work was to set the table and prepare the tossed salad.

In discussing the problem with her foods teacher, Emma was reminded of the Basic Four Food Guide she'd learned about in class. She decided to show the guide to Aunt Fern. She would try to persuade her aunt to use it in planning meals next week. Many of the simple-to-prepare, inexpensive foods on the plan had been prepared in class, and Emma was willing to make them herself.

THE INTERVIEW Q: Will Aunt Fern listen to your suggestion for next week's meals?
A: I hope so. If I volunteer to do some of the cooking, there will be less work for her. Maybe then she won't mind trying something new.
Q: Have you helped plan meals before?
A: No, but the menus the class planned are good ones and I'd like a chance to try them with my family.
Q: Does Aunt Fern want your help?
A: Yes. It's just that we've all gotten into the habit of cooking a certain way. Each of us has a definite job to do at mealtime, and things get done quickly then. It might be difficult to change.
Q: What makes you so interested in improving family nutrition?
A: In class we learned what happens when nutrition is poor. And we practiced making meals that tasted good and were easy to prepare. It's not as difficult or boring to prepare nutritious meals as I expected. Eating correctly is beginning to make sense to me.

REACT What additional problems must be overcome in improving nutrition? Whose responsibility is good family nutrition?

---

products which give about the same amount of calcium as an eight-ounce glass of milk are: one serving (one and one-fourth ounces) of cheese; two servings of ice cream (one-third pint per serving); three servings of cottage cheese (one-half cup per serving).

The Fruit-Vegetable Group

Fresh fruits and vegetables are good sources of carbohydrates. They are also the most dependable sources of vitamins A and C.

Since vitamin A is fat-soluble (and is found in fatty foods and fish oils) and vitamin C is water-soluble, the method of preparing foods containing these vitamins will have a bearing on how much vitamin value you actually obtain from the fruits and vegetables you may eat. The recommended serving of those fruits and vegetables which are good sources of vitamin A (see page 126) is one every other day. Additional servings (to make up four or more daily servings) may be selected from any other foods in this group. Recommended daily for adequate amounts of vitamin C is a one-half cup serving from "good sources." (See page 130.)

The Bread-Cereal Group

Foods in the Bread-Cereal Group are good sources of carbohydrates. They also contain the all-important B-complex vitamins. To contain their full quota of B-complex vitamins, breads and cereals should be whole-grain, enriched, or restored.

All food products made from cereal grains —wheat, rye, corn, rice, millet, barley, and oats—belong to this group. These include bread, pancakes, crackers, cake, and cookies. They also include rolled oats, grits, and spaghetti. The daily recommended serving from this group is four or more a day. An average serving includes one slice of bread, one ounce of ready-to-eat cereal, one-half to one-quarter cup of cooked enriched cereal, cornmeal, grits, noodles, or rice.

CHOOSING BETTER NUTRITION

Nutrition knowledge is essential to sound decision making at mealtime. If your goals are good physical, mental, and social health and a vital, wholesome appearance, an awareness of the important role that nutrients play in providing these is important to you. Brief reflection makes clear that "you are what you eat."

THINK BACK

Nutrients for adequate nutrition are supplied by the foods we eat.
Discuss: *What nutrients are present in the food you most commonly eat? Is this an adequate supply?*

No single nutrient is responsible for the total health of the body.
Discuss: *What are the different functions of the different nutrients?*

Using the Basic Four Food Groups in meal planning helps insure adequate nutrition.
Discuss: *How does one use this food guide in meal planning?*

The amount of nutrients needed daily depends on one's age, activity, and general health.
Discuss: *Why is it best to consult qualified professionals for a weight loss or weight gain program?*

LOOK AROUND

1. What foods help to supply the body's needed water supply?
2. Plan a meal for a person on a high-protein diet. When do you think such diets are recommended?
3. In what instances is a low-fat diet an important consideration in planning meals? Prepare a menu for such a diet.
4. What are polyunsaturated fats? What products on the market qualify as such?
5. Discuss with class members today's most popular "fad" diets. If possible, have a nutritionist participate. Why do people so readily accept these fads? What are potential problems associated with each?
6. What different cooking principles must you apply if you wish to retain the vitamin value of various foods?
7. What are the Basic Four Food Groups? How many servings of each help meet a teenager's daily nutritional requirements?

FOLLOW YOUR PATH

PATH ONE: Design an Advertising Campaign

Step 6 Make up an ad for the next issue of the same magazine. Using the same slogan or idea, illustrate your ad with three well-balanced meals which use your vegetable.

Step 7 Ask two members of the intentional family in Path Two to read your ads. Does this vegetable fit their present food plans? If not, find out why. Do these reasons apply to other families? Should you change your slogan or idea?

Step 8 Create a one-minute television commercial which will show your product being prepared as part of a meal. Using the resources you have available, create some artwork, collect props and costumes, and get whatever else you will need. (It is not necessary to actually cook the food. You may pretend—do it in pantomime. It may be easiest to work with hand puppets.) Rehearse your commercial privately. At the end of Chapter 9, you will act it out before the class.

PATH TWO: Feed an Intentional Family

Step 6 How many of the planned menus are balanced? Agree on the way you will balance each main meal.

Step 7 Are you preparing meals in such a way that the water- and fat-soluble vitamins are not lost? Make a chart illustrating each vegetable that will be served. Illustrate also how it can be prepared so that no vitamins—or not too many—will be lost.

Step 8 Plan a birthday party for the family member whose birthday is nearest. Do not tell him about the menu. Base what you do on what you know about him so far. Privately, he should plan his own party as he would like it. Everyone should think not only about the food, but also about the circumstances under which it will be served.

PATH THREE: Operate a Restaurant

Step 6 Does your menu offer a variety of foods from each of the food groups? If necessary, revise your menu to allow for a greater variety of balanced meals. As much as possible, consider your questionnaire or interview results.

Step 7 Organize your menu. Draw it up. Make it look as professional as possible.

Step 8 Either through drawings or a cardboard model, show how your restaurant looks. Also draw a floor plan, showing the complete seating arrangement.

PATH FOUR: Study Your Food Habits

Step 6 Examine the list of foods you ate (Step 2). Are you getting too much or not enough of any nutrient? Make up a poster showing the long-term effects of your diet. Separately explain the effects of each nutritional deficiency.

Step 7 Take a long piece of brown paper. With a felt pen or crayon, divide it into seven equal sections. At the top of each section, write in the days of the week. With your "meals" from Step 6 and with other magazine pictures, illustrate a well-balanced diet for each day. Include snacks and beverages. Indicate the time of each meal and snack. Plan meals so that you will have enough "fuel" for the most active parts of your day. (Refer back to Step 4.)

Step 8 If you are missing out on certain nutrients, select several foods which you like and which contain these nutrients. Add those foods to your diet. Go through magazines. Cut out pictures of these new foods and of the foods you usually eat. On separate pieces of paper or paper plates, combine these foods to show well-balanced meals that you feel have both eye and taste appeal. (Some of these meals should be what you would consider suitable for breakfast.)

CHAPTER 9

Mealtime Decisions

Someday it may be possible for all our food to be in capsule form. For the present, however, food comes in a great variety of shapes, tastes, and colors. This variety can be extended even further by the way in which food is prepared. Foods can be ground, sliced, or mashed; or they can be combined with other foods to make something which looks entirely different from any of the individual ingredients.

People differ greatly in how they regard various foods. Some who would enjoy eating slivers of coconut would never eat a single frosted ant. Certain foods are associated with specific types of occasions. To some people, lobster is "something special," while hot dogs are fine only when a person is "on the run."

The successful cook is aware of the variety not only among foods, but also among the ways different people think of foods. From among the foods available to him and the preparation techniques with which he is familiar, he creates a plan. The cook's work, however, need not end there. He might also concern himself with creating a "good" atmosphere—an atmosphere in which his food will be enjoyed.

A cook, then, can have a number of goals. He combines them, just as he might combine ingredients in a bowl, shaping the total social occasion of which eating is a part.

MAKING THE CHOICE: PLANNING FOOD OCCASIONS

The usual goals of food occasions arise from physical, psychological, and social needs. When and how food can be used to meet these goals depends on the occasion and on the people involved. If you are eating alone and are not too concerned about the taste or appearance of food, your goal might simply be a well-balanced diet. You might have different objectives if you are planning breakfasts and dinners for a family over an extended period of time. Then, you would probably consider not only nutritional balance, but also the needs and preferences of each family member. For a special occasion, your goal might be to serve an unusual food.

Consider planning the food and the surroundings at the same time. The kind of food served should be appropriate to the nature of the occasion. If you are considering a formal dinner, hot dogs might be the "wrong" food to serve. If friends are coming over to listen to records, hot dogs or tacos might be quite appropriate. No matter how simple or complex, food occasions offer opportunities to satisfy esthetic needs. All menus can be planned to have visual and taste appeal.

Remember that your choice of food and setting is the choice of a social environment.

The guests you invite will interact with this environment. Guests would tend to dress up to attend a formal dinner where pheasant under glass was served. They would most likely eat with forks, knives, and spoons. At a picnic, however, people would more likely appear in casual clothing, and they would probably eat many foods with their hands.

Whatever the nature of your food decisions, you should be aware of all the factors that are involved.

Planning the Surroundings

A clever meal planner can create a pleasant feeling almost anywhere. Still, different mealtime surroundings have different feelings about them; they help create different atmospheres. Kitchens do not generally have the same atmosphere as dining rooms. Dining rooms do not generally have the same atmosphere as public parks. You form one impression from ten people in tuxedos and evening gowns. You would probably feel otherwise about ten people in dungarees and sweatshirts. When planning to serve food, keep in mind that the surroundings will influence the way people will feel about the occasion. This applies as much to routine food occasions—like family dinner—as it does to special parties. However formal or informal the occasion, planned hospitality tends to be more successful than haphazard entertaining. Even apparently casual entertaining tends to be more successful if it comes from a general plan. To carry it off, you need to know who and how many are going to be there. You need to know what refreshments you are going to offer to your guests. You also need to know what activities they could participate in and enjoy.

Imaginative table settings add to mealtime atmosphere. In this combination of formal and informal elements, the arrangement of the glasses, candles, and fruit replaces a traditional centerpiece.

On formal occasions, there are recognized standards for the way food is eaten and served. These standards influence the way people behave, as well as the way they expect others to behave.

Formal occasions Any gathering where food is served provides an opportunity for people to meet their need to belong. Formal occasions can be used by people who wish to satisfy their need for status. There can also be an esthetic pleasure in arranging and displaying the items on the table.

Formal occasions require you to follow certain established guidelines for dress, food service, seating, and introductions. These rules are intended to promote, rather than to restrict, comfort and relaxation among people who may not know each other. Young adults often prefer spontaneity and informality. However, even they sometimes choose a formal wedding. They recognize that it provides guidelines for a complex and ceremonious occasion. The socially established routines of formal events permit the planner to save time and energy.

The formal table may feature an artistic centerpiece of fresh flowers or fruit. The table might also be set around a candelabra. The guests might eat with silverware from dishes of fine china. The glasses might be crystal. All this is often set on a tablecloth of linen, fine cotton, or lace. In truly formal dining, the food is usually served by paid assistants; the host and hostess remain seated with their guests.

Informal occasions The relaxed atmosphere associated with informal dining may be more comfortable for routine meals, like family breakfast and dinner. The advantage of informality is that it encourages many people to feel more relaxed and natural. If a host or hostess is sufficiently skilled and confident, it is possible to combine both formal and informal elements to create a warm atmosphere.

Should an **informal seated meal** seem best to meet your goals, you might begin with colorful tablecloths or mats. Brightly colored earthenware or plastic dishes might also help create the proper atmosphere. When meals are served "family style," serving dishes are placed on the table. They are passed from one person to the next. Another alternative is to fill plates in the kitchen. In such cases, bread, butter, and salad are generally passed at the table.

If you do not have the space for an informal seated meal, you might choose to have a **buffet**. At a buffet, guests serve themselves. (A buffet is also called a "stand-and-serve" or "cafeteria-style" meal.) Unless trays or small tables are provided, guests hold their plates on their laps. For this reason, foods that need to be cut with a knife should be kept to a minimum. The dishes and tableware at a buffet can be elegant or simple, depending on the occasion. Paper cups and plates are often appropriate.

Casseroles and stews are popular main courses at buffets. For large crowds, several such dishes can be offered.

Barbecues and **picnics** are other popular forms of casual eating. You might choose to have a picnic, for example, if you wish to feed more people than you can comfortably seat indoors. A picnic should, of course, be an event that you feel your guests would enjoy. Some people may dislike eating outside. Others may love the sky and fresh air, and even think that being outdoors makes the food taste better. If the guests enjoy active sports, the party could be planned around hiking, swimming, or boating.

The foods you choose should be appropriate to the occasion: if you plan a picnic, consider foods like shish kebab, which are easy to prepare and eat outdoors.

CASE STUDY: JACK

THE SITUATION *Beth and Jack invited George and Pat, friends they had not seen for a long time, out to dinner. They went to The Quiet Corner, an elegant restaurant with authentic Victorian furniture.*

On arriving at the restaurant, the two couples were seated promptly and given menus from which to order. After much indecision, orders were given and the four settled back to await appetizers and soup.

"I haven't been to a place like this for quite a while," remarked George. "It certainly is loaded with atmosphere. I like the low lights and these private little tables."

The waitress brought the appetizers and, shortly thereafter, the main course. The couples laughed and talked throughout dinner, enjoying the good food and service. At the end of the main meal, before dessert, George leaned across to Jack and said, "Pass your plates over here. I'll stack them up for the waitress to take."

"Oh, that's not necessary," replied Jack. "She can get them easily." He was a little disturbed by George's suggestion. It was not exactly the procedure to follow when eating out.

George ignored Jack. He reached across to collect all the empty plates on the table. By the time the waitress returned for the dessert order, there were three neat piles of used plates waiting to be removed.

THE INTERVIEW *Q: Did you enjoy your evening with George and Pat?*
A: Oh, yes. George and I have always gotten along well. But I was embarrassed when he decided to stack up all the dirty dishes.
Q: How did your wife feel about it?
A: She agrees that to stack dishes when eating in a restaurant is not an acceptable practice. She also said that he probably was instructed to do so by his mother when he ate meals at home with his family. Now he is continuing the habit without thinking. I'm still bothered that he did it, though.
Q: Would you call that an example of bad manners?
A: I don't think I'd call it bad manners. It's more in the category of lack of poise or social know-how. It's just one of those things that a person may not see as offensive until someone points it out to him.
Q: Will you tell George you were embarrassed?
A: No. Then I would make him embarrassed and ill-at-ease. But I certainly don't think he should continue to stack his dishes like that. I don't know what to do.

REACT *What would you have done if you were Jack? What is the difference between "bad" and "good" manners? Did George really show "lack of poise"? Would the situation have been different in a diner?*

Planning the Food

In making food choices, nutrition should be a basic consideration. For most occasions involving an entire meal, try to plan a nutritionally well-balanced menu. Consider both the needs and preferences of each person. A well-balanced meal means nothing if the people for whom it was prepared will not eat it. The eye and taste appeal of different foods varies with individuals. (Cultural background has a lot to do with such appeal.) Nutritional requirements vary according to age, sex, level of health, and activity.

Eye appeal People look at their food before they eat it. If they do not like what they see, they might conclude in advance that they will not like the meal. Thus, even a well-balanced and tasty meal might go unappreciated.

What do people see when they look at a meal? Most often, they see a number of foods, each of which has its own size, shape, and color. Foods also have textures. Mashed potatoes are smooth; celery is crisp.

What makes a meal look appealing? There is no single answer that applies for everyone. People from India may enjoy looking at a dish of deep green and yellow-brown vegetables which have been cooked to a smooth consistency. The same dish would be less likely to excite many North Americans, who might prefer to find more variety in the color and texture of the foods in their meals. Bright colors—like red, yellow, and green—would probably be more appealing to them.

A one-colored meal of creamed cauliflower, baked whitefish, boiled potatoes, milk, and rolls may appear monotonous and unappetizing. Some yellow cheese in the cream sauce, paprika on the fish, parsley on the potatoes, and chocolate in the milk could liven up the same combination of foods. The creative cook uses his imagination; he considers color contrasts in advance. The cook

An attractive buffet can be set up in the kitchen near the range, thus eliminating the need for special food warmers. For any kind of buffet, it is important that food and dinnerware be arranged so that guests can serve themselves easily, with a minimum of "traffic" problems.

Eye and taste appeal begin when you plan your menus. As you choose foods that will make a nutritionally balanced meal, consider color, texture, shape, and flavor combinations. Garnishes add interest, as does the way food is arranged on the plate.

who planned the whitefish and cauliflower meal could have substituted tomatoes and carrots for potatoes.

Taste appeal Foods vary in sweetness, sourness, bitterness, and saltiness. They vary in the intensity and quality of their aroma. These characteristics combine to give foods their familiar flavors. Your senses of taste and smell work together.

Taste contrasts can be as obvious as the contrast of sauerkraut with pork, or spicy sauce with rice. These contrasts can also be subtle: a cook may add a pinch of salt to applesauce or a trace of sugar to spaghetti sauce. The use of seasonings (like herbs and spices) can enhance flavor in unexpected ways. Used creatively, especially in convenience foods, seasonings can make many taste variations possible.

Contrasts in texture and consistency can add enjoyment to a meal. Raw fruits and vegetables offer contrasts in shape and texture. Both can be served attractively without time-consuming preparation.

The temperature of food affects its taste and aroma. Heat brings out some flavors and aromas. Chilling enhances others. Temperature also affects texture and consistency. As it warms, a molded salad loses its shape; a cold baked potato is no longer light and flaky. Planning a meal so that hot foods are served hot and cold foods are served cold requires practice in kitchen management.

Seasonings and garnishes make everyday meals more inviting. Can you image a pizza without aromatic oregano? Cranberry sauce is served with turkey; a sprinkling of cinnamon frequently dresses up French toast. Hamburgers are often served with mustard,

141

Whether you eat breakfast is more important than what you eat, as long as it supplies one-fourth to one-third of your daily nutritional requirements. You need not eat traditional breakfast fare.

relish, onions, or ketchup. Plan in advance the accompaniments that you think will add taste appeal to your meals.

Nutritional requirements Food helps to serve so many functions that it is sometimes easy to forget its essential purpose, nourishment. A food occasion may be marvelous fun; the foods may be tasty and brilliantly colorful. If there is limited nutritional value in what the people eat, however, the planner might well question the "success" of what he has done.

When planning meals, consider the nutritional needs of those who will be eating. This is easiest and most important when planning meals for the same people on a regular basis. Then you are likely to know

the food intake of everyone concerned. You will be better able to plan meals that will help fulfill everyone's minimum daily requirements.

To simplify the nutritional aspect of meal planning, many nutritionists advocate that all meals be balanced. They feel that every meal should contain something from each of the Basic Four Food Groups. Then, of course, everyone would almost automatically be well-nourished.

As you know, each of the Basic Four contains a great variety of foods. From them, menus can be devised which will satisfy nearly every personal and cultural taste.

FOOD PREPARATION RESOURCES

Like all other human activities, food preparation requires using some resources. These resources can be rather modest. To roast marshmallows outdoors you need only a wood fire, marshmallows, and a stick to run through the marshmallows. Food preparation resources can also be quite elaborate. Some modern kitchens are filled with a variety of specialized appliances. They contain an array of cooking utensils. The contemporary cook relies on this equipment when preparing meals. Quite often he also relies on another resource: recipes.

Regardless of your level of interest in food preparation, try to master these resources. Skilled use of recipes and equipment can save you time and energy.

Recipes

A *recipe* is a detailed set of instructions for preparing a dish that will serve a certain number of people. It includes a list of the ingredients and specifies how much of each will be needed.

Well-developed recipes offer precise directions, and they generally have good reasons for doing so. If unsalted butter is required by the recipe, it is probably because regular butter would yield a dish that would be much too salty.

Recipes are also quite specific about the amounts of ingredients that should be used. Leavening agents like baking powder, for example, are added to mixtures to make them rise. By adding more than a recipe calls for, a cake or muffin may burst through its crust and burn while in the oven.

The amounts of ingredients are always geared to the number of servings. By multiplying and dividing, you can adapt some recipes to different numbers of servings. If a recipe "serves four," you can use half the amount of each ingredient to prepare a meal for two. Also, you might be able to reduce the cooking time, though not quite by half.

This rule does not necessarily apply, however, to large groups of people. When foods are cooked in large quantities, the proportions of ingredients sometimes change. To serve large groups, use a "quantity recipe."

Equipment

Food preparation equipment includes kitchen fixtures, appliances, utensils, and tools. Sinks, counters, and cabinets are kitchen fixtures. They are the "built-in" part of kitchens. Most kitchens also contain a range and a refrigerator. They may also contain some small appliances, like electric mixers and blenders.

Saucepans, baking sheets, and similar containers and surfaces are cooking utensils.

COMMON FOOD PREPARATION TERMS

Baste   to moisten food while it is cooking

Beat   to make a mixture smooth by rapid, regular motion that lifts it up and over

Blend   to combine thoroughly two or more ingredients

Cream   to make soft and light by beating with spoon or electric beater

Cube   to cut into cubes ½ inch or larger

Cut-in   to distribute solid fat in dry ingredients

Dice   to cut into cubes less than ½ inch

Fold   to combine ingredients by using a gentle under-and-over motion with a wire whisk or rubber scraper

Knead   to press and work dough with hands

Marinate   to let food stand in a spicy, often acid, mixture (marinade)

Mince   to cut or chop into very fine pieces

Parboil   to boil until partially cooked

Pare   to cut away the outer surface

Poach   to cook in simmering liquid

Precook   to simmer for a short time before cooking by some other method

Sauté   to brown, or cook gently, in a small amount of fat in a frying pan

Scald   (1) to heat to just below the boiling point (2) to pour boiling water over food or to dip food into boiling water

Score   to cut shallow slits or gashes in the outer surface of food

Simmer   to cook slowly over very low heat

Steam   to cook in steam with or without pressure

Stir   to mix foods with a circular motion

Whip   to beat rapidly with a rotary beater, electric mixer, or wire whisk

utensils have copper bottoms. Each conducts heat differently. Glass, for example, absorbs and holds heat better than metal. Consequently, for baking in a glass dish, manufacturers recommend that the oven be set twenty-five degrees lower than the temperature recommended for baking with a metal dish. Some differences among ranges, refrigerators, and small appliances will be discussed in Chapter 19.

When you buy kitchen equipment (especially appliances), read and save the manufacturers' instructions. When following a recipe, pay special attention to the equipment they tell you to use. Ask experienced cooks about utensils and appliances. Cook things yourself; learn from your mistakes. In time, you will acquire a knowledge of kitchen tools that will simplify most of your mealtime decisions.

Cleaning up as you go along is a useful practice. It helps you to organize the rest of the meal preparation, makes it easier to serve the food smoothly, and simplifies cleaning up after the meal.

The cookware you need to buy depends upon the way you eat. People who plan many low-cost stew and casserole menus will equip their kitchens differently from those who practice gourmet cooking.

Measuring cups and spoons, spatulas, and mixing bowls are among the many kitchen tools.

How much kitchen equipment a person needs depends on how much and what kind of cooking he actually does. Whatever your food goals, you will be helped in reaching them by learning something about the equipment you have to use.

It takes time to acquire this knowledge. Two pieces of equipment that seem similar at first glance may actually perform quite differently. Cooking utensils provide a good illustration. They may be made of aluminum, steel, cast iron, or glass. Some other metal

When you cook, do you make sure that handles do not extend beyond the range? Do you use potholders, and open lids away from your face? Do you wipe up spills immediately and disconnect appliances by the plug, not the cord? These precautions help ensure kitchen safety.

ACTIVATING THE CHOICE: MANAGING MEALS

Meals can be managed. They can be prepared in such a way that time, energy, and money are used to best advantage. (We will discuss money in the next chapter.)

Some people get great satisfaction from meal preparation. They enjoy the opportunity to work with food. These people must have not only strong interest, but ample time and energy to devote to lengthy meal preparation.

Whatever the goals, meal management usually involves organizing the food-preparation tasks. This means performing these tasks as cleanly, neatly, and safely as possible.

Work flow can be organized for one or more persons, depending on the kind and the amount of food.

Cleanliness and Neatness

Cleanliness and neatness are assets to every part of kitchen work. Personal cleanliness is extremely important. Germs can contaminate food and cause illness. Clothing, besides being clean, should be simple. A ruffled blouse is more likely to catch fire. Strings and scarves may end up dangling in the food. Food, of course, should also be as clean as possible. Fresh fruits and vegetables should be carefully washed to remove

CASE STUDY: KATHY

THE SITUATION *"Before we begin the actual cooking, I'd like to show you how to work the gas and electric ranges."*

Kathy listened as Mrs. O'Hare began the class period. Cooking was a new experience for Kathy, a high school junior. She had enjoyed the introductory part of the foods and nutrition unit, but was a little hesitant about actually preparing food. She was in a work group of students who had taken foods courses before and she worried that she would appear unknowledgeable and inexperienced. Already Mrs. O'Hare had used terms unfamiliar to Kathy and had suggested a kitchen work plan that sounded like a tremendous amount of responsibility. How would Kathy ever do the required work?

The class followed Mrs. O'Hare to one of the kitchen units. Many girls and boys had notebooks and were preparing to take notes about the operation of the ranges. Kathy had left her notebook at her desk and decided she could probably remember most of what Mrs. O'Hare would tell them. As it turned out, the explanation seemed simple. A range was not really so complicated.

As the group was moving to the next kitchen unit, Mrs. O'Hare noticed that a burner had been left on. Because Kathy was close to the control button, the teacher asked her to turn it off.

"Me?" asked Kathy, as she moved away from the range. "I don't know how to do it!" She joined the rest of the group before Mrs. O'Hare could reply.

THE INTERVIEW *Q: That was a surprising thing for you to say, Kathy.*
A: Why should I be expected to do something I know nothing about?
Q: But the teacher had just finished a demonstration of how to work that range. How are you going to learn to operate it if you don't practice when given the opportunity?
A: I'll have plenty of time to practice tomorrow when we cook. I'm not going to be the "guinea pig." She should ask someone who knows how to do it.
Q: Are you worried about cooking class?
A: I've never cooked before. My mother doesn't want any of us in her kitchen. She doesn't want it cluttered up. Everyone in this class knows more than I do.
Q: How are you going to learn to cook?
A: I'll watch everybody else and do what they do. If something sounds too difficult for me, I just won't volunteer for that job. If everything is too hard, I'll drop the course.

REACT *What should Mrs. O'Hare say to Kathy about her behavior? How could you help Kathy learn to cook?*

---

dirt and pesticides. Work surfaces should be kept free of clutter, as well as dirt.

Your work area should be clear for use. All needed utensils should be clean and close at hand. By doing this, you can use a limited number of utensils. Keep a container handy for wastes, and dispose of them as you prepare the food.

Organized cleanup following the meal includes disposing of garbage, storing usable leftovers, and washing dishes.

Organization

The approximate time that a meal will be served is usually determined before the preparation of the meal begins. Consequently, the cook generally works against a deadline. He needs to plan the work flow so that most foods are ready to serve at the same time and at the right temperature. This involves his planning the best use of his own time and energy. It involves his having a clear idea of just what foods, equipment, and tasks the preparation of a particular meal will require. (Well-developed recipes are a great help in this regard.) Such advance organization eliminates confusion. It can eliminate unnecessary work.

There are three basic phases of food preparation: assembling, preparing and combining, and cooking. Consider the time required for each of these phases for each of the items you plan to serve.

The gathering phase involves assembling all the ingredients and utensils. This is a sure way to see that you have everything you need. If you should be missing an ingredient or not have the proper size pan, you can make an early adjustment. You can either find another recipe or adapt the one you have. At any rate, with all the ingredients at hand, you can proceed more efficiently with the next two phases.

The preparing and combining phase involves everything from opening cans or shredding lettuce to mixing the ingredients for a cake. The cooking phase could involve baking a cake or broiling a lamb chop.

The more frequently a person serves meals, the more he can routinize these phases. He can then better organize the flow of his work. He can better prepare more foods at one time. He is more likely to have everything ready to serve at the same time.

Dovetailing tasks Most meals include more than one item, each requiring its own kind and extent of preparation. The cook often finds it necessary to do several things at once. Part of the art of cooking, in fact, is the ability to harmonize a number of different tasks.

This is possible because there are two different kinds of time involved in meal preparation: active time and waiting time. To understand the difference, consider the example of tomato sauce: First, whole tomatoes are poured from the can into a pan. Then, onions, salt, pepper, a little sugar, and cloves are added. The contents in the utensil are stirred and the heat is turned on. From time to time, while the sauce is cooking, the sauce is stirred again. Most of the cooking time involves no effort on the cook's part. It is *waiting time*. All the preparation time and the stirring time involves the cook's participation. It is *active time*. The well-organized cook plans so that while he is waiting for one menu item, he is actively involved with another.

Getting everything ready to serve at the same time is a difficult meal-management skill to acquire. The inexperienced cook can make it easier by sticking to simple menus and familiar recipes.

Planning backwards Many foods must be served soon after they are prepared. A tossed salad, for example, will lose its crispness if it is kept too long. A juicy steak will dry out. Plan backwards. Have all foods ready at the same time. Make first those foods that require the most advance preparation.

For example: You wish to prepare an informal family dinner. You plan to serve meatloaf, baked potatoes, yellow summer squash, and a tomato and lettuce salad. You will be free to begin at 5:00, mealtime is 7:30. From your recipes and general knowledge, you know the preparation times for each dish that you are planning.

The meatloaf will take the longest to prepare—one hour and thirty-five minutes. You should probably start the preparation before six o'clock. When should you begin to prepare the other items? Write up a schedule. Consider dovetailing tasks. Allow time to set the table.

Menu item	Active time	Waiting time
Meatloaf	20 min.	1¼ hr.
Baked potatoes	5 min.	1 hr.
Yellow squash	10 min.	10 min.
Salad	15 min.	none

Preparing ahead Not all foods need to be prepared immediately before mealtime. A pudding, for example, can easily be prepared the night before. It must be left in the refrigerator to set and to cool to the right serving temperature.

Not only cold dishes can be prepared in advance. Stews and casseroles can also be made ahead of time. Their flavors improve when they are stored in a covered container and served after a day or two. Breads and cakes can be made in advance and frozen.

Dishes which can be prepared in advance fit conveniently into meal plans. Though they do not necessarily reduce overall preparation time, they do increase the time a cook has available immediately before a meal. This can help the working parent whose children wish to eat early dinners. It can help the party host who wishes to prepare elaborate dishes. It can help anyone whose menu includes a number of items requiring a great deal of active time.

Sharing tasks So far, we have been talking mainly about situations in which one person is doing all the food preparation. Such is not always the case. Many households have more than one member. Often several—

It is important that foods be properly packaged for storage in the freezer. Hot foods should be quickly cooled, and all should be wrapped or put in airtight containers labeled with the contents and date.

male and female—share in food-preparation tasks. Working together can be an enjoyable experience. It can add another dimension to the social aspect of food.

Tasks can be divided in many ways, depending on the authority pattern of the household, the interests of the members, and the preparation time available. One time-saving division of labor might be to have one person preparing a main course while another makes the salad.

PLANNING FOR BALANCED NUTRITION

An important aspect of independent living is the opportunity it offers for making your own mealtime decisions. Many new dormitories for college and nursing students are equipped with kitchen facilities. Mealtime decision making involves young adults in questions not only of what to eat, but of when and where to eat. Sometimes a main meal will be eaten out, and breakfast and lunch will be prepared at home. A lunch prepared at home can be carried to an office or a school cafeteria and supplemented with a fresh beverage. For cost- and calorie-conscious young men and women, the carried lunch can provide foods of a kind and quality not always available in a restaurant or cafeteria. Even though you may not be able to plan every meal, you can control your on-the-spot choices to maintain a nutritionally balanced diet.

THINK BACK

Choice of formal or informal food service depends upon your time, space, energy, equipment, and goals.
Discuss: *What are the advantages of each kind of service?*

Dining out can expand your knowledge of food preparation and service.
Discuss: *In what ways does eating in a restaurant differ from eating at home?*

More needs can more easily be met at mealtime when the meal served is pleasing to the diner's taste, when it is nutritious, and when it varies in color, texture, and shape.
Discuss: *What problems might arise from inviting people of many different cultural backgrounds to a meal?*

Successful meal management involves organizing your resources well before and during food preparation.
Discuss: *What resources are available to you for meal preparation?*

LOOK AROUND

1. What setting would you be most likely to plan when arranging a meal? Why?
2. Design a mobile illustrating a nutritionally balanced meal that would appeal to your eye and your palate.
3. What is your favorite fruit or vegetable? From magazines, cut pictures showing this fruit or vegetable prepared in different ways. Rank these pictures in order of your preference.
4. What is your favorite dish? Go through several cookbooks and copy several recipes for the same dish. How do they differ? If possible, prepare two of these recipes. Which do you prefer? Why?
5. After interviewing classmates, develop a "What? Me Eat Breakfast?" bulletin board on which are recorded their reasons for neglecting breakfast. Include appropriate solutions.
6. Where appropriate, develop and prepare breakfast menus that solve some of the "What? Me Eat Breakfast?" problems encountered by class members.

7. View a gourmet cooking program on television. Are the recipes demonstrated easily understood and followed? Are meal management procedures demonstrated similar to those discussed in this chapter?

8. What are common problems encountered by class members when working in the kitchen? What are possible solutions?

9. What kinds of tasks can be shared by your family members in meal planning and service?

10. At what age should young people be encouraged to learn to cook? How can adult objections to children working in the kitchen be overcome?

11. Plan one menu for a high-income family of four and another for a low-income family of four. What are the major differences between the two? Evaluate the nutritional value of each.

FOLLOW YOUR PATH

PATH ONE: Design an Advertising Campaign

Step 9 Act out your commercial before the class.

Step 10 Assign one member of the agency to go among the audience with a "microphone," asking people to react to the product. Would they buy the product? Why?

Step 11 Have a meeting to evaluate the results of the class discussion. Should you make any changes in your ad campaign? Which ones?

PATH TWO: Feed an Intentional Family

Step 9 Compare the group's plan for the birthday party with the individual's plan. Adjust any differences.

Step 10 Discuss the family menu plan in terms of taste and eye appeal. Make any changes.

Step 11 Make an illustrated chart — perhaps with pictures cut from magazines — showing the day, the time, and the foods for each meal.

Step 12 Discuss who will perform what preparation and cleanup tasks for what meals.

Step 13 Make up a chart to assign tasks.

PATH THREE: Operate a Restaurant

Step 9 Discuss whether you feel your menu and your restaurant are formal or informal. Are they appropriate to your potential customers? If not, what changes do you feel should be made?

Step 10 Does your menu offer foods that have eye and taste appeal? From magazines, cut out pictures and illustrate dishes that you feel are especially appealing and also balanced.

Step 11 How many people would be required to prepare and serve the food? List the tasks that each would perform.

PATH FOUR: Study Your Food Habits

Step 9 Watch the television commercial for Vitalveg (Path One). Write a letter to the president of the company, telling him whether the ad convinced you to buy their product. Tell why.

Step 10 Select two days from Step 1. Note the meals you picked for those days. With the help of recipes, determine how long it would take to fix each meal. Choose the meals you will prepare with convenience foods. Chart how you will dovetail tasks. Indicate active and waiting times.

Step 11 If necessary, reorganize your activities for each of the two days in order to allow yourself time to prepare the meals.

CHAPTER 10

Buying Food

Supermarket shelves are filled with cans and packages, each of whose labels has its own special visual appeal. Small wonder that it is so easy for even the most rational food shopper to lose sight of his goals. Yet the foods for almost any purpose are there—available in a wide variety of sizes, qualities, and prices. Frequently the packages contain printed information that will help you to select or reject their contents. The necessary information can be had. It is up to the shopper to find it and to keep it in mind. This chapter discusses some food-purchasing strategies open to you, whatever your food preferences or nutritional requirements.

PREPARING A MARKET ORDER

A *market order* is a list of the kinds and amounts of food you wish to buy. When considering only a few items, you might easily keep such a list in your head. If you plan to buy many items, write them down.

The *amount* of food you will need to buy depends on the number of people you will have to feed. It also depends on the number of meals you will have to prepare for each of them. The amount of food you buy could also be influenced by the amount of food you already have on hand. You might have decided that leftovers could be attractively prepared for one of the meals. You may already have canned or frozen foods for one or two meals.

Storage space is important. In planning the amount of food to buy, you could choose to buy more than you will need before the next time you go shopping. You could plan to store foods for future needs. Your storage resources affect the amounts of foods you list on your market order.

The *kinds* of foods you might buy depend on a number of factors. Among these are the amount of food money, coupons, food stamps, or other food-purchasing resources you have available.

The type of the food occasions is another consideration. Suppose you are planning four dinners and a lunch. Three of your four dinners might be routine family meals. The fourth might be a birthday—a special occasion meriting special foods and perhaps a higher proportion of the budget. The luncheon might be special, too. Perhaps it is to welcome back a friend who has been away. If you first plan the menus for each of these meals, you can then include all the items needed in your market order.

The kinds of foods you place on your market order should reflect the amount of time you can or will devote to meal preparation. You would not list the ingredients for a casserole if you were not interested in later taking the time to prepare it. In making your list, consider also the equipment you have available.

In weighing these considerations, you should have some knowledge of what is available to be bought. You might know precisely how much of something you want; but does a package just that size exist? Some foods come precooked and need only to be heated. These foods cost extra. Do you want to adapt your budget to meet the extra cost? Also, some foods might be high in cost at one time of year. Knowing this, you might plan your menus around those foods which are less expensive at that time.

Consider the Quantity

Unit price is the price for a certain standard of quantity. When figuring the unit price of canned food, the ounce is one common standard. To figure the unit price of a can of corn, you calculate how much you have to pay for each ounce in the can. The total price of a larger can would almost always be more. As a general rule, the unit price would be less. This is what people mean when they say: "The more you buy the less you pay." If you have the storage or freezer space, you may save money by buying in quantity.

For packaged foods, quantity buying means buying the larger package. A gallon container of milk is usually cheaper than four quarts. For unpackaged foods, quantity buying means simply buying a greater amount.

Consider Convenience

Today it is possible to purchase foods for which some of the preparation has been done. Such foods are called *convenience foods*. Frozen pizzas and canned peas are convenience foods. They need only be heated before serving. A cake mix is another convenience food, although some active time and a few other ingredients are required to transform the mix into a cake.

When preparing a shopping list, study newspaper ads and write down prices, so you won't forget them. Listen to the radio and TV to find out what is in season and plentiful. Before buying, check to see what you have in the refrigerator, freezer, and cabinets.

Items such as magazines, toys, and cosmetics are sold in food stores. They are not part of a food budget, although they often cut into it. The cost of nonfood items should be deducted from the total bill.

Convenience foods can save you time and energy. They also save you the trouble of buying and storing a variety of ingredients. The disadvantage—for some—is that they often cost more money.

When choosing between a fresh and a convenience food, you are choosing between two *forms* of the same food. Fresh peas in the pod and shelled, frozen peas are two different forms of peas. It is not always useful to compare the unit cost of different forms by weight. Instead, figure their cost per serving. (Packaged and canned foods often list the average number of servings they contain.)

Convenience foods are time-saving standbys. They are also excellent emergency reserves when company arrives on short notice. Many recipes feature novel uses of convenience foods.

Consider the Season

In the United States, almost any food is available at almost any time of year. The cost, however, varies according to supply and demand. For certain foods, the price is lower during certain seasons. Fresh fruits and vegetables are in greatest supply right after they are harvested. In summer, they are generally less expensive and of higher quality.

CHOOSING A MARKET

You cannot consider using a market unless you have some means of getting there. Of course, the question of availability is partly subjective. Some people would not travel a mile to shop. Others would go much farther.

Large city neighborhoods often have a number of food stores within walking distance. These might range from supermarkets, which sell a whole range of foods, to small stores which specialize in meats, fruits and vegetables, or the foods of one particular ethnic group.

Smaller communities might lack many of the specialized stores. There, however, anyone with a car can travel to a number of markets. If the community is in a farming area, fruits and vegetables might be available from roadside stands during the harvesting season.

There are people who use a market simply out of habit. In terms of wise money management, this is not always a good idea. Some stores consistently charge more for all food products than do other stores. Some are generally higher for certain kinds of food. Many stores have sales from time to time. Purely from a money standpoint, it makes sense to shop around, to buy at each available store those items which are least expensive there.

How can you learn the most economical places to shop? Experience is a fine teacher. You might at first explore a number of stores, to form a general idea of the prices that they charge. You might also rely to some extent on the advice of neighbors. (Be careful here. Your neighbors might have entirely different goals when shopping.) Some stores advertise food "specials" in newspapers and on radio. You might tear ads out of the newspaper and take them with you. Be aware that not all advertised prices are sale prices. In selecting a market, it might be helpful to keep a record of key prices from week to week.

Of course, money is not the only consideration in choosing a market. Shopping at a variety of stores takes time—a resource which is limited for most people. One-stop shopping may be the best solution. The extra cost may be worth the saving in time.

BUYING FOOD

If you have planned what to buy and where to buy it, you will have an easier time when shopping. Even then, however, not all your problems will be solved. Most markets stock a number of similar, but not necessarily identical, food items within each food group. Each of these might satisfy a particular pre-planned menu requirement, but not all would satisfy it equally.

A wise food shopper has certain basic information about what to look for in unpackaged foods of each of the Basic Four groups. He knows how to judge quality in everything from meats to grains. He reads the labels on packaged goods and can evaluate the information he finds. Among similar food items, he asks which one is most appropriate.

Sometimes the most appropriate food is not the least expensive. It need not be the highest quality, either. (For example, canned vegetables may be fine for certain recipes.) Some items on the store shelf might be better suited for your purpose and less expensive than others. These same items might also require more preparation time. Can you invest that time? "Most appropriate" means different things to different meal managers. All who approach food buying rationally will pay attention to both food labels and prices before making a purchase.

Buying Meat-group Foods

Meat is the muscles and organs of animals. In the United States, all meat and meat products intended for shipment across state lines are subject to inspection by the United States Department of Agriculture (USDA) to insure wholesomeness. This means that the animal was slaughtered under sanitary conditions. Once inspected, meat is then stamped with a circular mark. This mark may appear on a particular cut of meat you buy. States and some cities have laws that also require inspection of meat.

The USDA also sets standards of quality for meat. They assign it a certain grade level, like Prime, Choice, or No. 1. There are different numbers and kinds of grades for different meats. The standard of quality appears within a shield which is stamped on the meat. Meat quality does *not* refer to nutrition. A high grade of meat may contain exactly the same amount of nutrients as a lower grade. High quality meat is, however, generally considered to have better eye appeal. Usually it is more tender.

Tenderness is related to the age of the animal. Meat from a young animal is usually tender. It can be recognized by its porous, red-streaked bones. The bones of an older animal are flinty and white. The texture of meat from younger animals is of a finer grain; meat from older animals is usually more coarse and darker in color.

Tender cuts generally cost more per pound. When buying meats, consider the cost per serving, not the cost per unit of weight. If two different cuts of meat cost and weigh the same, the one with less fat and bone is usually a better buy. You will get more servings per pound.

Of course, depending on the purpose for which it is intended, you may or may not need tender meat. Less tender meat is quite satisfactory when cooked by a moist-heat method. The moisture helps soften the connective

The federal inspection stamp (left) assures the buyer that the meat is wholesome. The grade stamp (right) refers to the quality of the meat. Different grades designate high and low qualities.

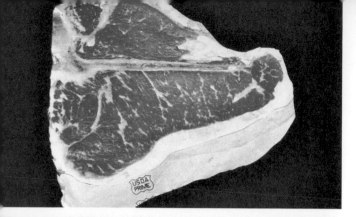

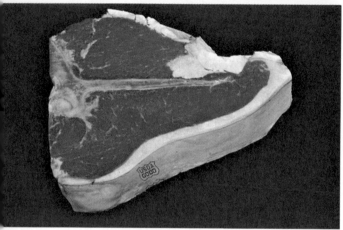

The "prime" cut of beef (top) has a higher proportion of fat to the meat, or lean, than the "good" cut (below). The streaks of fat, called marbling, indicate that the meat is tender and juicy.

High quality pork has less fat in proportion to lean, or meat. Fresh pork should be cooked to an internal temperature of 170° F. Pork is grey in color when it is fully cooked. No pink color should remain.

tissue. Tender cuts may be cooked by dry heat. Whether buying beef, pork, or lamb, adapt your cooking method accordingly.

Meat is expensive. In the United States, many people spend more on meat than on any other food. (Consider such alternate sources of protein as poultry, fish, and eggs.)

Beef Beef is the meat from cattle at least one year old. There are eight USDA grades for beef. Top quality beef is USDA Prime; it is sold mostly to restaurants, but may be found in a few retail stores. The next three grades, in descending order, are USDA Choice, USDA Good, and USDA Standard. Retail stores usually stock only one or two of these grades. The lower grades are seldom available directly. They are used in processed meats, like frankfurters.

The tenderness of beef does not depend only on the grade. If the meat is from an active muscle, like a shoulder or a leg, it will be relatively tough. If it is from a less active muscle, like the back, it will be relatively tender. Tender cuts of beef include cuts from the rib, porterhouse, T-bone, sirloin, and tenderloin steaks. Chuck, flank, and round are less tender.

A higher quality—and more tender—cut of beef will have a higher proportion of fat to meat. It will also have more streaks of fat—it will be better *marbled*.

Pork Pork comes from pigs and hogs that are generally younger than one year old. The grades are seldom stamped on the meat; when buying pork, you must know what to look for. Remember that higher quality pork has less fat in proportion to lean, or meat; the fat it does have is white and relatively firm. It is also better marbled.

The names of the retail cuts of meat taken from these wholesale cuts vary across the country. If you learn the retail names in your area, as well as proper cooking methods, varied menus can be inexpensive.

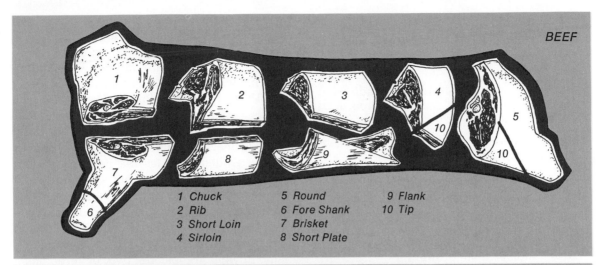

BEEF

1 Chuck	5 Round	9 Flank	
2 Rib	6 Fore Shank	10 Tip	
3 Short Loin	7 Brisket		
4 Sirloin	8 Short Plate		

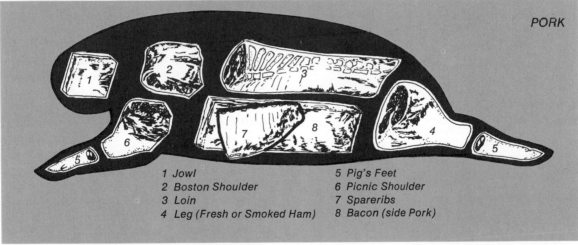

PORK

1 Jowl	5 Pig's Feet
2 Boston Shoulder	6 Picnic Shoulder
3 Loin	7 Spareribs
4 Leg (Fresh or Smoked Ham)	8 Bacon (side Pork)

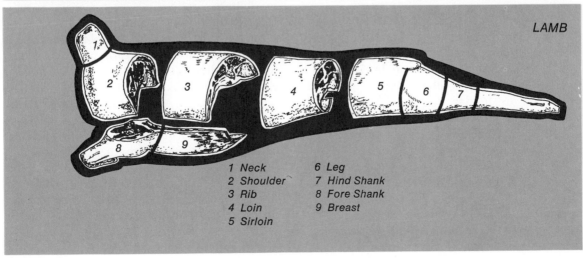

LAMB

1 Neck	6 Leg
2 Shoulder	7 Hind Shank
3 Rib	8 Fore Shank
4 Loin	9 Breast
5 Sirloin	

157

Pork is available in a wide variety of cuts. These range from roasts, chops, and bacon, to hams, hocks, and spareribs. Pig's feet, backbones, and the head can each be the basis of many fine dishes. Unlike beef, all pork cuts are tender.

Cook fresh pork to an internal temperature of 170° F. One can get a disease called *trichinosis* from eating pink, undercooked pork.

The pink color of hams and picnics is not the result of too little cooking. Rather, it is caused by a process called *curing*. Originally, curing was done to preserve the meat. It is now done as much to give the ham or picnic a particular flavor.

Lamb Lamb comes from sheep less than one year old. Meat from older animals is called *yearling mutton* and *mutton*. There are five grades of lamb and yearling mutton. The highest are USDA Prime, USDA Choice, and USDA Good. In addition, there are grade yields ranging from one to five. The grades for mutton are the same, except that there is no Prime. The lamb you buy may or may not be graded. Besides the usual characteristics for high-quality meat, look for color if you want a better piece of lamb. The color of lamb varies from light to dark pink; in yearlings it varies from medium pink to light red. The fat is chalky white. Higher-quality lamb in yield grades one, two, or three has a higher proportion of meat to fat.

Because it is younger, lamb is more tender than mutton. It also has a more delicate flavor. Leg of lamb and lamb chops are the most popular cuts. Lamb shanks, shoulder, breast, and neck are economy cuts.

Poultry Poultry refers to chicken, turkey, duck, goose, guinea hen, and squab. It is inspected and labeled for wholesomeness, and may be graded for quality. The highest quality is U.S. Grade A. This poultry is well-fleshed and meaty, and has a good overall shape and appearance. It is practically free of defects. Most of the poultry found in supermarkets is Grade A.

The tenderness of poultry is indicated by class, not by grade. This class, which is shown on a label, is determined by the age of the poultry. Young birds are more tender than old ones. Young tender birds (broiler fryers, roasters, young turkeys, and ducklings) are hence better to fry, broil, roast, or barbecue. Older birds (hen, stewing chickens or fowl, yearling or mature turkeys, and ducks) must be cooked with moist heat.

You may buy chicken, turkey, and duckling whole or cut up in parts. Compare differing costs. The whole bird usually comes with giblets (liver, heart, and gizzard) packed inside. Whole birds are usually less expensive.

Eggs Top quality eggs are U.S. Grade AA (Fresh Fancy). These are produced under a special USDA quality control program which assures that they reach the market quickly. Cloudiness of the egg white is a sign of freshness. Out of their shells, Grade AA eggs cover a small area. Both white and yolk stand firm and high. Eggs are also graded A and B. Grade A eggs spread slightly more. The white is reasonably thick and stands fairly high. The yolk is firm and high. Grade B eggs may be a wise choice for general cooking and baking. There, appearance is not important.

Eggs are sized according to minimum weight per dozen. There is no relation between size and quality. Eggs may be sized Jumbo (30 ounces per dozen), Extra Large (27 ounces per dozen), Large (24 ounces per dozen), Medium (21 ounces per dozen), Small (18 ounces per dozen), or Peewee (15 ounces per dozen). When buying eggs, figure their cost per pound. Compare the cost per dozen of different sizes. If one size costs over seven cents more than the next smaller size, it is probably a less economical buy. Note the difference between the cost of eggs and that of more expensive protein foods like meat.

Fish and shellfish Sole, cod, mackerel, flounder, halibut, snapper, salmon, and lake or brook trout are among the most popular finfish. Oysters, clams, mussels, scallops, prawns, shrimp, crab, and lobster are popular shellfish. Per pound, finfish are often an excellent buy. They contain high-quality protein and little waste.

Fresh fish should have bright, clear, bulging eyes, a clean, slime-free surface, firm flesh, and a fresh, pungent smell. If oysters or clams are purchased alive in the shell, the

Chicken is one of the most versatile meats available. It is an excellent choice for family or festive meals, for healthful snacks, for diets, and for virtually any occasion that calls for food. Because it is a short-fibered meat, it is easy to digest.

Fish is available fresh, frozen, and canned. It may be purchased whole, as fillets (below), or as steaks (top). Fish is rich in protein and low in fat. It is tender, as even large varieties do not develop tough muscles, but it becomes tasteless when it is overcooked.

shell should be tightly closed. If the shell gapes, the fish has lost its liquid and is dying.

You can buy fresh fish in a number of forms: whole, *drawn* (with entrails removed), and *dressed* or *pan-dressed* (with head, tails, fins, and entrails removed). *Fillets* are cut lengthwise from the backbone, with or without skin removed. Fillets are popular because they are practically boneless. *Steaks* are cross-section slices of large dressed fish with one large, central backbone. Fish is also available frozen, canned, canned and pasteurized, or dried. The careful shopper will watch the prices of canned tuna and salmon, which are sometimes excellent protein buys. In some groups, such specialties as dried or smoked fish are popular.

Buying Milk-group Foods

We will limit our discussion of Milk-group foods to milk and cheese. The kinds of each differ significantly both in price and in nutritional content. Very often people deprive themselves of these valuable foods because of their expense. In some form and at some price, however, they can be readily incorporated into any food budget.

Milk The U.S. Public Health Service has established standards for milk quality. It is up to local authorities to enforce these standards. According to these standards, milk is graded A, B, or C. These grades refer to the number of impurities the milk contains. Most milk is Grade A, pasteurized, and homogenized. The term *pasteurized* refers to a process in which milk is heated to kill any harmful organisms which might be present. The term *homogenized* refers to a process in which the fat particles of milk are broken up and spread evenly through the milk. They become too small to rise as cream.

Milk may be purchased in many forms. *Whole, fresh, fluid milk* contains at least 3.25 percent milk fat, and at least 8.25 percent milk solids other than fat. The proportions of each are subject to local control.

Skim milk is milk from which most of the fat has been removed. Since Vitamin A is contained in the milk fat, many dairies add Vitamin A to skim milk. Vitamin D is usually added to both skim and whole milk. The container will inform you if milk is *fortified* with these vitamins. *Buttermilk* is generally made from skim milk and a lactic-acid-producing culture. It is also low in fat, and has a tangy taste. Skim milk and buttermilk are lower in calories than whole milk. Fresh milk may be purchased in gallon, half-gallon, quart, and smaller sizes.

Dry whole milk is milk without water. When reconstituted by adding water, it has the same food value as fresh whole milk. *Nonfat dry milk* (dry skim milk) is milk without its water and most of its fat. When reconstituted, it has the same food value as fresh skim milk. Dry milk is a good buy.

You may also purchase evaporated or sweetened condensed milk, both of which come in cans. *Evaporated milk* is made from fresh, whole milk, with slightly more than half the water removed. Because the milk is sealed in cans and sterilized by heat, it

There are over 400 varieties of cheese sold in this country. A good budget food, it has little or no waste and is a good source of protein and calcium. It can be used in main dishes, appetizers, and desserts. High heat and overcooking toughen cheese and lessen its flavor.

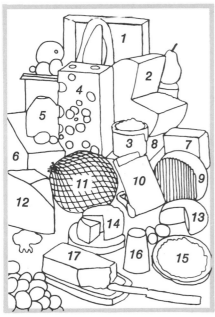

1. Cheddar
2. Blue
3. Ricotta
4. Swiss
5. Scamorze
6. Brick
7. Gjetost
8. Mozzarella
9. Edam
10. Colby
11. Provolette
12. Parmesan
13. Gouda
14. Camembert
15. Cottage
16. Sapsago
17. Cream

requires no refrigeration until opened. When mixed with equal parts of water, it is equivalent in food value to fresh whole milk. *Evaporated skim milk* is also available in many areas. *Condensed milk* contains 40 to 45 percent sugar, which helps preserve it.

Remember that heat and light destroy many of the nutrients in milk. Fresh milk should be stored in a refrigerator at 40° F. or less. At this temperature, it will keep for a week or ten days. Once canned milks have been opened, the unused portion should be kept in the refrigerator. When using dry milks, reseal the package. To prevent milk from absorbing surrounding odors in the refrigerator, keep the container closed. Freezing does not change milk's food value, but it may detract from taste and appearance.

Cheese Cheese can be made from many kinds of milk. It contains most of the milk nutrients in concentrated form. On some cheeses, the protective coating, or rind, must be removed and discarded. The rinds of other cheeses are entirely edible. Most cheeses are excellent sources of high-quality protein, and can be used as alternates for meat. However, cream cheese contains a high amount of fat and is not a good source of protein.

There are hundreds of varieties of cheese. They differ in aroma, flavor, body, and texture. Cheeses are of two basic types: natural and process. *Natural cheese* is made directly from milk. The kind of milk, seasonings, and the method of production, ripening, or curing makes the difference in the final product. Many cheeses on the market are *process cheeses*. These are made by melting one or more kinds of natural cheese. They are pasteurized and blended to obtain a smooth, uniform texture. *Process cheese spreads* and *process cheese food* are made by adding cream, milk, skim milk, nonfat milk solids, or whey to process cheeses.

Cheese is a perishable food and should be kept refrigerated in an airtight container or wrapped tightly with plastic film or aluminum foil. This keeps the cheese fresh and moist and retards the growth of mold.

Buying Fresh Fruits and Vegetables

Fresh fruits and vegetables are called *produce*. There are Government standards for grading produce, but these are not generally available to the buyer.

Mature or ripe produce will have a deep or rich color. It should feel firm, yet slightly yielding, to the touch. (There is no one standard of maturity for all produce.) It should look fresh and be reasonably free from blemishes and signs of decay. As a rule, mature produce has the greatest eye appeal.

When it is to be prepared in such a way that it will not be directly seen, slightly over-ripe produce might be satisfactory. This is sometimes—but not always—a better buy. Avoid buying produce that is too mature. After you have removed the decayed spots from such fruits and vegetables, you may find that what remains is no bargain at all. Also, as produce deteriorates—and it happens quickly—it loses its vitamin content.

Different fruits and vegetables are sold in different ways. Citrus fruits are often sold by the dozen. Melons and lettuce are often sold individually. Beans and apples are often sold by weight. Berries are usually sold by volume. When buying fresh produce that has been packaged, you can be reasonably sure that it has not been handled by other shoppers. (Squeezed produce spoils more quickly.) Try to see if the packaging hides spoiled parts of produce.

Many fruits and vegetables also come processed—frozen, canned, dried, or dehydrated. Standards of identity as well as standards of quality have been established by the U.S. Food and Drug Administration. The prices of processed fruits and vegetables vary greatly. Do not assume that corn or beans in one form are necessarily a better buy than those in another form. Read labels and compare costs per serving.

Buying Bread–Cereal-group Foods

You may purchase grains in a variety of forms. Among them are whole and partial grains, breakfast cereals, flours, and breads.

Rice   You can buy regular milled white rice, parboiled rice, precooked rice, or brown rice. Rice that has been milled—so that the hull and a small amount of the bran has been removed—is called *brown rice*. (When cooked, it has a chewy texture.) *Regular milled white rice* is created when the remaining bran layer is removed by polishing. *Parboiled* rice has been steamed with the hull and bran layers on. After cooking, its grains will be fluffy, separate, and plump. *Precooked* rice has been completely cooked and dried. It cooks quickly, and is the most expensive form of rice. To *enrich* rice, some of the vitamins lost in polishing are added: niacin, iron, thiamine, and sometimes riboflavin and calcium. These are added to the outside of the grains and can be lost if rice is rinsed before or after cooking. The three types of rice are short-, medium-, and long-grain. Long-grain rice cooks fluffy and separate. Short- and medium-grain rice cook tender and moist, and the grains tend to cling together.

Breakfast cereals   Breakfast cereals, both the ready-to-eat and hot varieties, are made in a number of flavors, textures, and forms. "Puffed," "shredded," or "rolled" cereals usually contain the whole grain. Others, called "restored," have had thiamine, niacin, and iron added to the cereals to make sure they contain as much of these nutrients as the whole grain did before processing. Many other cereals have been fortified with larger amounts of thiamine, niacin, and iron, as well as other vitamins, so that they provide more of these nutrients than the whole grain. Additional amounts of protein have been added to some cereals. Thus, these contain a higher percent of protein than others. The package label provides information about added nutrients, and also lists all ingredients. Since cereals are sold by weight, the net weight is clearly shown on each package. Because cereals differ in densities, packages of the same size may contain different net weights of different cereals. Compare net weights and servings per package.

Flour   Flour is a ground-up whole-grain or partial-grain product. In the United States, the term *flour* refers to wheat flour. Flour from other grains should be referred to with the name of the grain. (Corn flour, for example.) Whole-grain flour is less commonly found. Most partial-grain flour is enriched.

You may purchase enriched all-purpose flour, cake flour, or self-rising flour. (Leavening agents and salt have been added to self-rising flour.) Cake flour has a lower protein content and does not develop as much elasticity. However, it is more suitable for baking cakes. It is commonly sold in two-pound boxes. All-purpose flour is packaged in two-pound, five-pound, ten-pound, and larger sizes.

Bread   Flour is the principal ingredient in bread. The most nutritious breads are whole-wheat and enriched white bread and rolls. There are federal standards governing how much of which ingredients goes into these items. Some breads weigh considerably less per slice than others; they have more *air tunnels* in them. You may prefer them for some purposes. To get the most for your money, first compare the weight of different loaves. By weight, bread is usually less expensive than rolls.

Buying Packaged and Canned Foods

In discussing what to look for in foods from the Basic Four Food Groups, we have emphasized foods that are fresh and that can be inspected directly. As we have suggested,

Pasta, the family name for a group of cereals usually known as spaghetti, macaroni, and noodles, is frequently enriched with three of the B vitamins and iron. Pasta is an inexpensive "stretcher" for meats.

not all foods meet these criteria. Some foods are fresh but covered. Some packaged and canned foods are preserved. You will often find it necessary to buy a product you cannot directly see. You will have to buy it merely on the basis of a label. It will help if you know what to look for.

By law, a label must provide certain information. Besides the name of the food, it must inform you of the name and address of the manufacturer, packer, or distributor. The label must tell you the net weight of the food—the weight excluding the weight of the container. It must also tell you if the package contains certain chemical preservatives or artificial coloring.

Ingredients need not be listed for certain products for which federal *standards of*

identity have been established. Such federal standards assure you of consistency in a product, whatever its brand. These standards cover many fresh and convenience foods. Some of these products are mayonnaise, macaroni, bread, jams, ketchup, hot dogs, corn beef hash, and orange juice. The list of foods for which standards of identity have been established is constantly expanding.

The labels of products without standards of identity must tell you the contents. In such cases, ingredients must be listed in *descending* order of volume. As an example, take chicken stew. If the vegetables are listed ahead of chicken, then the can contains more vegetables than meat. For some products, mainly canned fruits and vegetables, certain descriptive details are required. The variety (white or yellow corn, for example) also must be specified. The style of pack (whole or diced) must be given. So must the substances in which the food is packaged (perhaps sugar, syrup, or water).

If a canned food is made for people with certain dietary restrictions—such as diabetics—all relevant information must be given. In addition, if the food is an imitation, this fact must be clearly stated. Any picture of the product within must be an accurate representation.

Baby foods must state the nutrients they contain. If they are strained, a list of the ingredients must be included on the label.

Although it is not required, the labels on packaged foods generally state a brand name. If you found that a certain brand of canned peaches met your standards, you might then be more disposed to try canned beans of the same brand.

A NOTE ON FOOD ADDITIVES

A *food additive* is a substance which is added to food. Food additives are made of chemicals, as are all foods; but the chemicals referred to on food packages are generally man-made. There are other additives which occur in nature. Additives range from common table salt to monosodium glutamate, commonly known as MSG.

Different food additives perform different functions. Some add flavor. Some add color. Some add nutrients. Some preserve a crop while it is growing. Some preserve the quality or certain characteristics (like texture) of a processed food. Some make a food easier for the manufacturer to package or for the cook to prepare.

In 1938, the Food, Drugs, and Cosmetics Act was passed. This law contained many provisions to protect the food consumer. In 1958, the Food Additives Amendment was passed. Under this amendment, the GRAS list came into existence. The *GRAS list* names substances which have been added to foods for a long time and which are *Generally Recognized As Safe*. The list includes over six hundred items, including substances as different as water and sodium nitrite.

The amendment further provided that before food manufacturers could add any new substances to their products, they would have to prove that these additives were safe.

THE MEANING OF CHOOSING FOODS

Although government and industry agencies work to protect him, the informed consumer is still his own best protection. It is up to him to buy foods that are nourishing and within his price range. It is up to him to buy foods that suit his purposes.

Of course, the consumer's decisions also influence the ways he will utilize his resources of time, energy, skill, and creativity in meal preparation. Beyond this is the effect food choices have on the environment and on the lives of others. Waste products related to food and household upkeep affect the quality of life for every member of your community.

THINK BACK

Planning ahead and organizing food-buying procedures beforehand make food shopping more satisfying.
Discuss: *When should a young person first assume responsibility for doing this kind of thinking?*

Knowing the variety of foods available in each food group makes menu planning easier.
Discuss: *What are examples of uncommonly used foods from each group?*

Following recommended methods of selecting and preparing certain foods helps insure adequate nutrition and wise use of the food dollar.
Discuss: *What is the reasoning behind various recommended methods of food preparation in each food group?*

Consumers, as well as government and private agencies, are responsible for the quality of our food supply.
Discuss: *How can a consumer exert influence on the quality of our food supply?*

LOOK AROUND

1. After checking food prices in a newspaper or market, plan a week's menus suitable for your family food budget. What foods require the greater share of your food budget? How can you reduce expenses in this area?
2. Interview several family food shoppers. What problems do they encounter when shopping? What solutions can you suggest to their food-shopping problems?
3. Inventory the packages and canned foods available in your family's kitchen.

Plan a week's menus, utilizing as much of that food supply as possible. How has this cut down on family food spending for the week?

4. Arrange the foods on the menu plan in questions 1 or 3 according to the shelf arrangement in the store where you usually shop. What foods might you not buy in that store? Why?

5. What foods are your "best buy" at this time of year? Are they a better buy in a canned, frozen, fresh, or dried variety?

6. What shopper services are offered by the markets in your area? Do these additional services affect food prices in the markets which offer them?

7. What is *unit pricing*? What stores in your area use this pricing system? How effective is it in helping food shoppers choose the best buys?

8. Develop a "How Now, Brown Cow?" bulletin board illustrating cuts of beef available in local supermarkets. For each cut, include a recipe you might use in one of your activities.

FOLLOW YOUR PATH

PATH ONE: Design an Advertising Campaign

Step 12 Visit a local television station. Ask them at what times of day a product such as yours is usually advertised. On what kinds of shows? Ask why this is. Does this change your ideas about who will buy your product?

Step 13 Go into at least ten grocery stores and price all the products similar to your own. Note the sizes in which the products are sold. Note also any information about different qualities. How much do you think your product will sell for?

Step 14 Design three different labels for your product. You may wish to consult the food researcher.

PATH TWO: Feed an Intentional Family

Step 14 Make a market order based on the foods in your family and birthday menus. List the number of servings you will need.

Step 15 Each family member should take a copy of the list to a different store. List the brand of the food, the type (like canned or precooked), and the standard of quality that you would buy if price were not a factor.

Step 16 Make up three market orders, one listing the most convenient items, one listing the least expensive items, and one listing the highest quality items. Total and compare prices. For each list, figure the daily cost per person. Note which items appear on two and three lists.

PATH THREE: Operate a Restaurant

Step 12 Refer to your menu. Visit a local supermarket or grocery store. Check the cost of all the items on your menu. Make any changes in your menu plans based on new cost and quality information you obtain during your visit. You may allow a 20 percent discount on all food items, since a food service operation buys at quantity prices.

Step 13 Determine how much you would need to charge for each item on your menu to cover *just* the cost of the food.

Step 14 Select six or eight of the food items from your menu. Find out how much restaurants charge for these items.

PATH FOUR: Study Your Food Habits

Step 12 Determine which of the meals in the chart in Step 7 you would probably eat at home. List the foods and the approximate quantities you would need.

Step 13 Take your market order to three stores. Proceed as in Path Two, Step 16.

CHAPTER 11

Careers In Foods

Your food has passed through many hands on its way to you. Many people did many different things to bring food to your store. (The farmer and the storekeeper are just two.) The value of this work to you is obvious.

What is the value to the people who did these jobs? Indirectly, they get to eat, too. They earn money from what they do, which permits them to go out and purchase food the same as you do.

Of course, many are committed to their jobs. Their jobs suit their personalities, and a number of other needs are satisfied by working. Could there be a career in foods for you? Read about the careers in foods described in this chapter and see if any might satisfy your expectations.

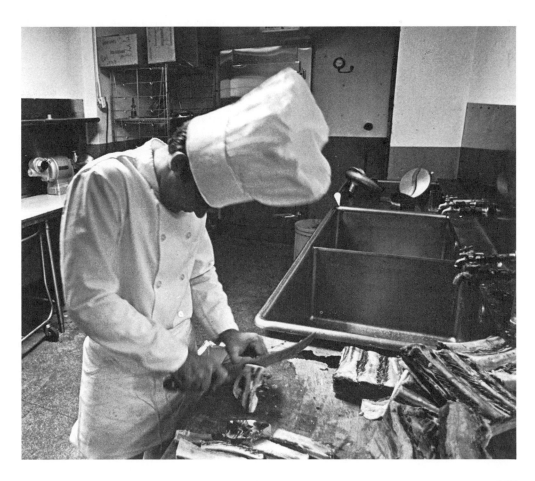

THE FOOD INDUSTRY

The modern Western world is a world of specialization. It is one where most people work at jobs that concentrate on one particular kind of activity. Consequently, they must depend on other people to supply them with the means to satisfy many of their needs and wants. For example, those who do not grow their own food must depend on the food industry.

The food industry itself should not be thought of as one single block. It is complex. It is composed of a number of interrelated industries which are also complex. First among these industries are those which are concerned with the production of food. From these the food passes to those industries which are concerned with food processing. Next, the food must be *distributed*; it must be sent out to all those places where the people are who will buy it. Finally, the food must be *merchandized*; it must be sold.

Food Production

Many of the plants and animals from which our food comes can produce—or reproduce— themselves quite well without our help. Fish, for example, live and breed according to their own life pattern. Human "producers" then come with nets and fishing poles to take the fish from the water.

In our specialized world, however, it is not always possible to let our food grow in its own way. A relatively small number of people are responsible for producing large quantities of food. In order to perform such a function resourcefully, it is necessary for them to breed cattle and grow corn in a fairly concentrated area. Imagine a corn farmer having to search far and wide for each stalk of corn. At such a rate, he might not even be able to feed his own family.

Fishing, livestock breeding, and fruit and vegetable growing are among the more commonly known food-production industries. Others are not very well known. Fish, for example, can be "farmed." When this is done, fish are hatched under artificial conditions and kept in special enclosures. Scientists are now experimenting with ways to convert even cloth and paper into food.

Food Processing

Food processing refers to whatever is done to food between the time it is grown and the time it is distributed. The most essential reason for processing food is to preserve it, for unlike the products of many other industries, food spoils, some of it quite quickly. Food is also processed to standardize it. A can of high-quality peas, for example, contains only peas of the same size.

Some processing operations are concentrated in certain parts of the country. Much of the meat packing industry, for example, is concentrated in Chicago and Omaha. The processing of milk—pasteurizing, homogenizing, and bottling it—must, however, be done locally. Bottled milk would spoil before it could be shipped across the country.

The many processing industries are largely responsible for our having varied and high-quality foods available to us all year round.

Merchandizing and Distributing

From the producer or the processor, the food must come to us, the consumers. This is the task of the merchandizing and distributing industry. Sometimes the producer or processor is himself involved in food distribution. Farmers, for example, might join together in cooperatives, and ship their own goods. Often a wholesale firm is involved. They buy the food from the producer, or from someone else, and they sell it to the store or restaurant that will sell it to us. Large food chains often try to avoid some of these "middlemen." They employ their own buyers, who may specialize in the purchase of meats, produce, or packaged foods.

Industries use techniques to produce items in great quantity, in a relatively short time, and with a minimum of human effort. Factory-based industries have assembly lines. In large-scale farming, massive harvesting equipment is employed.

LADDERS AND LATTICES

Food-industry jobs are available at all rungs on the career ladder. An outstanding advantage of entering this field is the real possibility of upward job mobility.

Positions near the top of the ladder usually require advanced or special training, but on-the-job experience is often as valuable as special schooling. Two- or four-year college training is a short cut to most of these jobs. Large hotel chains usually require advanced training for middle- and top-management positions; these companies often feature training programs within their organizations.

Of course, there are also professional careers in foods. Home economists and veterinarians require special college training.

For some careers in foods, high school provides job-preparation courses. Among these are courses in agriculture, home economics, and food service. In some cases, these can lead directly to employment. One girl who completed a high school agriculture course in shoeing farm animals was able to earn a good living doing this work, which she enjoyed.

At one time, most food was distributed within the local community, and it was frequently merchandised by the producing farmer or rancher. Today, vending equipment is used in food distribution, providing new jobs in packaging food and servicing and stocking machines.

Might a career in foods appeal to you? We discuss here only a sampling of the jobs in the food industry. Perhaps this can suggest to you what a wide range of jobs exists, and what kinds of abilities and interests a person might need to enjoy them.

Entry-level Jobs

The food industry has many entry-level jobs. These are jobs that require only a willingness to learn, or a limited skill that one can learn in a fairly short time. Some, like cook's helper, offer excellent opportunities for advancement. With others, such as migrant farm worker, there is considerably less chance to "get ahead."

Waiters and waitresses   You have all seen waiters or waitresses at some time in your lives. They take orders, bring food, and total up the bill. They need clean work habits. They must have the ability to work under pressure, for restaurants are quite hectic during mealtimes. They also must be able to add up a check. Waiters in formal restaurants must have more knowledge. They must, for example, know the etiquette for formal service. They must also be prepared to recommend good wines to customers.

Stock clerks   A stock clerk is a clerk who keeps track of stock. The stock may be of buttons or tractor parts; it may also be a stock of food. The stock clerk in a super-

CASE STUDY: VAL

THE SITUATION *"Summertime and beaches go together, don't they?" Val stood at the window of the North Shore Inn during the morning break. She had finished her waitressing duties, but had not yet left the dining room for her free time. This was her second summer as a waitress at this resort hotel, and she loved her work. The atmosphere of the Inn was homey, and the people she served were friendly and appreciative of staff efforts to please them. Some of her friends at home felt she was silly not to apply for a higher-paying job, but Val wanted to return to this job every summer while in school.*

"It's nice, Val, but it's spoiled when you have a dining room hostess like ours to deal with. Where'd she come from, anyway?"

Val turned her attention to her friend Kay's remark. This morning, because of a misunderstanding, the hostess had scolded Val for a poorly set table. She had also accused Val of deliberately arriving late to work, not realizing that the hotel manager had asked Val to do a lengthy job for her beforehand. Both misunderstandings might easily have been cleared up if the hostess had spoken to Val privately. Instead, she had begun her criticism within earshot of a group of guests and waitresses already in the dining room. Embarrassed, Val said nothing. She was relieved when Kay had approached the two, directing their attention to guests waiting to be seated.

"We got that problem taken care of after breakfast," replied Val. "Everything is all right now. She really gets upset easily, doesn't she? Thanks for interrupting."

THE INTERVIEW   *Q: I see you're back this year again. You must enjoy this work, Val.*
A: I do. I like to help people and make them happy. By being a waitress here, I also get to make new friends—not only among guests, but also among staff members.
Q: How often has a situation like the one this morning happened to you?
A: Never before. It was embarrassing, and I wouldn't want to go through that again. A lot of people were listening to her.
Q: Would you quit if it happened again?
A: No, I like working here. In this kind of job, with so many different personalities involved, you can't expect everyone to be perfect. I would be angry with her, though, and would probably tell her so. There are good and poor ways of working with people. She has as much to learn about being a good hostess as I do about being a good waitress.

REACT   *What would you have done in Val's situation? What are some of the "good" ways of working with people?*

---

market is probably the most visible to the public. (Most of the others work in warehouses.) He is responsible for checking the number of each of the food items on the shelves. Should there be fewer than a certain number, he brings more out. Before putting merchandise on the shelves, he marks the price on it.

A stock clerk in one part of the food industry may just as easily be employed in another part, or for that matter in another industry. The skills involved—primarily a mastery of arithmetic—are the same. A stock clerk may also advance. The job above his is that of a shipping clerk. This job requires a person to take responsibility for ordering

Bilingual young adults who are interested in food service may have special opportunities in the many restaurants that specialize in the cuisine of a particular country or culture.

Some schools train high school graduates in the art of cooking. Students learn about the foods of many cultural groups, as well as the skills of food service and restaurant management.

new stock when the old stock is running out. Most stock clerks are high school graduates.

Special Food-vocation Skills

Every industry has its skilled workers— workers who have mastered certain difficult tasks. Very often it is possible to become a skilled worker through experience gained on the job. It is quite possible, for example, for someone to climb an occupational ladder into a career as a cook or meat cutter. The more adventurous can use one of these jobs as a springboard into businesses of their own. Many good cooks and meat cutters have opened successful businesses of their own.

Cooks Cooks prepare food. There is a great variety of places and ways in which different cooks go about their jobs. Abilities also vary. The person behind the swinging doors in a luncheonette or cafe, for example, may show good skill in preparing lamb chops and boiled potatoes. The great chef in a French or Chinese restaurant, however, may be more than skilled. He may be an artist who creates dishes of his own. In fact, the fame of certain restaurants rests on such chefs. Some of these people are themselves internationally famous. They rate salaries equal to those of some bank presidents.

The smaller and less formal the restaurant, the more different jobs the cook is likely to perform. Some cooks do everything from ordering the food to deciding the size of servings and trimming the excess fat from steaks. Some large restaurants employ cooks who specialize. A soup cook and a vegetable cook, for example, might work in such an establishment. There are also cooks who specialize in preparing the food of particular countries. The more specialized cooks a restaurant has, the more it needs an *executive chef*. As the name suggests, this person serves more as a manager than as a cook. It is rare, however, that he is not an experienced cook himself.

Many cooks learned their jobs first hand; they started their careers as kitchen helpers. Others began their careers in high school, where they took food-service courses. Such courses can help one to start on a higher rung of the career ladder.

Perhaps the most essential requirement for becoming a successful cook is an understanding of food. All cooks must be willing and able to do physical work. They must be able to work quickly and precisely. Those cooks who supervise others must be able to demonstrate how a job is done. Those who plan menus must be able to apply the decision-making strategies we discussed in Chapter 9.

Meat cutters You are probably familiar with the meat cutters who work in meat shops or grocery stores. It is their job to cut meats to the sizes and shapes which you are used to buying. They trim off fat, remove bones, and roll and tie meat into roasts. In some stores, there is one meat cutter who supervises all the others.

There is also another kind of meat cutter, or butcher, who works for meat and poultry packers. The first part of his job is to slaughter the animals. He then beheads them, skins them, and removes the insides. He may clean those parts of the insides which can be sold as variety meats. He may clean animal hides, as well.

OPENING YOUR OWN RESTAURANT

The food-service industry provides a person with many opportunities to be his own boss. Here are some beginning steps.

Learn about lending and borrowing requirements. Start a savings plan now for a restaurant of your own.

Get a job in an established business. Choose one that is similar to what you want to operate, and that has a variety of job opportunities for you to try.

Sample the service and food selections in different restaurants offering the kind of service you want to perform. Note the menu, decor, and number of employees. Enroll in a food-service training program. Find out about purchasing new or used equipment. Check out "businesses for sale" in the newspaper. Find a site that needs the services you can offer. Locations near office buildings, shopping centers, financial districts, or wharfs are often good places to begin small operations.

Start small. Offer food selections that you can prepare and serve singlehanded.

Learn to read contracts. Pay a lawyer to review any contract to avoid later financial problems.

Learn to prepare foods that are appealing and tasty. Charge fair prices. Return business is very important, particularly in a small enterprise. If you open a new business where the need exists, the word will travel, and your enterprise should grow and prosper.

People become butchers after serving a three-year *apprenticeship*. This means they must work for three years under the close supervision of an experienced butcher. In many of these programs, the apprentice must be a high school graduate. Physical strength is necessary; animal carcasses are often heavy. These butchers must learn to work exactly. The wrong cut can ruin a good piece of meat.

Management Careers in Foods

We have discussed what management means in terms of your personal resources. In the world of work, management has a similar definition. It means managing the human

There are a variety of specialized careers in food preparation. In this baking school, students gain experience in dealing with recipes for large-scale baking and in handling large equipment.

and material resources of a business operation. This may involve managing a sales or production operation. It always, however, involves supervising other people. Management careers are not always separate from the other categories of work we are discussing here. The administrative dietician, for example, besides being a professional, is involved in management.

It is the job of all management people to pull together information and then to make decisions. The educational requirements vary from position to position.

Farmers When we speak of farmers here, we are referring both to those who own and operate their farms, and to those who operate farms owned by others. The latter are often called *farm general managers*. They must consider the wishes of the owners when making decisions. Those who own their own farms are of course accountable only to themselves. Both perform essentially the same kind of work.

Farmers hire and supervise workers. If they need money, they go to the bank and arrange for credit. They find out what crops are needed before deciding how much of each crop they will grow. Sometimes they sign contracts with food processors to grow only a certain crop. Farmers buy equipment and supplies. They keep financial records.

Most farmers grew up either on or near farms. The education they receive is a practical one. Increasingly, they attend college, where they study agriculture. Other qualifications for becoming a farmer include those we discussed for managers in general. Farmers must also be handy; farming involves a great deal of physical work.

Restaurant managers Whether a pizzeria, a formal restaurant, or a catering hall, every place in which you have eaten has had someone, somewhere, who managed its affairs. The functions these people perform are essentially the same. The emphasis that is

CASE STUDY: HARRY

THE SITUATION Harry had helped his father with work on their small farm for several years. There had been good years and bad years, depending on weather and family health. Harry had seen his father work all night to harvest a field of wheat that was threatened by an impending storm. He had accompanied his father to distant states in search of secondhand equipment for trade or sale. He had held odd jobs after school to supplement family income.

Now, with high school graduation less than a year away, Harry had to decide what he was going to do for the next few years. Would he remain with the family and continue to help run the farm? Should he think about other work and further education?

"There's not much money in farming nowadays, Harry," said the guidance counselor. "If you have a lot of land, good equipment, a good business sense, and are willing to work hard, you might do all right. But the little farmer has to struggle hard to pay his bills."

Harry thought of his father's disappointment if he were to leave the farm. The community was made up of small farmers, many of whose children had already chosen work or education elsewhere. Many once-productive fields were going unused or were being bought out by large farm owners. Harry's father didn't want to sell the farm; but he might be forced to do so.

The decision was a difficult one to make. Harry delayed making a choice by deciding to talk over the situation with his father at a convenient time.

THE INTERVIEW Q: What kind of work do you think you would prefer to do, Harry?
A: I'd love to have my own farm and be my own boss. It's very satisfying to plant seeds and work towards a good harvesting. But I know the guidance counselor is correct about farming. Dad says the same thing himself.
Q: And he still wants you to farm?
A: Yes. It's the idea of the son following in his father's footsteps.
Q: Is there something you can do that relates to food production? Something that would satisfy both your and your father's interests?
A: You mean a compromise? Something where I could continue doing farm work for him without worrying about my income?
Q: Yes. Of course, that type of job may require special training or more schooling.
A: It would be worth it if I could find something that keeps me in agriculture. I started to think about the possibility of food-related work some time ago, but I got sidetracked. Now I will find out what is available.

REACT What possible occupations might Harry explore? To what extent should thoughts of future income influence Harry?

placed on different functions varies from one kind of eating place to another. In a fancy restaurant, the manager would be more likely to devote more time to greeting and speaking to his customers.

Most restaurant managers are responsible for hiring workers. All keep some sort of records of the money taken in and disbursed.

If the restaurant has a menu that changes daily, the manager plans this menu with the chef. It is also the manager's responsibility to see that the place is kept clean.

Experience is as vital as formal training in a restaurant or cafeteria. This experience is gained by working up through the lower-level jobs.

Catering is one area of food service that requires management skills. Caterers prepare food for special groups. They make attractive, and sometimes elaborate, displays. They may supply china, glassware, and flatware. Depending on the occasion, they may also serve the guests.

Professional Careers in Foods

The term *professional* is usually reserved for those careers which require specialized training at the college level or beyond. One seldom gains access to a professional career without this training. One does not usually work his way up the career ladder to such a position. Once there, however, a person may be able to move across a career lattice. Home economists and dieticians, for example, can be employed in many areas of the food industry.

Home economists Your teacher is a home economist, so you are aware of the classroom role of the members of this profession. Having read this unit, you are also aware of the scope of what home economists can teach you about food. Perhaps you are not aware of their role in the food industry.

Home economists working in the food industry (or in any other industry, for that matter) are known as home economists in business. They may belong to an association known as HEIB. They may work for food processors or for advertising and public relations agencies handling food accounts. In these jobs, they develop and test food recipes. They may give demonstrations to community groups and schools. They may write anything from advertising copy to cookbooks and television programs. An important part of their job may be to give new information about a product to the consumer.

Home economists must have bachelor's degrees in home economics. Whatever their job, it generally involves working with people. It also requires them to pull together and organize different kinds of information. Public speaking ability is another asset.

Dieticians As the name suggests, dieticians are concerned with people's diets. Most dieticians work in hospitals, although they may be employed in such other institutions as restaurants and schools. *Administrative dieticians* are responsible for the food that everyone eats. They plan menus. They oversee the purchasing of food and the preparation of meals in quantity. They make sure that all this is done in a safe and sanitary environment. They supervise the selection and training of food-service workers.

The tasks involved require the ability to handle other people. They also require a certain kind of knowledge. This is attained in acquiring a bachelor of science degree in home economics. As part of their course of study, dieticians-to-be must study nutrition, food chemistry, bacteriology, and human growth and development. Then they must serve a one-year *internship* in a hospital or other institution. There, they gain practical experience under professional supervision. After this, the intern may be *licensed*—approved by the American Dietetic Association.

Therapeutic dieticians must first fulfill the same requirements of education and internship as administrative dieticians. The work they end up doing, however, is more personal and less administrative. They work with doctors to provide diets for individual patients—diabetics, perhaps—who have special dietary needs. They also discuss with the patient and his family ways that the patient can stay on the diet after leaving the hospital.

Agricultural engineers The trend in farms is for them to become larger. As this has happened, farms have become increasingly dependent on machines to do work. They have also come more and more to use techniques in the selective breeding of livestock and plants. In all these activities, agricultural engineers play a part. It is up to them to recognize the need for new farm equipment and structures. They design such equipment

and structures, and they supervise its manufacture. They might be responsible for seeing that a farm has enough electricity to keep its equipment running. They might design equipment to control insects or animal disease, or they might be concerned with the machines that turn up the soil, plant seeds, or harvest the crop. They might design buildings for farm animals or even farmers.

Some agricultural engineers are concerned with soil conservation and with the maintenance of an adequate water supply. Others develop food-processing equipment.

An agricultural engineer needs a bachelor of science degree.

Since proper nutrition is essential to physical and mental health, dieticians perform a vital human service. The challenge is made greater when they must work with low budgets and food prejudices.

FOOD FOR ALL

Some human beings see only an abundance of food. Others see only dried-out fields and shriveled crops; they see only the face of hunger. We have the technology to make this face disappear. Part of the answer lies in the ways in which food is produced and distributed throughout the world. Part of the solution lies in the attitudes which we all have towards food and the way that it is used.

In the past, lack of sufficient food has caused whole groups of people to migrate from one part of the earth to another. It has caused suffering, disease, and war. The decisions that we human beings make—as individuals, through our government, and through those who produce and distribute our food—can help relieve the misery of others.

THINK BACK

Job opportunities exist within the food industry itself, as well as in satellite occupations.
Discuss: *How does one decide which area of job possibilities to investigate?*

Chances of job satisfaction are greater when we know the variety of job choices available to us.
Discuss: *How does a person get "locked into" a job situation?*

Different job opportunities in the food industry require different levels of education, training, and skills development.

Discuss: *What is the meaning behind the phrase, "A job worth doing is worth doing well"?*

Self-employment offers personal satisfaction in serving others, gaining skills, and being "your own boss."
Discuss: *What are some ways in which a person can become self-employed?*

LOOK AROUND

1. Consult the yellow pages of your telephone directory. Which of the three main industries within the food industry are in your community? Give examples

178

of each. Include full names and addresses.

2. Which of the jobs discussed in this chapter best fits your self-concept? Why?
3. What food products are grown and sold locally in your area? For what reasons do you think farming is considered a profitable or unprofitable business in your community?
4. What are major responsibilities associated with restaurant management? What training is required for such a position?
5. If you were an employer interviewing young adults for a position as a stock clerk, what would be the first five questions you would ask them?
6. Name three industries that are related to, but not directly part of, the food-service industry.
7. What food-related education or service programs are offered to community residents in your locality? Does the community need them? Are they of any use to you personally?
8. What training for food careers is available in your school?

FOLLOW YOUR PATH

PATH ONE: Design an Advertising Campaign

Step 15 Have the class vote on the three labels. Why do you think they selected the one they did?

Step 16 Make a chart showing all the businesses with which you had some contact during this unit. With what other kinds of businesses might an ad agency work?

Step 17 Might a career in advertising suit your vocational goals? Write a short theme on this. If it would be helpful, consult your guidance counselor.

PATH TWO: Feed an Intentional Family

Step 17 Consult with the restaurant owner from Path Three. What food tasks performed in the home are training for jobs in restaurants? How do they differ? What at-home food tasks might be training for other food careers?

Step 18 Make up a chart. Show the family in the center and all the food industries that support it around the outside. Draw lines to show how these relate to one another.

Step 19 Which food-homemaking tasks suit your personality? Which do not? Write a short theme explaining why you would or would not like to become a homemaker.

PATH THREE: Operate a Restaurant

Step 15 Visit a government or a private employment agency. Interview the owners of several restaurants similar to yours. Are restaurant jobs organized the same way you did it in Step 11? If necessary, revise your work in Step 11. Figure how much you would have to pay in wages for a month.

Step 16 Visit a real estate agent. Show him your drawings or model and ask how much it might cost per month to rent such a place if it existed. To cover odds and ends, add $40 per month to this figure.

Step 17 Total Steps 15 and 16. This is the amount of money you would have to take in just to break even. About how many meals do you think you would have to serve to do this? If you are poor at math, ask a teacher or friend to help.

PATH FOUR: Study Your Food Habits

Step 14 Same as Step 17 of Path Two.
Step 15 Same as Step 18 of Path Two.
Step 16 Same as Step 19 of Path Two.

Perspectives on clothing

Man is both mobile and fragile. He can and has moved to inhospitable places, to places where the climate has severely challenged his chances for survival. One way he has protected himself from his environment is by wearing clothes.

He also uses clothing to meet higher needs. With clothing, he adorns himself— he makes himself look more attractive. Through the way he dresses, he may identify himself as a member of a group.

Today, we have an immense variety of clothing. In making clothing choices, we have a large number of options. The size and complexity of the clothing and textile industries help provide us with these many options. You may explore the wide scope of the clothing world by reading this unit and following one path below.

PATH ONE: Provide a Wardrobe Consultation Service

This path involves making up a number of characters, describing how and why they select their clothes, making clothing budgets, choosing fabrics and styles, visiting stores, and examining magazines.
Step 1 List three sets of your clients (for example, a newly married couple or teenage twins). Assign ages and complete names to each.
Step 2 Represent each of your clients, using stick figures, drawings, or magazine pictures. Show or tell the height, body proportions, and hair and eye coloring.
Step 3 Discuss each client's job, activities, and income.

PATH TWO: Manufacture an Apparel Item

This path involves group decision making. It involves selecting a company name, designing labels, making an apparel item, keeping records, creating a pamphlet and an ad, and visiting stores.
Step 1 Hold a company meeting. Assess the useful talents of each member. Determine a form of company organization. How, for example, will decisions be made?
Step 2 Determine at least five different clothing items you would consider manufacturing. These must be made from some kind of fiber or cloth. Consider only those items which your company can make while you are studying this unit. Also consider cost. Perhaps you can recycle material from old garments.
Step 3 Join Paths Three and Four to survey class clothing preferences. Include questions about the items you are thinking about making.

Step 4 Considering the results of the survey, choose the item you will make.

PATH THREE: Open a Clothing Store

This path involves finding the clothing preferences of your class, deciding what you will sell, and setting prices. You will also have to collect pictures from magazines, create model window displays, prepare and make sales presentations, visit stores, and create a credit policy. Follow this path alone or with others.
Step 1 Make up a list of clothing items you think you would like to sell. You may wish to model your store after a store in your community.
Step 2 Join Paths Two and Four in surveying class clothing preferences. Include questions about whether the class would buy the items from Step 1.
Step 3 Considering the results of the survey, choose the items you will sell.

PATH FOUR: Plan a Fashion Magazine

This path involves examining fashion magazines, determining the clothing preferences of your class, naming your magazine, designing a cover, and writing articles. Prepare a picture essay and lay out your magazine.
Step 1 Ask your school's journalism teacher or a fashion editor for hints.
Step 2 Study current fashion magazines. Do some rough sketches or layouts of how you want your magazine to look. Show the width of the column(s) of type and the kinds and sizes of illustrations. Ask for your classmates' opinions of these layouts.
Step 3 Join Paths Two and Three in surveying class clothing preferences. Determine favorite styles, garments, fabrics, colors, and patterns. Write an article on each favorite. Coordinate the survey.

CHAPTER 12

Background for
Clothing Decisions

She was sitting in the kitchen, reading a fashion magazine. Suddenly a gust of wind slapped the window pane.

"It's going to be winter, soon," she said, "and I'll be cold again."

"You need a winter coat," her mother said. "Why don't you buy a warm one?"

"I had hoped to," she said, pointing to her magazine, "but here are the winter fashions, and none of the coats look warm."

"Do you have to buy one of those?" her mother asked. "I know where you can buy a warm coat."

Her daughter shook her head. Already she was resigned to shivering through another winter.

Not everyone would share this young adult's desire to be fashionable, especially at the expense of being warm. Still, like her, most of us do not use clothing merely to satisfy our need for protection from the environment. We use it to satisfy psychological, social, and spiritual needs, as well. In this respect we are like peoples from other times and places. It was among their goals, too, to adorn their bodies with clothing and ornaments.

CLOTHING AND HUMAN ECOLOGY

The natural environment yields certain materials which we use for clothing. We then often wear this clothing as protection from the same environment that gave it to us. To make clothing we use the earth's resources; we thereby can risk altering the balance of nature. When we are finished wearing clothing, we discard it; we thus create the possibility of pollution. In these and in other ways, clothing affects the quality of our lives.

Nature to Clothing to Nature

Until less than a century ago, most clothing materials came directly from plant or animal sources. Cotton and linen, for example, come from plants. Wool, leather, furs, and silk come from animals. Sometimes, raw materials undergo great changes of appearance in becoming a fabric. A woolen jacket looks different from what the average sheep carries around on his back. Nevertheless, the molecular structure of both is the same. No complex chemical process is needed to transform one into the other.

A garment made from natural materials can be discarded without endangering the environment. Gradually, it will disintegrate. No harmful substances will be left behind. The material may even serve a useful purpose to some living creature. Cotton and linen, for example, may *mildew*; tiny plants called *fungi* may inhabit their surfaces. Moths consume the soil on wool and in the process damage the material.

Many such natural materials could also be *recycled*—they could be put to other uses. For example, cotton and linen could be used in making fine paper.

Today we use the same natural fabrics, sometimes treated with chemicals to improve their wearability. We also have man-made fabrics, such as rayon, acetate, nylon, and polyester. Man-made fibers may be *blended* with natural fibers. Chemically treated natural fibers, man-made fibers, and blends offer different advantages to the clothing wearer. Some resist wrinkles. Some resist fire. Others resist mildew or moths. From an environmental point of view, however, these materials may raise new problems. Most do not readily disintegrate. Satisfactory ways to recycle them have not yet been found. For example, cotton-and-polyester blends—out of which most "cotton" garments are now made—cannot be used for making paper, as could pure cotton.

Climate and Clothing

Many people wear clothing as protection from the environment. Different climates, in fact, have influenced the development of different styles of clothing. *Tailored* clothing, like trousers, is made to follow the shape of the body. Some anthropologists believe that such fitted garments originated among people who lived in cold climates. Fitted clothes help shut out the cold. Air in the narrow space between the body and the clothing acts as insulation. This layer of air, warmed by body heat, acts as protection from the cold.

The clothing styles of a people can be influenced by the values of another culture. That missionaries did not appreciate the Tahitian view of climate and clothing is evidenced in Gaugin's "Women With Mango."

H ow proud we are! how fond
    to shew
Our clothes, and call them rich
    and new!
When the poor sheep and silkworm
    wore
That very clothing long before.

from "Against Pride in Clothes" (Isaac Watts)

Loose-fitting garments are believed to have originated among people of warmer climates. Such garments would allow air to circulate freely around the body. This would keep the body cool.

Today, wherever they may live, people have a wide choice of what to wear. In making such choices, we need not pay as close attention to the weather as did primitive man. We have many climate-controlled buildings—homes, offices, schools, and stores—which are pockets of protection from the weather. Once inside them, we have a certain freedom with regard to clothes. We do not have to adjust our dress to the extremes of the weather outdoors.

However, what control we do have over our environment does not alter the range of weather to which we are subject. Different parts of the globe have different seasons. A person must still, through his choice of clothing, cope with variations in the weather. New York, Chicago, and Madrid, for example, have cold winters and hot summers. As a result, residents of these cities can use seasonal clothing. San Francisco and Calcutta each have a fairly constant temperature throughout the year. Both cities, however, have rainy seasons. Their inhabitants do not need a very wide variety of seasonal clothing.

HOW CLOTHING
MEETS BASIC NEEDS

That clothing can help meet physical needs is known—and nearly forgotten—by almost everyone. Outerwear protects us from the cold. Brimmed hats shield our eyes from the sun. Shoes protect our feet from sharp objects and dirt. Clothing is like a "second skin"—a tougher skin that guards us from the dangers of our environment.

Clothing has also been called a "silent language." What we wear "speaks" to others as surely as do our words. Whether consciously or not, we and others know, to some extent, clothing's language. Clothes help us meet psychological and social needs. From what others wear, we can begin to form an idea of what they want and how they go about reaching it. Your clothing says something about who you are as an individual and about the groups to which you belong. Clothing can also be used, as a symbol, in meeting spiritual needs. Consider the special garments worn in religious ceremonies.

Psychological Needs

Who are you? Who is he? What do you think of yourself? What does he think of himself? What different kinds of feelings does he have? As soon as we meet someone we find "interesting," we try to find out more about him. The clothing he wears is one place to begin. It does not, of course, tell us everything we want to know about someone. (In fact, it is misleading and unfair to judge someone solely by externals.) Nevertheless, people do use clothing to meet their needs. Two psychological needs which most people use clothing to meet are the need for identity and the need for stimulation and variety.

The need for identity Clothing can "fit" you psychologically, as well as physically. You can select clothing that you feel expresses the real you, that conforms to your self-concept. A person who considers himself to be casual, for example, would be likely to dress differently from a person who thinks of himself as being formal. You can drastically alter your public image by changing the style of clothing you wear.

Those who like themselves and their world are likely to reflect positive feelings in their clothing and grooming. Those who are dissatisfied with themselves and the general order of things often express their negative feelings by deliberately wearing clothes that shock or offend others. Sometimes a rejection of certain accepted ways of dress reflects independence of choice. Indifference to clothing may be an expression of such positive personal values. It may reflect the pursuit of goals that do not at first appear to be directly related to decisions about clothing and appearance.

Clothing can speak a "silent language" that others interpret and sometimes misinterpret. Although most people dress in a way that reveals something about them, others use clothing as a kind of disguise.

Clothing and grooming have long played a role in defining sexual identity, although not as much today. Other characteristics, such as beards and the shape of the body, still identify male and female.

The need for stimulation and variety There are many aspects of our daily environment over which we have no control. We cannot change or control these aspects from day to day. Clothing offers opportunities for both control and change. Through clothing and accessories, we can satisfy our need for stimulation and variety as often as our imaginations and pocketbooks will allow. Such changes may be as simple as the way in which we tie a scarf. They may be as complex as a complete change of wardrobe. Clothing changes can reflect our moods: we can appear daring one day and conservative the very next day.

187

Clothing sometimes identifies the work and societal roles of individuals. Uniforms, especially, can tell you immediately what kind of work the wearer does and what authority he or she has.

Social Needs

Clothing identifies groups as well as individuals. In fact, most cultures have some clothing that strangers identify as a national costume. (The Japanese wear kimonos.) When people wear the accepted garb, they are signaling to others that they belong. Clothing and grooming can be used to make a social statement; consider, for example, the "Afro" hairstyles of recent years. Clothing and grooming can express social positions.

The need to belong Accepted garb in some societies may amount to no more than a string around the waist. In other societies it may include layer upon layer of clothing. Even the face may be covered. However much or little clothing is involved, all societies have clothing standards. Individuals conform to these standards to help meet their need to belong.

In the United States, many teens and young adults reject the standards of dress and grooming of the older generation. Still, the need to belong has a strong influence on what they choose to wear. Even the most "nonconforming" young adult may accept without question the clothing standards of a peer group.

The truly mature person feels inwardly secure and does not always need to conform in every detail of dress to what others expect.

The need for recognition Clothing can confer "instant status." Rich fabrics, fine or rare materials, and elaborate or exquisite workmanship can suggest that the wearer is a person of wealth or position.

"Name" labels in garments and a "known" designer's name printed conspicuously on a scarf may become status symbols. (Prices of some status items are often pushed up by manufacturers who keep the output low. This creates an artificial supply and demand situation. Only a few can afford the "new look.")

Today, prestige clothes can be worn by anyone who has the money. This was not always so. At one time, only royalty was allowed to wear purple; only noblemen wore silk or satin. Now, purple comes into fashion periodically, and jockeys' "silks" are part of their traditional garb.

INFLUENCES ON YOUR CLOTHING DECISIONS

Different people perform different tasks in our world. They feel different about what they are doing and about themselves. Some wish to be up to date; others are less con-

Clothing and adornment meet people's need to belong and to be recognized. Complying with the standards of any one group tells others that you value that group and want to be a part of it. Within a group, the way you adorn yourself or wear your clothing often has a certain meaning.

cerned. All, however, to one extent or another, are influenced in what they wear by the prevailing customs. These customs are different with different groups of people, and they change with time.

Personal Attitudes

We all have certain personal attitudes that are reflected in what we wear. Some people spend a great deal of time deciding what to wear. They check every detail of what they put on and may try a number of different combinations before settling on one. Others are relatively indifferent to the details of dress. Even those who are most meticulous—most careful—have some lapses. They may at one time or another be too rushed to give their appearance close attention. Even the easygoing dresser may become quite fussy when preparing for a special occasion.

Clothing is so visible that it is one of the first standards by which we measure "conformity" in others. But conformity, whether highly valued or despised, is in the eye of the beholder.

189

CASE STUDY: STEVE

THE SITUATION *"Hey, Steve! Here they come!" Steve turned nonchalantly in the direction Earl pointed. Sure enough! There were three of his best buddies marching attentively along with the group of thirty children they worked with. Most of the children were dressed in clean uniforms, complete with scarf and hat. What really surprised Steve was that each of his friends was also dressed in a uniform. He stared as they flashed wide grins in his direction.*

"I didn't know they wore uniforms," he commented to Earl. "When did they get those?"

"When you join a group like this, you usually buy a uniform, right? What's wrong with that?" asked Earl.

"Now they look and act like thousands of other people in the same situation, that's all. It takes away their individuality."

"Are you kidding?" returned Earl. "They're the same now as they were before they joined this group. Just because they put on uniforms one day a month doesn't mean they change personalities. Uniforms might affect little kids, but not someone our age. Come on! Let's catch up to them."

THE INTERVIEW *Q: Do you think a uniform affects a small child more than it does a teenager, Steve?*

A: I know it affects little kids. My brother is nine, and when he puts on his baseball uniform he shapes up right away. No one can tell me it doesn't affect my friends that way. They grinned, but they were still acting the way the uniform suggested. You'll never catch me wearing a uniform as part of a group.

Q: Your feelings are strong on that issue. Don't you know any true individuals who have joined one group or another?

A: When they're alone and by themselves they're individuals, yes. When they're in a group, no. Why do you think groups end up buying outfits that are all the same? To take away from individuality, of course. The less individuality, the stronger the group. I'll continue to decide for myself what to wear and when to wear it.

REACT *Why do certain groups require uniforms of their members? What is your reaction to dressing like other members of a group?*

The person who makes rational decisions about clothing understands his own attitudes in terms of his own wants and needs. He establishes priorities in the items of clothing that he will acquire.

Customs and Roles

Our personal ideas of what is modest, beautiful, and appropriate reflect the values of the society (and of the groups within that society) to which we belong. These values differ from society to society; and within a society, they differ from subgroup to subgroup. They also differ within a society according to the particular roles that society sets. As an example of all this, consider the tuxedo. The tuxedo is traditionally worn by well-to-do men in Western society on certain formal occasions, and it has increasingly been adopted by other groups. Still, there are formal occasions when a man from an Oriental or African nation would wear other garb.

Work roles are often reflected in dress. Consider the variations in on-the-job clothing worn by firemen, judges, nurses, and astronauts. Sex roles, too, often involve one kind of clothing considered appropriate for men and another kind considered appropriate for women. Men and women have traditionally worn strikingly different kinds of clothing. Today in the Western world, however, many sex distinctions in clothing are blurred.

Fashions

Clothing customs change. Clothing worn at any one period in time is said to be *in fashion* or *in style*. When a fashion lasts for an extremely short time—a single season, perhaps—it is called a *fad*. Most fashions tend to recur through the years in what is termed the *fashion cycle*.

Fashions may be distinguished from one another by the *silhouette*, or outline. The silhouette of women's dresses may be either full or narrow at the hips. The beltline may be above or below the wearer's natural waist. The skirt may touch the floor or rise above the wearer's knees.

The source of new fashions may be the people at the peaks of society. When kings

Clothing reflects customs. This tea gown was the first maternity garment sold in this country. By 1911, there was maternity wear for the street, as women no longer secluded themselves during pregnancy.

Cultural definitions of feminine or masculine clothing do not necessarily carry over into other cultures, as shown by the uniform of the Royal Guard of Athens. What other examples can you think of?

The relationship of modesty to function in clothes changes as societal values change. In the early 1900s, a premium was placed on modesty. Today, we value comfortable and functional clothes.

At one time, little boys couldn't wait to wear long pants and adolescent girls dreamed of the day they could wear their hair up. What change in emphasis do you see in the way people dress today?

ruled the Western world, it was they, and the nobles who surrounded them, who set the fashion standards. The most dominant court was that of France. Today, France is still influential in the world of fashion; French clothing designers like Yves St. Laurent are internationally known. They design expensive, one- or several-of-a-kind outfits for wealthy patrons. In turn, these designs eventually affect the styles of clothing available to a great many other people.

Fashions may also originate with a cultural subgroup. In France after the French Revolution, certain men rebelled against the simple clothing that was the main style of the time. They were called *Incredibles*, and they dressed in costumes that were flamboyant, to say the least. Today, the "youth culture" begins many clothing trends.

CLOTHING VALUES AND GOALS

Clothing may or may not "make" the man or woman. It does, however, cover a large part of a person. Consequently, it affects the way you appear. You can use clothing to make yourself look the way you want to look. You can use it to project your personality.

You can also use clothing to be creative. You might show creativity by making your own clothing. You might also be creative in the way you combine clothing and accessories.

Appearance

You may be tall or short, underweight or overweight. Perhaps you are physically average (whatever that means).

Through wise choices about what you eat, you can control your weight. Through your habits of cleanliness and neatness, you can further influence the way you look. Beyond that, there is not much that you can do to change your body. It is a given resource.

You can, however, affect the appearance of your body by covering it in various ways. You can choose clothes to spotlight those parts of you that you may want to show off to the world. You can also choose clothing that de-emphasizes other parts of your body. You can even choose clothing that seems to alter height, weight, and body proportions.

Personality

"Clothes are clothes," some people say. "It doesn't matter what you wear." Yet, some clothes are bright, and attract attention. Other clothes tend to blend with their surroundings. Some outfits are unique. Others are very much what "everyone" is wearing. Some people look favorably upon people dressed a certain way. Others dislike people

These silhouettes illustrate what is known as the fashion cycle. You can see that some of the styles of recent years echo earlier fashions. Although the basic silhouette is the same, current styles are usually modified so that the earlier style is reflected, but not copied.

Probably every new and eagerly expected garment ever put on since clothes came in, fell a trifle short of the wearer's expectation.

from *Great Expectations* (Charles Dickens)

just because they are wearing certain garments.

Remember that some clothes may suggest —however fairly or unfairly—that the wearer is a certain kind of person. Keep this in mind when you are choosing clothes to express who you think you are to the rest of the world.

Creativity

Throughout history, personal adornment has given men and women opportunities to express creativity. At times, clothing has shown imagination at the expense of usefulness. For example, during the sixteenth century, people wore starched, ruffled collars that were so wide they had trouble seeing their plates when they sat down to dinner. They could eat soup only with the aid of long-handled spoons.

There have been times when people had little choice about what they could wear. This was sometimes because of limited materials for clothing. Such restrictions have also come about through law. At certain times in history, people went to jail if they wore the "wrong" outfit.

Today we have great freedom in what we may wear. We also have more clothing from which to choose. If we wish to make our own clothes, a vast variety of materials is available to us. The opportunities for creativity in clothing are nearly boundless.

A NOTE ON BODY CARE

We cannot consider clothing without also considering body care. By this we mean both your habits of cleanliness and the way you carry yourself. These affect the way you look as much as what you wear does.

Your clothing belongs to you. You choose and wear it every day. For these reasons, your clothing can be considered your "nearest environment," one that you design to please and express yourself.

Grooming

Grooming habits include habits of personal cleanliness and neatness. The primary purpose of grooming is health; the cleaner you are, the more likely you are to resist certain diseases. Grooming is also a vital part of clothing decisions. When people form a first impression of you, they consider the appearance of your hair, face, and hands, together with the clothing you are wearing. Grooming serves another purpose. In our society, it is important not to have body odor. To avoid this, all one's skin should be cleaned at least every forty-eight hours. (Our society also places a positive value on pleasant scents. Hence, many people use perfumes and colognes.)

Complexion care Complexion care means care of the facial skin, which may be dry, average, or oily. Skin type depends on the amount of body oils, especially around the hairline, nose, and chin. Each type of skin calls for a different type of care.

If your skin is dry, it has few oils. In caring for your face, therefore, you should try to keep the oils you have. Since soap dries up the skin, it is not a good idea to wash with soap. Dry skin is better cleaned with a *cleansing cream.* You may then use a *lubricating cream,* which will help restore some oils to your skin. A few drops of a mineral oil will also serve this purpose. Clean average skin with soap and water at least once or twice a day. A lubricating cream may be helpful, especially if you live in a very dry climate. Oily skin should also be cleaned with soap and water at least twice a day. After washing, one can rub on an *astringent,* like rubbing alcohol, which helps further clean dirt and oil from pores.

Regardless of your skin type, always splash cold water on your face after washing. Cold water helps to close the pores and keep dirt out of them. (An astringent also closes pores.)

Complexion problems, such as acne, are

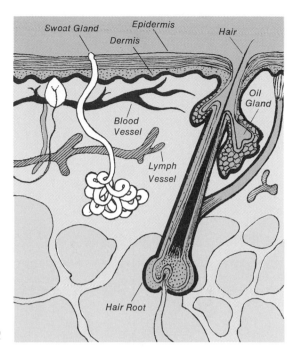

The skin serves several functions, among which are protection, temperature control, and waste elimination. It consists of two layers: the epidermis, or outer layer, and the dermis, or true skin.

common during adolescence and the early years of young adulthood. Skin doctors, or *dermatologists,* attribute these problems to a variety of causes. In young men, skin problems are almost certainly related to the changes in body chemistry that take place at this time of life. Such may also be the case in young women. Nervousness may be another cause, as may inadequate amounts of sleep and infrequent shampoos. Many doctors believe that a diet that includes many fatty and greasy foods can be a further cause of acne. Some believe people inherit the tendency to have acne.

Regular complexion care is basic for acne control. There are preparations on the market which can help further. For all serious skin disorders, consult a doctor. Never pick or squeeze skin eruptions. Doing so may cause an infection. It may also leave a scar.

Like clothing, makeup goes through fashion cycles, and you probably modify the way you use cosmetics from year to year. Whatever the fashion, you can find cosmetics that will enhance your personal coloring.

Care of hands and feet   Dirty, ragged fingernails and toenails are unattractive and potential carriers of infection. Rough, broken skin and dried cuticles can be painful as well as unattractive. Breaks in the skin can easily become infected. Keep your hands and feet clean. Wash hands thoroughly and frequently. Use lotions or creams if your skin or cuticles are rough. Keep your fingernails clipped and smoothly filed. Gently push cuticles back from the nails once or twice a week.

Your feet naturally perspire when covered. For this reason, everyone needs to wear clean socks or hose daily. Air footwear nightly after wearing. Toenails need regular clipping and trimming. To avoid discomfort, cut or file toenails almost straight across.

Hair care   Your hair, like your skin, needs cleansing, moisture, and attention. Brushing your hair daily stimulates the natural oils in your scalp, and removes broken hair shafts. Cosmetic preparations for dry or oily hair are available. Remember that tints, dyes, and chemical permanents can weaken and dry hair shafts. Sprays and lacquers also dry hair. Chemical treatments for curling or straightening may be better done by professionals. Considerable damage can occur if you are careless in using chemicals on your hair.

Posture

Posture refers to the position of all the parts of the body in relation to one another. It refers to these positions whether you are standing, sitting, or moving. Clearly, the way you carry yourself reflects your self-concept. It also projects a public image. A person who slouches when he walks might give the appearance of being inattentive to the way he looks. A person who walks erectly is thought to be more conscious of the impression that he creates.

Besides its effect on your public image, your posture can affect your physical well-being. It can affect your digestion and your muscle tone. In terms of health, the best posture is an erect posture. This is one in which an imaginary straight line could be drawn from the ear lobe, down exactly through the shoulder cap, hip bone, kneecap, and ankle bone. A slouching posture may stretch certain muscles and leave others virtually unused. It may cramp certain internal organs and thus interfere with digestion.

To find out if your posture is healthful, answer the following questions: Do you slouch or sprawl when you sit? Do you shuffle or drag your feet when you walk? Do you cross your arms and stand on one hip when you talk to people? Do you clench your fists? Do your hands and arms dangle or fling about? Does your head bob as you walk?

Recognize these habits. Try to replace them with more healthful habits.

FOCUS ON CLOTHING CHOICES

Your clothing choices tell much about you. So does the attention you pay to good grooming. Do you feel self-assured when you have finished dressing and grooming yourself? Positive feelings of self-respect are not to be confused with vanity or conceit. Being concerned with the way you look and the way you impress others reflects pride. Remember that clothing and grooming—even though they are external—can project to others the real inner you.

THINK BACK

Conditions in our natural environment help determine our clothing choices.
Discuss: *Dark-colored clothing absorbs heat; it helps keep the body warm. Light-colored clothing reflects heat; it helps keep the wearer cool. Should people be advised to buy dark colors for cold weather and light colors for warm weather?*

Clothing selection and grooming procedures often indicate our attempts to satisfy basic needs.
Discuss: *For what reasons is clothing now considered a "second skin"?*

Individuality in clothing selection is achieved through a combination of personal preference and cultural pressures.
Discuss: *How can one be truly individual in clothing selection?*

Suggested grooming procedures not only insure cleanliness, but also set standards for personal appearance.
Discuss: *What is the meaning of the statement, "If you care for yourself, you give yourself care"?*

LOOK AROUND

1. How are wool, linen, and cotton naturally recycled?
2. How does climate affect your personal habits of dress? What specific items of apparel might you wear if you lived in a colder climate? In a warmer climate?
3. What basic needs are reflected in the clothing choices we make? Among your classmates, which needs seem most predominant? How are these indicated?
4. Ask your classmates what clothing means to them. Are young men as in-

terested in appearance as young women are? Develop a newspaper article about the responses of the two groups.

5. Collect ten pictures of individuals wearing various styles of clothing in various settings. Interpret the personalities reflected by the people in the pictures.

6. What is an individual? What is a nonconformist? How are they different? How are they the same? Develop a display showing some possible clothing choices for each.

7. What does society consider appropriate attire for teenagers? For adults? For small children? How have these standards of dress changed in your lifetime?

8. What customs, attitudes, and beliefs are reflected by clothing choices of various groups in your community?

9. Who is most influential in helping you make clothing decisions? How can young people be encouraged to assume responsibility for their own clothing?

10. Collect ads which offer remedies for dry skin and ads which offer remedies for oily skin. On the basis of what you have learned in this chapter, comment on these remedies.

FOLLOW YOUR PATH

PATH ONE: Provide a Wardrobe Consultation Service

Step 4 Pick one basic social need. Explain, in words or pictures or both, how each of your clients uses clothing to meet it. Explain both the similarities and the differences.

Step 5 Describe as specifically as possible the basic clothing goals of each client.

Step 6 Make up an annual budget for each of your sets of clients. Allocate money for food, clothing, housing, and other expenses. Show the clothing budget for each individual client.

PATH TWO: Manufacture an Apparel Item

Step 5 Choose a name for your company. Choose a particular style of lettering in which your company's name will appear. Print up the name. In this form it will appear on labels and in ads. This is a *logotype*. Why do companies have logotypes?

Step 6 Discuss who will do what jobs in making your item. All items must be made by the time you finish reading Chapter 14. Keep a record of the hours worked.

PATH THREE: Open a Clothing Store

Step 4 Interview the owners or managers of clothing shops. Ask how they select merchandise. Which items did not sell? Try to explain why. Examine displays. What catches the eye? Does this have anything to do with the needs and goals discussed in this chapter?

Step 5 Think up a name for your shop. Have it suggest what kind of clothing you think you will sell.

Step 6 Show how your store will look. You may wish to make a cardboard model. Indicate the floor plan and decor. Show where each of the items will be displayed. You will need storage, office, and selling space.

PATH FOUR: Plan a Fashion Magazine

Step 4 Choose a name for your magazine. This name should appeal to young adults. It should suggest that the magazine will help them reach certain clothing goals.

Step 5 Find a picture for the cover of your magazine which you believe will appeal to young adults. Explain your choice.

Step 6 Write an editorial for your first issue. In it, explain the purpose of your magazine. Explain how you hope to influence readers' clothing decisions. Explain how you hope to help them reach their clothing goals.

CHAPTER 13

Clothing Materials and Design

When something is made, it is made from something else. The final product has a certain shape. Perhaps it has a certain color. The materials of clothing are fibers and fabrics. The designs may be close-fitting or loose-fitting. They may be bright and noticeable, or dark and subdued. Different clothing materials have different characteristics. Different designs affect your appearance differently. In making clothing decisions, you may find it helpful to master certain facts about clothing materials and design. You might think of this information as one of the first steps toward acquiring the clothes that are right for you.

CLOTHING MATERIALS

Clothing is made from *fabrics*, or *textiles*. Fabrics are usually made from long strands, called *yarn*. Yarn, in turn, is made by twisting together *fibers*. Fibers are hairs or hair-like substances; there are many different kinds. They are combined into yarns and fabrics in many different ways. The variety of fabrics is further increased by certain treatments. Different treatments may make two pieces of the same fabric look and respond as though they were entirely different fabrics.

Not all clothing materials are made of fibers. Leather is one natural material that is not. Various plastic materials are also in this category.

Fibers

Fibers vary. Some occur in nature; others are made by man. Some are very long and are called *filaments*; others are short and are called *staples*. Fibers vary in *luster*, or shine, in thickness, and in strength. Some wrinkle; some stretch; some tend to break when bent.

Natural fibers   *Natural fibers* are fibers that come directly from plants and animals. The two plant fibers you are most likely to be familiar with are cotton and flax. The two most common animal fibers are wool and silk.

Slender fibers surround and protect the seeds of the cotton plant. These fibers are called **cotton**. In different species of cotton, the fibers are of different lengths. They

Cotton fabric is available in a wide selection of weights and textures. Heavyweight cottons, such as corduroy, have a look and feel that is suitable for winter apparel. Cotton is cool in warm weather. When blended with man-made fibers, it is less apt to wrinkle.

range in length from one-half inch to about two inches. The shorter kind is referred to as *short-staple* cotton; the longer is called *long-staple* cotton.

Cotton fibers are *absorbent*; they have the ability to soak up water. This makes cotton fabrics easy to wash, which is convenient because cotton soils quite readily. Cotton fibers are *flexible*; they can be bent in any direction, and they resist cracking. They do, however, tend to wrinkle. In damp climates, cotton fibers tend to mildew. Left in hot water, they tend to shrink. They are good conductors of heat, which means that they can carry heat away from the body. This makes cotton useful for summer garments. Perhaps for this reason it is the most popular fiber of all.

Up until two hundred years ago, this position was occupied, at least in Europe, by **flax**, the fiber from which linen is made. Flax fibers are contained in the slender stem of the flax plant. The longer fibers are generally between twelve and twenty inches long. Flax, like cotton, tends to soil, absorb water, wrinkle, and mildew. However, flax resists shrinking. It is also different from cotton in another way; it lacks cotton's flexibility — when folded, it tends to wear along the fold.

The most widely used animal fiber is **wool**, which comes from the coat, or *fleece*, of sheep. Wool clipped from living sheep is called *fleece wool. Pulled wool* comes from slaughtered animals; it lacks the very springy quality of fleece wool. This *resilience* makes wool garments hold their shape.

Wool is resilient and durable if cared for properly. Wool is warm, but because it "breathes," lightweight fabrics made from it are also cool. Thus, woolen garments are comfortable in winter, as well as in spring and fall, when temperatures are likely to be inconstant.

The characteristics of yarns made from natural fibers depend on fiber length and the preparation for spinning. Man-made fibers can be produced in any length desired to achieve a variety of effects.

Wool fibers are highly absorbent. They are also fairly strong, but they weaken when wet. Wool fibers do not attract soil as easily as cotton and flax do. Once soiled, however, they cannot easily be cleaned. Wool shrinks. Further, it is attacked both by moths and mildew, creating a problem when it must be stored. Wool garments are very warm.

Another well-known animal fiber is **silk**. It has been favored throughout history by kings and others of wealth and fame. In some ways this is amusing, for silk is the product of a lowly caterpillar, the silkworm. At one point in its life, the silkworm spins itself into a cocoon. Later, it emerges from this cocoon as a moth. Perhaps we ought to say *should* emerge, for silk is the thread of which this cocoon is made. Should the moth emerge, the silk would be damaged. Hence, the moth is killed with hot water or dry heat. The silk filament—which can be anywhere from five hundred to sixteen hundred yards long—can then be unraveled.

Silk filaments absorb water as readily as do wool fibers. They are quite smooth; dirt does not easily cling to them. While silk filaments are washable, they are usually dyed with substances that are not. Silk is not affected by moths, and only under extreme conditions is it subject to mildew.

Man-made fibers   Man has admired not only the product of the silk worm; he has also admired the process whereby it spins its slender filament. By the end of the nineteenth century, he had learned to imitate this process. He began to make a long, smooth filament called *rayon*. Rayon was produced, and is still produced, with a *spinneret*—a device that looks something like a shower nozzle. It has a flat face punctured by tiny

holes. In making rayon—or any other synthetic fiber—a syrupy liquid is forced through these holes. This liquid comes out in long, continuous strands. In the case of certain liquids, these strands may harden on contact with the air. In other cases, these liquids must be forced out into a chemical bath if they are to harden. The thickness and shape of the filament depends on the size and shape of the holes in the spinnerets. The length can be varied from an inch to a mile. The other properties of the filament depend on the kind of "syrup" from which it is made.

Rayon and acetate are man-made fibers that resemble plant fibers in their molecular structure. Others—like nylon, acrylic, and polyester—do not.

Wood fibers or cotton fibers too short to be used for cotton yarn may be used to make **rayon**. These fibers are changed into a liquid and then forced through a spinneret. Under a microscope you could see that the molecules in the resulting rayon fibers were exactly the same as those in the fibers from which they were made. This would not be apparent, however, from a comparison of the appearance of the two fibers.

Long rayon fibers can be made into fabrics as lustrous as silk. Short fibers are spun into yarns resembling wool or cotton. Some rayon fibers are extremely strong. Others are quite weak. (All are weaker when wet.)

Like cotton fibers, rayon fibers are absorbent, flexible, and shrinkable. They have the same ability to conduct heat and the same tendencies to mildew and wrinkle. However, they resist soil better than cotton.

As with rayon, the principal ingredients in **acetate** are cellulose fibers, like wood pulp. Unlike rayon, acetate fibers also contain other substances. Hence, acetate fibers behave less like cotton and other plant fibers.

New man-made fibers, such as the new, silk-like nylon shown here, are constantly being developed. Chemists believe that a fabric that will change colors with the weather will someday be popularly used.

Acetate fibers are not as strong or absorbent as are some rayon fibers. They are weaker wet than dry. They drape themselves easily over any shape.

Acetate is *thermoplastic*. This means that it can be softened by heat without changing its molecular structure. When soft, the shape of the fiber may be changed; it may, for example, be bent. When cooled, the fiber hardens, retaining its new shape.

A more familiar thermoplastic is **nylon**. This was the first fiber to be made entirely from substances that never were fibers. Members of the group of fibers known as nylon are highly regarded for their strength. They are also quite *elastic*—after being stretched, they return to their original shape. Nylon fibers do not wrinkle. They are not attacked by moths or mildew. Nylon attracts dirt, which can easily be washed away. It also attracts dyes. Hence, light-colored nylon fabrics should be laundered separately from dark fabrics. Nylon does not absorb water. In addition, though nylon is very flammable, it does not conduct heat.

Other thermoplastic fibers, called **acrylic** fibers, take their name from the chemicals

Although acrylic fibers have good bulking properties, garments made of them are lightweight and wrinkle-resistant. Acrylic sweaters are less warm than wool, but most can be machine washed and tumble dried.

Modacrylic fibers have general characteristics similar to those of the acrylics, although they are more flame resistant. They are also very heat sensitive. They are used chiefly in products that are not ironed, such as washable, no-set wigs, and deep-pile fabrics.

from which they are made. Their most distinguishing characteristic is that they are bulky. Acrylic fibers resist wrinkling and stretching. They are not too absorbent and they are not attacked by mildew.

Acrylic fibers are frequently cut in short pieces so that they resemble wool. Left in long filaments, they have a silky quality.

Yet another group is made up of the **polyester** fibers. These are resilient and especially resistant to wrinkling, stretching, and shrinking. They do not absorb water and they are easy to clean. Mildew presents no problem to them.

Yarns

Yarns are made by twisting fibers together. The fibers may be staples or filaments, many or few. They may be twisted tightly, loosely, or in special ways. All these factors influence the characteristics of the yarn that is produced.

Tightly twisted fibers are harder than loosely twisted fibers. Up to a point, they are stronger. (Beyond that point they are strained and may break.) Loosely twisted filaments have more luster than tightly twisted ones. Luster in yarns made from staples depends on how long and how nearly parallel the staples are.

Yarns made from cotton staples (or from cottonlike man-made staples) that are of different lengths and are lined up to be roughly parallel are called *carded* yarns. Yarns made from long staples of cotton (or similar man-made fibers) that are lined up almost parallel are called *combed* yarns. Carded yarns are rougher and duller in appearance than the more lustrous combed yarns; they may be quite strong. Short, carded, wool fibers that are not parallel are made into the rough, fuzzy *woolen* yarns used in sweaters. Wool fibers longer than those in woolen and cotton yarns are made almost parallel, and twisted tightly into *worsted* yarn. Worsted yarns have a smooth texture.

Polyesters resist wrinkling and wash and dry easily and quickly. These characteristics make them ideal for wash-and-wear garments. Polyesters, either alone or in blends, pack and travel well.

Just as fibers may be twisted together, so may yarns. A yarn that is made up of two or more yarns is called a *ply yarn*. A double-ply yarn, for example, is made up of two single yarns. Ply yarns are stronger than single yarns of the same fiber content, weight, and thickness.

Yarns may be blended or combined. A *blended* yarn is one made from more than one kind of fiber. A *combination* yarn is made from more than one kind of yarn. (The combining may also take place when the yarn is made into a fabric.) The purpose of this is

Double knits can be used successfully for almost all styles of clothing. They have the ease and comfort of single knits, but they have more body and durability. They are less likely to sag or lose shape.

to combine the advantages and minimize the disadvantages of all the fibers used. The classic blend is cotton and polyester: such a yarn (and fabric) is soft and absorbent like cotton and wrinkle-resistant and easy to care for like polyester.

Fabrics

The strength, texture, appearance, and other characteristics of a fabric depend partly on the fibers and yarns from which it is made. These characteristics also depend on the way these fibers and yarns are held together in a fabric. Woven fabrics differ from knitted fabrics. Both differ from other kinds of fabric constructions.

Woven fabrics Woven material is made up of crossed yarns. The vertical yarns are called the *warp* yarns. The horizontal are called the *filling* yarns. The warp and filling yarns are intertwined. Each filling yarn goes over one or several warp yarns, then under one or several, and then the pattern is repeated. Each warp yarn also makes a pattern, going over and under the filling yarns. The nature of the pattern influences the texture—and therefore the appearance—of the cloth. It also affects the strength.

The most common weave is the *plain weave*. In this weave, the filling yarn passes over one warp yarn and then under one. Each warp yarn passes over one and then under one filling yarn. This weave can make strong cloth, especially if the yarns are close together. Its texture is fine and flat.

In all other weaves, some warp threads "float" over two or more filling threads or some filling threads "float" over two or more warp threads. In *twill weaves*, the floating threads create diagonal lines on the surface of the fabric. In *satin weaves*, the floating threads are arranged so that no surface design is visible.

The difference in weave affects the characteristics of the fabric. The greater the un-

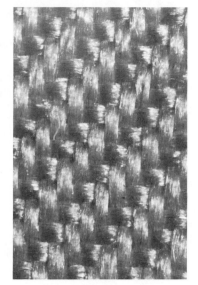

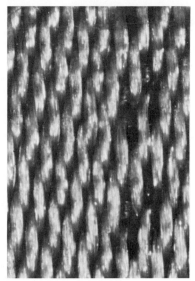

Plain Weave	*Twill Weave*	*Satin Weave*
Burlap, Canvas, Chiffon, Crepe, *Oxford Cloth, Taffeta*	*Gabardine, Covert, Serge,* *Denim, Whipcord*	*Antique Satin, Crepe-back Satin,* *Panne Satin, Sateen*

The basic weaves are the plain weave, the twill weave, and the satin weave. A few of the common fabrics woven in each are listed below them. Satin is both the name of a weave, as well as of the fabrics woven in it, but each type of satin has different characteristics.

interrupted length of a yarn that is exposed, the more lustrous will be the fabric. Such fabrics, however, do not have the strength of plain weaves of the same yarns.

Knit fabrics   Another common way of constructing fabrics is by knitting. In *knitting*, the yarn is attached by looping it together. There are a number of different kinds of loops, or *stitches*. Each can create a different textural effect. Sometimes different stitches are combined.

Basically, there are two kinds of machine knitting: filling knitting and warp knitting. The main difference is in the direction in which the looping is done. Filling knitting is done with one continuous yarn; warp knitting is done with many yarns. The kind of

knit affects not only the appearance, but also other characteristics of the fabric. All other things being equal, a warp knit is usually stronger. However, it is not quite as elastic as a filling knit, which "gives" to fit the body. Filling knits tend to *run*. If the yarn is broken or a stitch is dropped in one spot, the knit tends to unwind. You have seen the effect of this in nylon stockings, which are filling knits. All knits may wrinkle, but with most fabrics the wrinkles come out when the fabric is allowed to hang. Both filling and warp knits tend to shrink and stretch. This partly accounts for the increased popularity of *double knits*. Besides resisting shrinking and stretching, these knits have a finished appearance on both sides. As opposed to this, regular knits are rough on one side. This makes them cling to the body.

Pile weaves are made by interlacing three sets of yarns so that the third set forms loops, or pile, on the surface of the material. These loops may be left uncut, as they are in terrycloth. In other fabrics, such as corduroy, velvet, and velveteen, the pile is cut.

Other types of fabric There are also other means of producing fabrics. One method is *felting*. Felt is made from wool fibers or from a combination of wool and other fibers. Felting involves the locking together of these fibers to form a fabric. This is possible because of the nature of wool fibers: they have a series of scales (like fish scales) all along their surfaces. In the presence of heat and moisture, these scales open up. They catch on one another and the fibers interlock.

Felt has a flat texture. It is weaker than woven fabrics and uneven in strength. The kind and distribution of fibers differ from one part of the material to another.

Other nonwoven fabrics are constructed by a process of *binding*. The fibers are spread out, and then some sort of glue is added to hold them together. Fabrics are also made by *bonding* or *laminating*—two different, but similar, processes. These involve "cementing" two layers of fabrics together by applying heat or glue. This makes possible fabrics possessing two or more entirely different qualities. Waterproof plastic with a fabric lining is one example.

Finishes

Finishing is whatever is done to a fabric after it becomes a fabric. Finishing may involve applications of heat, pressure, or chemicals. Special finishing adds a desirable quality that the fabric would not otherwise have.

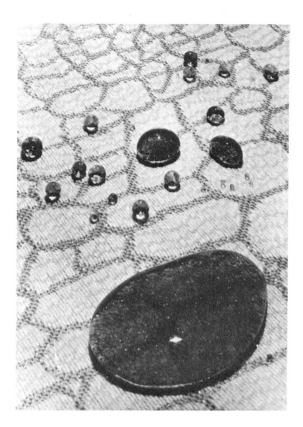

Stain-resistant finishes prevent spilled substances from being absorbed into the fibers immediately. Some of the available finishes effectively resist both oil and waterborne stains; others do not.

Lace is an old, but still popular, type of nonwoven fabric. Once considered a fine art, lacemaking was done by hand until 1813. Use of man-made fibers has made lace less expensive and easier to care for.

Fabrics finished with chemicals may be resistant to moths and mildew.

Linen and certain cotton fabrics may be pounded to give them a flat appearance. This is called *beetling*. There are other finishing processes which make fabrics more lustrous. One of these is *degumming*. This involves soaking silk fabrics in a solution which removes a natural gummy substance from the filaments. In the case of certain other fabrics, a chemical must be added to give a lustrous quality, or perhaps even a glazed effect. Pressing the fabric between two rollers, called *calendering*, is a way to give some fabrics a glossy finish. There are finishing processes that add weight, stiffness, or

CASE STUDY: DEAN

THE SITUATION *Dean hurried into the kitchen, anxious to show Aunt Marion his new shirt. "Look what I bought on the way home from school today. It was the only one left in my size."*

Marion stopped her work to look at his purchase. Dean continued. "Don't worry. It's a knit shirt and doesn't require much care. Just wash it and hang it up to dry!"

"I'm glad I won't have to iron it. Look at that basket of clothes over there! Every single thing in there belongs to you. I don't know when I'll ever get time to take care of all those shirts and pants."

Dean glanced in the direction of the basket. He knew there were many items of clothing there. He had worn something different for every activity so far this week. Though Aunt Marion spent hours caring for his clothes, he couldn't bring himself to wear the same thing twice. The laundry mounted up.

"I was talking with Mrs. Anderson this morning," said Aunt Marion. "She mentioned that her son occasionally does his own washing and ironing. She said he can press things very quickly now." Marion looked at Dean, who was examining the pocket of his new shirt very carefully. "It's not a bad idea, Dean. How would you feel about doing your own washing and ironing?"

"I don't know how to iron a shirt," replied Dean. "I don't really have time, either, with school, basketball practice, and my job."

"Time is a problem," agreed Marion. "But we all have that problem. I think, since you're so interested in clothes, that you should also care for them. You can't imagine how discouraged I get when I see your clothes and all the rest of the family's clothes waiting to be taken care of. After supper tonight, I'll give you your first lesson in ironing."

THE INTERVIEW *Q: Do you think you'll be able to learn how to iron a shirt, Dean?*
A: Sure. There's nothing to it. This is really going to cut into my free time, though.
Q: But you're not the only busy person in your family, are you?
A: I know that. I just think that these kinds of tasks should be done by Aunt Marion. I don't know too many guys who wash and iron their own clothes.
Q: Are you going to go along with your aunt's plans?
A: Yes, for a while. It is fair that I should care for my own things, and I do have more clothes than anyone else in this family. But Aunt Marion is tired now. She'll change her mind after a while. Maybe I'll be able to get out of this job after all.

REACT *Should Dean care for his own clothes? What fabrics and finishes might make the care of his clothing easier?*

---

strength to a fabric. There are finishes that make fabrics resistant to flames, stains, bacteria, or perspiration. There are finishes that keep fabrics from slipping and from shrinking. Some finishes are temporary and may be lost in laundering or dry cleaning. Other finishes may be permanent. Check labels to be sure.

CLOTHING DESIGN

A number of philosophers, psychologists, and painters have thought a great deal about what the eye takes in. Out of all their thoughts have come certain generalizations: you can reduce everything you see to lines, shapes, colors, and textures. Since clothing is something visible, you can see it in terms of these four elements.

The fact that you are seeing these elements in clothing, however, does not mean that you are seeing a clothing design. A design suggests a plan. It suggests that these elements are consciously and deliberately put together. It suggests that, as they are combined, certain principles are considered.

Elements of Clothing Design

What does it mean to say that the elements of clothing design are line, shape, color, and texture? Texture is the way a fabric looks and feels; it refers to a fabric's roughness or smoothness. We discussed the specific textures of different fabrics above, and we need not discuss them further here. It is easy to understand that a costume is made up of

materials of one or a number of colors. However, it is not always easy to understand that an outfit contains lines.

Imagine a woman's outfit composed of a plain sweater and a plain skirt. Where are the lines in this? Before answering, consider that in our minds we sometimes imagine lines where none exist. We do this when we see two shapes side by side. To keep them separate, we "draw" a line between them.

Line and form The *silhouette* of a garment is its essential outline. The silhouette of a dress, for example, would show its length, fullness, and the position of its waistline and neckline.

Most clothing also has lines and shapes that a silhouette would not reveal. A shirt, for example, could be made of material that has a pattern. The pattern could, for example,

The eye tends to follow the direction of a line. In general, horizontal lines create an illusion of width; vertical lines, an illusion of height. But when vertical lines are widely spaced, the eye is apt to move across, from one line to another, rather than up and down.

COLOR AND CLOTH

Dye is a colored substance that, when dissolved in a fluid, can be used to give color to clothing material. Dyeing can be done at different stages in the textile manufacturing process. Man-made fabrics may be dyed before becoming fibers. Dyes may be added to the liquid before it is forced through the spinneret. Dyeing may occur in the fiber stage, the yarn stage, or the fabric stage. As a general rule, the earlier materials are dyed, the better they hold the dye—the more *colorfast* they are likely to be. This is because the dye will have a better chance to spread throughout the material.

Dyeing is a good way to make a one-color fabric. It can also be used to make cloth that has a pattern. This can be done when the dyeing is done at, or before, the yarn stage. This way, different kinds of yarn can be combined to make the fabric. A plaid is one kind of woven fabric pattern that can be made in this manner.

Patterns can be dyed into some blended fabrics. This is possible because certain fibers will accept some kinds of dyes and others will not. A fabric made of two such fibers is placed first in a dye that one of its fibers will accept and the other of its fibers will reject. Then it is placed in a different colored dye that the other fiber will accept but which the first fiber will not.

Patterns can also be printed on a fabric. This can be done in many ways. Printed fabrics have their color clearly on only one surface.

have lines that are curved, straight, or zigzag; it could have lines that are thick or thin.

The pattern could also have shapes. These could be standard and familiar—like circles, triangles, and squares. They could also be irregular and unusual forms.

Color A number of terms have been developed to describe the differences among colors. *Hue, value,* and *intensity* are some of these words. We will see how they can be used to distinguish colors from each other.

When you combine colors in various ways, you create a color scheme. The three basic types are monochromatic, analogous (or related), and complementary (or contrasting). A monochromatic scheme uses only one color, but in a range of values and intensities. Hues that are next to one another on the color wheel form an analogous scheme. A complementary scheme uses colors that are opposite one another on the color wheel. Monochromatic and analogous color schemes are generally restful. Complementary schemes are lively and vibrant and are often more successful if one of the colors dominates.

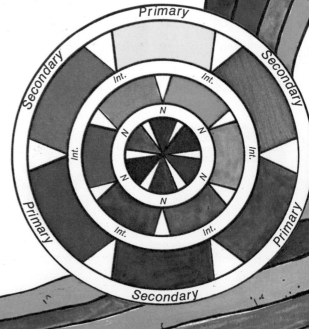

The name of a color is its **hue**. There are three primary hues: red, yellow, and blue. These *primary hues* cannot be made from other hues. Other hues can, however, be made from them. When equal parts of red and yellow are combined, the resulting hue is orange. Mixing equal parts of red and blue yields violet. Equal amounts of blue and yellow produce green. Orange, violet, and green are called the *secondary hues*. The relationship between the primary and secondary hues can be seen in the color wheel.

Note the *intermediate hues* between the primary and secondary hues. The color wheel does not show every color you have seen. It does not show black and white. It does not show more than one kind of each hue. While it does, for example, show orange, you know that there are oranges that are yellower and oranges that are redder.

You may sometimes see lighter or darker examples of the same color. The lightness or darkness of a hue is called its **value**. The lighter the color is, the higher is the value.

CASE STUDY: STAN

THE SITUATION   Sitting around the municipal swimming pool usually led to conversations with friends from neighboring apartments. Today Stan and his neighbors were talking about their various jobs. Because they were young men, all had held their present positions for two years or less, and they liked to "compare notes" about work.

"Stan, do you think you want to do this work all your life?" asked Ted.

"I doubt it," replied his friend. "I had interviews with various companies and liked this one best for a start. Did you ever notice the different impressions of a company you get by just looking at the person who interviews you?"

"You mean by actions and language?"

"I was thinking more of general appearance," replied Stan. "Most of the personnel men who talked with me were average looking. They were dressed conservatively and inconspicuously. I was more impressed with those who wore up-to-date clothing. They seemed to be the ones who were more outgoing and interested in me."

"You probably noticed them because you like to dress boldly yourself," remarked Ted. "Some people who interviewed me were less stylish, but I enjoyed my conversations with them. I didn't choose my place of employment based on the looks of the interviewer."

"Neither did I," laughed Stan. "At least I don't think I did. Maybe I am more impressed by a person's appearance than I realize. There was one company that was just starting out in business. It required its employees to wear brown shoes and pastel shirts with their suits. The competition for their product was heavy, and they didn't want to offend potential customers by appearing overconfident or pushy. I didn't even consider working for them."

"Who knows?" replied Ted, jokingly. "You probably turned down a one-in-a-million chance to become company president just because you didn't like their color preference. Better luck next time."

THE INTERVIEW   Q: Stan, do you agree with the company feeling that conservative dress is best for business?
A: It depends who they want as customers. I think clothes do create an impression about the wearer and his associates. I also agree that some people are offended by personal appearance.
Q: Why would a person be offended by another's personal appearance?
A: Some people see a snappy dresser as a show-off. Some see a sloppy dresser as disrespectful. Some associate bright colors and fashionable clothes with liberal or young ideas. Clothing is a highly personal thing, whether it's worn by you or someone else. We all have definite attitudes, prejudices, and preferences when it comes to clothes.
Q: Does a company have a right to tell its employees how to dress?
A: Some people disagree, but I think it does. If I don't like that particular rule, I don't have to work there. A company is in business to make money. Its employees are the tools it uses for this purpose. For myself, I prefer to work where I'm free to make my own decisions about clothing.

REACT   How do clothing colors affect the way you think of someone? Should a company feel free to tell its employees what colors they can wear?

Value can be explained as the amount of white or black mixed with the basic hue. The higher values have more white. Lighter values are also referred to as *tints* of a color. (Pink is a tint of red.) Darker values are also called *shades*. (Navy is a shade of blue.)

Another term that is applied to color is **intensity**. This refers to the brightness of a color. When a color is dulled by adding either grey or its *complementary* color—the color directly across from it on the color wheel—it is said to be less intense.

In addition to its intensity, a color may have **warmth** or **coolness**. Yellow and red are considered warm. Blue and green are considered cool. We interpret colors in relation to our experience. When we see a piece of yellow cloth, we automatically think of the most obvious things in nature which are yellow. Nothing is warmer than the sun. Blue is usually associated with water and other cool things. Black, grey, and brown are considered neutral. Sometimes they are called *earth colors*.

Our definition of "pleasing" proportions may vary, within a certain range, as fashions change. But when proportion is grossly distorted, the effect is comic, as Charlie Chaplin well knew.

Principles of Clothing Design

Although all outfits can be seen to have the four elements of design, not all can be said to be designed. The word "design" suggests a plan. It suggests a conscious and deliberate attempt to put something together. Those who attempt to design clothing generally consider four principles: proportion, emphasis, balance, and rhythm. At times, they may choose to bypass balance or rhythm; but they are at least conscious of the purpose each could have served in their design.

Proportion Considering proportion means considering each part of a garment in terms of the others parts. A high-waisted dress has different proportions from a low-waisted dress. Each "breaks" the body into upper and lower areas of different sizes. A man's outfit consisting of a short vest with slacks has different proportions from a similar outfit with a long vest or jacket. Equal proportions are generally considered less interesting than unequal ones.

Emphasis To *emphasize* something means to call attention to it. A line, shape, or color in a garment may stand out. It may emphasize a particular part of the garment or some part of the wearer. The best way to determine what the elements of design are emphasizing is to look. As you look, you might find it helpful to keep in mind these few rules of thumb: The more intense the color, the more it will stand out. White and higher value colors are more noticeable than black and lower value colors. Black and lower value colors, however, reveal more prominently the shape of the area that they cover. Warmer colors give the illusion of coming toward you; cooler colors seem to move away. A shiny texture is seen before a dull one. A thick line is seen before a thin one. The busy lines in a lace collar stand out on a plain dress. The eyes move upward to follow vertical lines, making these lines stress height. Horizontal lines usually stress width. (An exception to this is a series of short horizontal lines, which the eye "climbs up" like a ladder.) If one part of an outfit is marked by a strong texture or by a distinctive pattern, it will attract more attention.

Balance   Think of any outfit and draw an imaginary line down the center of it. Look at the right side and then the left side. If one side dominates—if one side attracts all the attention—then the outfit is unbalanced. There are two kinds of balance: formal and informal. Formal balance exists when one side is a mirror image of the other. If a blue shirt were to have a yellow pocket over each breast, it would be formally balanced. Informal balance is created when one side is different from the other, yet each attracts the same amount of attention. If the same blue shirt were to have a yellow pocket only over the left breast, it might be balanced by a vertical stripe down the right side. Generally speaking, an eye-catching decoration should be worn close to the center of a garment if balance is to be achieved.

A small area of intense color can be balanced by a larger area of less intense color.

When something is balanced, it is stable: opposing forces or weights are equalized. Clothing may have this stability without being static because the same lines or details that determine whether a garment is formally or informally balanced may also add a sense of rhythm.

A small area that is light in value can be balanced by a larger area that is dark. A small, warm area can be balanced by a large, cool one. A small area with a pattern or design can be balanced by a large, plain area. When two complementary colors are placed beside one another, both of them stand out equally.

Rhythm In music, rhythm means setting the same beat and constantly repeating it, perhaps with slight alterations. In design, *rhythm* means repeating or varying slightly a certain kind of line, color, or pattern. Rhythm may be accomplished by repeating the curved line of the collar of a jacket in the neckline and in the openings for the pockets. It may be achieved by a looping line which decorates the cuffs, hem, and pockets of a blouse.

The eye of a person looking at a "rhythmic" outfit will move from one similar line or form to another. Hence, the principle of rhythm can encourage a person to view the whole garment, to see it as one unified and esthetically pleasing design.

YOUR SECOND SKIN

You could not pick out your first skin; it was given to you. Your second skin, however, is something you can choose. You can determine its texture, its thickness, its colors, and—to some extent—its shape. Moreover, you can change this skin for another that is quite different. You can wear different clothing for your different moods. You can wear different clothing to satisfy basic needs in different ways. You can do this better if you apply the strategies of rational decision making.

The purpose of this chapter has been to provide you with some (and only some) of the information you will need to make clear clothing choices. Fabrics are the raw materials of clothing. Only by knowing something about the strength and appearance of different fabrics can you know which ones will best serve your needs. By understanding the elements and principles of design, you can develop certain guidelines which will help you to distinguish among different clothing styles.

THINK BACK

Different clothing fibers have different characteristics.
Discuss: *"I just want a white blouse. I don't care what it's made of."*

The characteristics of fibers are altered by the kind of fabric into which they are made. Finishing processes alter the characteristics of fabrics.
Discuss: *What makes a lustrous fabric shine?*

We can reduce everything we see to the elements and principles of design.
Discuss: *"That's funny. I was sure he was taller than you."*

LOOK AROUND

1. If all your clothes had to be made from one fiber, which one would you choose? Why?
2. Which fibers would you tend not to wash in hot water? What effect might this have on your caring for clothes made from such fibers?
3. Of which fibers are most of your clothes made? How does this affect the amount of time that must be spent caring for your wardrobe?
4. Using half-inch wide strips of construction paper, make magnified samples of various fabrics. Also, write a short paragraph on the structure of wool fiber, referring to these samples.

5. Why are undergarments made of knitted, rather than felted, fabrics?
6. Draw clothing silhouettes for ten men and women. Using line and color, create an informal balance in the clothes of each of the ten.
7. Go through magazines. Find five outfits that please you. Analyze each in terms of the principles of design.
8. Go through a magazine quickly. Stop at the first advertisement that strikes your eye. How is emphasis used in this ad?

FOLLOW YOUR PATH

PATH ONE: Provide a Wardrobe Consultation Service

Step 7 Select the fabrics that you think might be the best for each of your clients. Explain each choice.

Step 8 Draw or cut out pictures showing the lines, shapes, patterns, textures, and colors you feel each of your clients would like. If your clients are modeled after real people, you might ask them to help you with this step.

Step 9 On the basis of Step 8, cut pictures out of magazines that show garments you feel each of your clients would like. Consider the way you feel each would—or would not—apply the principles of design.

PATH TWO: Manufacture an Apparel Item

Step 7 What fibers or fabrics are you using to make your items? If you do not know, ask a teacher in your school who knows about this. What are the characteristics of these materials? For what activities do you think your items would be suitable? For what activities do you think they would not be suitable? Have someone in your company write up a pamphlet stressing the advantages of your items. Discuss how you think the limi-

tations should be handled. Should these limitations be mentioned in the pamphlet? If so, how would you mention them? Why?

Step 8 Go through magazines. Pick out garments and accessories (like shoes and gloves) which you think would go well with each of your items. Cut out and paste up on paper or cardboard at least one complete outfit for each of your items. Describe each outfit in terms of the principles of design.

PATH THREE: Open a Clothing Store

Step 7 Cut pictures from magazines showing the types of merchandise you wish to sell. Consider the price your customers can afford to pay. Select only items that are currently in season. Collect as much information as you can about the fabrics of which these items are made.

Step 8 Prepare a window display showing customers the advantages of the two fabrics of which most of the items you selected are made. In making this display, consider the elements and principles of design.

Step 9 Prepare a window display showing off one or two of your most attractive items. Include a slogan which you feel will appeal to the class.

Step 10 Show both window displays to your classmates. Ask them what they think of them.

PATH FOUR: Plan a Fashion Magazine

Step 7 Write an article telling the story of the most popular fabric in your class. Tell where it originates and how it is made into fabric. You may wish to tell something about the finishing processes used on this fabric. Discuss its advantages and disadvantages. Use illustrations.

Step 8 Begin a picture essay on the class's favorite color. Collect magazine pictures in which that color is used in many different garments and accessories.

CHAPTER 14

Wardrobe Decisions

Suppose it were possible to live one day twice. Presume that each time you would do precisely the same things. You would say the same words. You would eat the same foods. The only difference would be that you would wear completely different clothes. They would be different colors and styles. They would be considered appropriate for completely different occasions.

You might be surprised at the different reactions you would receive from people on each of these occasions. The different outfits you would wear would each give you a somewhat different appearance. Each might suggest a different life-style.

Keep this in mind: in making clothing choices, you are choosing more than clothes.

ANALYZING
THE CHOICE SITUATION

Before actually making clothing choices, you might first do some thinking about yourself. Look carefully at yourself—at your face, eyes, and hair. Look at the shape and size of your body. Those things you consider good points are your *assets*. Those you might wish were different can be termed your *liabilities*. You can learn to pick clothes that point up your assets and play down your liabilities.

Besides evaluating your appearance before making clothing choices, you might also evaluate your life-style. Your activities influence your clothing needs.

Evaluate Your Appearance

How do you look to yourself? "Fine," you might say, or "not bad," or "could be better." Your answer reflects the attitudes you hold toward your appearance. It might also suggest certain goals you could set toward altering the way you look. A self-description like "not bad" provides no clues to what it is about yourself that you might wish to improve. For such purposes, you might wish to see yourself in terms of the lines, forms, and colors that make you up. Ask yourself what you think of your own personal elements of design.

Your face and hair The colors of your skin, eyes, and hair combine to form your personal coloring. Many people feel that these colors form a certain "natural harmony." If the combination somehow displeases you, however, it is not a harmony for you. It is, up to a point, possible to modify your personal coloring. Hair may be dyed or covered with a wig. Skin tone may be subtly altered through the use of cosmetics. Tinted contact lenses can change the color of your eyes.

Besides its color, hair has texture. It may grow thick or thin. It may be lustrous or flat. It may be straight, or it may have a certain amount and kind of curl. Individual strands may be fine or coarse. The length to which the hair is cut and the way it is styled give it a certain shape.

In shape, your face may be more or less round, oblong, or square; it may be pear- or heart-shaped. If your facial shape pleases you, you may wish to emphasize it through the way you style your hair. You can do this by repeating the shape of your face in the shape of your hairstyle. A round face is emphasized by a rounded hairstyle; a square face is emphasized by a squared one. You may also choose a hairstyle that gives the illusion of changing your face's shape. Such a hairstyle might have lines and forms that differ from those in the face. If your face is too square to suit you, you might choose a wavy hairstyle. A hairstyle can also "build up" the shape of the face. A hair style that is full on top can make a round face appear more oval.

The design elements of your face, then, may be natural or acquired. In either case, you may choose clothes that stress them or play them down.

Your body type As a young adult, many of your physical characteristics are set. Compared to other people, you are tall or short, and you will remain so. You are large-boned or small-boned. Your body proportions are reasonably set.

Your body proportions refer to the amount of your total height that different parts of your body take up. Your head might be one-seventh of your total height, or it might be one-eighth. The distance between the top of your head and your waist might be three-eighths of your total height; it might be more or less. At different times in history, different body proportions have been considered ideal. In the early Middle Ages, the ideal body type seems to have been compact; in relation to the rest of the ideal body, the head was larger than it is today. The contemporary ideal body is topped by a head that is one-

Square

Round

Pear

Heart

Oblong

Straight

Concave

Convex

You can emphasize or camouflage your facial features with your hairstyle. As you choose a hairstyle, remember to consider the shape of your profile, as well as the shape of your face. You should also consider your body proportions, your personality, and your life-style.

221

eighth the body's total length. The waist is three-eighths of the way down from the top of the head. The body is evenly divided at the hips. As with other kinds of "perfection," few people have ideal body proportions. No one can acquire them. You can, however, through the clothing you choose to wear, give the appearance of coming closer to the ideal than you actually are.

You can also give the impression of coming closer to some other, perhaps more personal, standard. It might suit you fine to have a low waist. You might prefer to select clothes that represent you much as your are. You might select clothes that accentuate some part of you just because you like it.

Evaluate Your Life-style

The term *life-style* refers to the way you express your wants and needs. It refers as much to the roles you fill as to the way in

Your body type will influence how certain styles and fabrics look on you. If a fashion does not flatter you, can you adapt it to meet your needs? If not, will you choose to pass it by?

Your clothes and accessories will be more flattering if the patterns and styles are in scale with your size. Accessories that look dramatic on someone who is tall would overpower a small person.

which you fill them. Part of your present life-style is to be a student—a very particular student with very particular ways of doing what a student does. If you wish, you can wear clothes that reflect both your role as student and the fact that you approach this role in an individual way. You can dress to show that you belong to a group and to show that you are an individual within a group. Your clothes can tell people that you are a waitress, a clerk, or a teacher. They can suggest you are formal or informal.

CASE STUDY: GAIL

THE SITUATION *"It's that time of year again. What are we going to get your sister and brother-in-law for their birthdays?"* Every September, Peter asked the same question. He and his wife Gail would talk over possible gifts, though the final decision was Gail's to make. For Gail, giving gifts was always a special occasion. Whether holiday, birthday, or graduation, she insisted on buying or making presents for family members. Peter's family placed less emphasis on giving or receiving gifts. He would have been satisfied without either giving or receiving, but he usually went along with Gail's wishes.

"Clothes, of course! I think Bruce might look nice in a brightly colored dress shirt; and I don't think Sara has a hostess outfit yet. If I can find something reasonably priced, I'd like to get her one. What do you think?"

"Would either one of them really use what you've suggested?" asked Peter.

"What do you mean?" responded Gail. *"I think those are good gift suggestions."*

"For some people, yes," said Peter. *"But didn't your sister say that Bruce spends more time at his job than anywhere else? He loves what he's doing, and he even wants to work on weekends. He's usually so tired in the evening that he doesn't want to go out anywhere. Besides, he only has one suit, and he probably has enough shirts to wear with it."*

"And what about my sister?" asked Gail.

"She'd probably look very nice in something like that," answered Peter. *"But she seems to be someone who needs practical things to wear. We got her a long robe one year. It stayed in her closet for months. She said she was afraid she'd trip when wearing it. I think you should get both very useful, easy-to-care-for clothes. They can buy their own fancy things if they really want them."*

THE INTERVIEW Q: *Will you follow Peter's suggestions?*
A: They sound boring to me. I want these clothing gifts to be special.
Q: *Shouldn't you try to suit each present to the individual and his interests?*
A: Do you mean I should buy Bruce something to wear to work, for instance?
Q: *Is work his major interest in life? If so, use that knowledge as your guideline in making gift decisions. And what is his wife really interested in? Do the same for her.*
A: But work clothes just don't interest me.
Q: *Are you buying clothes for you, or for your sister and her husband?*
A: You're right. I was thinking of what I would like to have rather than what is right for them.

REACT Is clothing an appropriate gift item? What is the best way to shop for clothes that you plan to give to other people?

Because you are at the launching stage, this is a particularly good time for you to evaluate your life-style before making wardrobe choices. Soon you will leave school; your needs will change and you will adjust your life-style in various ways. In the future, you will fill some different roles. Before making any significant addition to your wardrobe, consider the kinds of activities you now perform. Consider also those activities you think you will perform in the future. Consider the personality traits you wish to project. Being consciously aware of who you are and what you do can help you to make clothing choices that will give you a great deal of personal satisfaction.

Before making new clothing choices, you may find it worthwhile to evaluate your past clothing choices. By doing this thoroughly and honestly, you may be able to avoid repeating clothing mistakes.

MAKING WARDROBE CHOICES

Making rational clothing choices means taking the time to consciously select garments that do for you what you want them to do. Each person will have his own idea of what that will be. Few people wear clothes only to cover themselves. Many people choose garments because they think they are attractive. Many choose clothes because they are considered to be the "right" clothes to wear.

There is another reason you might consider in making clothing choices. You might consider how useful a garment is to you. If, for example, you can get only one garment, are you getting the one that will give you the most service? Are you getting the garment that you most need? Before you can tell what

you need, you might do well to know what you have. Before you select new clothes, examine the ones you have. You might list everything in your present wardrobe.

Attractiveness

An attractively dressed person can look in a mirror and say, "That's me. That's the way I want to look." He can also, through the clothing he wears, project to others the impression of himself that he wishes to communicate. He can suggest the physical appearance and the personality that he desires. A person could do this by wearing clothes that are in the mainstream of contemporary fashion. On the other hand, a person who likes certain colors or patterns might choose his clothes according to his own tastes, regardless of whether the colors or patterns are in fashion. A person might feel that he can best represent himself by wearing clothes that will not call much attention to himself; or he might prefer to dress in such a way that everyone will look at him. In meeting his other goals, he can also select clothing that stresses what he feels are his physical assets and plays down his liabilities. He can do this through the way he uses the elements of design.

Choosing colors Applying the principles of rational decision making when selecting clothing colors involves consciously selecting colors that do what you want them to do.

To draw attention to yourself, you might wear bright colors. You might also wear an unusual color or an unusual color combination. To be less noticeable, you might choose colors that are dark or dull. To appear taller, you might wear a costume of a single color. Wearing one color above the waist and

The pattern of the material and the use of contrasting colors create lines and shapes that add to the style of a garment. Imagine how these clothes would look if they were made with fabric of a solid color.

CASE STUDY: HARRY

THE SITUATION Ben and Harry had finished painting the downstairs rooms of Harry's remodeled home. They were ready to work on the walk-in closet upstairs.

"Wait until you see the closet," commented Harry. "You'll wish you had never volunteered to help with painting."

As they reached the top of the stairs, Ben understood what Harry was referring to. One whole side of the big closet was jammed with clothes belonging to Bev, Harry's wife. There was barely room for another hanger on Bev's side of the wardrobe.

"She asked if she could begin using my side of the closet for her clothes," sighed Harry. "I don't know what to do about it. She has a closet full of clothes, and says she has nothing to wear to work. When we go shopping, she buys new outfits; and two months later it's the same thing all over again. She has things in here she hasn't worn more than twice. They're in excellent condition, and they're very much in style. She won't wear them, and she won't give them away. It seems like a waste of money to me."

"Well, we'd better start taking the clothes from the closet as we talk. Otherwise, we'll be here all day," replied Ben. "She does have a lot of clothes. Maybe you'll just have to put your foot down and say no one of these days. Either that, or you'll have to build yourself a new closet."

THE INTERVIEW Q: Was Ben serious about building a new clothes closet?
A: No, he was kidding. But he's right about one thing. I should say "no more clothes." This is getting ridiculous.
Q: Why does Bev buy clothes so often?
A: I don't know. We can't always afford it, but if we don't get something within a day or two of her request, she becomes grouchy and depressed. She has bought clothes ever since she first began earning her own money in high school. She buys whatever she happens to like as she walks through a store.
Q: What will happen if you decide to say no to her requests?
A: I've never done it before, so I don't know for sure. She'll probably get very angry. She might tell me that she will buy them anyway. On the other hand, maybe she'll go along.

REACT What is the best way for Harry to handle this problem? For what reasons might clothing become so important to a person?

---

another below creates two separate areas; the eye of the viewer is interrupted as it travels up the body. Hence, the wearer seems shorter than he really is.

Colors can also be used to focus attention on different parts of the head and body. Consider the case of a man who is proud of his red hair. To create the desired emphasis, he might recall that complementary colors emphasize each other. To complement his red hair, he might wear a bright green shirt.

If the same man wished to give the impression of being taller, he might wear slacks of a darker green. Because the slacks would be of the same hue as the shirt, they would create less of a "break" in the length of his body. If the same man's goal were only to make his shoulders appear larger, a shirt with a wide collar would do the job.

Perhaps the trickiest part of clothing color selection is in finding the "right" color for your skin tone. A complementary color close to the face emphasizes your skin tone; an analogous, or related, color will de-emphasize it. Very bright colors near the face will de-emphasize both very pale and very deep skin tones. If you have a favorite color that you feel is not flattering to your face and hair, wear that color away from your face

Choosing lines and shapes You can also use the lines and shapes of garments to create effects that will enhance your appearance. It all depends on the way you apply the principles of design. The principle that an unbroken vertical line stresses height, for example, can be applied in a number of ways. If a woman wishes to appear taller, she might wear an outfit with a straight silhouette. (If the dress were tight enough to cling to her, it would emphasize her figure, as well.) Women who feel their hips are too

large may wish not to wear such dresses. An A-line dress would help conceal their hips. Women who wish to emphasize their hips might wear skirts of bulky material, or they might wear skirts with pockets or pleats.

The similar decorative patterns and lines of two different garments—or on different parts of the same garment—can create a sense of rhythm. Embroidered trimming around the hem of a dress could be repeated in a similar way around the collar. Patterns can also be used to create emphasis: imagine a man dressed in solid matching vest and slacks and a bold plaid shirt.

Appropriateness

Society considers certain kinds of clothes to be appropriate, or proper, for certain occasions. Clothes appropriate for some occasions

Textile technology has increased the variety of fabrics that are appropriate for leisure and sportswear. "Luxury" fabrics, such as satin, velvet, and silk, are now durable and easy to care for. Also, man-made fibers can duplicate the look of almost any material.

CLOTHING CLASSICS

Clothing classics are time-tested styles of wearing apparel. Many are identified by the names of people who brought them to the fashion scene. Among these are the loose-fitted Chanel jacket, the velvet chesterfield collar, the casual, front-buttoned cardigan sweater, and the belted, boxy, Norfolk jacket. Some classics take the name of the place where they originated, such as argyle socks (Scotland) or the breton (a women's hat with a turned-up brim worn by peasants in Brittany)

Many casual clothes have become classics: some of these are caps, moccasins, trench coats, and blazers. Dressier women's classics include princess styles, opera pumps, contour belts, and bolero jackets. The tuxedo is a classic for men. Current fashions, and even fads, can put their stamp on clothing classics. For a time, pumps may have chunky heels, or they may have square or pointed toes. Bolero jackets may be fringed, made of leather, or crocheted. A tuxedo may have wide or narrow lapels, and it may be made of a variety of fabrics. In any variation, the classic style is still recognizable.

Fabrics, materials, and colors also become classics. Linen, crepe, suede, patent leather, velvet, seersucker, camel's hair, and corduroy rarely go completely out of style. Plaid, gingham check, and striped designs are classic patterns. Navy blue and charcoal gray are classic colors that are found in fashionable wardrobes year after year.

are not necessarily appropriate for others. The polo shirt a man might wear while visiting a neighbor might not be considered appropriate for his job at the bank. Appropriate dress for school generally differs from appropriate dress for special occasions like weddings and religious observances.

Appropriateness refers not only to how fashionable a garment is. It refers also to whether a garment has the strength and special characteristics to do the job expected of it. A worker is appropriately garbed not only when he wears overalls to work, but when those overalls are made from a sturdy fabric such as denim. When making clothing choices, consider those clothes that are appropriate for your life-style.

Choosing school clothes Most teenagers and young adults know what they consider appropriate clothing and grooming for school. Social acceptance of dress by peers (those in the same age group) is especially important in high school. Bright colors and casual mixing and matching are in order for some schools. Skirts, sweaters, trousers, wash pants, sport shirts, tennis shoes, and sandals are popular in wardrobes for school. Some schools establish standards for appropriate dress and grooming. Those set by students themselves are usually observed cooperatively.

You see the same people in school each day. Changing your appearance may help you to get recognition and approval. Clothes that mix and match, or serve dual purposes, offer more opportunities for variety. Is your time limited? You may prefer to select easy-care clothing. Wash-and-wear garments and knitted fabrics need less care than clothes of delicate materials in ornate styles.

Choosing work clothes Choose clothing that is appropriate for your job and conforms to your employer's standards for dress. In some occupations, special clothing is needed. White-collar jobs are usually performed in offices, stores, or in other places where the public is met. They are called *white-collar* jobs because at one time men working at such jobs had to wear white shirts. *Blue-collar* jobs are performed in factories, outdoors, or behind the scenes. These jobs receive their name from the traditional blue shirt worn by workers.

A sport jacket and slacks, along with a shirt and tie, are appropriate for some white-collar jobs and many types of professional and paraprofessional positions. Business suits are often more appropriate for conservative occupations, such as banking, investment, and insurance. Workers in creative occupations, such as communications or the

Many people, especially those in service occupations, must wear uniforms to work. There is a trend toward uniforms that offer several options within the prescribed dress, including pants suits for women.

This old motoring costume is an example of how leisure-time clothing styles develop to serve a particular function. Some sports clothes, such as tennis "whites," reflect the etiquette of the game.

MIX-AND-MATCH INVENTORY

Accessories	Footwear	Skirts or Slacks	Tops	Dresses or Suits	Footwear	Accessories
red belt red, white, and navy scarf	navy shoes	red plaid skirt red corduroy slacks	navy turtle-neck sweater	gold and navy tweed jumper	navy shoes	gold suede belt
				purple wool dress	black shoes	purple paisley scarf
brown leather belt	brown shoes	brown corduroy slacks	gold and brown cotton blouse gold knit vest	rust suit	brown shoes	gold chain

Completing a mix-and-match inventory like the one above will help you to determine the versatility of your wardrobe and to plan future purchases. The "Tops" column in the center can be read both with the columns to the left of it and with those to the right. So, one completed line might represent two different outfits, each accenting a different color combination, both of which go with the same top. Your personal taste will determine which garments you would put together as you consider the color, style, and fabric of each.

arts, may strive for more flamboyance and originality in their clothing.

Men can appropriately wear a sport shirt without a tie for some blue-collar jobs. Others require protective clothing like overalls. For women, casual daytime dresses or separates are appropriate for outdoor or behind-the-scene jobs. Waitresses, nurses, and stewardesses wear uniforms. The question of what to wear on the job is solved for them. Stores may have established policies concerning apparel for the job. Salespeople wearing tailored dresses in dark colors are easy for customers to identify.

Appropriate accessories also differ according to job. Tennis shoes, sandals, and casual shoes are usually worn only by people who work behind the scenes. People who are on their feet a lot may favor support hose to reduce fatigue; women doing such work generally select shoes with low heels.

Choosing leisure-time clothes Choose leisure-time clothes that are appropriate for your particular activities. Clothes for leisure activities, whether for sports or hobbies, are usually designed for comfort and ease. Some are designed for specific activities. Tennis togs, track shoes, ski pants, jodhpurs, bathing suits, paint smocks, sweatshirts, and gardening gloves are each meant for a particular activity. Each has a particular kind of strength and special characteristics. Blue jeans—once favored by hard-riding cowboys and farmers—are now worn for many casual purposes. Many of the things you wear for school are also suitable for informal social events and after-school jobs.

Choosing "at-home" clothes If your goal is to relax at home, choose clothes that are comfortable. They may be your oldest clothes—perhaps out-of-style leisure clothes that are easy to care for. House dresses are still marketed as an item of clothing for the woman at home. Many young homemakers do their housework in jeans or other casual clothes. People often get their last use out of clothing while doing messy household chores, such as washing the dog, polishing the car, or painting the house.

Many of us have degrees of "at-home" clothes. Some are for housework while others are for entertaining. In some life-styles, hosts and hostesses may choose elegant and elaborate "at-home" clothes. These may consist of hostess skirts, gowns, or robes for women, and smoking or lounging jackets for men.

Some young women begin careers and then marry and become full-time homemakers. They find that some career clothes do not adapt for "at home" or "roll-up-your-sleeves" wear. Career clothes often require dry cleaning. Young women who plan a brief period of work before full-time homemaking should consider their future home needs when making further clothing choices.

Choosing clothes for special events Gala, once-in-a-lifetime events usually call for special clothes. "Black tie" or "white tie"—written on an invitation or mentioned by a host or hostess—signals the degree of formality that is appropriate. "Black tie" means a tuxedo for men, and a formal dress for women. "White tie" indicates full dress suits (tails) for men, and floor-length gowns or skirts for women. Consider outer attire for

formal social events. Men may choose full length opera capes, top hats, and patent leather shoes, while women may select fur wraps or stoles.

Many young people plan formal weddings for which the bride and her attendants wear floor-length gowns, and the groom, the best man, and the ushers wear formal attire. Appropriate wedding clothing depends on

For some people, special events offer a chance to get outside their usual life-style, to wear clothes they do not often need. Others prefer to tailor the event, as well as the clothing, to their life-style.

Versatility can be an especially important consideration when you make a major purchase, such as a suit or a coat, for your wardrobe. Which of these coats is more versatile as a basic wardrobe item?

the hour and place of the ceremony and reception. A morning wedding in a church calls for semiformal clothes. A garden wedding should take the setting into account. An evening wedding with a reception and entertainment following requires more elegant dress. Increasingly, couples are choosing out-of-the-ordinary wedding locations and set highly personal standards of dress.

High school graduations may be informal, semiformal, or formal. Guests usually wear business suits or daytime dresses.

A special event, such as a confirmation, debut, "sweet sixteen," or bar-mitzvah, may require more elaborate clothing for the person being honored and that person's parents. The style of dress for guests is properly indicated on the invitation. It is always permissible to call your host or hostess about the appropriate attire.

Those who seldom wear formal apparel might consider renting it.

Versatility

Versatile clothes are clothes that have more than one use. A woman may have, for example, a sweater which she finds suitable enough to wear to work and to parties, and durable enough to wear at home. The same sweater may have a different kind of versatility: it may be useful in different kinds of weather. It may be light enough to wear in spring and autumn, and still be adequate to wear beneath a coat in winter. A coat would have this kind of versatility if it were water-repellent and had a lining which could be zipped in or out, depending on the temperature. Three-piece outfits can also help to make seasonal transitions.

A garment may also be versatile in the sense that it can be worn in combination with a variety of garments to make a number of different costumes. A man may have a shirt whose color, pattern, silhouette, and texture blend attractively with several suits and pairs of slacks.

Learning to mix and match by choosing a basic color for your wardrobe can help you provide more variety with fewer items. A wardrobe based on a red, white, and blue color scheme, for example, would offer many opportunities to wear different combinations of basic items. Too many colors in a small basic wardrobe can cut down on the number of pleasing combinations that are possible.

Among the most versatile garments are clothing classics in dark or neutral colors. A simple dress or suit stays in style in spite of fashion changes. A wardrobe which includes clothing classics can be small but up to date.

The versatility of a small wardrobe can be further increased by the way you use *accessories*. By changing his necktie, a man can make the same shirt and jacket look quite different. A woman can do the same by varying the necklaces, scarves, and belts she wears with the same dress. If a woman has selected a basic wardrobe color scheme, she might choose to buy major accessories, like shoes, which fit into that scheme. There is a great variety of inexpensive accessories.

SOCIAL CLIMATE AND CLOTHING DECISIONS

Sumptuary laws are laws which regulate, among other things, what a person can wear. They may do this by limiting the amount he is allowed to spend on clothes, or by forbidding people of a certain social rank to wear certain fabrics or styles. Laws like these were common in Europe from the thirteenth to the fifteenth century. They also existed among some of the early colonists of North America.

The social climate in which people select what they will wear has altered greatly. Today, we have more options in making clothing choices. Besides the increased variety of fabrics we have to choose from, we have a great variety of stores in which to choose them. We have also changed attitudes toward clothing. During the 1960s, a number of different clothing fashions remained in style at once. Women, for example, could select skirts and dresses of many different shapes and lengths.

THINK BACK

The elements and principles of design are useful tools in selecting clothing most complimentary to your physical features.
Discuss: *How can you help the person who insists he has "no artistic ability"?*

Clothing needs are determined not only by present life-style, but by future plans, as well.
Discuss: *What is your answer to the person who decides he "can't think that far ahead"?*

A knowledge of clothing items that are recommended for various activities guides clothing selection.
Discuss: *How does one avoid conformity in dress if this is so?*

Satisfying clothing decisions result from self-understanding and wise use of resources.
Discuss: *How can the statement "You are your own worst critic" apply here?*

LOOK AROUND

1. Analyze your face shape, coloring, and body proportions. List what you feel are your physical assets and liabilities.
2. Go through your entire wardrobe. List everything you own. Beside each item, put the length of time you think it will last. If you do not intend to wear an item anymore, put a zero next to it. Chart the clothing items you think you will need to buy during each season for the next two years.

3. What do you consider your most valuable personal resources to be used in wardrobe planning? Explain your use of each.

4. Do the clothes in your wardrobe accurately reflect your daily activities? Where should additions or deletions be made?

5. Begin to develop an "Especially For You" bulletin board that illustrates how present teen clothing styles can be adapted to various body types.

6. Go through magazines. Which designers are influential in setting clothing styles? How does the use of line differ among designers? Which designers' clothes are most suited to you?

7. What future plans are to be followed by your classmates after graduation? Develop a display suggesting basic wardrobe items appropriate to several of the future life-styles and income levels. Include color suggestions, prices, fabrics, and care instructions.

8. Interview several "best-dressed" classmates from various grade levels. What are their suggestions for achieving a satisfactory school wardrobe? Develop a "Try This!" bulletin board on which the best suggestions of each person interviewed are portrayed.

FOLLOW YOUR PATH

PATH ONE: Provide a Wardrobe Consultation Service

Step 10 List each client's physical assets and liabilities.

Step 11 On the basis of all the previous steps, collect from magazines pictures of five complete costumes for each client, including accessories. (Do not, however, choose more than two pairs of shoes.) Make your choices as attractive, appropriate, and versatile as possible.

PATH TWO: Manufacture an Apparel Item

Step 9 What would be the physical characteristics of one person you feel would look attractive in each outfit? Why?

Step 10 Make one rough drawing showing how you would change the colors of each of your items. Select colors that you think would appeal to people with different physical characteristics and personal tastes.

Step 11 Ask a group of classmates to judge your items. Would they purchase them? How much do they think they are worth?

PATH THREE: Open a Clothing Store

Step 11 Make up an advertisement for your store. In it, show three people with very different physical characteristics. For each, making use of the items you are selling, show three outfits that you feel look good on them. Write an ad that explains the advantages of shopping in your store. Place the ad in the fashion magazine in Path Four.

Step 12 Prepare for your customers a demonstration in which you present two of your items which are on sale. Try to convince these customers of the attractiveness, appropriateness, and versatility of these items.

PATH FOUR: Plan a Fashion Magazine

Step 9 Put together your picture essay from Step 6. The object will be to show how this color can be worn by young adults with many different types of facial features, personal coloring, and body proportions.

Step 10 Visit the apparel factory in Path Two. Examine their product. Write a short article telling your readers whether or not you recommend the product. Give reasons.

Step 11 Visit a number of clothing stores. Do a brief article on versatile garments that are easy to care for.

CHAPTER 15

Managing Your Clothing Resources

There have been ages in which life was in some ways simpler than it is today. When someone needed a new coat, he made it himself, or he bought it from one of only a few available places.

If we have the time, skills, materials, and interest, we can still make our own clothes. If we choose instead to buy, we have more options than people formerly did. More stores—and more kinds of stores—are available to us. These stores offer a variety of wearable merchandise. Included are garments and accessories that at first glance seem to be the same but which actually differ in price and quality. Clothing stores also offer a variety of services. The costs of these services are not specified on the price tag, but they are included in the garment's price. Which is the right garment for you? Are services worth paying for?

All these options present challenges to the consumer. He can meet the challenges by becoming informed about clothing materials and construction at the same time that he is learning how to buy. In clarifying choices, a wardrobe plan is useful. If you know what you have, it will help you to determine what you want. A clear idea of what you want puts you in a better position to evaluate your options. If you have an *overall* plan and have estimated your clothing needs and a clothing budget, you have a good idea of how much money you have to spend on any item. Choices made at home will provide background for the clothing choices you will make in the marketplace.

This "Fashion Mirror" allows a shopper to see if a garment is flattering before she trys it on for fit. The mirror reduces shopwear on merchandise, as well as the time and energy required for shopping.

ACQUIRING CLOTHES

Suppose you have a wardrobe plan that includes a new green jacket. How will you go about adding this article of clothing to your wardrobe? If you have the skill, you might make it; otherwise, you could buy it. If you have the money, you might go out and buy it immediately; if not, you might wait for a sale. Once you are sure that you want to buy the jacket, you may know a number of stores in which to compare merchandise. Different stores offer garments that appear to be similar but which may actually differ in price and quality. Not every available green jacket will meet your needs. Some stores might offer helpful services, like alteration and delivery. The cost of these services is passed on to the consumer. Judge for yourself whether you wish to absorb this cost. Not all stores insist that you pay in full before taking your jacket home. You might also have to choose the payment plan that best suits your budget.

Acquiring clothing, then, can be a very involved part of a rational decision-making process. It can call for knowledge and careful judgment.

Discovering Alternatives

To acquire clothes to fulfill your wardrobe plan, you will have to both discover and choose among several alternatives. You need not assume that you will buy what you wish to have. You may prefer to make it yourself. You need not necessarily acquire garments or fabrics at the moment you most want them. Clothes vary in price throughout the year. After you evaluate your clothing resources, you may wish to make a purchase earlier or later than you first intended.

Buying or making Most young adults have fluctuating resources to invest in clothing and grooming. Yet, if personal appearance has high priority, you will find some way to create the image you want. Money, of course, is an important resource; but skills are also important. Your skill in constructing and altering clothes can be a valuable resource in filling out and expanding your wardrobe.

Today, **ready-to-wear** clothing of all kinds is available in practically every size, quality, and price range. This was not always the case. At one time, all clothes were made by hand.

It generally takes less time and energy to buy clothes than to make them. It may even cost less money. To determine that, you would need to comparison shop for ready-made garments and for the materials needed to make similar garments. You may find high-quality clothing at reduced prices. Small, large, or irregular sizes are often featured in sales. Average sizes sell more quickly during the regular season.

If you have skill in sewing, knitting, or crocheting, as well as the time and interest, you may want to **make it yourself**. Many people consider sewing to be an enjoyable hobby. Others are taken by the creative aspect of making clothes for themselves.

In considering the cost of home sewing, include the prices of the material, the pattern, and the thread. Also include the prices of any zippers, buttons, and seam or hem tape that you will need. The cost and quality of each item in the garment may make the finished product more expensive than a comparable garment in a store. When the skilled amateur duplicates expensive details in workmanship, however, the overall cost may be less.

It is usually more economical to buy men's shirts than it is to make them. If you are skilled, however, you can "turn" collars and cuffs to get added wear from an otherwise serviceable garment. Pajamas, hose, and underclothing are usually cheaper to buy than to make. By comparison, children's clothing can often be made less expensively. Labor costs for manufacturing children's clothes are almost identical to those for making adult

Evaluate your skills when you consider making a garment. If the project is too difficult for the skills you have acquired, it may be wiser to buy it readymade. An unwearable garment is no bargain.

clothes, although less material is required.

For the person who values originality and creativity in dress—and who is unable to find the garment he wants in the appropriate design, size, fabric, or color—make-it-yourself clothing has many advantages. Those who find satisfaction in creating unique clothing may be motivated to master clothing construction skills and related crafts.

Considering sales Stores feature different garments and fabrics at different times of the year. This is especially true in regions where seasonal differences are great. In-season clothes are usually highly priced. Out-of-season clothes can often be found on sale.

If you wish to wear current fashions and if you have the resources to do so, you may want to buy clothes at the moment they become available in stores. If you are not too concerned about being "up to the minute" in style and if you have a wardrobe plan, you

Inspect sale items carefully. Minor repairs can be made and slight soil removed, but if a garment is poorly constructed or badly soiled, you may never be able to make it presentable enough to wear.

inventory. Sometimes, especially when business is poor, they have sales to attract customers. There are going-out-of-business sales and fire sales. (Some stores have "fire sales" all year long. You might question whether items in such stores are really being offered at a reduced rate.) Whatever the reason, sales are usually advertised in local newspapers. Some may also be advertised on local radio stations.

Choosing a Store

You may purchase clothing in a number of different kinds of outlets. Some stores sell many kinds of clothing. Others specialize in only a few. Some stores are very attentive to potential customers. Others leave the shopper to pick and choose for himself.

Each kind of outlet offers its own particular advantages to the consumer. The rational selection of a place to shop depends on your clothing goals. It depends on the time, money, and energy you choose to devote to those goals. In some cases, a department store or specialty store may suit your purposes. A variety store or a discount store may be fine for other clothing items. To reach still other clothing goals, a mail-order house may be satisfactory.

Department stores   A wide selection of articles is available in most department stores. The store may be organized so that the shopper can make quick comparisons. A glove counter might offer wool, cotton, and leather gloves, as well as sets of matching gloves and scarves. At another counter, men's socks might be displayed in cotton, wool, and blends, and in various colors, lengths, and patterns. Some stores have special departments for the teen or young-adult consumer, featuring styles that may have been selected by a representative advisory board. In a particular department, a woman might find a blouse, shoes, and other accessories which reflect the same fashion trend.

may be willing to wait to buy some basic items. You can plan your wardrobe on a yearly basis, taking advantage of seasonal sales. If you are a person whose weight fluctuates frequently, this may not be a good idea. You can take advantage of off-season clothing sales only after you have stopped growing, when you are maintaining a steady weight.

While change of season is the main reason for clothing sales, it is not the only reason. Stores sometimes have sales to reduce their

CASE STUDY: MRS. BRODY AND CHERYL

THE SITUATION   The 4-H clothing contests were considered valuable learning experiences for all participants. But as Mrs. Brody sat with her daughter Cheryl at the judging table, she knew Cheryl did not agree. Her daughter's eyes were beginning to swell with tears as the judge carefully looked over construction details of Cheryl's dress. The dress was not poorly made. On the contrary, it was beautifully done, as the judge indicated. Cheryl had tears in her eyes from nervousness. Mrs. Brody, rather than Cheryl, had done most of the work on the dress. She, not Cheryl, had insisted on attending this clothing contest. It had been Mrs. Brody's idea that her daughter learn to sew in the first place.

"The dress is beautifully made," remarked the judge. "Is there a part with which you're particularly pleased?"

As Cheryl hesitated, her mother answered for her. "She said she liked the way the sleeves were attached. They do look nice, don't they?" The judge nodded, a concerned look now replacing her smile.

"Cheryl, your 4-H clothing leader spoke with me earlier today. She felt that she could not honestly encourage you to enter this contest. She said you rarely attended the work meetings. She has no way of knowing how you learned to make a dress like this."

Cheryl was extremely embarrassed. She made no reply.

"Why, I helped her with the difficult steps," said her mother, hurriedly. "I think Cheryl learned a great deal in attempting this type of pattern. And now she wants to try something even more difficult, don't you, Cheryl?"

"Perhaps," interrupted the judge, "it would be better to make another garment in this same unit. I cannot give you a rating on your dress because of your leader's uncertainty. Why don't you try to attend more meetings so that your 4-H leader can help you with your work?"

Silently, Cheryl and her mother picked up the garment and left the table. Big tears rolled down Cheryl's cheeks.

THE INTERVIEW   Q: It seems that you insisted that your daughter learn to sew. Why did you do that?
A: Because it's a wonderful skill for a girl to know. She can select the patterns and fabrics that best suit her. She can make unique clothing less expensively than she could buy ready-made clothing.
Q: What were Cheryl's objections to learning to sew?
A: She didn't think she'd be able to make something nice. She doesn't really enjoy working with her hands. I thought that if she tried to learn and was successful with one garment, she'd want to continue sewing. I guess that I was wrong in doing what I did. The judge's decision was very embarrassing for both of us.
Q: Do you think that Cheryl will follow the judge's advice?
A: I'd like her to. She's angry with me now, though, and will probably stop sewing altogether. I created a very bad situation for my daughter. It will take a long time to repair the damage.

REACT   How do you think you would feel if you were put in Cheryl's position? Are some ways of learning how to sew more effective than other ways? What, to you, might be some of the "good" and "bad" results of requiring that a person learn to sew?

If you know exactly what size you wear without having to try on a garment and if you are willing to spend time sifting through disorganized merchandise, low-level service stores may offer clothing bargains.

Department stores carry clothing in a range of styles, qualities, and prices. Some stores emphasize higher fashion clothes. Some deal only in better constructed garments. In some stores, the price range is higher than in others. Not every department store will have the garments that you want.

The variety of apparel sold in a department store makes one-stop shopping possible. De-partment stores also offer a variety of services. They have knowledgeable salesclerks and can provide clothing alterations. Some stores that specialize in men's clothing will also have tailors.

Stores may also arrange credit and make deliveries. They generally have customer-service departments for adjustments and complaints, and information booths to help you shop efficiently. They provide dressing rooms. Services to the customer cost the store money, and the cost of these is passed on to the consumer. In some cases, you may consider the added cost too high. Even then, you might shop at the department store's budget shop, where lower quality and irregular merchandise is featured at reduced prices.

For some, location may be another disadvantage of department stores. They are often located in the centers of cities and larger towns. You may be unable or unwilling to go there. Parking may be too difficult or too expensive. Today, more and more department stores are opening branch stores in shopping centers. These stores generally offer merchandise of the same price and kind as the main store. Since the branch stores are usually not as large, stocks may be smaller and the selection more limited. Parking is seldom a problem at branch stores. In many cases, it is possible to shop by phone at the main store. You may be able to telephone in your order and have the store deliver it. Such services may be limited to customers who have charge accounts with a store. Some stores may deliver COD—cash on delivery—within a certain radius.

Specialty stores   Unlike department stores, specialty stores deal in specific kinds of merchandise. Stores that specialize in men's clothing or women's shoes, for example, are in this category. Some specialty stores concentrate on merchandise of a particular quality and price range. Some cater to a specific market. One specialty store may cater to tall men. Another may sell fashions for the "junior" or "petite" woman.

Specialty clothing stores can be found in most shopping areas. Salespeople in specialty stores may be especially knowledgeable about their lines of merchandise. If you feel you need advice about the quality or fit of a garment or accessory, you may patronize a specialty store. Most specialty stores allow you to try on garments. Those that do not will usually offer refunds or exchanges on unsatisfactory merchandise. Those that sell suits, dresses, and similar items can usually arrange for alterations and adjustments.

An item frequently costs more in a specialty store. Such stores may offer credit.

Variety stores Some variety stores are called "five and tens." This name comes from a time when such stores sold most items for

Many department stores have opened "boutiques" that centralize in one department all the apparel and accessories necessary to put together a total "look." Such departments are good choices for people who need help in coordinating their purchases.

Sales service may influence where you choose to shop. Are you allowed to make decisions without enduring unwanted advice? Are you made to feel uncomfortable if you choose not to make a purchase?

a nickel or a dime. Since then, prices have gone up. Variety stores continue to feature inexpensive items. Some have limited selections of outerwear or dressy apparel, but wide selections of leisure and work clothes.

Variety stores have salesclerks, although you cannot expect them to have information which will help you to make up your mind about making a purchase. These stores seldom have facilities where you can try on clothing. Only a few offer credit. Some will not permit you to return merchandise.

Discount stores Discount stores generally offer low prices. This is possible because they keep down their overhead. They may not spend extra money to decorate attractively their stores or to display their merchandise. Sale items may be piled on tables or in crates. Also, to keep down overhead, discount stores may hire fewer salesclerks. Customers must spend time searching out garments of the

right size. If there are no places for shoppers to try on garments, they may find it hard to select those that will fit. Discount stores may limit return privileges.

Many of the original discount stores were located in out-of-the-way places. Some were set up in warehouses. As these stores became more popular, they became more conveniently located. Today, they can be found in many shopping areas. Also, as they become more popular, their prices tend to rise.

Discount stores do not consistently handle items of the same brand name or quality. To get a "good buy" under such circumstances, one must be a good judge of quality.

Mail-order houses You can buy clothes from a mail-order house without ever leaving your home. These places supply potential buyers with illustrated catalogs which list all the merchandise available. The catalog describes each item and gives its price and the colors and sizes in which it is available. Some mail-order houses accept phone orders.

Browsing through a mail-order catalog frees you from direct sales pressure from salesclerks. You may be able to find what you want without investing much time and energy. If you need an item right away, however, remember that mail orders take time. When returning a purchase, repacking and mailing merchandise can be inconvenient and time-consuming. If you are an average size and refer to the size charts in the catalog, you are assured of approximate fit.

Because of their low overhead, mail-order houses sell many items at prices lower than the prices in department stores. (Remember to add on the mailing and shipping charges.)

Mail-order catalogs provide an excellent reference for price guidelines in shopping.

Selecting Clothing

Knowledge of fibers, fabrics, and finishes can help you choose garments that suit your needs. Knowledge of clothing construction—

of the way clothes are put together and finished—can also help you. Some guides to the quality of materials and workmanship are available in this and other books. Up-to-date information is circulated by manufacturers all the time. Newspapers and magazines may offer tips for better clothing buying. Mail-order catalogs contain much useful information. You may also learn some of what you want to know inside the store. There, you can examine carefully the details of a garment. You may be able to try the garment on to see if it fits to your satisfaction. If a salesclerk is knowledgeable, he may be able to assist you in your selection. Some labels and hangtags may also be instructive.

Reading labels The labels and tags on garments carry much useful information, some of which is required by law. Labels indicate the price and size of the garment. They may also include the manufacturer's or designer's name. These can help you judge the quality of a garment. If a woman was satisfied with a "Brand A" skirt, she might be more inclined to purchase a "Brand A" jacket. Brand names are also one of the best guides for comparison shopping. If the same brand of a garment costs less in one store than in another, you are sure that the lower-priced garment is a bargain (provided, of course, that both are in the same condition).

Labels and hangtags also tell the fibers of which the garment is made. Under law, the percentage by weight of each fiber in a blend must be given, provided that it is over 5 percent. There are, however, some exceptions to this rule. Since a small amount of spandex greatly affects the elasticity of a fabric, the name "spandex" is usually listed on the label. In the case of man-made fibers, the *generic* name—acrylic or rayon, for example—must be given. Each manufacturer also has a trade name for each man-made fiber he makes. The trade name is featured on the label. You might find Dacron polyester, Fortrel polyester, Kodel polyester, or Vycron

Mail-order catalogs have special sections that help you to determine your correct size. They include instructions for taking accurate measurements and size charts for all types of garments.

polyester. When considering more than one such fabric, remember that all are essentially—though not exactly—the same.

Labels carry information about fabric finishes. A label may call your attention to the fact that a garment is water-repellent or spot-resistant. It may tell you if and how much a garment may shrink. It may tell you if the garment is colorfast.

Increasingly, labels and hangtags offer suggestions about garment care. They may tell you whether a garment should be hand-washed, machine-washed, or dry-cleaned. If washed, the tag may tell you whether hot, warm, or cold water would be best. The tag may even suggest an ideal washing temperature. Some tags advise about the use of bleach. Some suggest ways for drying garments and temperatures for ironing them.

These suggestions give you an idea of the time, energy, and money necessary to maintain a particular garment.

Checking workmanship Checking the *workmanship* of a garment means looking to see how well the garment is made. Often, but not always, there is a relationship between workmanship and price. The rational selection of a garment does not necessarily mean choosing the garment that has the best workmanship. It means choosing a garment whose level of workmanship and whose price best suit your clothing goals. Do you need a ready-made garment that you hope to wear often or for a long period of time? Consider a selection that is well made and that you can expect to last. Do you need some clothes for only occasional or seasonal wear? Do you want a "high-style" garment that will soon pass out of date? Consider a less expensive item.

When examining garment construction, check it inside and out. Buttonholes may be reinforced with stitching or binding that will give added strength and longer wear. The tops of pockets may be reinforced—they

Permanent care labels are now required to be attached to almost all wearing apparel sold. The label, which must remain legible for the life of the garment, must state fully any regular care needed.

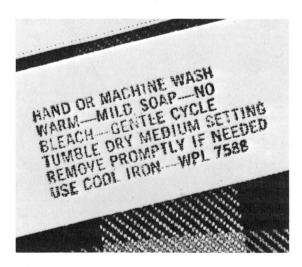

may have extra stitching to keep them from ripping out. In coats and suits, the buttons, snaps, hooks, zippers, and belt loops should be separately and securely sewn. There should be no loose threads. If the price and garment are otherwise right, you may wish to reattach buttons and hooks yourself. If the buttons are of poor quality, you may plan to replace them. Loose threads can be tied, and their ends can be cut off. Seams should be at least one-half inch wide. In better clothes, hems are at least two inches deep. Both seams and hems can be reinforced. The lining should be firmly attached, even at the bottom of the coat.

Checking fit The dressing rooms offered by department and specialty stores offer a key advantage to the shopper. By trying a garment on and moving around in it you can find out if the garment fits you properly. Bend and twist; move your arms and shoulders to make sure the garment gives you the freedom you need without pulling or straining at the seams. Check collars and pockets to see that they lie flat. There should be no pulling or wrinkling at seams or buttonholes. Fitted slacks do not sag behind; they fit comfortably in the crotch. The key measurements of a skirt are in the waist and hips. A skirt that is too tight may "ride up" and give a wrinkled appearance.

Making Payment

In buying clothing, as in making other purchases, you may have the option to pay cash or use credit. (See Chapter 5.) Two ways of delaying payment on clothing are layaway and charge.

Layaway A *layaway plan* allows you to place a small deposit on an item and to pay the balance in a specified time. The store holds the item for you. You may be able to make small payments until the article is paid for. If you have a rational wardrobe plan,

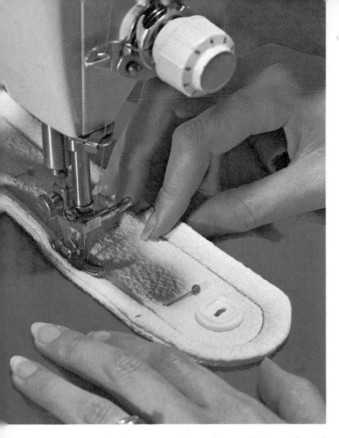

Whether you make your own clothes or buy them ready to wear, certain details indicate immediately whether a garment is carefully made. Top stitching should be straight and even, stripes and plaids should be centered and well matched at the seams, and zippers should lie flat.

layaway may appeal to you. Regular budgeting is essential when using layaway plans. Know what you want, and set aside regular amounts to reach your goal. You must pay for the entire item before you can have it. If you fail to complete the payments, you lose the garment. In some cases you may also lose the money you have already paid. The store owner may give you credit for another purchase. Rarely will you receive a refund.

Charge accounts When a store lets you open a *charge account*, it agrees to let you purchase items on credit. At the end of a month—or other agreed-upon time—the store sends you a statement telling you how much you owe. There are two types of charge accounts: regular and revolving. In a regular charge account, you have a certain period of time in which to pay for a purchase. This period is usually thirty days, though it may be as long as ninety days. Interest is not charged. In a revolving charge account, you are obliged to pay only a certain percentage of your total debt in any one month. The amount you must pay depends on the amount you owe. Suppose you must pay 20 percent. If your debt is fifty dollars, you must pay ten at the end of the first month. If your debt is one hundred dollars, you must pay twenty. Interest is charged on revolving accounts, although it may be waived if you pay your entire bill within one month. There is a limit to the debt you can carry.

Regular and revolving charge accounts are usually issued by department and specialty stores. Customers with charge accounts tend to favor those stores.

CASE STUDY: TONY

THE SITUATION *"I should be able to find something I like at this sale," thought Tony. "Here I am with a newly cashed paycheck, and I have nothing to spend it on. Dad will never believe this."*

"May I help you?" asked the salesclerk. "We have some trousers on sale that may fit you."

"I was more interested in a shirt or sweater, but you don't have either in my size. I don't really need trousers, but I'll look at what you have," replied Tony.

The clerk led the way to the trousers and indicated Tony's size. Looking through the selection, Tony chose three. After several minutes in the fitting room, he emerged, saying, *"The only one I like is this plaid one."*

"It's a great fit," interrupted the clerk. "You couldn't find anything better."

"But the plaids don't match at the sides," continued Tony. *"When I stand sideways, this blue line appears to be slanting towards the floor. It shouldn't look like that, should it?"*

"We'll alter this for you, adjust the seam. Everything will be fine."

"Will that really straighten the plaids?" asked Tony.

"People wear anything nowadays," urged the clerk. *"The front and back look straight, don't they? Wear one of our long sweater vests over the trousers. No one will ever notice the slanting lines. You won't find a bargain like this anywhere else in town."*

"I think I'd like to look around a little more," replied Tony, hesitantly. *"I like these trousers, though. I have several vests that will go with them."*

"Look, if you don't take it now, it will be gone when you return. Our merchandise is very popular with the younger crowd. Everyone is wearing that style of trousers now. Let me wrap it up for you."

THE INTERVIEW Q: Are you going to buy the trousers, Tony?
A: I'm not sure yet. We learned in school that one of the construction details to look for is plaids that match at seams. The sale price is reasonable, though, so maybe that's not an important detail.
Q: Do you need these trousers?
A: No. I already have enough trousers. I hate to go home without buying something, though. This sale is a good one.
Q: Can you afford to waste your money?
A: Of course not! But I could plan to wear the trousers often enough to make this purchase worthwhile. With all the other clothes I have, no one would notice the faults of these trousers.

REACT *Should Tony buy the trousers? What questions might you ask the clerk?*

The credit cards issued by banks represent the same type of credit arrangement as the revolving charge account. Some bank credit cards are honored at a number of stores. With these, you receive one bill for purchases made at different stores. Some people prefer to make one large payment rather than a number of small payments.

CLOTHING CARE

Clothing care means seeing that clothes are properly cleaned, stored, and maintained. It can involve anything from washing a scarf in the kitchen sink to tightening a button on a newly purchased sweater. Regular clothing care assures you that items in your wardrobe will be clean and neat. It also helps to extend the life of your garments and to stretch your clothing dollar.

Regular Care

If possible, do not wear the same suit or jacket two days in a row. Giving any item of clothing a rest will increase its wearability. Hanging allows fibers to resettle in the woven or knit shape and gives wrinkles a chance to fall out. If you must wear such a garment two days in a row, try to air it overnight.

Some garments require more care than others. Because underwear absorbs body oils and perspiration, it should be laundered after each wearing.

Different fibers respond differently to water. (Sec Chapter 13.) Consequently, some fabrics can be *laundered,* or washed in water. Others, which would be damaged by water, should be dry cleaned.

Laundering For best results, washable fabrics should be laundered in recommended ways. Most washable fabrics can be laundered in a washing machine. A washing machine can satisfactorily wash only a certain amount of clothing at one time; garments must first be divided into loads. Loads should consist of fabrics requiring similar washing conditions—water temperature, wash time, washing action, spin speed, and detergent. Dyes used in dark-colored fabrics may not be colorfast. If not, they will "run" or "bleed" in hot water. Dark-colored fabrics should be washed in warm or cold water, separately from white and light-colored clothes.

Most fabrics can be dried in a clothes dryer, according to drying instructions on tags and labels. Since different fabrics can withstand only certain amounts of heat, remember to sort drying loads according to fabric drying temperatures. Delicate fabrics may be rolled in towels to absorb some moisture, and then dried in the air. When drying fabrics on a clothesline, hang the items by

An organized closet is a help in caring for your clothes. Make as much room as possible for garments to hang, so that they will not be crushed and air can circulate. Cleaning bills will be lower, too.

main seams, such as shoulders. Drying forms —which can eliminate the need for some additional pressing—are available for trousers.

Fabric information like that in Chapter 13 can guide you at laundry time. Pay attention to information on clothing labels. You may also wish to acquire a chart that tells how different fibers and fabrics may be laundered.

Unless you have a washer, and perhaps a dryer, coin-operated laundries may offer you the best way to clean your clothes. The

Proper laundering methods keep clothes in good condition longer. Sorting clothes according to color and washing conditions and paying special attention to heavily soiled areas are important prewash steps.

original cost of a washer and dryer is usually high. The investment is worthwhile only if the appliance will be used for a long period of time. Use equipment in a coin-operated laundry as directed by the proprietor.

Dry cleaning Dry cleaning is a process in which chemical solvents are used to loosen soil from fabrics. Dry cleaning may be done by a commercial establishment, or you may do it yourself at a coin-operated dry cleaner.

Professional dry-cleaning firms may provide many services, including spotting, button removal and reattachment, and pressing. At your request, the professional dry cleaner

will make a garment water-repellent and crease-resistant. Services for cleaning and blocking sweaters, knits, and hats are often available. In some places, shirt laundering and leather cleaning may also be available.

Self-service dry cleaning is available at some laundries. Work space for spot removal and a hang-up service for completed cleaning may be provided. The management does not ordinarily provide a free pressing service. If one is available, you may want to use a coin-operated presser on some garments.

Removing spots and stains Give immediate attention to removing spots and stains. You might prefer to take the garment to a professional cleaner. A highly skilled spotter can possibly save your garment.

There are a few rules to keep in mind when removing spots yourself. Try to find out what a stain or spot was caused by before you try to remove it. Check on the fabric you are working with. If a garment has a "dry-clean only" label, heed the warning. On washable fabrics, cold or cool water will loosen most stains. If the stain is fresh, it is usually easier to remove. Hot water may set soil. Avoid using hot water on most garments until the stain has been completely removed. Chocolate, blood, water-solvent inks, and most food stains can be loosened with cool water. Apply soap and water for final cleaning.

Nonwashable fibers are more challenging. If you are using a chemical remover, try it first on a hidden seam. If it leaves a ring, the garment needs professional attention.

Locate a spot- and stain-removal chart. Accumulate and label the cleaning agents you find effective.

Storage Careful storage of clothing can add to its life. Hang your clothes up when you take them off. Close slide fasteners, buttons, and hooks. Hang garments with the shoulder seams squarely on the hanger. Hang slacks over padded hangers. Always empty pockets. Allow space between garments in your closet. A little space between clothes prevents wrinkles that are formed when clothes are jammed together. Air out garments regularly to keep them smelling fresh. You may wish to use closet fresheners. You may wish to make or buy special kinds of hangers and storage items. These include hangers with curved frames (for jackets), trouser hangers, multiple shirt hangers, tie racks, jewelry boxes, shoe trees, shoe bags, and hatboxes. These may help you to organize as well as protect your wardrobe.

Seasonal Care and Storage

Most of the United States has at least two seasons. The kinds of clothing for one season need to be stored while other seasonal clothes are worn. Stored garments should be cleaned, pressed, and covered prior to storage. Enclose moth balls or moth preventatives with stored woolen clothing. Sealed, airtight, moisture-proof containers are helpful in keeping out dust, moths, and mildew. Moving companies and variety stores sell large, airtight storage boxes. Those who have them can turn attics, garages, and basements into storage areas. (Only dry, airy space should be used for storage.)

MAKING INFORMED CLOTHING CHOICES

We have a wide variety of clothing and accessories from which to choose. To make reasonably informed clothing choices, we would have to know a great deal. Yet, we have a limited amount of time, energy, and money to spend acquiring clothing. We are fortunate to have certain industry and government controls. Because of these controls, we have some assurance that information on clothing labels and tags is accurate.

THINK BACK

Consider personal interests and resources in choosing to make or buy a wardrobe item.
Discuss: *Can a person really make something for less than it costs to buy it in a store?*

Your choice of a clothing store depends on your personal clothing goals.
Discuss: *Is it worth the extra money to buy clothing in a store that offers dressing rooms and tailoring?*

Immediate minor repairs can prevent the need for extensive future repairs.
Discuss: *What types of repairs can you be expected to make?*

Managing your clothing dollars includes selecting the payment plan best suited to your needs and resources.
Discuss: *Can you always "charge it"?*

Regular care is necessary to maintain the appearance and life of wardrobe items.
Discuss: *What would convince people to take better care of their clothing?*

Decisions to use commercial clothing care services depend on the availability of your personal resources.
Discuss: *Is it worthwhile to allocate money for dry cleaning?*

LOOK AROUND

1. Identify low-, medium-, and high-priced clothing stores in your community. Check labels in clothing stores. What added information would be useful?
3. Evaluate the prewear care required for several low-, medium-, and high-priced garments. Which choice would make best use of your own clothing resources?

4. What is the difference between layaway and charge plans? Which do you recommend for students? Why?
5. Develop a "How-To" bulletin board explaining common clothing repairs.
6. Inventory the contents of your clothing storage area. Develop a plan to reorganize items and save space.
7. What construction techniques are associated with better quality clothing items? What else might you need to know to determine the quality of a garment?
8. At what age can children best assume responsibility for clothing care? (Refer to Chapter 2.)
9. What are ways in which time needed for clothing care can be minimized?

FOLLOW YOUR PATH

PATH ONE: Provide a Wardrobe Consultation Service

Step 12 Visit different stores, including the kind in Path Three. Note what kind of services and credit are offered. Find garments that fit each Step 11 wardrobe selection. Look at labels and workmanship. Record the fabric, finish, price, and quality of each garment. Check those items which you feel best meet each client's goals.

Step 13 Write up a report for each set of clients. Tell them where you think they should shop. Mention store services and credit arrangements. Advise the clients about the use of credit. Make general recommendations about the kind of store you think might suit their particular clothing needs.

Step 14 Make up a purchasing chart for each set of clients. Down the left-hand column, list each item from Step 12 that had a check next to it. Across the top, show the months of the year. Check when you think the item might best be purchased. Ask your teacher for advice about sales.

PATH TWO: Manufacture an Apparel Item

Step 12 Visit stores that sell items similar to yours. Discuss whether you want your items to cost more, the same, or less than these items. Set a price.

Step 13 Make up a label and a hangtag for each of your items. Include all the information you feel the consumer will want to know. Use the logotype you designed in Step 5.

Step 14 Meet with your classmates who are working on the magazine in Path Four. Make up an advertisement that you feel is suitable for this magazine. Use your logotype.

Step 15 Visit the store or stores in Path Three. Try to sell them your items.

PATH THREE: Open a Clothing Store

Step 13 Give your demonstration from Step 12 before the class. Answer any questions.

Step 14 You are visited by a wardrobe consultant from Path One. Try to sell him items which you feel will meet his clients' needs. Have the class evaluate his behavior and your behavior.

Step 15 Visit a store like yours. If it has a credit policy, model your own after it. Make a poster explaining it to customers.

PATH FOUR: Plan a Fashion Magazine

Step 12 Visit the store in Path Three. Note some of the prices, and compare them with the prices of similar items elsewhere. Note the variety of goods offered. Write a short article about the store.

Step 13 Again, visit clothing stores in your community. Interview owners and managers. Ask about their principal complaints against customers. Write down the remarks that you feel are most important. Reproduce these remarks in your magazine.

Step 14 Type your articles, or have them typed. Begin to lay out your magazine.

CHAPTER 16

Careers in Clothing

Since the industrial revolution, great changes have taken place in clothing manufacturing. Before that time, clothes were made by hand. The entire operation —from spinning to weaving to sewing—was done in the home. The advent of power machines stepped up the pace of manufacturing. The growth of cities provided a concentrated labor force for the new textile and clothing industries. The apparel industry moved out of the home and into factories. Thereafter, textile and clothing manufacturing was focused in certain areas. With technological advances, it became possible to make a greater variety of clothing items.

Added to manufacturing, clothing merchandising and distribution became part of a complex industry. A surprising variety of interrelated jobs was created. Today, many of these jobs are highly specialized. Among them are jobs for people with many different personalities and interests. Might the wide world of clothing contain a career for you?

251

THE CLOTHING INDUSTRY

The clothing industry begins with the people who raise sheep for wool. It begins with those who dream of inventing new man-made fibers. It ends with people buying garments and wearing them. It employs millions of workers. These people operate sewing machines and tend huge knitting machines. They design fabrics and dresses. They pour buttons into boxes and hoist racks of clothing onto trucks. They are machinists and chemists, truck drivers and models, dry cleaners and pressers, salesclerks and home economists. Because of the varied efforts of those in the textile, apparel, merchandising, and distribution industries, you have thousands of clothing and accessory items from which to choose.

The *textile industry* produces man-made fibers. It conducts research to try to discover new fibers. It converts natural fibers into a condition from which they may be made into cloth. It makes, dyes, and finishes cloth. It prints patterns on cloth. In the past few decades, great changes have taken place in the textile industry. More new fabrics have been developed than in all of previous recorded time. Much of the textile industry in North America is concentrated in the southeastern United States.

The *apparel industry* designs and makes garments. The heart of this industry is a six-square-block area in New York City. Other centers are spread throughout the country. (Texas and California are two such centers.) Most garment factories are small. They specialize in making only a few kinds of high-, medium-, or low-priced garments. Manufacturers of high- and medium-priced garments place a great deal of emphasis on design. Manufacturers of low-cost garments often imitate higher priced designs.

The *merchandising* aspect of the clothing industry is closely related to garment manufacturing. For the most part, garments are not usually produced in quantity until they have been ordered by stores. It is the job of sales representatives to take orders from buyers who represent department stores. They show sample garments to these wholesale buyers. Most large manufacturers have showrooms in New York City for this purpose. For smaller manufacturers, this task is performed in bigger cities by agents who are sometimes called jobbers.

Most of the merchandising jobs in the clothing industry are on the retail level. These jobs are filled by the salesclerks and others who work in clothing stores. On a part-time or temporary basis, you may have had such a job yourself.

A key to financial success in the clothing industry is timing. It is the goal of many to have the right style of clothes on the market at the right time. This can be a tricky task. Fashion is fickle, and popular tastes change almost overnight. Because new fashions can create new sales, the clothing industry encourages such changes. The industry creates an artificial situation so that clothes appear "old-fashioned" before they wear out. The hemline is an indicator of such a change in women's fashions. Compare the hemlines over the past fifty years. They went up or down about every ten years. Such a change makes a deep impact on the clothing market. Every new style requires a host of items to complete the desired effect. Shoes, underwear, and accessories are needed to round out each "new look." Each season, colors in the women's fashion industry in the United States are set by a committee of designers, manufacturers, and fashion editors. The color choices are made six months or a year before they actually appear on the fashion scene. This gives manufacturers an opportunity to coordinate their products with textile and garment manufacturers.

Once a trend has been set, the public must be informed of it. The communications industry is essential to promoting fashions. Promotion is done through magazines, newspapers, trade papers, radio, and television.

It is in the showrooms of garment manufacturers and designers that wholesale buyers make decisions about what they will order. Buyers must have a keen sense of fashion timing, as well as thorough knowledge of the tastes and preferences of their store's customers.

LADDERS AND LATTICES

There is a wide variety of careers at each rung of the clothing industry ladder. There are jobs that appeal to different kinds of people. There are jobs for people with different personalities and with different interests.

Have you sold clothes, fabrics, or shoes? Were you ever a clerk at a dry-cleaning store? Have you planned a fashion show or modeled in one? Liking people is an asset in clothing sales, marketing, and promotion.

Are you happy working with tools? Do you like gadgets? Do you like to know how things work? People who answer yes to these questions may be suited to some of the skilled jobs in clothing production: machine operators, pressers, and seamstresses.

Do you like organizing data? Do you enjoy mathematics? Do you like to keep track of things? An order clerk, purchasing agent, department manager, and stockboy need these skills.

Are you happier working alone? This characteristic and artistic talent are needed in display, layout, designing, or gift wrapping.

Are you interested in art or writing? Do you enjoy spending some time working unsupervised? Copywriters, editors, and ad specialists often have these characteristics.

Different clothing careers demand different qualifications. For some, advanced college degrees are necessary. For others, a bachelor's degree is adequate. For many, on-the-job experience and technical training are the best ways to learn the work.

Training for clothing production is available in high school and at special schools following high school. It can also be acquired on the job. Most of the special schools—like the Trade and Technical School in Los Angeles and the Fashion Institute of Technology in New York—are located in large cities. Their programs include on-the-job experience and classroom instruction. Many garment workers learn their trades as apprentices. They start at the bottom, learning various jobs, and work their way up.

Entry-level Jobs

The clothing industry offers a wide variety of entry-level jobs. Some of these, like sewing machine operator, offer limited opportunity for advancement. From others, like sales clerk or model, one can move into a variety of careers in clothing.

Models There are clothing models of every size, shape, and age. Beauty is not always necessary in this line of work. New faces are always needed in the fashion business. Some models are successful because they have a single outstanding or unique feature, such as their legs, hands, or teeth. Models model all kinds and varieties of clothes. Some specialize in a particular kind of garment or accessory. A model might model only shoes, gloves, or rings.

Some models are trained at professional modeling schools. Most fashion models are quite tall and usually thin. (This is because

Today, with so many stores competing for customers, window display is an important retail merchandising tool. Window designers must create effective presentations of the store's merchandise, using decorative themes that enhance the items being displayed.

CASE STUDY: MRS. BUTLER

THE SITUATION   *Mrs. Butler rang the door-bell to the third home on her delivery list. She sold cosmetics door to door and had two purchases to deliver to Mrs. Orr.*

"I have your order," she said, as Mrs. Orr opened the door. She delivered the items, made change, and reached for the new catalog to show her customer.

"I don't think I want to order anything else now," said Mrs. Orr. "I'll call you when I need something."

"My goodness!" answered Mrs. Butler. "Christmas is coming. Many people are ordering now so that they'll be sure to have the merchandise in time for the holidays. Why don't you just look through the catalog?"

"No, thank you," was the reply. "I've spent enough money on these products, and I don't want to be tempted. I like them, but I have other things to buy, too."

"Well," returned Mrs. Butler, "I'll just leave the catalog with you. If you see something that interests you, just give me a call." When Mrs. Orr again declined to accept the catalog, Mrs. Butler placed it back into her sample case. "I don't know how people can make money today," she commented. "I have lots of things to sell, but people just don't buy. I think I have money left over and then find that all I have is enough to make ends

meet. Well, you should give me a call if you want to order anything."

THE INTERVIEW   *Q: Was Mrs. Butler suggesting you should help her out by ordering more items?*
A: Probably not, although that is the impression she gave me, too. She's probably very frustrated about her inability to make as much money as she wants. She probably made that comment without really thinking of its effect on me.
Q: How were you affected by the comment?
A: I don't think that's the kind of thing to say to a customer. We all have money problems. My reaction was to turn her off right away. I don't like being pressured like that.
Q: Will you buy from her again?
A: Yes, but not because she's a good sales-woman. I happen to like using the product. I think that a salesperson should present a positive, rather than negative, approach to selling. She should give a better impression of self-confidence if she wants to encourage sales.

REACT   *What is your reaction to Mrs. Butler's closing comment to Mrs. Orr? What are the personal characteristics of salespeople that influence you to buy?*

---

photographs tend to make people look heavier.) Flawless grooming is absolutely essential. Constant care of the skin, hair, face, feet, and hands is a time-consuming and expensive occupation. Modeling is highly competitive, irregular, and strenuous. Models must maintain excellent health habits of sleep, diet, and exercise.

Top models earn top money. There are probably only ten or twelve steadily working top models in the country at a given time! The

number of working years is usually limited. Many former models continue in the industry as stylists, promotional experts, modeling instructors, or directors of modeling agencies.

A modeling portfolio containing from four to ten glossy photographs is essential for all photographers' models. It enables the potential employer to see the model's photogenic qualities. Models pay for the pictures in their portfolios, and they must keep them up to date.

As they work, retail clothing salespeople become familiar with the stock and with what customers will buy. They may become eligible for management jobs or become wholesale buyers.

Clothing is modeled throughout the apparel industry. Large design houses show collections each season. A small modeling staff is usually employed on a regular basis. Large manufacturers, advertising agencies, magazines, catalogs, and newspapers use modeling services. Some department stores employ salesgirl models. This can be an excellent entry into the field. Most modeling jobs are not steady. Modeling agencies book assignments for their free-lance clients. A few exclusive stores retain the services of one full-time model to show custom clothing or designer originals.

Some models work behind the scenes. The designer drapes muslin around them as he tries to implement a new idea. These models tell designers how a dress feels. The designer may make changes according to their suggestions.

Sewing-machine operators As a general rule, the higher the quality of the garment, the more sewing is done by hand. In factories where moderate-priced apparel is made, most sewing operations are done on special industrial sewing machines. Usually, garments are made on an assembly line. In making a blouse, for example, one sewing-machine operator might sew on the cuffs. Another might sew on the collar. Still another might hem the garment.

Industrial sewing machines are larger than those used at home. They may have special attachments for specific production operations. One such device holds buttons while they are sewn in place. On industrial sewing machines, certain operations that once required special skill on the part of the operator can now be performed automatically. One machine does intricate embroidery, while the operator merely watches, making sure that nothing goes wrong.

Besides needing manual dexterity, sewing-machine operators must be able to work fast. Generally, they are paid by the piece. The more garments on which they perform their assigned task, the more they will earn. Skills required in performing one operation are not too different from those required to perform another. Operators can easily switch from sewing pockets on shirts to sewing slide fasteners on trousers. Frequently, they can move from one task to another which merits a higher pay rate. Advancement up the career ladder is not too likely. A few former sewing-machine operators inspect and supervise the work of other operators.

Special Clothing-career Skills

Special clothing-career skills range from those of the shoe repairman to those of the dry-cleaning machine operator. They include the skills of the tailor and the dressmaker. They include the skills of the highly trained mechanics in textile mills and of the cutter and the pattern maker in the apparel factory.

Shoe repairmen Shoe repairmen perform all kinds of repairs on all kinds of shoes. Their primary task is to replace worn heels and soles. They also resew loose seams and mend broken straps. They generally polish shoes before returning them to their owners. Some shoe repairmen restyle shoes. They remove the old polish from shoes and dye them a different color. They add new buckles and other ornaments. Most shoe repairmen mend handbags and other leather and canvas goods. A few highly skilled shoe repairmen make special shoes for people with foot problems: they follow the prescriptions of podiatrists, or foot doctors.

Shoe repairmen must have manual dexterity. Their job requires them to operate a number of machines. They use sewing machines, for example, and power-operated heel nailers. They also use hand tools.

Most who presently do this work learned it by spending several years on the job. Some learn the trade in vocational schools. The majority of repairmen operate one-man shops. There, in addition to their mechanical skills, they can use managerial and sales skills. They must keep records and write out sales slips. They must deal with customers. Some shoe repairmen employ helpers, whom they must supervise. Others work in large shops, where they may become foreman.

Dressmakers Dressmakers are capable of completely making women's garments. They can work either by hand or with sewing machines. They do custom work. Each garment is made to fit a particular customer. Some dressmakers can begin with only a picture of the dress to be made. Others need a pattern. All work closely with the woman who is to wear the garment. They take her measurements. If some modifications from the original pattern are necessary, they make them. They then cut, sew, fit, and press.

Home sewing is a rapidly growing industry in which pattern companies play an important role. Once a pattern is produced, there is still a need for artists who can represent on pattern envelopes and in catalogues what the finished clothes will look like.

Hair stylists and beauticians need special skills and training for their careers. Their education is a continuous process, since grooming techniques and hairstyles are likely to follow fashion trends.

Manufacturers of higher-quality women's garments employ dressmakers to make sample garments. Many dressmakers are self-employed. Generally, they keep on hand patterns for each of their customers. They adapt patterns to the particular fabrics and styles of garments which their customers want. Some dressmakers set up part-time businesses from their own homes. Others may teach dressmaking courses at a YWCA or YWHA. Still others are employed by department stores and dry-cleaning establishments, where they do alterations.

It is possible to learn dressmaking on the job. Some have learned it in apparel factories, beginning with simple sewing operations and working their way up. A much quicker way to begin to master the trade is by taking clothing-construction or career-training courses in high school or in evening school.

Management Careers

Successful management people in one line of work share certain qualifications with those in other lines of work. All have the ability to assess and deal with people. All have the ability to absorb large amounts of information and make decisions on the basis of it. These shared characteristics allow management people some movement from one kind of management job to another. They are limited in this lateral movement, however, by the fact that different management jobs require large amounts of highly specific information. A department store buyer and a factory production manager need to master different kinds of information.

Department store buyers The merchandise that is available to you in any store was purchased by a buyer. Department store chains employ regional buyers. Local department stores have buyers for each department. Buyers specialize in clothing for infants, children, teens, men, or women. Other special lines are shoes, handbags, hosiery, lingerie, jewelry, formal clothes, and furs.

Buyers usually begin as salespeople. They may progress through a department store's training program. Buyers decide what to buy. In making these decisions, they weigh, among other things, fashion trends, color coordination, the characteristics of their customers, and the price at which their store can sell the garment. They visit showings of new lines. They meet salesmen representing clothing manufacturers. They keep purchasing records. They check displays. They set up employee work schedules. They deter-

CASE STUDY: FRED

THE SITUATION *Fred had opened his coin-operated laundry ten years ago. Up until that time, the people in the neighborhood had taken their laundry as far as two miles in order to use a similar self-service facility. When the workmen began installing the washers, many people welcomed Fred, expressing their interest in using a facility so close to home. The laundry was in use the very first night and business prospered. Fred was always on hand to make change for customers, to mop up overflowing soap suds, or to make minor repairs on the machines.*

That was ten years ago. Fred remembered the conversations, the cooperation of his customers, and the late hours for last-minute laundry problems. Now things were different and he couldn't remember when the change had begun. He still mopped up, but the spills now resulted from smashed windows in the machines. He closed early because it was unsafe to remain open after dark. Customers refused to come at night because they disliked walking past the groups of young people gathered in front of the store.

As Fred unlocked the laundry door, he remembered his son's advice to him. "Close up, Dad. You're spending more money on repairs than this business is worth. It's a losing battle. You can't change the neighborhood back to the way it was ten years ago."

Maybe his son knew what he was talking about. Before him, Fred saw a morning's work to be done before the machines could be used. Someone had entered through the back and broken the door latches of several washers. Cleaning supplies were thrown around. Crayon marks had been rubbed over the washers and walls. Discouraged, Fred turned out the lights, locked the door, and walked away from his business.

THE INTERVIEW *Q: Aren't you going to clean the store today?*
A: What's the use? I spend all my time and energy putting the place back together, only to have it destroyed again. I can't afford to keep my business going anymore.
Q: Are you going out of business?
A: Yes, I'm quitting. I enjoyed this work and kept my customers happy. But I can't do it all alone anymore. I don't know what's wrong with people today. Some of the ones who use this laundry are also the ones who do the damage. They have no respect for property. I'll move out of town to some place where my customers and I get along better with each other. No use batting my head against a stone wall here.

REACT *Why do people damage such self-service facilities? What other advantages and disadvantages accompany ownership of such facilities?*

---

mine sale items. They handle customer problems, sign credit returns, train salespeople, and manage the department.

A high school course in distributive education, coupled with work experience, would provide a valuable beginning for a career in clothing sales and marketing. Community colleges offer sales training for potential buyers. The Tobe-Coburn School in New York City is a privately operated school for buyers. Colleges also offer sales courses. Their graduates may receive higher salaries.

Buyers work with people; persuasiveness and diplomacy are two helpful qualities for them to have. They also need foresight. They must be able to predict fashion trends.

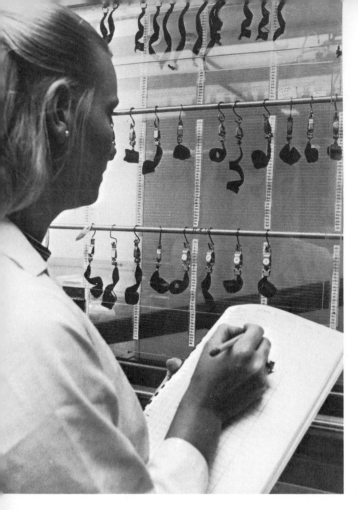

There are many opportunities for chemists in the clothing and grooming industries. In cosmetics research, chemists work to develop new products and run tests to determine that they are safe and effective.

Production managers Production managers in apparel factories oversee the entire production process. They estimate how much it will cost to produce a certain garment. They figure out how the work should move from one worker to another. They check the work as it is being done to make sure that standards of quality are being maintained. It is even their responsibility to hire new employees and to train them.

At one time, most production managers worked their way up through the ranks. It is still possible to become a production manager in this way, although the process takes many years. Today, a college education is increasingly important for this job. College graduates begin as management trainees.

Professional Careers

As in other industries, most professional careers in the clothing industry require specific educational training. The apparel industry in particular, however, has a long history of being highly competitive. Many professionals in this industry—clothing designers, for example—learn much of their trade as they are working their way up the career ladder. Their creativity, however, is something they have; it cannot be learned.

Home economists Home economists are connected with the clothing industry through their teaching and extension work. Some are employed directly by manufacturers.

Home economics majors with a specialty in clothing and textiles can teach clothing construction and textiles in public or private schools. Most teachers have had on-the-job experience. They teach custom construction, consumer education, and clothing selection.

A Cooperative Extension home economist serves the people of a community or county. She uses her technical clothing knowledge to prepare educational literature and special interest programs for homemakers, adults, and young people in the 4-H program, or any other person who asks for services.

Manufacturers employ home economists. These home economists develop promotional brochures, educational programs, and product information for consumers. Many also demonstrate new products. Experience in teaching, writing, fashion promotion, and industry are assets. Four years of college training is a prerequisite.

Textile chemists Textile chemists are trained to work in areas related to the technical aspects of fabrics. Working in laboratories, many undertake research to develop new products and processes related to fabrics. Some create new fibers in their test tubes. Others explore the characteristics of known fabrics: the temperature at which fabrics burn, the elasticity and durability of fabrics, and how fabrics react to dyes, bleaches, finishes, and cleaning solvents. Some textile chemists develop new dyes and finishes. Others improve the manufacturing methods used in making fabrics. Still others are engaged in testing manufactured dyes and finishes to make sure that they are safe.

Textile chemists are also employed outside the laboratory. They fill positions requiring a technical knowledge of textiles. Some in management positions supervise the research and product development being conducted in laboratories. Figuring the cost of producing a certain fiber requires knowledge of chemistry. Textile sales representatives benefit from having backgrounds in textile chemistry. A textile chemist might combine teaching at the university level with acting as a consultant to fabric manufacturers.

Textile chemists are employed in many industries. Manufacturers of textiles, manufacturers of laundry and dry-cleaning equipment, and makers of dyes, starches, detergents, and finishes all need textile chemists. A chemist's education begins with a bachelor's degree and often extends to the master's and doctoral levels. Work in industry provides additional job training. The higher degrees are increasingly important.

The chemist must be able to think abstractly and work with delicate and costly equipment. Those in management and sales need a knack for working with people.

Clothing designers Clothing designers come up with and express ideas for new garments. They may select elements from earlier de-

A career in textile design offers opportunity for creativity. Textile designers must have knowledge of textile properties and of the processes by which designs can be transferred to fabric. Some may specialize in a certain fabric or process.

signs and combine them. A few top designers have the talent to develop designs that spark new fashion trends. Designers work in different ways. Some begin by sketching their ideas. Some begin by adjusting muslin on a live model or a dress form.

Clothing designers specialize; because women's wear generally varies more than men's, designers of women's garments usually have the opportunity to show more variety in their designs. Men's clothing designers are often more knowledgeable about certain manufacturing processes. They would be more likely to know how to limit the amount of fabric required to make a stylish suit or sport jacket.

Successful designers—designers whose dresses sell—earn top money. The competition to reach such a position is quite heavy. The requirements for the job are hard to pin down. Designers need to understand clothing construction and know something about sewing. They need a feeling for fabrics and the way they drape. A sketch that suggests what they have in mind will do. Equally important is the ability to guess what the public will buy.

Clothing design courses are offered in schools of art and design. College courses in art history, anthropology, sociology, and other social sciences can offer the aspiring designer an understanding of what people have worn in the past and why, as well as of what makes people do what they are doing now. Particular courses in garment design can give someone a head start. Some models and workers in apparel factories have become designers in this way.

Designers free-lance or are on staff. They can move from one part of the clothing industry to another. For example, they may move from garment manufacturing to pattern manufacturing.

THE ENVIRONMENTAL COST OF OPPORTUNITY

Horatio Alger was a novelist who lived earlier in our century. He wrote tales of poor boys who overcame incredible odds to make good. In a way, this is the legacy of the garment industry. Sheer determination to become successful has helped a lot of people to the top. In this industry, many people have found opportunities to earn a living, opportunities to reach certain goals.

In the apparel industry, as in many other industries, taking advantage of opportunities often has an environmental cost. We might do well to ask how we can minimize this cost. In working towards our goals, we must consider the effect our actions will have on the world in which we live.

THINK BACK

Many levels of skills, talents, and education are needed in the clothing industry.
Discuss: *How can an individual decide if he "fits" a particular job?*

Interest in making, repairing, or selling clothes influences career decisions.
Discuss: *How can you help the person who "doesn't know where to begin thinking" about jobs?*

Experience, training, and skill improve chances of job satisfaction in the clothing industry.
Discuss: *How can the talented but inexperienced person get started in the clothing industry?*

Successful self-employment is related to background, experience, good business sense, and time.
Discuss: *Is there such a thing as a "self-made" man or woman today?*

LOOK AROUND

1. Which area of the clothing industry most appeals to you? Why? Which job within that area attracts you? What jobs are available locally?
2. As a customer, what do you consider desirable characteristics of a clothing salesperson? Which of those characteristics might reflect store policy? Which might be personality characteristics of an individual?
3. Interview classmates employed in various jobs related to clothing. What advice concerning their type of job can they offer to applicants for the position?
4. Develop a "Have You Thought of This?" bulletin board showing hobbies that might lead to future work in the clothing industry.
5. Make a display showing handmade clothing and accessory items that might be sold for profit. Investigate possibilities of placing items for sale in a local gift shop or clothing store.
6. What do you consider the "glamour" jobs in the clothing industry? Why are they so appealing? Tell the details of the work involved in one of these.
7. What is involved in selling cosmetics or clothing items door to door. What personal qualifications are required for such jobs?

FOLLOW YOUR PATH

PATH ONE: Provide a Wardrobe Consultation Service

Step 15   Which of your needs and goals do you think a job like this one might help you realize? How? Would you like to earn a living in an occupation related to this path? Can you think of a career in clothing that might suit you better? Which one? Why?

Step 16   What occupations in the clothing industry are related to this path? How? Gather information from the library and from your school guidance counselor.

Step 17   Which other parts of the clothing industry did you come into contact with as you followed this path? Make up a chart. Put your own service in the center. Draw arrows showing how these other industries relate to your wardrobe service.

PATH TWO: Manufacture an Apparel Item

Step 16   Same as Step 15 of Path One.

Step 17   Same as Step 17 of Path One.

Step 18   Add up the number of hours everyone in your company spent working. Add up the amount of money you would have if you had sold all your items at the price you set. Divide the total hours into the total money. The result is your pay per hour. Do you consider this a "good" wage? Discuss ways it could be improved.

Step 19   Visit your guidance counselor or the library for information about the garment industry. Does the way you organized your company differ from the way most apparel businesses are organized? If so, how? What improvements—if any—might you make in your company's organization?

PATH THREE: Open a Clothing Store

Step 16   Same as Step 15 of Path One.

Step 17   Same as Step 17 of Path One.

PATH FOUR: Plan a Fashion Magazine

Step 15   Same as Step 15 of Path One.

Step 16   Same as Step 17 of Path One.

Step 17   Show your magazine to members of your class. Ask them what they think of it. Does a magazine like yours exist? If not, would young adults buy it?

Perspectives on housing

Housing decisions occupy a more central position in people's lives than do decisions of many other kinds.

One reason for this is that housing is expensive. How much people spend on housing influences how much they have left to spend on other things.

Another reason is that almost no housing can be easily moved. In selecting a place to live, people choose more than ceilings, walls, and floors. They pick the communities in which they will live.

Still another reason is that people's dwellings—and the ways in which they furnish them—are reflections of who they are and who they think they are.

In this unit, try to gain some perspective on this influential world of housing. Begin by choosing one of the paths below.

PATH ONE: Make a Plan to Improve Your Own Home

This path involves evaluating your at-home activities, evaluating living space, possibly making collages, and making rough sketches and floor plans. You will also be looking through magazines, visiting a museum or library, going comparison shopping, looking at different types of housing, and discussing plans with your family and classmates.

Step 1 Write an essay describing your feelings about your home. If you wish, illustrate your essay.

Step 2 Draw pictures or make collages which express your ideas for your "dream residence." Write captions.

PATH TWO: Form a Family on the Move

This path involves acting out decision-making situations before the class, discussing plans with classmates and professionals, and clipping and organizing pictures from magazines.

Step 1 Have a meeting. Choose the family member you will play. Determine the age and interests of your character. If you have a job, find out approximately how much it pays.

Step 2 Announce to the class who you are and what you do. Act out the following situation: The principal wage-earner has accepted a job paying fifteen dollars more a week. The job is in the Path Four community, about which you know very little. Discuss the setting and your housing preferences.

PATH THREE: Be an Interior Designer

You may follow this path alone or with others. This path involves clipping and organizing pictures from magazines, making floor plans, making color and pattern combinations, expressing decorating ideas through drawings and collages, discussing decorating ideas with classmates, designing furniture, making model furnishings, and preparing a brochure.

Step 1 Cut out magazine photos and draw pictures showing the furnishings you like.

Step 2 Design what you feel would be an ideal living or family room for the Path Two family. Make a drawing or collage showing how it would look to sit facing each of the four walls. Make notes explaining the advantages of each feature to each family member.

PATH FOUR: Design a Community

Work with a number of your classmates to plan a new community. This path involves making decisions as a group and dividing tasks among yourselves with regard to such functions as laying out a community, naming it, designing houses, making model houses, doing research, writing a brochure, interviewing classmates and people in your community, and making plans with classmates.

Step 1 Hold a meeting. Elect a chairman. Elect a secretary who will take notes during meetings.

Step 2 Hold a meeting to decide what your community will need to be self-supporting (homes, for example, and places to work). Make a list.

Step 3 On several large pieces of paper, lay out your community. Will you restrict certain areas for homes and other areas for factories?

Step 4 Select a name for the community.

CHAPTER 17

Background for Housing Decisions

Members of the animal kingdom stake out a territory, an area in the environment that is theirs and theirs alone. They find some niche or corner of the world in which to mate and raise their young. Most will defend their nest, burrow, or grazing land from interlopers. Human beings, too, have a strong feeling about having a place of their own secure from intrusion. The primary purpose of housing is, in fact, protection from the environment. At the same time, our housing links us to the environment. Shelter is fixed in a place; water pipes, electrical wires, and telephone and gas lines tic housing to the resources needed to run a modern home. Housing becomes an extension of ourselves when it provides us with a means to express our personal tastes.

SHELTER
AND HUMAN ECOLOGY

You may live in the city, the country, or the suburbs. You may live in a high-rise apartment building or a single family home. The building in which you live may be new or old. It may be publicly or privately financed. It may be made from any number of different materials. No matter where and how you live, your housing probably reflects some of the advances of modern technology. Heating and plumbing, the wide variety of available materials—these and other technological benefits are so common that you may take them for granted. Yet the homes in which you live are made from natural resources. Housing occupies space. It is designed both to protect us from our environment and to provide a setting for daily living.

Environment and Housing

Housing can most readily and economically be made from locally available materials. When designed in harmony with local geographic and climatic conditions, a regional architecture tends to be created.

Climate and geography *Climate* refers to the range of temperature and amount of moisture and wind in a given region. *Geography* refers, among other things, to the physical features of the earth—to its hills and valleys, to its lakes and rivers. The climate and geography of a region may pose challenges of a particular kind to the physical well-being of those who live there.

As protection against cold, people have devised different types of housing. For example, certain Mongol tribes who must endure Central Asia's bitter winters live in *yurts*, which are circular dwellings built of felt-covered wooden frames. The felt acts as insulation, keeping out the cold and keeping in the heat. Europeans have traditionally kept out the winter by building houses with thick walls. One writer examined the thicknesses of walls throughout Europe, from England to Russia. He found that as he went east, where the winters are colder, the walls became thicker. The English found that nine-inch walls provided adequate insulation. In Russia, twenty-eight-inch thicknesses were not uncommon.

As protection from heat, desert Arabs live in long tents. The tops of the tents block out the sun, while the sides may be raised for ventilation. Arabs living in the cities and towns of Morocco approach the problem of heat differently. They live in houses built around central courtyards. Each room faces and is ventilated by the courtyard. As added protection, rooms on the second story often have covered balconies that block the sun.

The Cuna Indians of Central America face a different sort of environmental problem. The islands on which they live are partially or entirely flooded at high tide. They overcome this inconvenience by erecting their houses on stilts. After the sea comes in and goes out, their dwellings are left intact. Peoples from rain forest areas also commonly live in stilt houses.

Availability Materials used in housing are often those that are most available. In earlier times, available materials meant natural resources that were close to the site where the dwelling was being constructed. Plains Indians, for example, used the skins of animals they hunted for their wigwams and furnishings. The inhabitants of the African savanna used grass for their huts. The first North American settlers, who cleared the forests for farmland, used logs for their cabins. On the treeless prairies, settlers used

A scarcity of building materials, extremes of weather, and threats from enemies have forced societies to pool their resources in order to survive. Homes that have common walls conserve materials and create a closeness that comforts neighbors, as shown in "The Winding Path," by Maurice Sterne.

When building sites are planned without regard to the nature of the land or the local climate, the results can be disastrous. This house was built on a flat lot carved out of a hillside. After heavy rains caused a landslide, the owners suddenly found themselves with no backyard.

sod for huts. In timber-rich Finland, even in the cities and towns, over 60 percent of the dwellings are made mostly of wood. In other parts of Europe where the forests have long been gone, buildings of local stone and earth have traditionally been more common.

Today, partly because of improved transportation, home builders have a wide range of materials from which to choose. Furthermore, in recent decades, industrial materials —like steel, aluminum, plastics, structural glass, and concrete—have been developed.

New materials make possible new kinds of structures. The tall skyscrapers familiar to modern eyes could not have been built with the materials available at the time of the American Revolution.

New Control, New Responsibilities

Technological improvements have increased our options in deciding what, where, and how to build. At the same time, we now have more people to house. Matching our resources, our technology, and our priorities in housing is a basic challenge of the future.

Environmental control In planning housing, modern industrial man is less at the mercy of the environment than were his ancestors. He can establish communities far from his sources of food and water. Modern heating and air conditioning have made it possible to control extremes of temperature and humidity. Man can now maintain an indoor environment that he finds uniformly comfortable. In time, scientists expect that they may also be able to control some factors in the external environment. Architect-engineer Buckminster Fuller foresees a time when whole communities may be encased in plastic domes. Another architect, Paolo Soleri, has proposed whole cities designed in the form of bridges spanning canyons. He has made models of cities that float on water and cities that cling to cliffs. Each city is a single huge structure containing facilities for hundreds of thousands of people.

Conservation of natural resources To construct most modern houses requires many natural resources. These include the materials of which the house is made and the materials used to make the equipment which in turn is used to make the house. Houses take up valuable space. In building and operating a house, energy is used.

The home manager must be aware that as he turns a dial, flicks a switch, or sets a thermostat, hard-to-replace energy is being consumed. Within the home, decisions concerning the use of technically generated energy may be among the consumer's most far-reaching decisions. This is true for both people in a one-family dwelling and for people in multiple-dwelling housing.

Those involved in building dwellings ought also to consider the kind and amount of natural resources they use up. Conservation of space is one reason why Paolo Soleri has designed his concentrated cities. He feels that such well-planned cities will leave more natural landscape free for everyone.

Contemporary Homes and Habitats

Clearing forests, leveling hills, and building along riverbanks change the environment. Such actions, taken to construct housing, may in time change our climate. Indiscrim-

No house should ever be on any hill or on anything. It should be of the hill, belonging to it, so hill and house could live together each the happier for the other.

from *Autobiography* (Frank Lloyd Wright)

inate leveling of land for such purposes may result in floods, landslides, and other catastrophes. In recent times, men have built up much of the open space between settled areas. Roads, highways, the automobile, and mass transportation have vastly changed the face of our nation and the way people live.

Our crowded cities, spread-out suburbs, and rural areas offer widely different environments for living. The way you live will be strongly influenced by whether you live in the country, the suburbs, or the city. Some people live all their lives in one type of area. But more and more Americans—as many as one family in five—move their homes for one reason or another each year, experiencing rural, suburban, and urban living.

Living in the country Fewer North Americans today live the sort of isolated rural life that was once common. There are hardly any places left in the United States that are so remote that residents do not have easy access to some town or city. This is partly the result of the fact that towns and cities have grown and spread out. It is partly the result of improved communications. TV and the automobile have penetrated the countryside. Telephones are available almost everywhere. Because people in rural areas can get to and are in contact with cities and towns, their living patterns have changed. They are closer to the problems of urban communities.

Living in cities American cities are growing at a rapid rate. It is estimated that by the end of this century, some 200 million people will

271

be living in about 200 cities. If that happens, 80 percent of the population will be living on 10 percent of the land. This growth of our cities has been accompanied by the growth of urban problems. Among the major problems is how to create enough adequate housing for low- and middle-income families. Other problems can be traced to the economic and ethnic diversity of the cities' populations. When people with different values and goals are crowded together, conditions of stress are bound to result.

Problems increase as population increases. The problem of meeting the basic needs of large populations—of providing jobs, education, transportation, and health, welfare, and recreation facilities for city dwellers—is reaching monumental proportions. The budget of New York City, for example, is second only to that of the federal government. We can expect that the quality of life in our cities will remain a national concern.

Living in the suburbs Increasing numbers of people live in the suburbs, where they hope to avoid urban problems. They hope to live a life that combines the pleasures of a reasonably uncrowded outdoors with the comforts of a community that provides a wide range of services. Many have found, however, that the problems they hoped to escape have not been left behind. Instead, the problems have often followed them from the cities to the suburbs.

People are still drawn to a fireside, as they were in this nineteenth century scene. But in those times, the fireplace met physical, as well as social, needs. The fireplace was a source of heat and light, and sometimes the place to prepare food.

Because living quarters can be arranged or specially designed for almost any requirements, housing helps to meet the need for independence. Although an invalid, this woman is self-sufficient in a kitchen that has equipment, storage, and working space within her reach.

For some suburbanites, commuting to a job in the city may be a problem. Train or bus service may be inadequate; crowded roads during rush hour may make driving a car infuriating or impractical. Within their own community, schools, shopping centers, and playgrounds may not be close by. They often find, to their dismay, that urban problems are suburban problems.

HOW SHELTER
MEETS BASIC NEEDS

Housing helps us meet some needs directly, such as protection from the elements. It helps us meet other needs indirectly. Housing provides, for example, a place to store, prepare, and consume food. It provides a setting in which higher levels of needs can be met.

Physical Needs

We have already discussed the ways in which food and clothing help to maintain body temperature. Housing can also help to meet this basic need. Appropriate housing can shield our bodies from the extremes of heat and cold. It can also provide the necessary protection from wind, rain, and snow. Available within the shelter, or at least from the surrounding environment, must be such resources as air, space, light, and water. Facilities to meet the physical need to remove body wastes and to obtain proper sleep and rest are also necessary. To promote sound physical health, housing should protect the resident from disease-carrying pests, microorganisms, and excessive noise. Households and life-styles are built around meeting these needs.

CASE STUDY: SALLY AND DUANE

THE SITUATION *"How did you happen to hear about this house?" Jean asked Duane. She looked around, hardly believing the condition of the house. There was just a bare shell remaining of what had once been a farmhouse. Plaster had fallen off the ceilings and walls. There were no inside bathroom facilities or heating. And the house was miles from even the smallest shopping center. Only after at least two months of steady work could anyone possibly live there.*

"A realtor told me about it," answered Duane. "The owner was going to tear it down because no one has lived in it for seven years. He said that if I agreed to fix it up inside, we could rent it for a bare minimum each month. We took him up on his offer. I think it's great!"

Jean wondered how Duane's wife, Sally, liked the idea of "building" a home so far away from everyone. She had heard Sally refer to the place as "Duane's house." And Duane had complained that Sally rarely offered to help him with any of the work.

"Sally isn't as happy about it as I am," continued Duane. "She'd like to live in an apartment. The other day she visited a furnished model of a townhouse and became enthused about that. I just wouldn't be happy in any kind of housing but this. I can make this into exactly what I want it to be. In fact, I'm going to feel bad when I've done all the work on the inside. Then what will I work on?"

"I've noticed that people seem to be able to adjust to many situations," commented Jean. "You could live in an apartment."

"Oh, I'd get used to it," replied Duane. "But I certainly wouldn't be happy there. This is what I want."

THE INTERVIEW *Q: What do you think of Duane's choice of a home, Jean?*
A: I think it has a lot of potential. The thing that bothers me is the one-sidedness of the situation.
Q: Will that cause problems?
A: Not if they can compromise. For instance, they might agree to rent the house in the location pleasing to Duane and furnish it in a style pleasing to Sally. But they don't seem to have reached any kind of compromise. A home is a big part of life. For some people, it's their way of telling others about themselves. Sally doesn't seem to feel that way about this house.
Q: Do you think Duane should give up his ideal house?
A: Someone needs to give in a little. I think that two people should be able to come to some kind of agreement satisfactory to both.

REACT *Who should make the final decision in selecting a home? What do you think will come of this situation between Duane and Sally?*

Psychological Needs

Housing provides the setting for personal growth, as well as physical development. A home that offers family members opportunities to grow mentally and emotionally provides a foundation for psychological health.

The need for safety and security. Housing is the principal feature of most people's near environment. To most, housing becomes a home—a symbol of the safety and security necessary to psychological health. Freedom from intrusion is considered by most of us to be a basic human right. The Founding Fathers of the United States thought so, too.

They built into the Constitution guarantees against illegal search and seizure.

Within the home, personal safety involves protection from falls, electrical shocks, fire, and other hazards. Thus, regular maintenance of the home and safeguards against injury meet the need for safety and security.

The need for identity Housing always tells something about the people living in it. It becomes an extension of their personalities. It is part of their public image. It reflects their self-concept. The place in which you live, the things with which you furnish it, and the way that you arrange these furnishings all say something about you.

The need for love Each home has an emotional climate created by the people who live there. In a positive climate, people feel some closeness toward each other. Ideally, each person is accepted by others for being who and what he is. In such an atmosphere, feelings of love—which can be shown in many ways—can develop. Each person derives some strength from these positive experiences in home living.

The need for independence. Housing that offers opportunities for independent activities to those who live there helps to create self-sufficient personalities. In such homes, furnishings and equipment are arranged so that young children can safely learn to meet their basic need to explore and to learn about the environment. There they can learn to feed, clothe, and groom themselves. A well-planned home takes into consideration the layouts and arrangements of furnishings, thus enhancing the independence of those who may be handicapped by age or illness.

The need for stimulation and variety Within the home, an individual or a family can devise many ways to meet the basic need for stimulation and variety. Although certain basic features, such as the layout of the rooms and

Y ou have not known
 Men's lives, deaths, toils, and teens;
 You are but a heap of stick and stone:
 A new house has no sense
  of the have-beens.

from *The Two Houses* (Thomas Hardy)

the placement of fixtures, will probably stay the same, there are many ways to create interest in the near environment. Chapter 19, which deals with home decorating and furnishing, will help you understand how this need can be met.

Social Needs

Housing provides a resource for meeting social needs. The basic social unit served by housing is the family. As we have just seen, housing provides the setting for human growth and development. As contacts and interests expand with maturity, housing begins to meet more complicated social needs for young adults.

The need to belong Housing places you in a neighborhood and a community. Interest in the surrounding environment helps to bring about improvements in housing. Involvement in neighborhood and community affairs helps to meet your social need to belong to a special group.

Manufacturers of furnishings and home appliances often appeal to the need to belong to stimulate sales of their products. Some householders may try to meet this need by buying the same style of home furnishings or the same appliances as their neighbors.

Community resources such as recreation centers and clubs also meet the basic need to belong. Many people who have the opportunity to choose where and how to live will take the social opportunities available in a given community into account.

The sense of being "at home" extends beyond the actual housing that people occupy. They are "at home" in their neighborhoods and communities, as well. The use of recreation facilities and other community resources draws people together and helps to meet their need to belong.

Spiritual Needs

Housing can provide the means to refresh and uplift the human spirit. To reach his spiritual potential, the individual needs privacy. To the degree that housing provides privacy and opportunities for reflection and meditation, therefore, it can be said to contribute to meeting the individual's basic spiritual needs. In those homes in which religious activity is a focus of family life, symbols of faith may also be present.

Overarching Needs

The quality of housing has much to do with the ability of individuals and of families to reach their full potential. Housing that provides opportunities to explore one's interests and to test one's talents makes a positive contribution to self-actualization. Allocating space for study, hobbies, and other personally satisfying activities helps to meet these needs for self-fulfillment.

INFLUENCES ON HOUSING CHOICES

Current housing decisions can have a great influence on the quality of your future life. Individual and family needs change over time, and housing may have to be flexible enough to meet such changing needs. The plan to buy a house may be the most important financial investment a person will ever make. The decision to purchase housing is related to present and future income. Rental housing, while not requiring a large initial investment, still takes a considerable portion of a person's monthly income. Housing provides a setting for day-to-day living. Housing, furnishings, and equipment must be planned with present and future needs and interests taken into account. Some people acquire furnishings and equipment before they move into their own home. They will want housing adequate for their possessions —and for future possessions. Others may only wish to live in housing that comes furnished. Family size, health, and income are among the factors influencing housing choices. Housing shortages in many parts of the country seriously limit the freedom of choice in securing shelter. Many families move, and housing may not be permanent. If you know that present housing may not answer your long-range needs, you will need to consider moving costs.

Your Present and Future Needs

For a person living alone, space needs are fairly simple to determine. For young couples living in their first home and planning to have children, housing may quickly become inadequate. In such cases, it can be important to estimate present and future space needs.

Other needs are also involved. In selecting housing, you are also selecting your neighbors—the people with whom you can expect to meet some of your social needs. If a family has children, the choice of housing will affect their choice of friends and playmates. It may also determine what sort of schools the children will be able to attend.

Your Present
and Future Income

Housing and home furnishings represent a considerable financial outlay. A person can use credit to acquire either. How much an individual or a family is willing and able to pay for housing is related to present needs and long-range goals. If a high rent is paid, for example, it may not be possible to

accumulate the down payment needed to reach a goal of home ownership. Paying for a home makes heavy demands on income. It limits the amount of money available to spend on other things. For this reason, it is important to give serious thought to the source and stability of income when considering home ownership. You may decide that renting is the soundest way for you to pay for housing. You may find that some form of *government subsidized* housing best suits your purposes. In such housing, the government, in effect, pays part of the rent. In order to be eligible to live there, your income must fall within certain guidelines.

Your Present
and Future Interests

Many "extras" provided in certain types of housing may seem very attractive at the outset; but how often will a resident actually

People often adopt a standard of living that is not based as much on their personal values as on those of society, creating a wide gap between their standard of living and their level of living.

use recreation rooms, swimming pools, laundries, and other conveniences which are included in the cost of rental? How well does housing offer opportunities to pursue interests and hobbies? For example, pets are not permitted in some kinds of housing. If your hobbies generate noise and disturbance, you may have to seek special types of housing.

A life-style will influence not only the choice of housing, but the furnishings, as well. For example, some people will not buy matching furniture. They get more satisfaction out of using "odds and ends."

You may otherwise have trouble with neighbors when you run a power saw or play the piano at odd hours of the day or night.

Availability of Housing

There are wide differences in the availability of certain types of housing. Some regions are chronically in the grip of housing shortages. This is often true of the more desirable locations in major cities. Housing shortages contribute to making housing a difficult need for some to meet adequately. Thus, in considering housing, you will have to be realistic about whether all your needs can be met with the resources you have available. It is often necessary, when housing is in short supply, to make compromise decisions.

GOALS AND VALUES IN HOUSING

Because your choice of housing influences your way of living in so many ways, housing decisions have a high priority for individuals and for families. In making housing decisions, consider the values and goals that housing may be used to reach.

The term *standard of living* embraces the values and goals you seek in living. Among other things, it refers to your attitudes toward privacy and companionship, toward comfort and leisure. It refers to the goods and services you most want to have. The availability of resources in the household determines the level of living possible within it. Your *level of living* is the standard of living you actually achieve.

While they live with their parents, most young adults adapt their living style to their family's level. Their parents' standard of living influences their own. When young adults establish homes of their own, they sometimes reject the style of the parental home in favor of one that more closely reflects their own values and goals.

CASE STUDY: MARLENE

THE SITUATION *The class assignment had been to find a small wooden object that could easily be refinished. As Mrs. Hayes looked around the room, she noticed Marlene carefully examining a wooden rocker. She walked over to her. "That's a beautiful little chair," she commented. "Where did you find it?"*

Marlene looked up and smiled. "My mother found it in the basement of our building. It needs a lot of work, but she said I could bring it to class to paint."

"To paint?" asked Mrs. Hayes. "You mean you would rather antique this than refinish it? Will that go with your other bedroom furnishings?"

"It's not for my room," replied Marlene. "Mother wants it placed in the living room. And instead of caning the seat, she wants me to put a red velvet cover on it.

Mrs. Hayes thought the idea sounded nice. "I hope she doesn't get upset when people sit in it," she commented. "The velvet may get worn down more quickly than another fabric might."

"Sit in it?" Marlene asked in disbelief. "No one will sit on this chair. It will just be for decoration. Anyway, my mother hardly uses the living room. She has it decorated just for show. My friends and I aren't allowed to set one foot in that room. When someone comes to see me, we have to go into the den. The living room will be the place for this chair."

THE INTERVIEW *Q: Do you think most people are as strict as Marlene's mother is about home decorating, Mrs. Hayes?*
A: A few of my older friends fall into that category. They've raised their families and now feel they should be able to live the way they want. Once they decide where furniture is to be placed, they want the room to remain looking like a picture.
Q: Do you decorate this way?
A: No. I feel that setting up such rigid rules about a home creates a strain on the people living there. How can they relax if they must be concerned about the impression created by a room?
Q: Does that mean people should not worry at all about how their place looks?
A: Of course not. I don't mean that sloppiness is acceptable. With all the confusion of everyday living, we must be able to go to some place that is calm and peaceful. A neat home can provide that calm atmosphere. But such strict concern with the way a home looks indicates that the home and things in it may be more important than the people in it. I don't think that's a healthy situation for a happy family life. Maybe Marlene's mother feels differently, though.

REACT *Do you agree with Mrs. Hayes' ideas about home furnishing? Would you like to live in Marlene's home?*

Everyone's standard of living is partly determined by the surrounding culture. Living standards are strongly affected by the type of housing, its location, and even by the size and arrangement of the space within the home. Space that is broken up into a number of rooms tends to compartmentalize people and activities. Closed space promotes privacy. Open space promotes interaction.

Comfort and Convenience

Most people hope for some degree of comfort and convenience in their housing. What their idea of comfort is varies with culture, life-style, and individual preference. In Japan, people sleep with wooden blocks under their heads. Most Americans would consider this a hardship. For a person with a health prob-

It may not be practical for many young homemakers to live in or visit the country to provide safe and healthful outdoor play for their children. These people may choose to live in neighborhoods that have "pocket parks" and small playgrounds convenient to their homes.

lem, a walk-up apartment may be inconvenient. The mother of small children could also find such an apartment unsatisfactory.

In many industrialized countries, plumbing and electricity are generally regarded as essential to comfort and convenience. In colder climates, many feel uncomfortable without central heating. Some feel cramped in a small space that others would regard as cozy. To some it would seem inconvenient to use a dining area for other activities—like hobbies and study.

Basically, whatever their style of living, most people find certain features contribute to ease of living. Among these are clear "traffic lanes" for easy movement through the home, fixtures placed where they are needed and used, and storage facilities adequate for a household's needs.

Privacy

Some people seem happier with large numbers of people around them continually. Others prefer to spend a good deal of time alone. Everyone seems to need some privacy. There are different ways in which they attain it. Some achieve privacy by withdrawing into themselves. Others seek a separate room. In crowded households, privacy may be hard to arrange. It should nevertheless be considered in evaluating housing.

Companionship and Communication

When a number of people live in the same household, they usually find different ways in which to communicate with one another.

Some communication takes place on the run. Much occurs in special parts of the home. Some homes have a living room or a family room that provides an area for sharing ideas and experiences. In such a room, members of a household may share activities, like games and hobbies. The dining area, during meals and at other times, may also serve as a place for talk and togetherness.

Housing may also be the setting in which friends are entertained.

Beauty

Esthetic values in housing are among the most personal. Some people have a highly developed sense of color, line, form, and scale. People react differently to various textures and to different styles of design and decoration. A few are more aware of standards of craftsmanship and workmanship. The importance that an individual places on beauty in the near environment (as in the natural environment) varies with exposure, experience, and education. What some people seek and enjoy for the home others may find tasteless and uninteresting. Some people show great creativity and resourcefulness in turning "hopeless" housing into warm and inviting homes.

GOALS AND STYLES

A person's housing, then, is an integral part of his life. It is the focus of his near environment. It is a reflection of who he is. This is not only what housing is today; it is what housing was in the past, as well. The differences in housing over the centuries are partly attributable to changing ideas about privacy, comfort, companionship, and beauty. As these ideas have changed, so have styles of architecture, furniture, and interior design. In the next chapter, we will discuss these styles and suggest ways to use them.

THINK BACK

Housing helps us adapt to and control the effects of the natural environment upon our lives.
Discuss: *Has man been able to "conquer" nature completely?*

Concern for the preservation of our natural environment ought to accompany all plans for fulfilling housing needs.
Discuss: *What would a blueprint for such a "balance of power" between man and nature include?*

Adequate housing helps fulfill many of the basic social, physical, and emotional needs of each family member.
Discuss: *How does a person make a "house" into a "home"?*

Satisfying housing decisions result from careful thinking about present and future needs, goals, and resources.
Discuss: *What thoughts about the future might be most influential in housing decisions?*

Where you live greatly influences the comfort, health, and growth of family members.
Discuss: *What are the possibilities of a person being able to "live anywhere"?*

LOOK AROUND

1. What community problems have an effect on the lives of you and your family? What are the advantages of living in your community?

2. What is the difference between adequate and inadequate housing? What are the ill effects of inadequate housing upon family members?

3. How can your school be made more "homey"? Devise and display plans showing how.

4. Illustrate, through magazine pictures or drawings, the different ways in which people of different developmental stages use housing to meet needs.

5. What additions or changes would better suit the housing needs of each family member?

6. Discuss with adults in your family their reasons for choosing the place in which they live. In what ways do your ideas of adequate housing differ from theirs? Why? What will influence your future choices of housing?

7. How can residents of problem areas encourage solutions to the problems? How can young people help?

8. What is the "urban crisis"? What is being done to reduce the seriousness of the situation?

9. What is the difference between *standard of living* and *level of living*? Why does a family's level of living sometimes fail to meet its standard of living?

FOLLOW YOUR PATH

PATH ONE: Make a Plan to Improve Your Own Home

Step 3 Using the work you did in Steps 1 and 2, make a list of the basic needs you use your home to satisfy. List those you would like it to satisfy, but which it does not.

Step 4 What housing goals did you suggest in Step 2? Which do you think you might reach in your present home? Outline a plan showing how. Discuss it with your family. Report what they had to say.

PATH TWO: Form a Family on the Move

Step 3 What values and goals were discussed in Step 2? What conflicts arose? Were they resolved? How? What conflicts remain? Can these be compartmentalized?

Step 4 Examine the illustrations from Step 2 of Path Three. Discuss their esthetic and practical merits. If more than one set of drawings are involved, pick the set you like best. Arrange to see that designer.

PATH THREE: Be an Interior Designer

Step 3 Submit your drawings or collages to the family in Path Two. Solicit their reactions. Make requested changes.

Step 4 Prepare a portfolio of fabric swatches.

Step 5 Get color folders from paint stores.

Step 6 Make a display using combinations of materials from Steps 4 and 5. Describe the effects different combinations achieve.

PATH FOUR: Design a Community

Step 5 Have the class vote on the names for your community. Use the name which receives the most votes.

Step 6 Prepare a brochure showing how your community can help meet basic needs. Make the brochures appealing to people who wish to live in the city, the suburbs, or the country.

Step 7 Interview people of various types and ages. Include some from Paths One and Two. Find out what resources and services they expect from a neighborhood.

Step 8 Using the yellow pages of your local phone book, determine the variety and kinds of resources available in your community.

Step 9 Discuss your layouts from Step 3. Choose one. Make any additions, changes, or refinements you feel are necessary.

CHAPTER 18

Housing and Home Furnishing: Materials and Design

The American architect Frank Lloyd Wright once said that it was easy to get him to design a home. The problem was to find someone to build it. Wright's ideas about design and the use of materials were so unique that many builders did not believe that they would work. They did work, however, and a completed Wright home, no matter what the difficulty in erecting it, was the only one of its kind. Even the furniture was specially designed and made. The house was a living space that was at once the expression of a brilliant mind and of the needs of those who had it built. It made a very special imprint upon the environment.

Most of us employ less spectacular means in choosing and furnishing our housing. Yet, our dwellings, too, are very individualized places. They reflect us. They tell people something about who we are. The impression a home creates can be accidental, or it can be consciously created. The more we know about the kinds and styles of housing, furnishings, and the elements of design, the more control we may be able to exert over the appearance of our homes.

HOUSING THROUGH HISTORY

Like all arts, the art of architecture is reinterpreted in each generation. Sometimes, new architectural styles and construction techniques appear. Classic themes are restated and repeated in ways that "speak" to the new generation.

People in different periods of history thought differently of living space. At one time, living space was multipurpose. Today, many people prefer to use particular rooms and areas for specialized purposes. However, partly because of the housing shortage, multipurpose space is increasingly common.

Living Space

Many contemporary books on housing describe how interior space could and should be used. Many of these discussions assume that space within a home should be divided up into distinct areas—like kitchens and bedrooms—to serve more or less distinct purposes. In actual practice, many of us, out of preference or necessity, do not use space this way. Even in larger homes, bedrooms often double as studies. In our cities, with their housing shortages, a single room must often serve varied purposes. Nevertheless, having separate bedrooms, kitchens, dining rooms, and living rooms remains an ideal for many people. It is an ideal that has been prominent for the last several centuries.

Prior to that time, people thought differently about interior space.

In Europe in the Middle Ages, there were two basic types of housing. There were small houses in which a few people lived, and there were large houses where a great many people lived. In both cases, the same living space served a variety of purposes. Everyone was in the constant company of other people. Everyone ate, slept, socialized, and sometimes worked in the same room. Much of the furniture that was used—notably beds and small tables—could be folded or taken apart and removed from the room when not needed. It was centuries before most people began to set aside different areas for special functions. As early as the fourteenth century, some castles had bedrooms. Not until the eighteenth century, however, did average dwellings (dwellings not occupied by royalty) feature floor plans and room arrangements essentially like those used today.

Architectural Styles

In its broadest sense, the word *architecture* refers to the art and science of designing and constructing buildings. Each period in history is distinguished by a particular style of building. Sometimes the word architecture is used to refer generally to those structures which are most characteristic of an age.

Our European heritage The best known early examples of European architecture are from ancient Greece and Rome. The Greeks are famous for the temples they built to honor their gods. Most of these temples are rectangular and are built of stone. They are bordered on one side, two sides, or all four sides by rows of tall columns. The gently sloping roof extends just slightly over these columns, creating a kind of roofed porch between the columns and the walls. Roman architecture also made use of columns. Often they used these columns for the same purpose that the Greeks used them: to hold up

Many of the architectural styles found in the United States were inspired by European architecture. The Villa Rotunda (left) was built in Italy about 1550. Monticello (right), the home of Thomas Jefferson, was completed about two hundred and seventy-five years later.

the roof. Sometimes they used them for decoration. A number of Roman structures have "half-columns" which seem to emerge from the walls. Unlike the Greeks, the Romans favored rounded surfaces. Many Roman buildings had arches and domes. Some were built on a circular plan.

During the Middle Ages in Europe, another distinct architectural style was developed: the Gothic. Although not tall by today's standards, Gothic churches are known for the feeling of height which they convey to the viewer. This feeling was created by emphasizing the vertical lines of the structure. Narrow windows, for example, ran almost the entire height of the walls. A distinguishing feature of the Gothic style was the pointed arch.

Later periods in European history, down to the twentieth century, were also marked by distinct architectural styles. These styles differed from country to country. The Renaissance, Baroque, and Rococco styles made use of Greek or Roman *motifs*, or design elements, like columns and arches. From about the middle of the eighteenth to about the middle of the nineteenth centuries, what is known as revival architecture became popular. Neo-classic and neo-gothic were two popular styles during this time.

American architecture Early settlers brought to North America not only the architectural traditions of their homelands, but also their skills as carpenters, builders, and furniture makers. They applied these skills

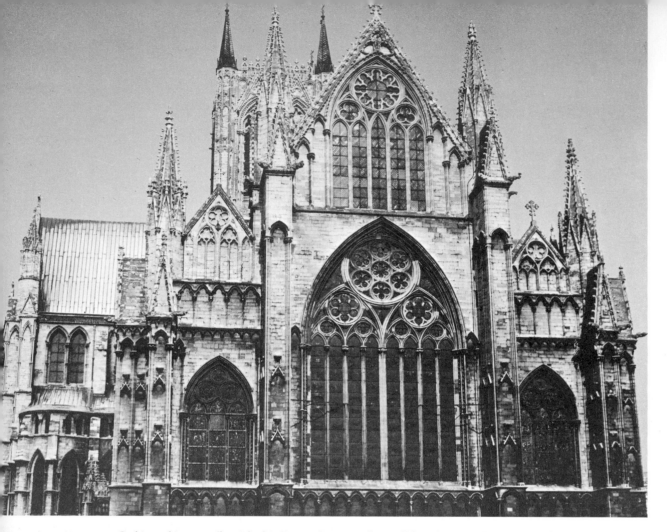

Gothic architecture flourished in Europe between the twelfth and sixteenth centuries. Its pointed arches and spires gave a feeling of aspiring to the sublime, and thus it was very appropriate for cathedrals and universities. Gothic castles and manor houses were also built.

to the materials they found at hand. Architecture began to take on regional distinctions in colonial America.

The Dutch colonists of New Amsterdam (New York) brought their steep roofs. The houses of well-to-do colonists in Maryland and Virginia resembled those of typical English country homes. In the northern colonies, styles had to be adapted to the more severe winters to conserve heat. Thus, the New England saltbox or Cape Cod house had a compact plan with low ceilings and small rooms. Smaller houses were sometimes built around a single chimney, which often provided two or three rooms with flues for fireplaces. Larger houses needed more chimneys to provide heat for more and larger rooms.

In exterior style, these houses were usually symmetrical (balanced) in design, with the door at the center and evenly spaced windows on each side. Almost all early homes were made of wood. In the Middle Atlantic states, where fieldstone and limestone were more plentiful, houses followed a similar design using these materials. As brickmaking

became more widespread, architects began to use bricks in town houses in great abundance.

Contemporary styles Many twentieth century buildings suggest the architectural styles of earlier ages. Our century has also been marked by the appearance of new architectural styles and ornaments.

In the 1890s, a new style of ornamentation that tried to combine the new technology with the inspiration found in natural forms emerged. The sinuous lines and organic shapes of the style called *art nouveau* (new art) were introduced. It was to be in fashion again in the 1970s because it expressed the desire of that generation to return to the forms of nature without sacrificing some of

This is a New England home from the colonial period. It was simple and compact, with small rooms to conserve heat. It featured a central front entrance and symmetrical floor plan and windows.

The industrial revolution made it possible for architectural decoration to be mass produced. Victorian architecture was very ornate, often employing in one building all the styles of trim that were available.

the advantages to be found in technology.

In the 1920s, the *Bauhaus* group in Germany began to exalt the geometry of pure form. Their style of architecture popularized flat roofs, expanses of glass walls, and free-flowing, rather than clearly partitioned, space. A few homes experimented with this style of architecture, and it appeared in some communities in schools, public build-

ings, and in commercial and industrial centers and parks. A short time later, new technology in using concrete made even more dramatic construction of arched domes, shell shapes, and winged shapes possible.

Contemporary architects have tried to capture the modern spirit in their designs. They strive to combine exterior and interior design with modern concepts of construction, insulation, and the use of materials. They have favored such materials as plywood, glass, brick, stainless steel, and lightweight concrete. Many modern homes boast improved heating, ventilating, and air conditioning systems.

The goal of most contemporary architects is to provide homes that are easy to care for, convenient to move through, and pleasant to be in. Designers of custom-built homes try to create houses that will reflect the personalities and interests of the people who will live in them. Exteriors are designed to harmonize with the site and to provide privacy in crowded communities.

Architects still make use of materials native to a region to give homes in an area a distinctive quality. Thus, adobe is still used in Texas and the Southwest, redwood siding is used on the West Coast, and limestone facing is used in Pennsylvania. Today, these materials can easily be transported elsewhere. The total effect has been to allow a great deal of individuality—for those who can afford it—in the exterior style of housing.

THE HOUSING MARKET

The availability of housing varies with national and local conditions. In fact, "housing starts," or the number of new housing units that have gone into construction in a certain period of time, are one indication of the state of the national economy. In the United States, there has been a general shortage of housing since the end of World War II. This shortage has been most keenly felt by those in low-

and middle-income categories who live in densely populated areas.

Housing has not kept up with the growth of our population or with the mounting demand of young adults for independent housing. Age, condition, size, location, and quality of materials and construction influence the cost of housing. Housing is available in a variety of types: the single house and the multiple dwelling, housing that is fixed on a site and mobile homes, and high-rise city projects and spread-out suburban developments are just a few types.

Types of Housing

There are a number of types of housing available today. One of these is the conventional single home. There are also increasing numbers of mobile homes—homes on wheels that can be moved from one site to another. Multiple dwellings have been variously planned and designed. For the traveler, there are hotels and motels.

Single houses The most common form of housing in early America was the free-standing single-family unit. Some families "added on" when children married. Members of the same family might live together in two- and three-generation homes. As towns and cities grew, the space between single units decreased. In some areas, this meant the development of row or town houses. Some of these became two-family or duplex units, separated by a common wall. Each family had its own entrance to its own unit. The free-standing one-family home gives those who live there the greatest amount of independence and often the greatest amount of

This modern house is well integrated with its surroundings. It was designed around the hill and the trees. Although integration to this extent can usually be done only with custom-built homes, many subdivisions are now striving to preserve the nature of the site.

CASE STUDY: TOM AND MARY ANN

THE SITUATION   The move had been made and Tom and Mary Ann were deep into plans for their new apartment. There were many things to think about because the new home was more spacious and had more rooms than their first place. Living five years at their previous address, they had accumulated enough furniture and accessories to make their one-bedroom apartment look well furnished—crowded, in some cases. They became particularly aware of the quantity of goods they owned when it was time to load their possessions into the van rented for moving. It took all day to move furniture out of the old apartment and into the new one.

Once the furniture was placed, it was apparent to Tom and Mary Ann that there was much to be done to make the place "livable."

"Where shall we begin?" asked Mary Ann. "Every room needs a big item such as a rug, piece of furniture, or draperies."

"Why not start with each room separately?" replied Tom. "By making a list of all furnishings we feel we need, we will be better able to organize and budget our furniture buying. And we'll be able to plan the use of each room, rather than placing furniture just to fill up space."

There were two bedrooms, a living room-dining room, and kitchen to consider. Tom was anxious to furnish the study. Mary Ann agreed to begin there. "I like the idea of guests having a separate room all their own," Mary Ann said. "They will have a place to put their belongings and rest undisturbed by other people in the apartment. And you should have a place for your desk and papers. Our second bedroom could be both study and bedroom, couldn't it?"

"The room is so small, though," reminded Tom. "How can we fit a bed, dresser, desk, chair, and other necessary things into one tiny room?"

"Let's look at sofa-beds and studio couches. We should be able to find something we like. What other furnishings will we need for that room?"

Tom felt that bookshelves were a necessity. They would also need two lamps to provide light for reading and working at the desk. Perhaps they could find one piece of furniture to serve the dual purpose of dresser space for guests and table for the reading lamp near the couch. Pictures on the wall, a rug, and curtains would complete the room.

Mary Ann reached for three important home furnishing tools: measuring tape, pencil, and paper. After measuring the window, she decided that curtains from their previous apartment would be too short. "But I did see bamboo shades advertised at an end-of-summer sale. The price was so much cheaper than that for ready-made curtains or ones I

privacy in the use of the building and grounds. As residents share common walls, walks, and grounds, they have more responsibility for the comfort of their neighbors.

Mobile homes   The United States pioneered a new concept in housing, the *mobile home*. The distinctive feature of the mobile home is that it is factory-made and remains on wheels, at least long enough to be transported from the factory to a lot, site, or space in a mobile-home park. The mobile home, therefore, offers an alternative to single-family fixed-site housing. Because it can, in many cases, be moved from one place to another, it meets the needs of those who like could make myself. Let's look at them. And we could get a cheerful, cozy effect for our study by making a rug of colorful squares of rug samples taped together. That would also cut down expenses."

Tom liked all Mary Ann's decorating ideas. He showed her a picture from a popular home-furnishing magazine. "An arrangement of bookshelves like this might fit this room. Let me borrow your tape measure."

Before leaving the study-bedroom, Tom and Mary Ann had taken measurements for the height and width of bookshelves, the width and length of rug and sofa-bed, and the amount of space left for a dresser or similar piece of furniture. They had discussed possible color schemes, placement of furniture, and the approximate amount of money they wished to spend for new furnishings.

Final plans included a sewing area in part of the bedroom and a conversation-entertainment area for the living room. Tired but pleased by the planning, Tom and Mary Ann put aside their list of furnishings and measurements, preferring to complete the remainder of plans another day.

THE INTERVIEW   Q: *Tom, will you be able to get all the furnishings on your list?*
A: *Perhaps not. But the list gives us a good starting point for shopping. We will probably see many other ideas that are appealing. Some may become substitutes for plans we made today, if we both agree to the switches.*

The important thing is that we have decided on the purpose of each room; and we know the feeling we want to create in each room.
Q: *Why are those two achievements important?*
A: *Because we have guidelines for the selection of colors and furniture styles. We can say no to some things and yes to others more easily. And we have goals to work towards.*
Q: *Can you afford everything on the list?*
A: *No. We will try to take advantage of sales where possible. The kind of rug we want for the study is a good example of where do-it-yourself skills will be handy. We may have to buy unpainted or used furniture, and Mary Ann may decide to put her sewing skills to use. We know how much we can afford, and plan to shop around for the best deal, tiring and time-consuming though it may be.*
Q: *How long will it take you to make each room to your liking?*
A: *Some people say it takes two years to get even a small apartment to look homey and furnished. Since we already have a few pieces of furniture, we may be finished in a year. At least by six months, the place will be comfortable. We know that planning is important, but all home furnishing plans take time to fulfill.*

REACT   What is the advantage of planning home furnishing carefully? Where would you begin to plan? Do you agree that rooms in a home should serve a variety of purposes?

to change their place of residence but not their home. Some mobile homes can be transported by the owner. Others must be moved professionally. The width and length of homes that can be moved in this way are regulated by law. For some families, a mobile home allows the owners to live in two climates during different seasons. Some

mobile housing is moved to a site and then built in after its wheels have been removed. Used in this way, it becomes a permanent, fixed-in-place home. Mobile homes may be extremely elaborate. For those who need a lot of room, it is possible to join mobile homes. Such concepts are the basis of modern trends toward *modular housing*.

Row houses are enjoying a revival in many cities where space for single-family dwellings is limited. Although they have no front or side yards, they usually have small backyards with limited privacy.

Multiple dwellings As cities became crowded, it was no longer possible to spread out, so buildings went up. Dwellings that accommodated several families were erected. The term *tenement* came into use to describe a dwelling with a room or set of rooms tenanted as distinct and separate dwellings. As years passed and many of these early buildings began to deteriorate, the term was increasingly applied to buildings in run-down, overcrowded sections of a city.

The population explosion has resulted in a tremendous spurt of apartment construc-

tion throughout the world. Many of these are high-rise garden apartments. Some are in specially designed suburban complexes. American architects were among the first to explore the possibilities of designing large-scale apartment complexes. Such buildings are a fixed fact of both American and European life today.

Apartment living offers many life-styles to apartment tenants. Apartments range in size from one-room "studios," "efficiencies," and "bachelor" or "bachelorette" types, to spacious suites. Some apartments at the luxury level of living occupy two or three floors. They are called duplexes or triplexes. The suite atop a luxury apartment building, called a penthouse, has become the symbol of luxurious living enjoyed by only a few.

Housing for transients Many people require housing to meet their needs as they travel from one place to another. It is not surprising that a huge industry has grown up to meet the needs of people in transit. The hotel industry offers a wide range of housing, from single rooms to full-scale apartment service. The motel industry has also grown up to serve travelers. These two arms of the housing industry try to create a "home away from home" for their customers. Because they supply shelter, restaurant services, and many other conveniences to travelers, they have been called "the hospitality industry."

Methods of Construction

For many centuries, all housing was made by one of a few basic methods. Technological innovations of the last hundred years have made it possible to make whole houses and parts of houses in a factory and transport them to a site.

Traditional methods The most common form of construction for single-family houses in the United States is the wooden frame structure. Wooden frame houses can be

Mobile home communities are no longer simple "trailer courts." They may have paved streets and sidewalks, as well as spacious lawns for each home. Mobile homes offer all the conveniences of fixed-site housing at about half the cost per square foot of living space.

finished off with a single layer of brick veneer, with shingles, or with clapboard. Some may be faced with stone. Some larger houses may be built with stone or brick masonry in their construction.

After World War II, houses with walls of hollow cement blocks were built in large numbers. In modern apartment buildings, steel frame construction is now the rule. Such buildings may be faced with masonry of stone, brick, concrete, or marble. Interior partitions may be made of hollow tile.

The interiors of both small houses and apartment units are similar for the same periods. The interior finish of older struc-

tures is usually plaster on lath (thin wooden strips). Such plaster can be finished with paint or paper. Plasterboard, fiberboard, or gypsum board can also be used. These, too, may be plastered or papered. At one time, wood paneling was commonly used for interior finishes. Such paneling is now found only in older, well-kept buildings, or in expensive modern houses.

In place of natural wood, plywood paneling may sometimes be used. This type of paneling is gaining in popularity because it is easy to install, economical, and offers a wide range of colors, finishes, and textures. Floors are commonly made of hardwood boards which withstand heavy wear. Concrete, terrazzo, and other flooring can be used in utility areas. In the heavy-use areas of the home, ceramic, asphalt, rubber, vinyl, and linoleum tiles can also be used.

Industrialized methods Architects and engineers have combined their talents to develop new techniques so that housing can be constructed more economically and more efficiently. Some innovations have been blocked by outdated building codes that specify conventional frame or masonry construction. In prefabricated or modular housing, parts of houses are produced in a factory assembly line. Shipped to the site, the parts or units are assembled by skilled craftsmen. Such construction methods may, in the long run, help to solve some critical housing shortages by making it possible to apply mass production methods to home building. More housing could be produced in a shorter time. In some cases, mass production could result in a reduction of cost. Such methods may cut down on wasted time for labor (when weather makes outdoor construction difficult) and on the waste of materials brought to a site and not used. As techniques for such construction improve, we can expect to see more general acceptance of this method, even in the construction of town houses and apartment buildings.

Housing made from **precut materials** has an unpleasant connotation for many builders. It recalls a time, just after World War II, when walls and other sections of houses rolled off assembly lines that had been used to produce armaments and temporary wartime housing. For a time, such housing was flimsy, poorly designed, and lacked style or taste. Such houses were put up, seemingly overnight, to ease the nation's critical housing shortage. The attempt led to no satisfactory solution. Much of this housing deteriorated rapidly.

The quality of precut housing has improved greatly. Today, it is possible to select a home from a catalog displaying a number of styles and a variety of materials. A buyer may select those standardized wall, floor, and roof sections that suit his purposes. He may also select such finer details as doorknobs and decorative moldings. Although aluminum is widely used, a variety of exterior finishes may be available. The factory-made parts are assembled on the buyer's site.

Some such housing costs as much as, or even more than, other forms of construction. It is sometimes possible for the buyer to get more for his money with this kind of home. This is especially true in areas with chronic housing shortages or shortages of skilled labor in the construction trades.

A newer, even more sophisticated form of industrialized housing is called **manufactured housing.** The mobile home is one example of this. Modular construction is another. Individual *modules*, or units, are made on an assembly line. The modular unit may be a kitchen, bathroom, bedroom, or living room. The units are assembled on the buyer's site according to an arranged plan. Such construction results in a considerable saving of time and labor costs. Laws are being passed in many states today that exempt this form of housing from restrictive building codes and zoning regulations.

Some experts have predicted that by 1980, two-thirds of the housing built in the nation will be industrialized. Operation Breakthrough, authorized by the Omnibus Housing Act of 1968, was designed to speed this process and to reduce other restrictions that exist in our system of home building.

Modular units may be placed on top of one another or side by side. This makes it possible to expand or contract living space as needs change.

Degrees of Uniqueness

No two homes are alike. There are a number of ways in which each establishes its uniqueness. A few people hire architects to design homes to their specifications. Some live in more or less standardized homes, which they may have altered to suit their purposes. Many people's dwellings are very much like those surrounding them. Consciously or unconsciously, however, they adapt housing to their personalities.

Housing developments Housing tracts, or developments, put up by mass builders make up 60 percent of the new housing market. Most new suburbs have been built up in this way. A builder acquires a tract of land. He subdivides the property. He lays out the development with roads, sidewalks, and other features which may or may not be finished when the first houses are sold. He constructs a few houses in a few standard designs, with certain interchangeable features. He then sells the houses and lots as individual packages. The customer is usually shown a model home. It is completely furnished (down to wall-to-wall carpeting and decorative accessories) to give him some idea of what kind of a home it would make. (This kind of "dressing up" may also distract a buyer from construction features.)

Some mass builders have developed communities that are well planned. A builder who is conscientious about preserving the environment will save as many trees as possible. He will protect privacy and offer enough variety to assure a sense of individuality.

When development houses are well planned, they provide maximum convenience

Modules may be used to construct both multiple dwellings and single-family dwellings. This method of construction reduces costs of materials and labor and makes expansion much easier. Modules may be varied in size to meet the living needs of their owners.

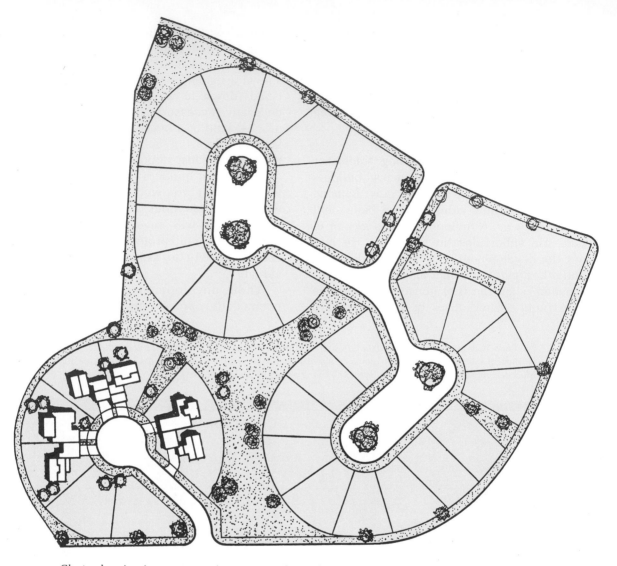

Cluster housing is a space-saving concept that is being used in housing developments today. This plan shows how individual homes are grouped, or clustered, around cul de sacs. In such a plan, through traffic is eliminated and the streets are quieter and safer.

and comfort. Many such homes are comparatively low in cost. This economy is made possible by a builder who takes advantage of new materials, purchases materials in quantity, and uses time-saving construction methods. By varying such obvious details as the color of bricks and the style of siding (clapboard and shingle, for example), some builders have been able to introduce an amazing variety into just a few designs.

If a prospective buyer decides to buy a home before a development is completed, he may have an opportunity to personalize a tract house to meet his own tastes. Such customizing may add from 5 to 20 percent to the cost of the basic design, but it will still be considerably less than the cost of a house that has been custom-built from an architect's plan. Some people have found that buying a builder's model home has provided them with many extras, such as carpeting and some extra "show" details, that they might not have been able to pay for if they had ordered them in advance.

Custom-built homes For the family with ample resources and for those who value individuality in the home environment, the custom-built home may be a long-range goal. Such housing is expensive because many skilled people are involved in its design, construction, and decoration.

In custom building, the owner, in consultation with an architect or contractor, can make every decision so that his home answers his needs. It will reflect his standards and tastes down to the last detail. A custom-built house may cost twice as much as a development house of similar size and materials. People with well-developed carpentry and other skills may reduce costs by doing some of the work themselves.

<h2 style="text-align:center">ELEMENTS
OF INTERIOR DESIGN</h2>

When you plan to create an environment for living, you will be making a number of furnishing and decorating decisions. In doing so, you will be dealing with all the design elements that concerned you in making clothing choices, but in quite a different way. A special element in the design of interiors is the importance of light. This includes both natural light flooding through windows and other openings and artificial light diffusing from a great variety of sources.

In today's smaller homes, many people wish to distinguish between spaces used for different purposes without actually closing them off. Here a shelf unit that is part of the living room furniture serves as a room divider that separates the living and dining areas.

CASE STUDY: DALE AND HIS MOTHER

THE SITUATION *Dale woke up to a scratching sound coming from the kitchen. Entering the room, he saw that his mother was already working to remove the paint from an antique trunk. Seeing Dale, his mother said, "The wood is beautiful. I couldn't wait to get started!"*

"At eight o'clock in the morning?" questioned Dale. "You must really enjoy doing this kind of thing."

"I do," replied his mother. "Even before Dad left for work, I was sanding the wood. Of course, he really didn't appreciate that. He grumbled his usual comment: 'I don't know what you see in an old piece of junk like that.'"

"He never has appreciated your interest in antiques," said Dale. "Yet, we have many in this apartment. You just didn't let his feelings bother you, did you?"

"I tried not to," answered his mother. "But it used to bother me. In the beginning, we would have arguments about my purchase of a piece of furniture. That's when I made up my mind not to tell him about a new piece. I'd go to an auction, buy what I liked, and have it delivered the next day. I'd leave it downstairs with Margaret for a few weeks. When I'd finally place it upstairs, I would tell Dad, when he asked, that the piece had been with Margaret. He wouldn't comment further. My goodness, Dale. If I hadn't gotten good furniture inexpensively at auctions, we could never have furnished this big apartment so nicely. The expense would have been too much for Dad's income. And I wouldn't have been happy living with inexpensive furniture. The surprising thing is that he really couldn't care less about the appearance of his home."

THE INTERVIEW *Q: You look surprised by your mother's comments.*
A: I am surprised. I never knew the whole story about this furniture. And I guess I was too young to hear them argue much about what she bought.
Q: What do you think of your mother's solution to the problem?
A: I don't think I'd like to be in my father's shoes. I wonder what he'd say if he knew how he has been tricked over the years! On the other hand, if he didn't care how the apartment looked, he should not have cared about her interest in home furnishing. Each of us must be able to develop the good hobbies and activities that interest us. I guess Dad really wasn't being fair to Mom.

REACT *Do you agree with his mother's solution? Should each family member feel free to develop his own special interests?*

The more developed your sense of design, the more likely you will make both practical and esthetically pleasing decisions.

Space and Form

The architectural lines of a room create the space that is enclosed. Lines create spatial relationships through which people move. This living space is defined by vertical, horizontal, curved, or diagonal lines. Each tends to create a different visual effect.

People respond to space differently. Conventional housing featured closed off spaces for separate functions. Modern architects may create free-flowing and open spaces. This arrangement invites the person who lives there to decide how to use space to express his own feelings about himself, the people he lives with, and the quality of his surroundings. People have strong emotional feelings toward different kinds of space. Some people feel more safe and secure in rigidly separated areas. Others feel more independent and imaginative when space is opened up and they can move through it without having to open and close doors, walk around furniture, or find their way blocked by too many objects. Your task is to decide what kind of environment you want to create. When you know the effects of line and space, you can create the kind of mood you want.

Light and Line

Clothing design is usually concerned with fluid, flexible lines. Housing, for the most part, is defined by solid, fixed lines. The body is the solid shape underlying clothing. In housing, the underlying shape is provided by the structure and framework of the building. Where surfaces join, planes and angles are formed to create additional linear elements. Open spaces through which light passes create a play of light and shadow through the space. These visual elements have a dramatic effect within a room.

Lines may form hard or soft edges. At the corners of rooms, on stairways, and in window and door frames, hard edges are formed. Edges may be softened by rounding them or by covering them with fabric or material, as when stairways are carpeted or materials are used to cover corners and edges. Edges can also be softened by spraying on plaster or plastic to provide natural shapes.

The invention of electric incandescent and fluorescent lamps has served to dramatize interior design. Lighting is a practical and an esthetic element in designing interiors.

Color

At one time, our inspiration for color came directly from the world around us. It was limited to what we actually saw in the environment. The development of chemical dyes added some colors rarely found in nature to manufactured materials. The "op" artists of the 1960s and 1970s used some colors that could not be seen under ordinary circumstances. These were colors from the invisible spectrum, the infrareds and ultra-violets that could be seen only in "black light."

Such experimentation challenged many previous assumptions about color. It ushered in a period when vivid "electric" colors were the rage, especially among young adults. It has expanded our awareness of the environment and the effects of color on mood.

The exteriors of high-rise buildings are much the same. Apartments in multiple dwellings and houses in some tract developments almost duplicate each other. In apartments, only the ornamentation of the interior is directly within the control of the residents. In rented premises, there may be strict limitations on what the tenant can do. Some landlords refuse to allow certain colors on the walls. Even with restrictions on the use of color on walls, however, there is a great deal that you can do with color to create an individualized near environment.

In planning a wardrobe, you can wear a different combination each day. However, if you paint a wall, buy a couch, or put down flooring or a rug, the colors will be there to be lived with day in and day out.

Coordinating colors The wild colors of a circus or carnival may be stimulating and exciting for a brief time. Many people, however, feel more comfortable and at ease if colors do not seem to fight for attention. Learning to coordinate colors and to discipline their use helps you to unify the appearance of a room or rooms. Planning keeps color from becoming a distracting element in the near environment. The same principles of color harmony discussed in Chapter 13 can be applied to interior design.

The use of color contributes as much to the mood of a room, as do the architecture and furnishings. The open design of the room at left is accentuated by the light walls and ceiling. In the cozy room at right, even the walls seem to be drawing themselves up to the fire.

For those with ample resources of time or money, seasonal rotation of slipcovers and other details may offer a "quick change" in some rooms. Most people in their first home have limited resources. Their choice of color in basic furnishings becomes a central decision that will influence satellite decisions for some time to come.

Colors in home furnishings, like colors in clothing, tend to reach a peak of popularity and then fade away. When a color is "in," it is easy to find "color coordinated" home furnishings. After its popularity subsides, you may have to do a lot of hunting to find things in the colors you want. Sometimes a color becomes a trademark of a whole design period, as when the Victorian era was dubbed "the mauve decade." (The color mauve was popularized by Queen Victoria.)

Creating mood We discussed the "warm" and "cool" properties of color on page 215. This quality of color can be used to establish a mood for a decorating scheme. You may wish to cool off a room that gets a great deal of light and warmth by using colors such as blue, green, and violet, from the "cool" side of the spectrum. In a room that already seems cold and that has little light, colors such as yellow, orange, and red may add a feeling of warmth. A room with little natural light may be livened up with the use of high-intensity colors. To bring the outdoors indoors, as you might wish if you had a city apartment facing a blank brick wall, you might favor blues and greens. In some decorating plans, the use of earth colors—brown, umber, and dull red—suggests a "back to nature" mood.

Creating illusions with color The apparent size of a room can be changed through the careful use of color. You may sometimes want a wall, ceiling, door, or other architectural feature to come forward or move back. Dark colors tend to make a room close in, unless relieved by other spots of color or light coming from windows, fixtures, or shiny surfaces. A bright color will bounce out at you. A dull one will fade into the background. Using light-value colors, such as neutral beige, gray, sand, or off-white, makes walls retreat, making a room seem larger. When such neutral colors are also used on walls, ceilings, and woodwork, the entire room will seem to open out. Thus, color can affect the feeling of space in your room.

Pattern and Texture

The space, surfaces, and objects in a room appeal both to your sense of sight and your sense of touch. That is, they have both visual and tactile appeal. Easy-care surfaces have invited people to touch more of the things used to decorate homes. The play of light and shadow can create a pattern that suggests the texture of grass, rock, or wood. Repeated lines and forms can create a feeling of rhythm and movement.

Pattern and texture can be introduced to interior design in many ways. Rough paint, repeated wallpaper or stenciled patterns, tiles, mosaic, or brick may provide many patterns and textures. Such soft surfaces as draperies, bedspreads, table coverings, and

The rather severe lines of the furniture in this room have been softened by the liberal use of texture and pattern on the walls, windows, and floor. The result is a very simple and stylish room.

wall hangings also introduce these elements. For example, a woven plaid fabric using flat and looped threads has both pattern and texture. A solid-color rug may have a rough texture. Vinyl or linoleum flooring may have a pattern or, if the design is embossed or cushioned, it may also provide a degree of texture. All the woods, fabrics, leathers, plastics, and other materials have characteristic patterns and textures. An additional factor in touch is the "coldness" and "warmth" of different materials. Take these into account in planning an interior.

BASIC FURNITURE STYLES

Many gifted craftsmen have turned their artistic talents to creating original furniture designs. Some have actually lent their name to well-known classic styles. Other furniture classics are known by the historical period in which they gained popularity. Originals of many of these designs are now prized as antiques. Many of these classics are now available as reproductions and adaptations.

Learning to identify furniture by designer or period takes a good eye for line and details of workmanship. Each fine designer has had his own approach to the form and function of furniture.

Traditional Furniture

Certain furniture styles have been used and enjoyed over many years. They seem familiar to most of us because we have seen them, in

Furniture should be in scale with the size of the room. Large, bulky pieces of furniture designed in the days of high ceilings look out of place in a modern, low-ceilinged room.

some form, for most of our lives. These traditional styles can be found in many stores.

European Traditional furniture styles are characterized by their high degree of craftsmanship, refinement of detail, and elegance of fabric. Such designs were not always suited to informal life-styles. More rustic, or "countrified," versions of these furnishings were created. French, Italian, and Spanish Provincial styles were designed for the relaxed rural living enjoyed by European gentry in their country homes. Because of their greater simplicity, Provincial styles have a strong appeal to some contemporary tastes.

French Provincial recalls the elegant designs of more formal court furnishings. Spanish and Italian furnishings are heavier and frequently more Gothic in style, featuring carving with pointed arches and columns similar to Gothic architecture. They recall the austere furnishings of monastery and convent life in the late Middle Ages.

Some styles became more ornate, but the general feeling of these furnishings is one of a life-style that valued solidity, simplicity, rough textures, and honest workmanship.

American American craftsmen had the example of English traditional furniture designs to follow. American settlers early showed a talent for innovative furniture design that used the native woods—notably pine and maple—and adapted them to the emerging life-style of the colonists.

Colonial furniture was simple and straightforward, with many regional variations. Authentic examples of these pieces are sought by collectors of antiques. Among the most imitated antique styles are the Hitchcock chair, Windsor chair, and Boston rocker by New England cabinetmakers. Shaker furniture, the product of the Shaker community, was stripped to essentials. The workmanship and life-style of the Shakers seem to have anticipated much that is valued by some young adults today. The Pennsylvania Dutch

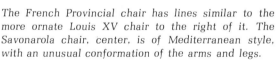

The French Provincial chair has lines similar to the more ornate Louis XV chair to the right of it. The Savonarola chair, center, is of Mediterranean style, with an unusual conformation of the arms and legs.

The Duncan Phyfe "lyre-back" chair is much more elegant than either of the earlier American styles shown. The Windsor chair (right) is of sturdy, simple design. The Hitchcock chair (center) is popular again.

furniture, the work of German immigrants, has strong simple lines. It features whimsical painted designs—which derive from German and American Indian designs—on such functional pieces as cupboards and chairs.

After the harsh beginnings of the colonial period, life became more leisurely. It was in such an atmosphere that Duncan Phyfe designed such furniture as his famous "lyre-back" chair. Phyfe's furniture reflects eighteenth century English and French designs.

Eighteenth Century English designers in the eighteenth century produced a wealth of furniture designs. Such designers as Chippendale, Hepplewhite, Sheraton, and the Adam brothers worked out basic furniture patterns and designs that have been copied and adapted ever since. These furnishings are chiefly executed in mahogany and other dark woods, most of them in high-gloss finishes. Most are noted for their light and often lacy construction. The backs of these

303

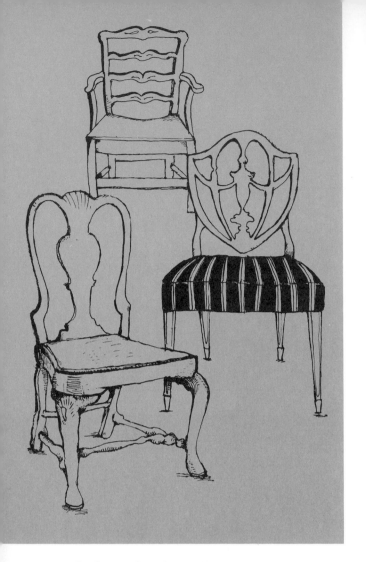

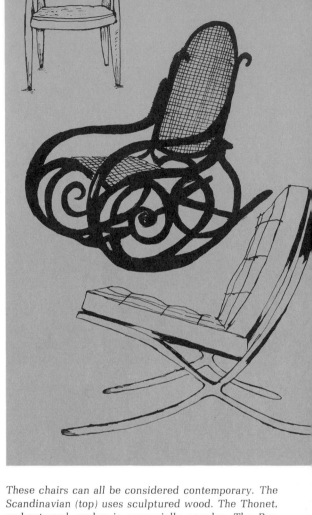

The legs and backs of these chairs identify three important eighteenth century styles. They are Chippendale (top), Queen Anne (left), and Hepplewhite (right). These styles go well together.

These chairs can all be considered contemporary. The Scandinavian (top) uses sculptured wood. The Thonet, or bentwood, rocker is perennially popular. The Barcelona chair (bottom) is a Bauhaus classic.

chairs are open and are often delicately carved. Many of them are higher at the center than at either side. Most chair legs of this period are slender.

Eighteenth century styles can generally be combined with one another and with contemporary furniture. The one exception may be the style known as Chinese Chippendale. This is considered by many to be too large, ornate, and distinctive to blend with the other English styles of its time.

Contemporary Furniture

The nineteenth century saw the coming of woodworking machinery and machine-made furniture. By the 1920s, furniture was being mass produced. New plastic materials for use in furniture began to be developed. They replaced the woods and fabrics used in traditional furniture. The move from large homes to small apartments made furniture on a smaller scale desirable. The increasing mobility of families also placed higher value on furnishings that could easily be moved from one residence to another. This resulted in smaller, lighter pieces as well as interchangeable and modular designs that could be assembled in a number of different combinations.

Contemporary furniture design showed a strong international influence. In the 1920s, the Bauhaus experimental art school and workshop sought to explore new forms and new uses of materials. The experimentation of the Bauhaus designers was geared to modern technology and industrial production. Utilizing chrome, glass, steel, and leather, they created many designs that have become classics. Used simply and severely, these designs reflected the architectural style of the time.

Scandinavian designers, who used light woods and sculptured shapes, also experimented with low-luster finishes. The Scandinavians introduced furniture that was oiled and rubbed, rather than mirror-finished. This treatment brought out the natural grain of the woods, especially the teak and birch with which they chose to work. The Scandinavian influence also sparked keen interest in all forms of texture—coarse weaving, rough pottery, and shaggy rugs. These softened the impact of the furniture's severe designs.

THE DEEPER MEANING OF DESIGN

Milo Baughman, a noted designer, has written in the *Journal of Home Economics* of "the threat to our emotional self of a disorganized and polluted visual setting." He feels that ugly surroundings are as damaging to our mental health as bad air and a nutritionally inadequate diet are to our physical health. He believes that our structured environment should "offer significant social and emotional benefits; it cannot simply look good." In making decisions about housing and home decorating, we can apply the elements and principles of design to these much broader ends.

THINK BACK

Uses of living space and styles of architecture have changed over the centuries.
Discuss: *Does housing "improve with age"?*

The different types of housing and methods of construction make it possible for people with many different values, goals and resources to satisfy their housing needs.
Discuss: *How can you answer the person who dislikes "rows of ticky-tacky houses"?*

Careful use of design elements brings satisfaction in "shaping" your near environment.
Discuss: *How can use of design elements create an impression for others?*

Furniture styles help reflect values and life-styles in the near environment.
Discuss: *What do the various furniture styles "say" to you?*

LOOK AROUND

1. Develop a time line showing how the use of living space has changed over the centuries. Explain what this tells us about the changing life-styles of people.
2. Compare the features of two different architectural styles. Which do you prefer? Why?
3. Which style of furniture would you choose to go with each of the above architectural styles? Why?

4. Develop a "Where Will You Live?" bulletin board illustrating the kinds of housing available in your community. Include a short description of the characteristics of each type of housing.

5. What is the difference between prefabricated and modular housing? A tract house and a custom-built home? In which might you prefer to live? Why?

6. What different methods of building construction can you find in your community? List an example of each.

7. Develop a picture quiz in which class members identify various pieces of furniture according to period.

8. Which different furniture styles would you combine? Which would you not combine? Explain.

9. Visit model rooms in a furniture store to see the variety of ways in which the design elements are combined. What new ideas resulted from your visit?

10. Develop a "Design for Living" bulletin board, illustrating the use of design elements in home decorating.

11. What guidelines for the use of color can be applied to room decoration? Collect pictures that illustrate suggested guidelines.

FOLLOW YOUR PATH

PATH ONE: Make a Plan to Improve Your Own Home

Step 5 Draw two sketches of the part of your home that most nearly belongs to you. (It may be your part of a bedroom or the part of the living room which you usually use.) In the first sketch, show it the way that it is now. In the second, consider the elements of design; draw it the way you would most like it to be. Retain most of the furnishings.

Step 6 Discuss both sketches with your family. Record their reactions.

Step 7 Visit a museum or library or review some magazines to find out how other generations managed to maximize space. Prepare a collage or bulletin board to illustrate your findings.

PATH TWO: Form a Family on the Move

Step 5 Discuss the "Living Space" section of this chapter in relation to your own ideas about living space. Ideally, how many rooms would you like to have? What purposes would each serve?

Step 6 Have each family member, independently of the others, go through magazines and clip out appealing furniture styles.

Step 7 Meet and discuss all these clippings. Make groups of furnishings that go together.

PATH THREE: Be an Interior Designer

Step 7 Design a piece of furniture that you feel "goes with" one of the traditional styles of furniture. Make up a poster showing your piece plus a traditional piece side by side. Use arrows or words to show similarities.

Step 8 Cut pictures of room interiors from magazines. Comment on the lighting. Would you do it differently? How?

PATH FOUR: Design a Community

Step 10 From your library, take several books on architectural styles. Examine them.

Step 11 Discuss the various styles. Select one or several that you would like to see reflected in the buildings of your community. Discuss the types of housing your community will have.

Step 12 Make rough drawings of model houses. Make floor plans which indicate the dimensions of each room.

Step 13 Do a report on various methods of construction. Discuss this report in a meeting.

CHAPTER 19

Housing Decisions

In a book called *Housing, People, and Cities,* authors Meyerson, Terrett, and Wheaton say: "The consumer cannot buy housing apart from a package of related goods and services: with the house go schools, churches, shops, visual environment, places to play, neighbors, status attributes, a municipal administration, a journey to work, (perhaps with it a commitment to a particular form of transportation), and even an orientation toward cultural, social, and commercial activities—in short, a way of life."

In addition to this community package, the living space itself may be considered to be a kind of package. It provides facilities which people can design to meet their needs and reach their goals.

Decisions about where to live and how to furnish living space affect many areas of your life. This chapter offers some information that may help you to make such decisions rationally.

DECIDING
WHERE TO LIVE

Most young adults live with their families, at least until they finish high school. For those who continue to live at home thereafter, some changes in living arrangements may have to be made. The young adult will want to accommodate his new study-, work-, and leisure-time activities. New arrangements will be especially important in the case of those who marry and live with one partner's family.

For those who leave home, decisions about where to live are usually related to decisions about study, work, and marriage. Most people like to live fairly close to their college, technical school, or job. Most have definite preferences about the kind of resources they would like their community to offer.

Choosing a Location

Individuals and families may hold different opinions concerning what is the most desirable location for housing. Some people want

This house was once part of a residential community. When change came, the owner refused to sell, preferring to remain in his home no matter what the surroundings. People who are sensitive to their surroundings will consider community stability before they buy or rent.

to live in the heart of a city. Others want to be away from crowds. Some families with young children may favor the suburbs, where they feel their children will have better opportunities for growth and development. Others may seek urban areas close to parks, playgrounds, day-care centers, nurseries, or schools.

In making rational decisions about the site of housing, physical, psychological, and social factors must all be examined.

Physical factors   The geographical location of housing determines that housing unit's exposure to the elements. Windows facing east will get the morning sun. Those facing north will get a cold, clear light. Those facing south will be bright and sunny at midday. Those facing west will be exposed to the strong afternoon rays of the setting sun.

Such geographic features as steep hills will have to be considered. A house set high on a hill may provide a magnificent view; but you must also consider whether your family and your friends will have the stamina to climb to it in all kinds of weather. Housing at the foot of a hill should be seen on a rainy day. Check for mud puddles and clogged drains that make walking and driving dangerous and that may flood the basement. Riverfront and waterfront housing may have considerable appeal on a bright, hot, sunny day; but consider the effects of tides and flooding. Some features, such as lakes or

Some decaying neighborhoods can be reclaimed by renovation projects. This may be done by individuals who buy property and restore it for their own use or for rental or resale. Private companies may also help to improve the community they serve.

COMMUNITY STABILITY

All communities change. Most people feel more secure in a community that remains fairly stable during periods of change. Controlled change can be assured only through responsible citizenship and decision making at all levels of federal, state, and local government. Special funds and projects are sometimes introduced to help communities remain stable. For those who join in such efforts, the results are often improved housing and improved communities.

Zoning laws and building codes contribute to community stability by preventing the rapid deterioration of residential neighborhoods to commercial use. The purpose of most such ordinances is to protect residents and property owners from irresponsible use of land, property, and buildings. Building codes help stabilize a community by regulating the size, height, purpose, and quality of new construction. When selecting housing, you will do well to be aware of the regulations affecting your neighborhood. Consider those zoning and coding laws that may be out of date, that may hold back community development. Make your voice heard through your vote.

pools, may be attractive to young adults or retired people. These same features may be extremely undesirable to the parents of wandering toddlers.

In evaluating the physical factors of a location, you will want to find out the distance in time and mileage from work—especially at rush hour. How far is the home from those of friends and relatives you may (or may not) wish to see often? Are recreational facilities and community resources easy to reach?

Psychological factors   In choosing a location in which to live, you are choosing an environment that stimulates psychological—including esthetic and emotional—responses. If you are a person who is extremely sensitive to the physical environment, you may find housing that faces a blank wall, a busy highway, or a refuse-strewn lot depressing. Your personal feelings about trees, flowers, wide streets and walks, or a view of trees or water may be the most important considerations in choosing a place to live.

A few people will overlook a location's lack of conveniences or run-down condition because they like the architectural features of a particular house. Some people have purchased deteriorated housing of a style they liked and have renovated it. Many city neighborhoods have been improved by such efforts.

Social factors   A major social concern in selecting housing is the opportunity to meet and be with people whose tastes and interests are similar to yours. The presence in a building, neighborhood, or community of others who share your interests makes it easier to meet your social needs. Some housing caters to "singles." The suburbs have traditionally attracted people with expanding families. Retirees look for others like themselves to make their well-earned leisure more stimulating and enjoyable.

The entire makeup of a community is the social environment for housing. More and more planners are making efforts to establish communities with a cross section of people of all ages, backgrounds, economic levels, and interests. Still, some people make better social adjustments in more homogeneous communities. They like living in a community where customs are familiar and their roles are clearly defined.

Economic factors The primary economic consideration in selecting housing is the cost of buying or renting. The cost of commuting (in time, energy, and money) will have to be added to the cost of housing. In some luxury areas, everything is more expensive. Is public transportation available or would the need for one or two cars involve additional expenses in moving to a particular neighborhood? Are facilities within walking distance if transportation fails? The answers to such questions will help you evaluate the convenience and economy of housing in a particular location.

Spiritual factors For many, closeness to the house of worship of their choice is a primary consideration in selecting housing. Their place of worship is the spiritual heart of the community in which they live. The absence of people of their own faith in a community could make some feel lonely and helpless.

Checking Community Resources

Like other resources, a community resource is a resource only to those who know of its existence, know how to utilize it, and do so to meet their needs. In making rational

Wherever you live, it is important to find out about the health services available in your community. What clinics, medical and dental centers, and private physicians are convenient for routine health care? What emergency services and accommodations are available?

decisions about where to live, evaluate community resources for physical and mental health, education and enjoyment, personal and property protection, and banking.

Health services What services does the community provide for medical, dental, and nursing care? Are there family planning centers? Nutrition counseling services? All of these services can contribute to family health. Some special community resources may include special treatment centers for the emotionally disturbed, handicapped, exceptional child, or the chronically ill.

Outdoor facilities such as parks, playgrounds, pools, and beaches that are properly maintained and supervised help to improve community health. Look for signs of pollution control in public places. Does the community have strict rules against burning garbage or leaves, fouling water, or making noise?

Family support services People will always have problems. Sometimes these problems may reach crisis proportions. Families are strengthened by the presence in the community of such public and private agencies as Alcoholics Anonymous and Alateen, which deal with the problems of alcoholics and their families. Each community will have a different approach to the drug problem, ranging from counseling to clinics and residential treatment centers. Gamblers Anonymous helps those with gambling problems. Some communities now support "crisis centers" where mental health counseling is available for troubled families.

Check with the local community service agency or look through the local telephone directory to gain some knowledge of the range of services available.

Educational facilities People can continue to learn all their lives. How good are a community's educational resources? Whom do they serve? Are there opportunities for academic, vocational, technical, or specialized education? Are there adult or continuing education programs? Is there a Cooperative Extension Service working with homemakers and youth in the community? Are there two-year or four-year colleges? Are there private as well as public schools? Are qualified teachers attracted to the school system? Do they remain? Are there active PTAs and other parent groups supporting the schools?

Cultural and recreational resources Does the community have such cultural resources as art galleries, crafts studios, libraries, or museums? Are there movies, theaters, or local dance or drama groups? Are there bandshells or fairgrounds that attract special events? Can residents enjoy such resources at low cost or free of charge? Are there flower clubs, stamp clubs, book discussion groups, or other groups engaged in activities of interest to you? Are there nearby swimming, skating, or other athletic facilities?

Are there groups of citizens and members of the business community actively engaged in improving the community? Are young people encouraged to participate in such events? Where do eligible young adults vote in local elections at the earliest opportunity? Do local civic groups sponsor teams, scholarships, or competitions of various kinds? Is there an active Chamber of Commerce, Jaycee, Soroptimist, or Junior Achievement group? Do such groups cut across community lines for cooperative participation?

Environmental protection Does the community show a lively interest in environmental matters? Does it have an environmental beautification program? Are public waste receptacles in evidence? Are they being used? Is the sanitation service efficient and well run? Do residents cooperate by sorting garbage for recycling? Is garbage packed securely? Are potential hazards to children properly fenced off and secured?

Banking facilities Financial stability in a community is revealed by the presence of full-service banks and savings and loan associations. Are residents encouraged to buy and remodel housing in the community? Is mortgage or home improvement money readily available to qualified borrowers? If such funds are short, it may reveal the banking community's lack of confidence in the stability of the area or the financial responsibility of local residents.

Fire and police protection Every person in the community is concerned with the level of law and order maintained there. Are police and fire departments efficient and well run? Do community residents cooperate with them? Are there volunteer services? Are there sufficient street lights, fire alarm boxes, and traffic lights? Are guards stationed at school crossings?

Some suburban communities have no central business district. They rely instead on shopping centers. Shopping centers may sponsor art shows or concerts, providing a cultural resource for the community.

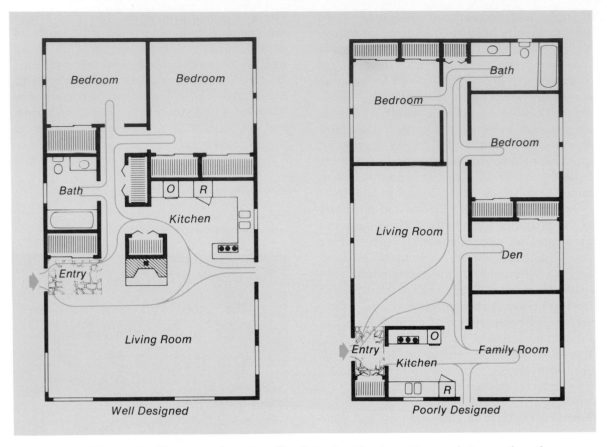

Labels within the floor plans:

Well Designed
- Bedroom
- Bedroom
- Bath
- Kitchen (O, R)
- Entry
- Living Room

Poorly Designed
- Bath
- Bedroom
- Bedroom
- Living Room
- Den
- Entry
- Kitchen (O, R)
- Family Room

A well designed traffic pattern channels traffic efficiently without requiring people to pass through one room to reach another. Ideally, the sleeping, living, and service areas should each be accessible from the entrance without requiring traffic through any other areas.

EVALUATING LIVING SPACE

A housing unit provides a certain amount of space which may be divided into a number of distinct areas. You can evaluate this space in terms of how well it might be used to satisfy the needs and wants of all the members of your household. Is there adequate space for preparing food, for eating, for sleeping, and for leisure-time activities? Is there room for privacy? Is there adequate space for the possessions you have and would like to have?

In making such an evaluation, you might find a floor plan or blueprint helpful. These are scaled-down drawings which show the size and proportion of the living space and the arrangement of the rooms. They show locations of doors, windows, and stairways.

In the case of new housing, a floor plan might be available from the owner. In the case of older housing, you might find it worthwhile to make one yourself. On a floor plan, you can arrange small pieces of paper which represent the furniture you have or would like to have. You can learn if it fits and if it can be arranged to your satisfaction. (This is easier than moving and re-moving the furniture itself.) By looking at a floor plan, you can also evaluate the probable traffic lanes in an area. With a pencil, trace the

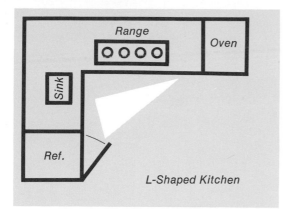

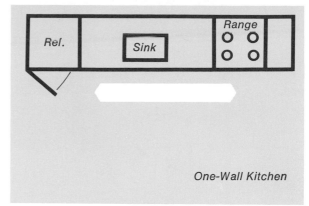

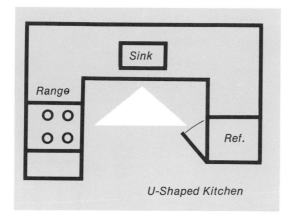

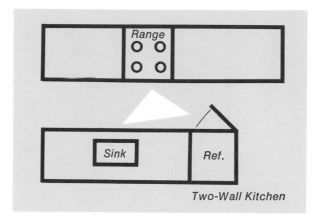

The four basic kitchen layouts can all provide efficiency if the work centers are appropriately spaced. The U- and L-shaped arrangements eliminate traffic through the work area. A two-wall kitchen is very efficient if "through traffic" is minimal.

routes you might follow in moving through the space. Whatever your goals, you will most likely find that some housing is more conveniently laid out than other housing.

Facilities for
Meal Preparation and Dining

The amount and kind of space needed for food preparation and dining depends on several factors. One of these is the number of people usually served. Another is the style and scope of entertaining that is expected. Still another is whether the members of the household usually eat in the kitchen, the dining room, or some other room. A clear

advantage in almost any case is having the food preparation and serving areas close together. Such an arrangement saves steps.

Space and size There are many possible kinds of kitchen arrangements. Two compact kinds are the efficiency, which occupies one wall, and the kitchenette, which occupies an alcove. Some houses and apartments feature a full, or "eat-in," kitchen. Principal considerations are the size of the work area and the amount of storage space. Counters, shelves, and cabinets should be at convenient heights.

Whether to seek a dinette for two or a dining room that will seat twelve depends

Storage areas may be at a premium in some kitchens. Displaying utensils attractively can overcome a storage problem. The frequently used items should be close at hand. The housekeeper should be mindful that utensils must be cleaned more often when they are displayed.

on the user's needs and life-style. Most modern apartments skimp on dining space. Many older homes have ample dining space in the form of a formal dining room. Such space is often used for other purposes — perhaps for studying or for pursuing crafts.

Location and layout A convenient kitchen location is near an entrance. This permits heavy groceries and supplies to be carried in easily and stored promptly. In many cases, kitchen layout is more important than size. A well-planned kitchen, even if small, can be a convenient place in which to work.

There are four basic kitchen layouts: the one-wall, two-wall, L-shaped, and U-shaped. Basically, any kitchen can be well arranged if work areas have been carefully planned. A convenient layout is generally considered to be one which requires the least amount of footwork on the part of the person working in it. This convenience is generally measured by the distance between the different work centers in the kitchen. There are five such work centers: storage (including refrigeration), mixing, cooking, serving, and cleanup. Cooking and serving utensils should be easy to reach. Space for food supplies should be close to the mixing center. Small tools, and especially handy utensils, should be reachable without too much walking, bending, and stretching. Supplies for cleanup should also be easy to reach. The food preparation and mixing centers should be near running water for ample sanitation. A door from the kitchen that swings both ways is a great convenience when food is being carried to the dining area.

Look for good lighting near all work areas. When a cabinet is above a work surface, overhead lighting may be blocked. Look for ample outlets for electric appliances.

Features and extras The kitchen usually gets a lot of attention from those looking at a housing unit. Many landlords and builders count on attractive kitchens to "sell" a unit. Kitchens that look good are not always the easiest to work in. Nevertheless, a kitchen should reflect an individual's own preferences and needs. The height and placement of shelves and cupboards for a tiny cook will not be appropriate for someone six or eight inches taller. Most homeowners will appreciate a kitchen arrangement that shields the rest of the house from cooking odors. Scratch-resistant counter tops and easy-to-clean surfaces may be counted among positive features. Home hunters should be aware, however, that many so-called "extras" and "features" may actually feature extra work and additional costs in maintenance, upkeep, and repair.

Facilities for Sleep and Rest

If you check real estate advertisements and advertisements for the sale of mobile homes, you will find that most units are described by the number of bedrooms they contain. Proper sleep and rest are basic to good health. Therefore, bedrooms or sleep and rest areas should offer quiet, sufficient heat, and adequate ventilation to assure comfortable sleep.

When living space is shared, as it often is, those sharing it must recognize that the sleep and rest needs of those living with them are important to health and comfort. People do not have the same sleeping patterns; not everyone sleeps with equal soundness. Therefore, the arrangement of the area and the consideration of those who share it is as important as the space itself.

Space and size In smaller efficiency apartments, separate facilities for sleep and rest may not be possible. There may be just enough room for a sleeping alcove with space for a single bed or convertible sofa. In a one-room apartment without an alcove, you will have to check carefully to see that there is enough space for the kind of dual-purpose bed you need. For those who need extra-size bedding, this may present a problem. You may have to decide on a three-quarter rather than a double-size bed. In a single-bedroom apartment, you will want to be sure that the space will accommodate a double-, queen-, or king-size bed, if such is included in your plan. Be sure that larger beds and sofas will fit through doors and stairwells.

Location and layout Sleeping space ought to be as far away as possible from the busiest areas of the home. In examining a place for sleep and rest, it is sometimes hard to picture bulky bedroom furniture in place. Bear in mind that beds, storage cabinets, night tables, and highboys take up considerable space.

In general, it is good to remember that beds are easier to make if you can walk around three sides of them. If space is limited, it may be necessary to check on the possibility of using compact or dual-purpose sleep furnishings.

Features and extras Closet and storage space is essential in sleep and rest areas. Any built-in dresser or special storage space for out-of-season bedding or clothing offers convenience. A walk-in closet or a cedar-lined closet for woolen storage may be valuable extra features in a home.

Facilities for Leisure and Recreation

Sleep and rest are basic physical needs. Provisions for leisure and relaxation meet physical, psychological, and social needs. These needs can be met either alone, with one's family, or with friends. Individuals differ greatly in the type of leisure and relaxation they enjoy. They also differ in the amount of leisure time at their disposal. Whatever their preference, they will gain more satisfaction from living space that affords them outlets for their interests and leisure-time activities. For some, this will focus on indoor-outdoor activities. Others will simply want enough room to entertain a group of friends for talk, dancing, or just listening to music.

Young people today may place a high priority on an "entertainment center." This usually includes a radio, stereo, and TV. Records and tapes go along with a stereo. For some, an entertainment center may also include books and games. All such items require storage space.

Space and size Most people would like a large and spacious living room. In a one-room apartment, the living room may be a multipurpose room—meeting the needs for sleep, rest, dining, and leisure. In such a room, the arrangement of furnishings be-

Since many children use their bedrooms as play areas during the day, furnishings should be durable and easily cleaned. When siblings share a room, furniture can be arranged to give some privacy. Each child should be provided with a space to keep his own belongings.

CASE STUDY: NEIL AND DIANA

THE SITUATION   *"We have already spent a lot of money on this house,"* said Neil. *"We can't afford to go out and buy brand new furnishings. We will have to be content with secondhand equipment until we have more money."*

He and Diana were looking at their new purchase, a small secondhand refrigerator. Diana didn't like it.

"Look at it," she admonished. *"There's hardly room for one pound of meat in the freezer, let alone a week's supply. I wanted one like my sister's. She has a separate, self-defrosting freezer compartment. It's about twice the size of this one."*

"Don't forget," replied Neil, *"that she lives in an apartment. Appliances are part of her rental package. And her refrigerator is not twice the size of ours!"*

When he and Diana had decided to rent an older home, they knew they would have to buy furnishings and accessories, as well as several major appliances. After pricing new items, they decided they could better afford secondhand appliances. Though the classified ads section of their local newspaper listed many refrigerators for sale, most were sold by the time Diana or Neil called the owners. Finally, fifty miles from their home, they located a refrigerator still available. After listening to a description and asking questions concerning the appli-ance, Neil agreed to buy it from the owner, sight unseen. He and Diana borrowed a truck from a friend and, one evening after work, picked up their new purchase.

THE INTERVIEW   Q: *Your wife is unhappy with this refrigerator. Does that mean you'll get a newer one?*
A: *We will have to get one eventually, but I won't agree to getting one in the near future. Before getting this one, we talked over the possibilities of purchasing a refrigerator and decided we couldn't afford a brand new one. So this is it!*
Q: *Did you question the previous owner about the size of the refrigerator and freezer?*
A: *Yes. We knew what we were getting. Diana said then that she wanted a larger freezer, but there just was nothing available. We couldn't wait any longer because of the inconvenience.*
Q: *Who made the final decision?*
A: *I did. And I think I made a wise decision. Diana will have to adapt her way of buying and preparing food to suit the equipment she has to work with in the kitchen. It can be done if she will just put out a little effort.*

REACT   *What food buying and preparation methods will make use of the new refrigerator more convenient? Was Neil's decision to buy a wise one?*

---

comes of primary importance in reaching many goals.

Most people settle for a living room that is smaller than they might have liked, but they can find ways to make it meet their needs. In a living room of any size, good lighting will add to the room's potential for leisure and recreational activities.

Location and layout   If possible, whether in a one-room home or a large and spacious one, the entry should meet a number of needs. First, it should provide some space for depositing outerwear—especially coats, umbrellas, and boots.

In both a house and an apartment, if the living room is laid out so that you do not have

When a home does not have a family room for the active and varied interests of the family members, the living room can be arranged to provide a game area, a place to display collections, and a quiet retreat for reading and conversation.

to go through other rooms to reach it, many steps will be saved. A living room should offer space for both quiet activities like reading and noisy activities like watching TV.

In evaluating any living space, the potential for room arrangement and decoration may immediately be apparent. Does the space include an interesting architectural feature, like a picture window, fireplace, or wall break? Such features offer opportunities to create interesting furniture arrangements or centers of visual interest. Because living areas (and especially living areas combined with sleep areas) use large pieces of furniture, there should be at least two long, rela-

tively unbroken walls. This will allow maximum flexibility of furniture arrangement.

Features and extras Built-in storage spaces for books, records, tapes, or other recreational materials are useful extras in a living area. A room with specially arranged lighting or lights with a dimmer may help to set the atmosphere for entertaining.

Facilities for Grooming

Good light, facilities that work, abundant hot and cold water, and good ventilation are essential for sanitary bathroom facilities.

Ventilation may be either by window or by ventilator fan.

Space and size Modern bathrooms may be very tiny. If they are well planned, well equipped, and their mirrors and lighting are well arranged, adequate facilities may still be provided. A handy medicine cabinet, storage space for paper and cleaning supplies, and a convenient hamper for soiled laundry may be built into modern bathrooms. Most families appreciate a full-length tub, but in housing in which there is not much room, tubs may be more compact, or the bathroom may have only a shower.

Location and layout To provide maximum privacy and freedom from interruption, a bathroom should be out of the main lines of household traffic. A well-planned bathroom will not have a window directly over the shower or tub unless it is specially insulated against water damage. Ideally, the bathroom will not be visible from such main living areas as the living or dining room.

Features and extras You can benefit from certain safety features in a bathroom. Such features include "no-skid" treads in the tub and, if possible, good hand supports near the tub and shower.

Modern bathrooms are more apt to have adequate lighting and built-in storage than older ones. Old-fashioned bathrooms can be made attractive and efficient without great expense. Added storage space can cover bare pipes and increase the grooming area.

CASE STUDY: PAT

THE SITUATION Pat was nervous and excited. She had spent three tiring days searching for a couch for her new apartment. She particularly wanted to purchase one this week because the manufacturer's sale was being held. It was so hard to select the best one! The price had to be right, as did the color and shape of the furniture. There were many couches on sale, some right off the floor of the store and guaranteed for immediate delivery if she selected one of them. After consideration of several, she made her decision and returned to a store she had visited on the first day of her search.

She approached a clerk with whom she had previously spoken. "I'm ready to buy a couch now. I'd like that one there in the corner."

"That's an excellent couch and the sale price is good," replied the salesman. "When you have selected the fabric, we'll order it for you right away. In six to eight weeks we should be able to deliver it to you."

"Six to eight weeks?" asked Pat. "I thought I'd be able to buy it right off the floor."

"Oh no, Miss," returned the salesman. "This particular couch must be ordered. I can show you the floor models we have for immediate delivery if you wish. Perhaps you'd like one of them."

"But this is the one I like! I've looked all over and have returned to this store three times, trying to make a decision. Are you sure I can't have this couch now?"

"I'm very sorry," said the salesman. "There are some couches we will sell off the floor, but when we get one that sells as well as this model does, we keep it to interest even more customers. We make more money by keeping it here for people to see than we would if we were to sell it to a customer."

There were tears in Pat's eyes. What a frustrating experience! She hurried away.

THE INTERVIEW Q: Did you notice how upset your customer was?
A: Yes. I'm glad that doesn't happen often.
Q: Why do you think she was so upset?
A: She is probably excited about decorating and expected everything to be completed right away. It doesn't work that way in the furniture business.
Q: What are your recommendations to customers?
A: Give yourself time to find what you want at a price you can afford. Comparison shop in a variety of reputable stores. If you want furniture to arrive near a particular date, either decide to choose only from floor models or begin shopping two to three months in advance. Try to buy at sale time, when items may be reduced 20 percent or more. Learn about construction and quality of fabric and finishes. And—be patient!

REACT For what reasons might Pat be upset about the delay in delivering the couch? What should Pat do now?

Look also to see that no electric outlets are placed where water is likely to accumulate. An electric outlet placed so that it will accommodate an electric shaver, dental irrigator, toothbrush, or sunlamp may be desirable. As a family grows, it may want a second shower or lavatory. In buying a house for a growing family, it is advisable to check to see whether or not there are plumbing lines adjacent to space that might later be needed for an additional lavatory or full bathroom.

DESIGNING
LIVING SPACE

Some apartments and houses come fully furnished and decorated. In mobile homes, some furniture may be built in. Many people consider such situations advantageous. They have the freedom to move from one locale to another without worrying about the cost and trouble of moving furniture.

Most housing is furnished by the inhabitants. The members of the household have the opportunity to choose items ranging from beds to wall coverings. They can make choices that reflect themselves and their life-style.

Those who have had more options in selecting housing may have an easier time in designing the interior. One of the advantages of examining floor plans in connection with evaluating living space is that furniture selection and placement can be carefully planned to suit wants and needs.

Selecting
Appropriate Furnishings

Few people plan to buy all the furnishings they need, or think they need, at the same time. If your first home away from your family home is a dormitory or furnished room, you will probably do no more than buy accessories and decorative items. If your first home offers minimal space, you will be planning a multipurpose room. That would include furniture for sleep and rest, a work surface, storage pieces, lamps, and possibly such accessories as draperies, spreads, linens, and towels. If you have special interests, you may have to make room for a large piece of entertainment or hobby equipment. Plan to buy basics first. Then choose the extras that will round out your plan.

Furniture   When selecting furniture, begin by knowing the size of the room or rooms you have to work with. A floor plan will help

to limit your choices. Be sure to note all architectural features that influence furniture placement. These include wall breaks, air conditioning and heating vents, doors (including the direction in which they open), and windows. Bear in mind that extra-large pieces of furniture may not be able to turn corners, pass through doorways, round stairs, or fit in elevators. You may have to scale down some of your planned purchases because of this limitation.

Wall coverings may vary within a room to add emphasis, create a certain atmosphere, or change the apparent dimensions. This alcove has been papered to set it off from the rest of the room.

Many young people must furnish their first home on a small budget and a big imagination. Comfortable furnishings need not be expensive. This sofa is made from a folding cot and home-made cushions. The wicker hampers used for tables also provide storage space.

As you make your plan, ask yourself whether your alternatives are to buy new, to buy furniture in a kit, to make it yourself, to buy usable secondhand, or to refinish secondhand furniture. Some furnishings may even be rented.

When you are fairly sure that you will be settled in one place and that you will have certain basic furnishings, cut out furniture shapes in the same scale as your floor plan. Move the cutouts around on the floor plan until you come up with an arrangement that satisfies your needs. You will find this easier than moving around actual furniture.

Wall coverings Your first problem in decorating living space will probably be what to do with the walls. The simplest treatment is

often a coat of paint. You can paint the surfaces in solid colors or graphically, with lines, circles, or other motifs. You can paint all your walls the same color. Light colors will make the room look larger. Dark colors will make it look smaller. If you choose to paper rather than paint, you can choose from among textured or patterned styles. If walls are old and plaster is cracked, a plastic-coated wall covering may be the best solution, unless you have gained skill in plastering. A large patterned covering will make the room look smaller. A delicate texture (such as a rice paper or a flocked velvet finish) will have the same effect as a light color.

If you are skillful, you may be able to apply fabric to your walls. Fabrics may provide rich textures, but it is best to remember that

This intricately patterned rug softens the starkness of the wall treatments and draws the room together. The unusual window coverings obscure an unsightly view but allow plenty of light. The plants become part of the window treatment, as well.

fabrics may not be washable on the wall, whereas washable paper or plastic-coated coverings can be kept free of spots and stains.

Inventive decorators have used aluminum foil, paper cutouts, egg boxes, and any number of things to create unusual effects on walls. If you are going to try something unusual, you will do well to test your idea on a small space first to see whether it works— and whether you have the right materials (such as glue or staples) to do the job properly. In rented housing, such work may need the landlord's approval before it is undertaken. Some will agree to such work if they see a sample of it done and are subsequently convinced that it will not cause any damage to their property.

Floor coverings The basic floor in most houses and apartments is hardwood. Some floors may have carefully worked designs, called *parquet*, which create a rich and pleasing pattern when properly stained and waxed. If flooring is old and unsightly, it may be scraped, stained, and waxed. It is also possible to give floors an instant renovation with sheets or tiles of such resilient floor coverings as vinyl, linoleum, and asphalt. These are available in a variety of colors, patterns, and shapes. They come in a wide range of prices. At one time, such floor coverings were used mainly in kitchens. Today, their use has become increasingly popular in all "hard-wear areas," such as entries and family rooms. Resilient flooring is easy to clean without a vacuum cleaner.

325

Rugs and carpeting are two other kinds of floor covering. A rug is trimmed on four sides, while carpeting is usually cut to measure and stretched from wall to wall. If your room is a regular size, you may be able to get a room-size precut rug at lower cost. Stores sometimes sell odd sizes of wall-to-wall carpeting as fully trimmed remnants. Area rugs cover only a part of the floor. They may be used to set apart one section of a room. By arranging chairs and a couch around an area rug, for example, you can make that part of the room more inviting as a place for conversation.

Decorating a room with posters and memorabilia is an inexpensive way to fill space and create atmosphere. Such accessories can be replaced as they lose their charm or as more permanent furniture is acquired.

Window treatments Basic window treatments include curtains, draperies, and shades. In cold climates, curtains and draperies may serve an insulating function as well as a decorative one. Shades may be an economical first step for a do-it-yourself project. Shades can be decorated with fabric, iron-on tape, fringe, and other trimmings that add texture or pattern to the room. Louvered wooden shutters, especially in older houses, may be left just as they are, painted or stained. If they serve the purpose of controlling the amount of light, additional draperies, curtains, or shades may not be necessary.

Accessories In some cases, it is the accessories—the smaller items like lamps, pictures, and pillows—that "make" the home. These add the finishing touches that can make a home attractive and individualized.

Many home accessories need not be bought. Found objects such as shells and stones of unusual shape and color can be placed in a bowl. A piece of knotted wood or dried pods or weeds can bring the memory of a walk in the woods or along the beach to a city apartment. Objects can be crafted of clay, fiber, or enamel. To some, anything that has the look of natural materials seems to contrast well with certain severe lines in modern furniture. Many mass-produced articles such as posters, glassware, and metalware can be obtained at low cost. Some original artwork can be obtained inexpensively. (If you have artistic talent, you may do your own painting or sculpting.) An attractive homemade lampshade can give a unique appearance to an otherwise ordinary lamp.

Arranging Home Furnishings

In general, it is easier to work with only a few major pieces of furniture and to keep space open than to try to cram a great deal into limited space. A first home, in fact, may center on a multipurpose room with differentiated areas rather than a full-scale living space with many rooms. You can apply the principles of design discussed earlier to create a center of interest that will help to organize visual elements. You can create activity centers such as "conversation corners" that will encourage people to communicate and interact easily and comfortably.

Activity centers For housing to be satisfying, it must accommodate the activities of the people who live there. In a people-centered home, furnishings will be arranged so that people can talk and enjoy each other's company. Conversation groupings are established when seating, such as chairs, couches, or hassocks, face each other in ways that encourage talk and contact. When the furniture budget is low, an arrangement of ottomans and pillows can provide seating. If interests include reading and study, a somewhat isolated "book nook" (where books, magazines, or papers are at hand) will be an important activity center. If music is a main interest, a stereo may be the major furniture in the room. Chairs and sofas might then be placed where listening is best. If you have an absorbing hobby, a work center that

Window treatments should carry out the decor of a room. The lattice pattern of the wallpaper and the use of floral prints create an airy, garden-like atmosphere in this room. Such an atmosphere would be undermined by a fussy or heavy window treatment.

meets your needs may have highest priority. If you start with the things that interest you, your living space will soon reflect your personality. It will begin to be a home that you find comfortable, convenient, and beautiful.

Overall esthetic appeal Esthetically appealing living space can be achieved by applying the elements and principles of design (discussed in Chapter 13 and Chapter 18) when furnishing and decorating a room.

Many people, in designing a living area, are predominantly concerned with creating a sense of **unity**. They want to have a room in which everything "goes together." Things go together when there is some discernible

Eclectic decor combines furniture and accessories of different periods and styles. The use of color helps to unite the items in such a room, but the key to successful eclectic decoration is scale. Most furniture of similar proportions and dimensions will combine well.

relationship among them. They may be related in shape, use, style, color, texture— or simply because the owner likes to live with them.

A room may be unified by having a *center of interest*, a focal point to which everyone's eye is drawn. The emphasis may be on an architectural feature, like a fireplace, window, or wall hanging. It may be a brightly colored wall or upholstered sofa. The center of interest can provide a theme for your other decorating choices.

Besides unity, consider the scale, or **proportions**, of the room and everything you wish to put in it. Each element of space, light, size, mass, and form will be experienced in relation to every other one. You can see certain proportions objectively. Things may or may not have the same length, size, or shape; but you also sense proportion in the weight, or mass, of different areas and forms. Be aware of the amount of one color in relation to another. Be aware of the amount of one texture or pattern in relation to another. Consider the size and heaviness of a piece of furniture in relation to the rest of the room. There are no absolute rules about what is "too big" or "too small."

THE COST OF COMMUNITY FACILITIES

The facilities and services which a community offers cost money. Part of the expense is paid by real estate taxes. If you rent housing, you will not be directly faced with these taxes. This is not the case if you buy housing. These and other financial aspects of housing are the subject of the next chapter.

THINK BACK

Community resources can help us to reach goals.
Discuss: *What community resources do you feel your community most needs?*

Physical, psychological, social, economic, and spiritual factors can be involved in deciding where to live.
Discuss: *Why are so many housing decisions compromise decisions?*

Rooms of a home should show potential for meeting basic and special needs of home-owners.
Discuss: *Is it possible to have "a place for everything and everything in its place"?*

The variety of basic home furnishings available enables us to make choices based on individuality, usefulness, and suitability.
Discuss: *How is individuality expressed in home decoration?*

LOOK AROUND

1. What is a "planned community"?
2. Collect pictures and words that illustrate the meaning of "home" to you. Design a collage expressing your feelings. Comment on your own collage as well as on those of others.
3. What area in your home would you like to decorate as a reflection of the feelings in your collage? Make a scrapbook illustrating your furnishing ideas for the room. Explain your selections.
4. What is the most important single factor in deciding where to live? Why?
5. What is a "building code"? What are "zoning laws"? What are the effects of each on your neighborhood?
6. Develop an "Inspection Checklist" of points to look for in evaluating the usefulness of various living areas in a home. Which room in your home most nearly meets suggested requirements? Which requirements are important to you?

7. What is the difference between "decorating" and "furnishing" a home? How can the two ideas be used together in housing?

8. Talk with your parents or other family members to learn their reasons for furnishing your home as they did. What values and goals were expressed in the conversation?

9. Of all the homes which you have visited, which are your favorites? For what reasons? What housing values and goals have you revealed by your selections?

10. What guidelines concerning proportion in wardrobe selection can be applied to room decoration?

11. What special interests do you and members of your family have? Using furniture cutouts and floor plans drawn to scale, show the possibilities of arranging one or more rooms in your home to suit the interests of several family members.

FOLLOW YOUR PATH

PATH ONE: Make a Plan to Improve Your Own Home

Step 8 Jot down your activities at home. What do you do daily? Weekly? Once a year? Roughly sketch the space and equipment you use in these activities.

Step 9 People often devote a good deal of space and equipment to activities that are infrequently done. Compare your sketches from Step 7. Suggest some alternatives that you might try in order to expand space for activities that you do frequently.

Step 10 Examine the housing models in Step 15 of Path Four. Which one of those comes closest to your "dream residence" from Step 2? Would you enjoy living in such housing? What single change would you most like to make in such a house?

PATH TWO: Form a Family on the Move

Step 8 Examine the plans from Step 12 of Path Four for total space and room arrangements. In a family meeting, discuss which plans would best suit the needs of each member of the family.

Step 9 Show a Path Three decorator your Step 8 plans and Step 7 furniture groupings. Ask for plans for decorating rooms and, if called for, altering floor plans. Ask for a cost estimate. (If you get more than one estimate, compare them.)

PATH THREE: Be an Interior Designer

Step 9 For a Path One client, do a rough sketch of a piece of furniture that serves more than one function.

Step 10 Show your sketch to your client. Ask him to suggest improvements. Make any necessary modifications in the design.

Step 11 Make a model—with paper, wood, clay, or plaster—of your piece of furniture.

Step 12 Using pictures from magazines or original drawings, make designs for the housing models for Step 16 of Path Four. Present them to the planning board.

Step 13 Meet with the Path Two family to discuss designing the interior of their home.

PATH FOUR: Design A Community

Step 14 Discuss the models in Step 12. Discuss possible changes and improvements.

Step 15 Ask those following Paths One and Two to examine your models. Ask them if any of the models suit their housing needs.

Step 16 Show your models to Path Three designers. Ask them to suggest improvements.

Step 17 Refine your brown paper model. Circle several "typical" sections. Draw these in enlargement, showing the locations of individual buildings. Tell the types of housing, the kinds of stores, and so forth.

CHAPTER 20

Buying and Renting Housing

Just as with every other commodity, the cost of housing is influenced by supply and demand. It is influenced not only by the supply and demand for housing units, but also by the amount of money available to finance home ownership and housing construction.

Housing costs more to produce, stays in use longer, and takes up a greater proportion of most people's savings and income than any other ordinary expense. Thus, the availability of housing, either for rent or sale, can have far-reaching effects on the economic lives of individuals, families, and communities.

Housing is the single most important investment that most people make in their lifetimes. Furthermore, housing expenses include the cost of supplies and utilities needed to keep a modern household running. They also include the cost of upkeep and repair for all things connected with shelter. In addition, the cost includes the price of any services required to maintain the home. If these fixed costs get out of line, it is not easy to bring them under control.

ALTERNATIVES IN PAYING FOR HOUSING

Sometimes housing is rented; sometimes it is owned. Because housing represents such a large and long-range financial investment, people must consider alternatives carefully. Individuals and families will have to evaluate their resources of money, time, energy, and skills to determine which type of housing best suits them at a particular time.

Not everyone is temperamentally suited to home ownership. Some people can create leisure-time activities out of household projects and gain satisfaction from do-it-yourself activities. Others consider such activities as intrusions on the "really worthwhile" things—such as reading, painting, golfing, fishing, or writing. Taking care of a home is not everyone's favorite hobby. Thus, interests, skills, goals, and values will strongly influence the decision whether to own or rent. They will influence the various forms of ownership that you will want to consider for yourself.

The upkeep of a home may be a complete surprise to the new homeowner who did not envision his walks and driveway covered with snow. Those beautiful trees need maintenance, and the homeowner may have to repair his lawn when utilities are installed.

Rental Housing

Rent is money you pay to use property that belongs to someone else. Today, all types of housing—including mobile homes—are available as rental units. Most people begin independent living in a rental unit of one kind or another. For young adults whose long-range goal may be home ownership, the appropriate choice of a rental unit may be an important short-range goal. If home ownership is a long-range goal, low rental may be a short-term consideration. Renting the most economical, rather than the most desirable, living space may then permit saving for a down payment on a home.

A tenant may make rental arrangements directly with the landlord or through the landlord's agent or representative. In some buildings this will be the building superintendent. If the landlord is a public agency or housing authority, there will be government representatives on the premises.

In places where housing units are scarce, it may be necessary for a would-be tenant to place his name on a waiting list. By doing this he will probably be advised of vacancies when they occur. Since housing turnover is slow in congested areas, some people have waited for years before being informed of an appropriate vacancy.

A formal agreement to rent is called a *lease*. This details the relationship—including the rights, privileges, duties, and responsibilities—of *landlord* (owner) and *tenant* (renter). These conditions of rental are in force for the term of the lease.

Forms of Ownership

Land and buildings may be owned entirely by one person. There are also a number of ways in which property may be owned by more than one person. Some states have community property laws. Whatever may be acquired during a marriage by the efforts of either husband or wife belongs equally

Apartment dwellers should check their lease to see what improvements they may or may not be allowed to make. Fixtures that are permanently attached to the wall may have to stay behind if the renters move.

The National Tenants' Organization in Washington, D.C., and neighborhood or city tenant groups give renters information on laws governing rents and landlord–tenant responsibilities. These New Yorkers are getting advice on rent increases from the Metropolitan Council on Housing.

to both. As a general rule, the advantage of such joint ownership is that in the event of death, the property passes to the survivor immediately. This avoids lengthy and costly court proceedings. Provisions of ownership may vary in detail from state to state, but the following are the most common forms of joint ownership.

Outright ownership   Outright ownership of a home is likely to be the result of long-range planning and the availability of sufficient resources to pay for the home (with or without money lent by a bank or government agency). It allows the greatest leeway under law for the use of property. An owner can make all decisions concerning his property as long as he does not violate any laws.

Tenancy by the entirety   In tenancy by the entirety, a husband and wife or other co-owners are considered joint owners of the entire property. In case of the death of either one, the title to the entire property goes to the survivor. Neither can sell without the consent of the other. Clearly, such an arrangement has both advantages and disadvantages. Among them is the fact that in most states, if people own a piece of property through tenancy by the entirety, a creditor who has a judgment against one owner could not force a sale of the property to collect the amount due him. On the other hand, neither of the co-owners could act alone to sell, mortgage, or rent the property. For a married couple, this might create problems if the relationship becomes strained.

Joint tenancy Two or more persons can own property as joint tenants. Title will automatically pass to the survivor or survivors. Any of the joint tenants can change the arrangement by selling his interest. There are advantages and drawbacks to this form of ownership also. Co-owners may act alone. In some states, property held jointly is subject to seizure if a judgment is entered against any one of the owners.

Tenants in common Tenancy in common is similar to joint tenancy, except that the ownership does not pass to the surviving owner or owners. Each owner can leave his share of the property to whomever he wishes. This form of ownership is common with business property. A businessman may want his share of the business passed to his heirs, not to others who have an interest in the business. This might also be the goal of couples who marry later in life and who have adult children. They may then want to be sure that they are providing for their children in some way. Depending on the individual's wants and goals, different forms of joint ownership may be agreed upon.

Cooperative ownership A cooperative is a multiple-dwelling building that is run by a corporation in which the tenants hold shares. At the head of the corporation is a board of directors elected by the tenants. This board of directors makes decisions about the maintenance of the property and the sale of individual housing units.

No owner of a cooperative unit can buy, sell, or rent without approval of a board of directors. The need for this approval can place serious limitations on the owner's freedom to dispose of his unit if and when he should wish to do so.

Condominium ownership In a condominium, a resident owns his own unit in a multiple dwelling. While owners have control of their own units, they share responsibility and ownership for public rooms and other commonly used areas. The owner of a condominium can buy and sell the unit in the same way as the owner of a free-standing unit. The new owner of the unit becomes responsible in the same way as the previous owner for the cost of maintaining the common property. This form of ownership is gaining acceptance because it gives the owner complete control of his own unit. He can sell it at any time and to anyone he wishes.

HOME OWNERSHIP

Home ownership does not mean that the owner actually lives "rent free," as some people think. It does mean that his outlay for living space and other expenses takes a different form.

When investing in a home, the purchaser may be able to consider whether to build or buy. In buying, he will have to consider new or old housing. He may buy a ready-built house from a builder or developer, in which case he will be the owner of a new home. He may buy a home directly from the previous owner or through an agent or real estate broker. In buying an older home, he may find it in "move-in" condition. He may also decide to fix up an older home. Such decisions will depend on the time, energy, skills, and financial resources available to bring the housing up to his standards.

Financing Home Ownership

Land and anything attached to it is referred to as *real property,* or *real estate.* Real property, as contrasted with personal property, cannot be moved by the owner from one place to another. The term *title* refers to the rights of an owner in a particular piece of property. The legal document that passes title (ownership) from one owner to another is called a *deed.*

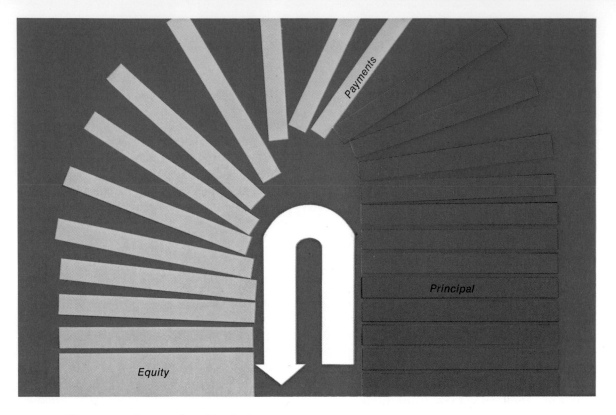

Payments

Principal

Equity

The amount of principal paid by the homeowner in his early mortgage payments may seem low by comparison with the interest he must pay. But with each payment of the same amount of money, a larger share goes toward reducing the principal debt. thus increasing his equity.

Home mortgages More than half of the owner-occupied homes in the United States are mortgaged. After making a down payment of from 10 to 30 percent, the buyer finances the balance by means of one or more mortgages. Money needed to buy a home or to buy into a cooperative or condominium is often borrowed. Financing may also be arranged for the purchase of a mobile home, but it differs, in most cases, from that used in buying a fixed-site home.

The agreement made between the lender and the borrower for the purpose of buying real property is called a *mortgage.* The lender is called the *mortgagee;* the borrower is called the *mortagagor.* The mortgage, signed by both the lender and the borrower, is a type of contract. It contains a plan, or schedule, for repaying the borrowed sum

(called the *principal*) plus interest at a specified rate within a specified period of time. It may contain other provisions agreed to by both parties. The property itself is the *security,* or pledge, that the loan will be repaid. If the mortgagor defaults on his payments, the mortgagee can foreclose on the property and, if he wishes, sell it to pay off the loan.

Mortgage payments Mortgage payments are usually made monthly, much like rent payments. They include repayment of the principal, plus interest at the agreed-upon rate, together with any other charges agreed to by the parties. Mortgage rates fluctuate. The borrower is wise to buy when rates are low, if he can.

In terms of cost, the smaller the amount

borrowed and the shorter the period of repayment, the more economical a mortgage is. Interest on a long-range, high-rate loan may, over a period of years, equal the actual price of the property. It may sometimes even exceed it. Therefore, those having home ownership as a goal will do well to save for as large a down payment as their resources will permit.

Decisions concerning repayment will take into consideration a number of factors. These include the borrower's age, income, and other plans for the future. Most couples have as a long-range goal a debt-free home at retirement. A prepayment clause allows the borrower, with certain penalties and restrictions, to pay his debt at a faster rate than the original schedule called for.

Payment of the mortgage reduces the principal. The process by which this indebtedness is reduced is called *amortization.* As the mortgagor makes his payments and reduces the principal, he begins to build up some rights, called *equity,* in the mortgaged property. The mortgagor's equity represents the portion of the property that he has paid for. The accumulation of equity is the actual value of the property to the borrower, who may want to sell the home before the payments have been completed.

Government-guaranteed mortgages Under certain circumstances and conditions, government agencies secure (that is, "guarantee") loans for home ownership. Among these agencies are the Federal Housing Administration (FHA), the Veterans Administration (VA), and the Farmers Home Administration of the Department of Agriculture (FHDA). The Federal National Mortgage Association (FNMA, sometimes irreverently referred to as "Fannie May") is an agency of the Department of Housing and Urban Development. It influences the amount of money made available for housing by buying, servicing, and selling government-guaranteed mortgages under certain conditions.

Such government guarantees help to stabilize the mortgage market. The guarantee insures the lender against loss in the event the borrower fails to meet his obligation to repay the loan. The proportion of the mortgage such government agencies are willing to guarantee varies with the type of housing, the amount of the mortgage, and the money market. The biggest advantage of FHA mortgages is that they usually require smaller down payments than conventional mortgages without this guarantee. Eligible veterans may be able to get a VA loan with little or no down payment and a low interest rate. All such guaranteed loans involve care-

Families of military service people have benefits that should be explored when they purchase a home. The Veterans Administration has offices to advise them of low-cost mortgages and tax exemptions.

CASE STUDY: ROGER AND SHARON

THE SITUATION   *After six weeks of house hunting, Sharon was losing her enthusiasm. She and Roger had found only two homes that interested them, and these were selling for more than they wanted to pay. They had hoped to find a three-bedroom home with a basement, recreation room, and big back-yard for their growing family. Would they have to settle for something less?*

After looking at individual homes, the couple turned to a tour of development homes. The homes were made of brick. They were situated on one-quarter or one-third acre plots—hardly the amount of space Sharon had envisioned for her children. For the price asked, the homes seemed to be cheaply made. There was very little individuality. Walls were thin. Kitchen cupboards were of soft, inexpensive wood. Baseboards in some were separating from the floor as the houses settled. It was hard to agree to pay thousands of dollars for what the couple considered inferior quality.

"Suppose we look at the town houses that are being built," suggested Roger. "They're not as private as we had hoped, but besides apartments, they're the only housing we haven't yet seen."

Town houses were new to their section of the country. They were three-story, single-family homes attached to seven other similar homes. There were private entrances to each home, with a private yard and terrace at the back of each. What pleased Sharon and Roger was the arrangement of the housing groups around beautifully landscaped garden areas. Playgrounds for children were distributed throughout the units, each safely reached by sidewalks that never crossed roadways. Other attractive features included the future construction of small shopping malls, office buildings, and adult recreation areas, all within walking distance of the housing groups. Everything seemed fine, except that the only available houses were for rent. None were for sale.

THE INTERVIEW   *Q: Would you prefer to buy or rent a home?*
A: We would rather buy. However, there is not much available that we would accept. Oh, there are many for sale, but we prefer certain features in a home, and none of the available homes had these features. And we just can't afford the asking prices of the two homes we did like. We're being shut out of the housing market in terms of the kind of home we dreamed of owning.
Q: How do the town houses appeal to you?
A: They were very nice. I liked the privacy, in spite of the fact that there would be homes on either side of us. And to us, the best features were the garden areas and playgrounds. We feel that children benefit from being able to play in open areas. There is less restraint on them emotionally and physically. In the single housing developments, there was such a feeling of confinement, even though everyone had a backyard! And besides, in the town house areas, children would be less threatened by traffic.
Q: What will your decision be?
A: We'll have to discuss the possibilities further. We don't like the idea of paying rent money and owning nothing in return. But the advantages that exist with renting a town house do not exist with owning the private homes we saw. If we agree to rent for several more years, a home we can afford and which suits our requirements may come on the market. We will try to decide soon.

REACT   *What would your decision be? How common is the problem they faced?*

ful appraisal of the property by specialized personnel who make sure that the borrower is making a reasonably sound investment.

Lenders are under no obligation to grant VA- or FHA-guaranteed loans. Conventional loans often earn higher interst rates for the lender. Lenders sometimes charge fees, known as *points*, as a prerequisite for granting a mortgage loan. Each point is 1 percent of the amount of the loan. By charging points, lenders can make FHA and VA mortgages as expensive as conventional mortgages.

Assuming an Existing Mortgage

It is sometimes possible to buy a house by assuming a mortgage that has not been paid off. In this way, you deal directly with the owner, bypassing the usual channels for securing a mortgage. The owner usually asks as a down payment the amount that represents his equity in the property. The buyer assumes the balance of the mortgage indebtedness. In some instances, the deal can be made without consulting the mortgagee. There is a drawback to this, however. The original borrower (mortgagor) remains responsible for the balance of the debt, unless he obtains a written release from the mortgagee. In that case, the new buyer will have to meet with the mortgagee's approval. That may be difficult if interest rates have gone up since the mortgage was arranged. The mortgagee may want a higher rate.

Sources of Home Financing

When the time comes to borrow money for home financing, some people may be able to borrow money from parents, other

Some communities seem to be impersonal. Yet, common causes do unite the residents. While property owners may have an obvious investment in their community, the environment could be tragically changed if all residents did not participate in "grass roots democracy."

It may be years before you use your property the way you will eventually want to, but the soil can provide immediate pleasures and economies like cutting gardens or vegetable patches. The younger members of this family are learning to take part in the plans of their parents.

relatives, or some other individual lender. Most borrowers, however, have to deal with a savings bank, savings and loan association, credit union, insurance company, or other institutional lender. The borrower should investigate each and compare the terms offered in relation to his resources and goals. There are usually a number of alternatives when making this major decision. The borrower may sometimes consult a mortgage broker for help in arranging the mortgage.

The money available for home financing fluctuates. In a "tight" money market, money is scarce. Interest rates are high. It costs the borrower more to finance a home. When the money market eases, money is "cheap." Interest rates come down. It costs the borrower less to buy a home.

Other Costs

The mortgage payment is not the only money outlay the prospective home buyer must consider. Lawyers and others involved in the transaction must be paid. Repairs, taxes, and insurance are other costs that add up.

Search of title When a title is *searched,* the history of its ownership, through deeds and other documents, is traced all the way back to its original owners. In the United States, this history can go back to the original Indian owners. Some titles go back to royal grants. Others go back to when the government opened land for settlement.

A careful search of title may disclose that others have some claim to the property and some rights of use. For example, some previous owner may have sold the mineral or water rights. A power company may have been given the right to put utility poles on the land. A neighbor may have the right to drive cows right through it. Such restrictions may hamper a future owner's plans for the property. Such rights (as well as outstanding legal judgments and unpaid mortgages) are called *encumbrances*. Unless they are fully known and understood, the new buyer may find himself the owner of a piece of property that is useless for his purposes.

The *title search* is most generally performed by a real estate lawyer or by employees of a *title guaranty company*. After careful examination of related records, the accuracy of the deed, which is legal evidence of ownership, is assured. This protects the lender against any future claims. *Title insurance* protects the lender against any flaw in the deed that might jeopardize his rights of ownership. It may be taken out by the buyer to protect him against future claims.

Closing costs   At the *closing*, when the deal (or arrangement) is formally "closed," the buyer becomes the new owner of the property. If a mortgage is involved, the property simultaneously becomes security for the loan. A number of costs arise at this time. These may include the lawyer's and real estate broker's fees and the cost of filing records. The buyer should be prepared to pay closing costs. Provision for payment of these costs is often overlooked. The buyer is expected to have with him at the closing a certified check to pay these costs. Buyer and seller sometimes share closing costs.

Repairs   In the course of time, ground shifts and, with it, houses shift and settle. This may create stresses and strains on the structure. The materials in the house expand and contract with heat and cold. Wind and water take their toll. As one writer put it, "Wood and mortar have more enemies than friends."

Among these enemies of wood are any number of pests—including termites. Before buying a home, the prospective buyer should have the premises inspected for these destructive winged ants. He may even request a written guarantee from the previous owner that the premises have been examined and found free of such infestation.

All this is to say that a home (no matter how attractive or how well constructed) is "used up" and "wears out" just like anything else. This may result in the reduction of the value of the property. This is called *depreciation*. Depreciation makes repair and upkeep a major cost in home ownership. This is an area where "do-it-yourself" skills can effectively reduce the cost of housing.

The Internal Revenue Service permits a depreciation allowance based on the assumption that a house will be "worn out" in forty

Drainage, zoning regulations, traffic hazards, transportation, building regulations, and laws governing pets and animals are a few items that should be considered by prospective homeowners.

INVESTING IN APPLIANCES

Whether buying or renting, you may find it necessary to purchase some appliances. You would do well to consider such purchases carefully, for appliances are expensive and you will want them to last for many years. In some circumstances, you may wish to consider secondhand, rebuilt, or reconditioned models. Look for a warranty which covers repairs and replacement parts for a reasonable amount of time.

Refrigerators and freezers Many tenants are asked to supply certain appliances. In an older home, the refrigerator may often have to be replaced. You will have to decide whether you want a conventional refrigerator, a combination refrigerator-freezer, or separate units. Your answer will depend on family size, the number of meals eaten at home, food shopping and storage patterns, and social needs. Extra features such as ice makers may not be necessary for those in their first home. Special storage space for eggs, butter and cheese, meats, and vegetables may help to preserve freshness if they are well designed and properly used. If there is a choice, be aware that appliances come in right- and left-hand door models. Choose the one that suits you and the place where your appliance will be put. A door opening in the wrong direction can be a daily irritation.

Ranges A wide selection of ranges in both gas and electric models is available. Ranges may be free-standing, built-in, console (an eye-level oven with a countertop range), and drop-in models that give the appearance of built-ins. In addition to conventional ovens, microwave ovens are now available. These cook foods in only a fraction of the time needed for most customary cooking methods. Such features as self-cleaning and automatic timing may be worth the additional investment for some homemakers. Check for ample drip pans under heating units or burners to make cleaning easier.

years. More realistically, the exposed and used areas of a home may be replaced on the average of every twenty years.

Equipment within the home is even more prone to wear and tear. A homeowner will want to replace appliances that may be run down or broken.

Property taxes Real property and some kinds of personal property, such as home furnishings and equipment, are subject to taxes of various kinds. Tax rates vary from place to place. Real property—both land and buildings—is *assessed*. It is given a dollar value for tax purposes. The assessed valuation may be higher or lower than the purchase price. The buyer must bear in mind that improvements he plans to make will raise the taxes on his property. In some areas, for some types of housing, special tax incentives have been offered to encourage renovation and rebuilding. The buyer must get as much information as he can and weigh it in terms of his financial resources.

Dishwashers In considering a dishwasher, you ought to know whether you have a sufficient supply of hot water to use it effectively. Dishwashers come in both built-in and free-standing models. In small apartments, a portable dishwasher may be used. This requires no installation.

Laundry equipment Many people use coin-operated and commercial laundries. Many wish to have their own washers and dryers. You may be able to choose from among automatic, semi-automatic, and hand-operated washers. You will also have to consider whether you want a front-loading or a top-loading washer. Experience will dictate a preference. Installing a dryer requires special air venting. In crowded apartments, certain space-saving washer-dryer combinations may be a possibility.

Cleaning equipment The proper care of rugs and carpets requires the use of a vacuum cleaner. This appliance also offers attachments for care of draperies, upholstery, and floors. Small crevice-cleaning attachments may increase the utility of a vacuum cleaner. Light cleaning may be better accomplished with a hand-powered carpet sweeper. Floor washers and polishers may help keep large, frequently used areas clean.

Small appliances Portable appliances are available to meet a wide variety of needs and tastes. They usually help with manual tasks such as mixing, polishing, blending, cutting, cooking, and sharpening. Such jobs, unless done often, may be done more efficiently by hand—if you consider the cost of electricity, time spent in cleaning, and space used for storage as economic factors. Some functions of the blender cannot be performed by hand. Table appliances such as toasters, electric skillets, and other cookware may conserve fuel if they are used in place of full ranges for certain purposes. Small appliances should be examined for the UL (Underwriters' Laboratory) seal. This indicates the appliance has been tested and is considered safe.

Special assessments Homeowners may be assessed for the use of such community resources as beaches and parks. They may be assessed for libraries and special community health facilities. They may also be assessed for such community improvements as sewers, sidewalks, roads, and water pipes. They may also be assessed for such essential services as waste and trash removal and for police and fire protection.

The homeowner may also be assessed for improvements made on his property. These may include such things as a finished basement. Such improvements usually add to a home's assessment for tax purposes, also.

Property insurance There is a risk involved in any kind of ownership. A homeowner wants to protect his investment to the best of his ability against loss or damage. Insurance helps to reduce the risk of loss to a few by spreading the cost among many policy holders. Many kinds of insurance are available. Insurance rates vary widely for different kinds of in-

Large home-repair jobs are best done by established contractors who guarantee their work. Consumers should be wary of repair offers made by door-to-door salesmen who may not complete—or start—the work.

surance in different parts of the country. A homeowner's basic insurance usually provides coverage against loss from fire, windstorm, and burglary. A homeowner may also carry insurance against other forms of loss. In buying insurance, he ought to consider the likely types of loss. He also should consider whether other forms of protection—like a burglar alarm—might offer adequate protection at a lower cost.

Financing the Mobile Home

A mobile home is usually thought of as personal property rather than real property. Financing a mobile home is much like financing a car. The payments are covered by a *chattel mortgage*. This usually requires a down payment of from one-third to one-quarter of the total purchase price. The balance is payable in a shorter period of time than for a conventional home. The payments include the cost of the home, its furnishings, and insurance on the property. In some cases, the mobile home dealer himself may arrange for financing the purchase.

Costs sometimes overlooked by those contemplating the purchase of a mobile home are the rent for the lot on which it is placed and the cost of utilities. If the home is to be moved, consider the cost of transporting the home from one site to another.

Financing Repairs and Remodeling

Some people meet their housing needs by repairing and remodeling the home in which they live. Some buy older homes with the intention of remodeling. The attraction of older housing is often that the homes are more available and more spacious; some can be found in well-established, well-developed neighborhoods. Further, older homes may have fine details of workmanship and craftsmanship lacking in mass-produced homes.

Repairing and remodeling of housing is not to be undertaken lightly. It can involve a tremendous investment of time, energy, and skills—as well as money. If older housing is fundamentally sound, investment in updating it may be a practical alternative. In buying older housing, there are costs to consider over and above monthly mortgage payments.

Obtaining money to remodel an old house may present problems. Lenders often prefer to make loans on new houses that are easier to sell and that increase in value more rapidly. You may, therefore, have to settle for a second mortgage of shorter term and higher rate if you choose to buy an old home.

Families and individuals set their own priorities for repairs and remodeling. These will depend on their standard of living and their own goals and values related to housing. Prospective buyers should consider the time, money, and energy necessary to clean up an old home. They should anticipate the delays that may take place before the house is really habitable.

Among the repairs that may have to be considered in older housing are refinishing floors, replacing steps, and fixing railings. It may be necessary to insulate attic floors and ceilings to prevent excessive heat loss. Providing adequate plumbing, wiring, and heating may involve major outlays of money. Other expenses may include replacing roofing, siding, and gutters, and replacing or repairing a furnace or water heater. Putting a fireplace in working order may involve replacing a chimney.

Remodeling costs may involve such large-scale projects as adding rooms or even a full second story, including stairs, structural improvements, finishing off an existing basement or attic, remodeling bathrooms and kitchens, replacing fixtures and major appliances, and installing air conditioning.

Home improvement loans Most institutional lenders offer loans for home improvement. They are usually available at high interest rates, so it is wise to shop for the least expensive arrangement. It is sometimes possible to arrange for financing directly with or through the contractor who is doing the work. Some FHA loans are available for projects in a certain cost bracket. Such loans are usually for projects that make homes more useful and livable. Not all lending institutions handle FHA loans, however. It may be wise to check first through the nearest FHA office, Better Business Bureau, or local builders' association.

Fire, theft, and liability insurance are generally needed by both apartment renters and homeowners. A wide variety of insurance programs are available to cover the needs of all homemakers.

For small home-improvement projects, you may be able to get a personal bank loan at a rate slightly lower than a home-improvement loan. You may have to put up some form of security. With satisfactory credit and income, your signature may be ample security.

Open-end mortgages If, at the time you buy a home, you already have plans for future remodeling, you may wish to arrange

345

for an *open-end mortgage*. An open-end mortgage allows you to borrow additional money from the original lender after some part of the original debt has been paid. The additional loan is repaid either by increasing the size of monthly payments or extending them for a longer period of time. The interest paid on the new loan will depend on the terms of the original contract. It will also depend on the availability of money at the time you borrow.

Second mortgages Additional money for home improvement may sometimes be obtained through a second, or junior, mortgage.

In the event of default, the first mortgage must be paid before the second mortgage. Thus, the lender is taking a greater risk. For this reason, rates for second mortgages may be higher than for original mortgages.

Construction loans It is sometimes possible to borrow money in the form of a construction loan, based on the value of property before and after remodeling.

For example, if you wanted to buy a house appraised at $20,000 and you wanted to make $8,000 worth of improvements, raising the anticipated value of the house to $28,000, you might investigate this kind of loan. If the

When major alterations or repairs are planned, their long-term use should be considered. Is the room to be a laundry or nursery forever? Does a garage location increase or decrease yard space? What effect will improvements have on the assessed value of the home?

CASE STUDY: DOUG AND FRANCINE

THE SITUATION   Francine just didn't feel like talking anymore. There seemed to be no easy way to make decisions about buying a house. After so much discussion, the biggest problem was still the financing of their home.

"My parents will lend us the money," she said to her husband. "They've done it often enough in the past."

Francine and Doug had thought of this possibility themselves, and were at first pleased by her parents' offer. The couple would be able to have the money right away so that it would be available the moment needed. The amount offered them exceeded what they had hoped to spend for a home, widening their choices in real estate. And the payments and interest rate charged by her parents would be lower than those charged by a commercial firm. This last advantage was enticing, particularly when coupled with the long period of time in which they could repay the loan. But the more he thought about it, the more convinced Doug became that this was not the best answer.

"Well, why not let them help us?" argued Francine. "It makes them happy."

Doug agreed that this was so, but he was beginning to think of his own happiness, too. He wanted to be able to support his family himself. Though he worked hard, he sometimes wondered when he'd ever have money to spend for more than bills. He knew he could do it eventually.

As Doug tried to make Francine understand, he could see she felt differently. All her life, his wife had been dependent on her parents. Though she had held jobs and been encouraged to solve her own problems, Mother and Daddy had always been there for support. When Francine and Doug married, they rented an apartment only thirty miles from Francine's home. Monthly visits to Mother and Dad continued the dependency. Maybe now was the time to change.

"Think about it," reminded Doug. "We would be in debt to them for a long time. Sure, we'd have a nice home in a nice neighborhood to show for it, but it's time we were on our own. We're adults, not children. We might not be able to afford the type of home we want at first, but who says we have to live there for the rest of our lives? People move around a lot."

"We'll hurt them," replied Francine.

"Maybe at first," answered Doug. "But in the long run, I think paying for our home ourselves is best for all four of us."

THE INTERVIEW   Q: Will Francine agree to seek money for your home elsewhere?
A: I hope so. Just because I don't want to accept the offer doesn't mean I want to stop associating with her parents. We're still part of the family, and I still love them both. It's just so easy to continue taking the easy way out. We have to do this ourselves.
Q: Why does your need for independence center on house buying?
A: Because buying and furnishing a home is a long-term project involving lots of discussion and decision. It's the time when two people can work together on a common goal. It can unite and strengthen a family because the members are meeting problems and finding solutions together. If Mother and Dad lend us the money, they will keep their hold on Francine and she'll be their "little girl" for a long time. Our family should start out with two of us, not four of us.

REACT   Do you agree with Doug's reasoning? What are your recommendations for financing the new home? How does a person gain independence from his family?

bank approved, it would give you $15,000 (75 percent of the lower appraisal). It would also make a total commitment of $20,000 (75 percent of the $28,000 improved value). The difference between the two loan amounts is $5,000. The bank would release this sum to the contractor doing the remodeling as his work progresses. You would pay the difference between $5000 and the actual cost of the work. You would come out with a $20,000 mortgage on a house worth $28,000; and you would be paying off the improvement cost at the same interest rate as the mortgage carries.

PROTECTING THE HOME BUYER

When making such a major investment, how can the consumer protect himself? In general, he must rely on the skill and honesty of the builder and other professionals with whom he is dealing. This is especially true when he buys a new house. If he can, he should look at other examples of the builder's work. He can talk with people who live in other homes he has built. They will usually be glad to talk about their experiences.

If you deal with a builder who has established roots in a community, he will still be

The Triton City Project, conducted by the Triton Foundation, is made up of floating neighborhoods designed to be anchored off large cities. Each neighborhood would be a single "building" into which modules for homes, schools, stores, and offices could be plugged.

there if a problem comes up. Your local Better Business Bureau and the National Association of Home Builders can make some information available to you. The other professionals with whom you deal are likely to give you sound advice. This is true of the mortgage officer at the bank you deal with. He can give you the bank's estimate on the reliability of builders they know, and an estimate of the future value of a piece of property you intend to purchase.

In buying older housing, you will not be dealing directly with the builder. You will most likely have to deal with the owner of the premises or his agent. You may want the objective opinion of a professional appraiser who can tell you about the quality of materials and construction and the present condition of a home you are contemplating.

The buyer must really be his own first line of defense. He must look, listen, and learn as he investigates the housing market and the money market related to home buying.

HOMES OF THE FUTURE

Concepts of housing, of environments for living, and of home ownership may change over time. People may develop new forms of living space based on the new frontiers of space and the oceans. It is possible that housing may be provided on these new frontiers as it was once provided on the "old" frontier of the West. It is not unlikely that the moon will one day have settlements. Explorers have already lived under the sea. If the seas can provide food, it is argued, why not an environment for living, as well?

As physical space becomes crowded, air rights have become more important for housing. Housing has been built over bridges, over waterways, and over highways. As new technology develops, it may be possible to move larger modular units of housing from place to place. The future of housing can be expected to change with our expanding technical and social environment.

THINK BACK

Decisions to rent or buy housing depend on your goals, your resources, and on the availability of housing.
Discuss: *Can you live where you want to live?*

Buying or remodeling a home should be undertaken only when the buyer thoroughly understands all the costs involved.
Discuss: *What is "reading the fine print"?*

Home ownership involves an understanding of the legal rights of ownership.
Discuss: *Does a home "belong" to all family members or only to adults in the family?*

Consumer protection in housing is largely dependent on the reputation of the people with whom you deal.
Discuss: *Must the "buyer beware"?*

LOOK AROUND

1. What information does a lease contain?
2. What are the legal rights of landlords in your state? Tenants?
3. What are the different forms of ownership of housing? Which would be ideally suited to you? Explain.
4. What are the legal rights involved in various types of joint home ownership? What arrangement might suit you best?
5. What information must be in a mortgage?
6. What is the advantage to the mortgagee of a government-guaranteed mortgage?
7. What are the regulations involving the purchase and use of a mobile home? What features make it an acceptable alternative to other types of housing?
8. Define depreciation. Does only real property depreciate, or does personal property depreciate as well? Explain.

9. Which method of financing home repairs seems to you to offer the most advantages? Why?

10. Interview older adults to learn of their experiences with their first housing rental or ownership. Develop a "Compare This" bulletin board illustrating similarities or differences between their experiences and those of people today.

11. What is the down payment needed for home ownership in your community?

FOLLOW YOUR PATH

PATH ONE: Make a Plan to Improve Your Own Home

Step 11 List the new furnishings in your second sketch in Step 5. Go comparison shopping for these items. Report your findings.

Step 12 Interview people who share apartments, live in mobile homes, and so on. Find out about such things as costs, advantages and disadvantages, furniture needs, and conveniences. Record your findings.

Step 13 Make arrangements to see one or two apartments and mobile homes. Note size, convenience, and furniture requirements.

Step 14 Prepare a display for each type of housing you would consider as a first home of your own.

Step 15 Present your displays to the class. Explain each according to an individual's needs and resources.

PATH TWO: Form a Family on the Move

Step 10 Find out from the Path Four committee how much the home you selected would cost.

Step 11 Discuss the decorator's plans and estimates. If you have more than one to choose from, make your choice.

Step 12 Visit a banker. Ask him the conditions for financing the home and its decoration. What would mortgage payments be?

Step 13 Present your findings to the class.

PATH THREE: Be an Interior Designer

Step 14 If possible, show your design plans for the Path Two family to an interior designer. Ask how much they would charge a client for such an interior. Submit a comparable estimate to your client.

Step 15 Survey some stores in your community to see if the item you designed in Step 11 would sell.

Step 16 Create a newspaper advertisement for your business.

Step 17 Furnish a model room for Path Four.

Step 18 Prepare a brochure showing do-it-yourself home furnishings.

PATH FOUR: Design a Community

Step 18 Evaluate the Path Three design suggestions. Consider the suggestions from Paths One and Two. Finalize the design.

Step 19 Out of cardboard or another material, build the models.

Step 20 Arrange all the houses as though they were on a single street. Make trees, shrubs, and whatever else you feel you need to create realistic surroundings.

Step 21 Commission Path Three designers to completely furnish rooms.

Step 22 Show your plans and models to an architect, a builder, or a real estate agent. Ask how much such structures would cost. Ask for comments on the design.

Step 23 Visit a banker. Find out the necessary conditions for financing such housing. What might the monthly payments be?

Step 24 Consult again with traffic managers, the recreation department, and the street department in your community. Ask them to criticize your design.

CHAPTER 21

Careers in Housing

Thus far we have discussed what housing and home furnishings are. We have discussed some of the strategies involved in deciding where to live and how to select and pay for housing and home furnishings. In this chapter we will take a look behind the housing and home furnishings decisions that many of you are on the verge of making. We will examine some of the many and varied jobs which people perform to bring you the goods and services relevant to these decisions. Could one of these jobs launch you into a satisfying career?

HOUSING
AND RELATED INDUSTRIES

In one sense, the housing industry begins in the forests, with lumberjacks cutting down trees. It begins with the mining of iron and other metals. It encompasses the manufacture of glass and steel and concrete. The architect works in the housing industry. So does the builder.

Related to the housing industry are the home-furnishings and appliance industries. These include everyone involved in the manufacture of everything from slipcovers to freezers. They include everyone who transports raw materials to the factories and the finished product away. They include store managers and salespeople.

Those who work designing, producing, and distributing doorknobs, light bulbs, electric wires, soap dishes, and mattress springs also support the housing industry.

The United States Census Bureau projects that our population will grow from 200 million to 300 million within the next twenty years. This means we will need to vastly increase our already short supply of housing. The creation of so many new households will generate jobs for millions of workers.

LADDERS AND LATTICES

Housing and related industries offer a wide variety of career opportunities at every level. These range from the tree pruner, whose main qualifications are an appreciation for the outdoors and an enjoyment of physical work, to the architect, who spends years learning his profession in school and on the job.

Entry-level Jobs

There are entry-level jobs in housing and related industries for people of almost every type. Those who like to work with their hands may become involved with making draperies and slipcovers. A wide variety of sales jobs are available. There are also careers for those who like to work outdoors.

Slipcover and drapery makers A person with manual dexterity and some knowledge of sewing may wish to earn his living making slipcovers or drapes. Some companies employ a number of sewing machine operators to mass-produce these items. The work is similar to other sewing-machine operator positions. Many stores employ people to make slipcovers and draperies to order. It is possible for someone to offer such service from one's own home. The work can be done on a part-time basis to fit in with other duties.

Furniture sales Certain aspects of most sales jobs are the same. Most involve showing merchandise to customers and answering their questions. Most involve accepting cash payments. Some involve accepting payment by credit cards or charge accounts. A basic knowledge of arithmetic is required. Because of the close contact with people, an agreeable personality is important.

Hence, someone may become a furniture salesperson after working in another sales area. Furniture sales careers also have their specific requirements. The salesperson must have a knowledge of furniture quality, styles, and construction. He needs this knowledge to inform customers of the desirability of the products he is selling. Because of the expense of furniture, customers may be cautious about making purchases. Salespeople must frequently devote a good deal of time and patience in making sales. Furniture salespeople earn more than unspecialized clerks.

Distributive education courses in high school can be helpful to those interested in this career. Possibilities exist for moving on to careers as buyers and store managers.

Experience in furniture sales is valuable for those who wish to open their own businesses.

Furniture movers Moving furniture requires physical strength and the ability to work carefully. Movers use special boxes and packing materials for delicate items like glassware and dishes. Some householders hire movers to come in to do their packing before moving.

Inside the truck, skilled movers arrange furnishings so that they form a compact load. They use ropes and padding to make sure that nothing gets broken or scratched.

Workers may become movers by starting out as helpers. They may also enter this line of work after having performed other tasks requiring a good deal of physical strength. Large moving companies will

THRIFT SHOPS:
A COMMUNITY SERVICE

The refurbishing of household goods and equipment has long been one of the services that Goodwill Industries and Salvation Army Thrift Shops have provided for communities. In addition, skilled craftsmen who perform the remodeling are provided with jobs. Training programs are usually available in these organizations. There, trades and crafts for occupational choices can be learned.

Today, when more members of the household go out to work, small businesses perform what were the heavy household tasks of families. With modern equipment and new techniques, these skilled servicemen can do most work more efficiently than the homemaker.

usually train their employees. There, specialization is more common. Movers may, for example, be piano movers, appliance movers, or dish packers. Small firms usually expect one mover to be able to perform a wide range of jobs.

Refuse and sanitation workers The refuse and sanitation worker performs a service directly related to human health, ecology, and environmental protection.

One of the most valuable services to any household, commercial building, or community is performed by sanitation crews. They provide protection against disease. Uncollected waste materials create many potential hazards to health.

Appliance repairmen may specialize in the maintenance of a few name-brand appliances. Major manufacturers train them. Large appliance dealers usually recommend local repairmen to their customers.

Waste collectors usually work in the early morning hours. They often are not seen by their clients. Their service provides immediate and direct benefit to homes, commercial buildings, and communities.

Special Skills and Talents

Many jobs in the building trades require special skills. Among these are plasterers, carpenters, electricians, and plumbers. Skilled workers are also employed in making and repairing furniture and appliances. A few such jobs are considered here.

Furniture upholsterers Reupholstering furniture usually involves more than removing the old fabric and putting on a new one. It involves rebuilding furniture. The process includes sewing and tying new springs in place. Several layers of materials (padding and reinforcement) are then secured to the springs and the frame. Finally, the upholstery material is cut and sewn. In large upholstery shops, these functions may be performed by several people. Those in business for themselves can perform all these functions.

The usual way to learn the upholstery trade is on the job, either in a large reupholstery shop or in a furniture factory. There, one can begin with the simpler functions and work up to the more complex ones. Some special courses are offered at the high school level in this field. A few people join apprenticeship programs, which take three or four years to complete. Upholsterers use a variety of hand and power tools. They must be able, on occasion, to do fairly heavy lifting. Many upholsterers are self-employed.

Appliance servicemen The term "appliance servicemen" refers to those who repair everything from toasters to refrigerators. Few people actually repair such a wide variety of items. Most repairmen specialize in either gas or electric appliances. Many specialize in a single type of major appliance.

CASE STUDY: MERLE AND ROGER

THE SITUATION *Merle had already checked the venting system and thermostat in his home several times. He was glad that Roger, the repairman, could come today. It was getting warmer and warmer, inside as well as outside. As he watched Roger turn bolts and screws, he marvelled at his knowledge of this kind of machinery. Merle had absolutely no interest in learning about motors. He would prefer to pay a repairman rather than try to fix something in his home himself. Curious, he wondered how Roger had gotten into the repair business.*

"I don't repair everything that has a motor," explained Roger. "I'm strictly an air-conditioning man. Someone else would have to fix a broken dishwasher or electrical appliance if you had called for that type of repair."

"Did you learn your trade on the job?" asked Merle.

"I had an air-conditioning business of my own," replied the repairman. "Before that, I attended a training school. When I went into business for myself, I received more training from the air-conditioning company."

"Didn't you enjoy having your own business?" questioned Merle.

Roger chuckled slightly. Merle knew he shouldn't have asked the question. He listened to Roger's answer, embarrassed by his own curiosity.

"Well, how shall I say this? The best way to put it is to say there was too much cut-throat competition. You know what I mean? But I'll try again someday."

Merle nodded and did not pursue the issue further.

THE INTERVIEW *Q: What did Roger mean when he answered your question?*
A: I guess he meant that he went out of business. It takes some experience and business know-how to compete in a job that involves self-employment.
Q: What kinds of problems might he have had?
A: There are any number of things that could have happened. Maybe the men who worked for him were not expert repairmen. Or there could have been too many other men, better established then he was, in the same business. They might have been getting all the business. Roger may not have known how to get the attention of potential customers and give them good service. Maybe customers didn't pay their bills, or his prices were too high—or too low. Who knows?
Q: How would a person who once had his own business feel about working for someone else?
A: That probably depends on the person. Some people might feel a lot happier because they no longer had all the responsibility of the business. Others might dislike taking orders, especially after being their own boss for so long. Some people might just use the situation to hold them over until the time they could enter into business for themselves again. Many small businessmen fail each year. And there are also many which succeed. Roger is an excellent repairman. He might do well the second time around. He probably learned a lot from his first unfortunate experience.

REACT *How does a person in business for himself succeed?*

Plumbing is important in both the construction and building maintenance industries. The great variety of buildings that require plumbing should suggest the complexity of such work and the skills and knowledge it requires. There are opportunities for small and large businesses.

At least half of the appliance servicemen are self-employed. Many run shops where they sell used and reconditioned appliances. Most other servicemen work in service centers run by large stores or appliance manufacturers.

Customers usually bring small appliances to a shop. Servicemen visit homes to repair major appliances. Because of the customer contact, a pleasing personality is as important in this line of work as is mechanical skill. It is not unusual, for example, for a repairman to show a customer the recommended way to use a washing machine or dishwasher.

Most employers prefer to hire high school graduates whose school records indicate that they have a working knowledge of elec-

tricity and mechanics. Much can be learned on the job by beginning with simple repairs and working up to more complex ones.

Gardeners and landscapers Once builders or construction workers leave a building site, gardeners and landscapers may be needed. Building and construction firms usually do not employ landscapers; they subcontract this work to smaller firms or individuals. Owners of public buildings and private homes need the services of gardeners or landscapers from time to time. Many large companies and government agencies employ full-time gardeners. They may hire many people just for the summer, too.

Most landscapers and gardeners know local growing conditions and plants. They can plan attractive outdoor settings. People who enter this field enjoy working out of doors and helping plants grow.

Carpenters Carpenters comprise the largest group of building trade workers. There are basically two kinds: rough carpenters and finish carpenters. When they work on housing, *rough carpenters* erect the wood framing, including subflooring and rafters. Their primary concern is that their work is strong and structurally accurate. *Finish carpenters* must be concerned with the appearance of their work, which includes installing doors, cabinets, and windows. Some carpenters specialize in one kind of carpentry. Some may only lay hardwood floors or build staircases. Some may primarily do paneling. All must be skilled with a wide variety of hand and power tools. Carpenters either work for contractors or are self-employed. Many alternate between the two.

Some people acquire their carpentry skills in vocational schools. A great many learn carpentry informally. The National Joint Carpentry Apprenticeship and Training Committee recommends a four-year apprenticeship program. Besides on-the-job training, this includes classroom instruction.

Management Careers

There are a variety of careers in housing and in related industries. These range from plant managers in furniture and appliance factories to apartment house superintendents. Here we consider three careers that require some management skills: real estate brokers, contractors, and hotel managers.

Real estate brokers A broker is an independent businessman who sells real estate. Many brokers specialize in real estate of a particular kind—private homes or commercial properties. Many deal only with property within a particular price range. Some brokers also rent and manage properties.

When a property owner gives a real estate broker the right to sell or rent a property, he is said to give him a *listing*. A real estate broker or his employees spend a good deal of time on the phone obtaining listings. Listings are also obtained through personal contacts and through advertisements.

One reason why real estate brokers specialize is that selling each kind of property involves a particular kind of knowledge. A broker selling farms, for example, would need to know about local soil and weather conditions. All must know about tax laws, insurance, and other relevant financial matters.

People who like plants and know how to care for them may work in or own garden shops and greenhouses. Some of these businesses specialize in "indoor landscaping" and offer various maintenance services.

Architects can be defined many ways, according to the services they perform. More and more, they are becoming custodians of the environment. Their responsibility to their clients is intertwined with their responsibility to society.

As a businessman, a broker needs to keep orderly records. He also needs to know how to work with people. He must be convincing and a good negotiator. He may have to act as a middleman between a buyer and a seller.

Many brokers employ *real estate salesmen* to sell and rent property. Both brokers and salesmen must be licensed by the state in which they work. They must pass a test which includes questions about real estate laws and procedures. The test for brokers is more inclusive than that for salesmen. In some states, the broker must first have worked as a salesman or taken college courses.

Most real estate businesses are small, consisting of only a few people. Some people combine real estate with other enterprises, like law or insurance. A great many people

sell real estate part-time. Housewives, among others, are able to do this because they can adjust their working hours to fit into their family's schedules. Many colleges offer courses in real estate. Some large firms have training programs.

Contractors   A contractor is a businessman who accepts responsibility for constructing or repairing buildings. He may also take care of related work, like paving driveways. Some contractors specialize. One may do only restaurants. Another may concentrate on doing alterations inside homes.

Contractors get their names from the fact that they sign contracts. These contracts define the kind and amount of work that must be done. They also state the amount

CASE STUDY: JERRY AND UNCLE DON

THE SITUATION *Getting up at six o'clock on a summer morning never did appeal to Jerry. He had taken this construction job because he needed to earn more money before school started again. Uncle Don owned the company, needed extra help, and was willing to hire Jerry for the remaining three weeks of summer.*

Being new to construction work, Jerry was the lowest paid. He was an aide to the more experienced men. So far, he had worked with lath, masonry, roofing, plastering, and wiring. The work was hard, and he always welcomed his hour's break for lunch.

Today, as on previous days, Jerry had eaten lunch and rested in the shade of a tree near the construction site. His next sensation was that of a boot gently rocking his leg and a voice saying, "Get up, Jerry! Day's only half over!" Jerry had fallen asleep. He opened his eyes to see Uncle Don grinning at him. "What's the matter with you, kid? We have mortar to mix and bricks to lay."

Jerry struggled to his feet. "Uncle Don, I can't keep up with you. I like to work steadily, but slowly, taking a break now and then for a rest."

"Can't do that here," replied Don. "This house has to be built before the end of the month. Best thing to do is to work hard and fast, get it all done, and then sit down for a rest. Come on. The men are waiting."

THE INTERVIEW *Q: Uncle Don works his men hard, doesn't he, Jerry?*

A: It seems that way to me. He's a strong, hard worker himself. He expects his employees to be the same way. He doesn't realize we're not all like him.

Q: Was he angry that you fell asleep on the job?

A: Oh no! He is pretty easygoing and has a good sense of humor. He'd say the same thing to one of the other men. Being a relative of his doesn't give me special privileges. I have to earn my wages.

Q: Would you recommend that a person work for his father, uncle, or other relative?

A: It doesn't bother Don or me that I work for him. Like I said, he treats everyone the same and I'm glad of that. If I were treated special, I think the other men would resent me. Hard feelings would be created because the men would consider the situation unfair. Sometimes I get angry that Don does work me as hard as he does the others, but that's really the best way all around. It's only for three weeks, anyway. I can keep up for that long.

REACT *Should a person expect his relative to hire him? What are advantages and disadvantages of working for relatives? Should employees be expected to work as hard as their employer does?*

of money to be paid. In order to get a job, a contractor must sometimes bid. A *bid* is an estimate of how much a contractor will charge to do a job. Contractors sometimes bid against each other. The architect, or whoever else is seeking the contractor, reviews all the estimates and often picks the lowest.

Contractors often arrange financing from banks or other lending institutions. They buy the necessary building materials. Small contractors may do some of the actual work themselves. Larger contractors either supervise or hire others to supervise for them. They hire the necessary skilled people.

The contractor must be able to write and understand contracts. He must be able to follow blueprints. States license building contractors. State licences can be obtained only after long experience in the building trades.

Hotel managers Some hotel and motel owners manage their own businesses and set their own policies. Other managers are salaried. They carry out the policies of the owners. All take responsibility for seeing that their facilities are run profitably and that their guests are comfortable.

In smaller hotels, the manager may also be a part-time desk clerk, registering guests and showing them to their rooms. In larger hotels, most of the manager's time is spent coordinating the activities of all the departments—from dining room to accounting to maintenance. In some hotels, a special food-service manager is hired to supervise the preparation and serving of food. Some hotels have *banquet managers* who oversee special events. Large hotels and resorts have managers who travel around promoting the facilities and services of the hotel or motel.

The manager sets room rates and determines credit policies. He allocates funds to different departments; he helps them plan their budgets.

People may enter hotel management from another management career. Some may move into it from other jobs in the hospitality industry. Young people can gain valuable experience by working at such entry-level jobs as bellmen, busboys, maids, or cashiers, either part-time or during summers. Today, a number of colleges offer courses in hotel management.

The Housing and Environmental Services Professional

Professionals in the housing industry have far-reaching influence on the quality of life enjoyed by individuals, families, and communities. They make contributions that influence the lives of the present generation and generations yet to come.

Representative careers are those of architect, urban planner, and interior designer.

Architects The job of the architect often begins with a visit from a client who wants some sort of building to be constructed. The client will explain what functions he wants the building to serve and how much he is willing to pay. He may have a notion of how he wants the building to look. The architect then comes up with an idea for the building and makes preliminary drawings. He discusses these with the client, making requested adjustments. At this point, a final design can be made. This consists of floor plans and drawings showing the precise location and size of every aspect of the building.

The architect may also act as a kind of counselor to the client. He may help him find a contractor to construct the building. He may advise his client as to a reasonable price to pay. He also keeps informed as work on the building progresses, to make certain that the plan is being followed and that the specified materials are being used.

An architect who is part of a large architectural firm or who works for a government agency may specialize in one function.

A wide variety of skills and talents are required of the architect. He must have the artist's ability to come up with ideas. He must have the engineer's aptitude for mathematics and an ability to work precisely. He must have the businessman's knack for working with people.

Professional architects are licensed. To obtain a license, an architect must pass an examination. In most states, he is eligible to take this examination after receiving a bachelor's degree in architecture (frequently a five-year course) and working in an architect's office for three years. In some states, a longer period of practical experience is accepted as a substitute for a college degree.

Interior decorators must consider the tastes and values of their clients, although the extent to which they encourage clients to participate in the actual selection of furnishings may vary. Decorators have shopping resources that are not available to most homemakers.

Urban planners An urban planner is involved in trying to solve some of the problems that plague our cities. He specializes in evaluating the kinds of buildings and other facilities that exist within a given metropolitan area. He may analyze such things as the age of buildings and the width of streets. In making his evaluation, he will consider the current needs of those who use the area. He will try to project the future housing, transportation, recreational, business, and industrial needs of that area. To do this, the urban planner makes detailed studies, including maps and charts that show the exact location of everything from schools to sewage pipes. Based on these studies, the urban planner determines what appears to be the best use of space. Decisions are made concerning the area's most urgent needs. At this point, he supervises the preparation of proposals setting forth his plans.

Most urban planners work for local governments. They are in frequent contact with people and must be tactful in dealing with them. They begin their work as instructed by elected officials. They work with private builders and community leaders.

In smaller communities, only one or two urban planners may be employed. These planners perform a variety of functions. Large cities may employ large staffs. There, individual urban planners may specialize. One may concentrate on plans for rehabilitating run-down neighborhoods or business districts. Another may spend all his time on research or on community relations. There are a few urban planners who direct their energies toward the creation of plans for entirely new communities. These planners must have a good sense of spacial relations.

There is a growing need for urban planners. Most are expected to have a master's degree in urban planning, landscape architecture, architecture, or a social science like sociology. Some master's degree programs in urban planning involve an apprenticeship.

Interior decorators and designers Interior decorators and designers select all the furnishings—from rugs to chairs to wallpaper to pictures—that go into living space. They arrange those furnishings in an artistic and functional way. They work in close consultation with their clients. The spaces they decorate range from living rooms to airplane cabins. They often supervise the workmen who carry out their plans.

Interior designers may be more involved in space planning. They may be responsible for deciding where all the interior walls of a building will go. (They do this in consultation with an architect.) Some of them also design furniture.

Interior decorators and designers must be good judges of people. They must be able to assess their clients' values, goals, and tastes. They also need some talent with the pen or brush. Most begin an assignment by making sketches or paintings of the way they want a finished room to look. They need to be familiar with the various styles of furniture, as well as with available floor coverings, wall coverings, and fabrics. A thorough sense of design is also necessary.

Many interior decorators and designers are self-employed. Some own their stores. They may sell furniture or accessories. They may also be employed by department stores, architectural firms, or furniture or textile manufacturers. Some magazines that feature garden and home information employ decorators and designers.

At one time, formal training was not necessary for these careers. Today it is difficult to get a job in these fields without some sort of certificate. Some people take a two- or three-year course at an art school or at a specialized institute. Some have degrees in architecture or home economics.

THE CHANGING HOUSING INDUSTRY

A slump in housing construction can mean a slump in related industries. The housing industry is large enough that such a slump has a significant effect on the national economy. Yet, in spite of the size of the housing industry and the amount of its activity, there is a housing shortage which shows no sign of lessening. Many people attribute this to the relatively slow, nonindustrialized methods of construction still largely used. They feel that the only hope of closing the housing gap is a wholesale adoption of industrialized methods.

THINK BACK

There are career opportunities in the housing industry and in related industries to suit people with many different kinds of interests and with many different kinds of skills and training.
Discuss: *How can an individual go about determining whether or not a particular job is really "for him"?*

Jobs in housing are found in both the near and external environments.
Discuss: *How much responsibility should one take for solving environmental problems?*

Self-employment opportunities range from skilled, highly specialized work to work requiring only interest and imagination.
Discuss: *Do we have "self-made" men in today's society?*

LOOK AROUND

1. Name five different entry-level jobs in housing and housing-related industries. Which of these jobs do you feel would suit you best? Which of these jobs do you feel would least suit you? Explain your reasoning.

2. What is the difference between a real estate salesman and a real estate broker? What training is necessary for each job?

3. What are the jobs of the architect, contractor, real estate broker, interior designer, and interior decorator? In what ways is each affected by problems of environmental protection and preservation? What are solutions to problems they face in these areas?

4. Develop a "Who's Responsible" bulletin board based on a diagram of the room in which class is held. Include a one-line job description for the craftsmen responsible for constructing various parts of the room.

5. What seem to be general qualifications needed by people interested in professional occupations in housing, skilled trades, and semiskilled trades?

6. Visit a new building or development under construction. How many different jobs are represented by the men working there? What are your observations about each job?

7. What new jobs have been created in your community as a result of the emphasis on environmental protection? Name several jobs you feel ought to be created.

8. Develop a "Job Opportunities" index identifying possible housing-related work available in and around your county.

FOLLOW YOUR PATH

PATH ONE: Make a Plan to Improve Your Own Home

Step 16 With what housing and housing-related careers have you developed some familiarity in following this path? Do any interest you as career possibilities? What are the educational and other requirements for those careers?

PATH TWO: Form a Family on the Move

Step 14 Same as Step 16 of Path One.

PATH THREE: Be an Interior Designer

Step 19 List the job functions you personally have performed. Check those you think you might like to pursue further. Visit your guidance counselor. Find the careers in which those functions are involved.

Step 20 Make a chart showing the jobs of those with whom you came into contact in performing your work.

PATH FOUR: Design a Community

Step 25 Display your neighborhood model for the class. Tell about the features you have incorporated and explain why you believe they are important. Will your neighborhood be adjustable to changing needs over future years? Explain.

Step 26 Same as Step 17 of Path Three.

Step 27 Draw a fairly large circle in the middle of a large piece of paper. Inside that circle, list some of the careers related to the kind of things your committee did. Around the outside of this circle, write the jobs of some of those with whom your committee came into contact. Display this chart before the class.

Perspectives on living

"No man is an island," the poet John Donne wrote. No one lives completely independent of his fellow man. Mothers and fathers, brothers and sisters, friends and neighbors, wives or husbands, and children—whether our own or others'—may play important parts in our lives. They influence the things we do; they influence the decisions we make.

Unit Five is about the people who will soon be in your lives. It is about what it means to become acquainted with them, to love them, and to live with them. Here we will discuss some of the implications of marrying and having children.

PATH ONE: Form a Newspaper

Alone or with one or two classmates, create a newspaper for young adults. You may wish to have your paper duplicated and distributed, or you may make only one copy and display it on a bulletin board. This path involves interviewing classmates and others, visiting stores and dwellings, and writing articles and reviews.

Step 1 Find out what papers and magazines your friends read.

Step 2 Select a name for your paper that will appeal to young adults.

PATH TWO: Plan and Operate a Community Center

This path involves conducting surveys in your class and community, visiting community centers, making a floor plan, describing services you would offer, creating and performing TV commercials, creating a newspaper ad, making a small model of a mural, making posters, and inviting guest speakers.

Step 1 Meet with the other members of your community center. Discuss how your center will be organized. Will you have a president or director guiding you? Will that person have the final say in decisions made in your center? How much say will each member have? Someone should take notes at this and every meeting.

Step 2 Survey your classmates and people of various ages in your community. Ask them what facilities they would like to have in a community center. Would they like theater, hobby areas, or food service? Would they be willing to pay? How much?

Step 3 Visit at least three different types of activity centers in your community. (For example, visit church centers, private clubs, apartment centers, or outdoor facilities.) What services and activities are provided? What costs are involved? How do the centers get people to participate?

PATH THREE: Form a Family Court

Follow this path with at least five classmates. This path involves playing roles in various court situations, interviewing professionals in this field, reading about family courts, and writing a report.

Step 1 Visit a family court or read about one. If possible, talk with a judge, a lawyer, a representative of a probation agency, and a representative of an adoption agency.

Step 2 From among yourselves, select a judge and two lawyers. You may switch roles later.

Step 3 Interview at least one person who has recently been involved in a family court case. Find out the procedures required of the person. How did the person feel before, during, and after the court experience?

PATH FOUR: Produce a TV Soap Opera

Follow this path with at least four classmates. This path involves creating characters, discussing them, planning soap opera episodes, enacting the episodes, interviewing young adults, conducting an informal debate, leading class discussions, and developing and performing a television commercial.

Step 1 Name each of your characters. Determine the age, job, and educational experience of each of them.

Step 2 Survey young adults you know. Ask them their principal concerns about the near future.

Step 3 Among yourselves, talk about the things these young adults say. Choose several challenges you feel almost all young adults have to face.

Step 4 The action of the soap opera will revolve around a romance between a young man and woman. Discuss what will happen in the first two fifteen-minute, live, unrehearsed broadcasts.

CHAPTER 22

Launching Your Life

We use the term *launching* to describe young adults who are becoming more independent. The word suggests a break with a previous stage of life. Being launched means taking over the controls of your own life. Successful launching requires a certain break with the past. You will gradually change your relationships with your parents, family members, friends, and even your community.

CHECKING YOUR READINESS
FOR LAUNCHING

You are about to be launched. Have you a conscious end and a conscious image of yourself in view? Reflect before answering the following questions. Your answers will suggest the degree of maturity you have attained so far. They may give you some insights into how ready you are to take control of the life that lies ahead of you.

Emotional Readiness

How well do you know yourself? Do you accept the fact that other people, including your parents, feel much as you do? Are you aware of the important part you play in the emotional lives of others? Have you ever comforted, encouraged, or praised your parents when you knew they felt troubled, discouraged, or unappreciated?

Is your attitude toward other people open and relaxed or suspicious and hostile? Do you give and receive trust, sympathy, understanding, approval, and love? Readiness for emotional independence means that you neither cling to and depend on others all the time nor avoid close contacts completely. It means that you would not set out to prove your independence through rebellious and irresponsible behavior. It means that you can enter into human relationships at many levels of emotional involvement.

Social Readiness

Are you aware of how and when your decisions affect the welfare of the group or groups in which you function? Are you willing to put some effort into achieving socially desirable goals in your home, your school, your community, and your world— even if you do not stand to gain from them directly? How willing are you to accept the fact that all progress requires some form of effort and physical or mental energy? How often have you accepted responsibility for another person? How often do others turn to you for advice? Have you ever shown someone how to be more independent?

Have you ever made a friend of someone you did not like at first? Have you ever worked quietly to make amends if you thought you had wronged someone—even unintentionally? Do you enjoy the company of young children? Do you seek out the company of older people? Can you count any adults outside your family circle as your friends? How much have you added to the welfare of others through working in community or church programs? If you have ever participated in a charity drive, an ecology drive, or an election, you have demonstrated your social readiness for launching.

Readiness For Relationships

How ready any person is to establish close relationships depends a great deal on the success or failure of earlier relationships with family, friends, schoolmates, teachers, and fellow workers. Are you ready to invite people into your life and to enter into theirs? Are you willing to give something of yourself to others? Are you willing to share? Do you know how to exclude some people, politely but firmly, if you feel that their goals and values conflict with your own?

In a brisk, impersonal world, the warmth and tenderness of a relationship is extremely important. The true capacity for relationships is the capacity to care for and to love others. A person must have relationships if he is to meet his basic needs. He must have them if he is to become a complete human being.

Launching your life means taking over the controls of your life. Your sense of responsibility changes when you realize that your new freedom is tempered only by your own standards, judgment, and maturity. This painting by Sir William Orpen, "Leading the Life in the West," shows a young man who has perhaps mismanaged his independence.

Social readiness is indicated by your ability and your willingness to meet the needs of others. The dependence of others on your skills and talents gives you the opportunity to use these resources.

Educational Readiness

How well have you understood and mastered the work you have been given in school? Were you able to find in any area of your work something that you enjoyed so much that you would not call it work? What have you learned on your own because you wanted to satisfy your curiosity about people, events, and ideas? What have you learned in school that you are actually applying in your daily life? No one can find every teacher and every kind of schoolwork equally interesting. Still, educational readiness for independent living involves, at the very least, mastering the skills you need to live and work effectively with others.

Occupational Readiness

Have you begun to formulate an idea of your place in the world of work? Occupational responsibility is shown in willingness to see through to completion any task that you

undertake. It also requires such habits as getting to work on time, dressing appropriately for the job, completing assigned tasks, and not interfering with the work performance of others. Once you have become oriented, responsibility involves seeing what needs to be done and doing it in an acceptable way.

Occupational responsibility involves caring for the tools, equipment, and supplies used for a job. It includes an awareness of how your work fits into the work being done by others. It includes finding some degree of satisfaction and pride in what you do. Any well done job can be a source of satisfaction to a worker. Every honest worker respects the work of others at every rung of the career ladder, both above and beneath his own.

Financial Readiness

When you have reached a reasonable degree of emotional, social, educational, and occupational readiness, you have the tools to establish financial readiness for independence. Do you take pride in having earned or saved the money you use to satisfy a particular want or need? If you have ever borrowed money, have you paid it back? Have you ever made a budget and stayed on it? Are you aware of the cost of your food, clothing, and shelter?

Do you take the use of such utilities as electricity, gas, and the telephone for granted? If you have the use of a car, do you always, sometimes, or never pay for your own gasoline? Do you pay for upkeep or other repairs? Do you know how much it would cost to live the way you want to live? Do you know what things you would be willing to do without if you were not able to pay for them yourself?

Are you aware of the changes in the cost of goods and services in the marketplace? Are you aware of your own value in the job market? What is your worth in relation to your education, skills, experience, and effort on the job? Have you learned the workings of a savings account, a checking account, a charge account, or some other aspect of financial management? Are you in the habit of spending all the money you have available? Do you keep a reserve for emergencies? Do you pay your bills promptly and remain reasonably clear of debt? If so, you are showing financial readiness for independence.

Moral Readiness

Each person who is ready for launching has developed his own system of moral or ethical values. How secure are you in your convictions? How well do you act on what you believe? Are you prepared to accept responsibility for your own physical, mental, and spiritual health? How would you handle the

---

STAYING HIGH ON LIFE

Mood-altering substances—such as tobacco, alcohol, and drugs—have been known to man throughout history. These substances have been classified as narcotics, stimulants, and depressants. They affect the body or the mind, and sometimes both. A *narcotic* is a drug that relieves pain and brings about sleep. A *stimulant* is a drug that activates body processes and causes an elevated mood. A *depressant* is a drug that slows down body processes and creates an aura of tranquility.

Only recently has the use of such substances—especially among teenagers and young adults, as well as some preteens—reached epidemic proportions. Continuous use of drugs may cause dependence resulting in serious personal and social problems. To be sure, not everyone who uses mood-altering substances becomes dependent on them. The tendency for them to become habit-forming is, however, widely recognized. The psychological desire to use mood-altering substances, including dangerous drugs, results in some people experiencing an easing of tension, a feeling of well-

being, or a "high." Continued use leads to physical dependence, or addiction. The addicted person develops a tolerance. He needs increasing amounts of the drug to produce the same illusion of well-being. When use is stopped, the individual experiences the shock of withdrawal. Using such substances as "props" in life indicates a lack of self-control and self-direction.

People use drugs to temporarily escape from frustration, to reduce feelings of depression, anxiety, or loneliness, or just to escape from a self they do not like. Such flights from reality produce no satisfactory solutions to the problems of everyday living. Instead, drug abuse represents an avoidance mechanism— a way to dodge responsibility to oneself, one's family, and one's community. You cannot be both a drug abuser and a self-actualizing human being. Such self-destructive behavior is only a temporary and illusory way to solve problems. Only you, with the right information—including information on drugs and drug abuse— can make the decision. Ask yourself, "Why not stay high on life?"

EXPERT ALTERATIONS

Some of your work skills may have to be learned on the job. Occupational readiness involves being aware of what is going on around you, so that you can learn the necessary skills as quickly as possible.

temptation to be daring in the use of drugs, alcohol, or cigarettes, which can be damaging to mind and body? The time has come to think about yourself in these terms. You have to know who and what you are to know where you are going and why.

CHANGING LIFE-STYLES

No two people live their lives in just the same way. No two generations have lived their lives in just the same way, either. Each culture is distinguished by its own life-style. Young adults in every generation have found ways to express individuality. They reflect their values and goals in the ways they live.

Changes in Society

The range of life-styles people adopt today differs somewhat from the range of life-styles chosen by people one hundred or even fifty years ago. This can be partly accounted for by changes in society; the society in which a person lives helps shape his life-style. Today, in the Western world, it is common for young people to live alone for a time. It is generally accepted that some of them will never marry. In our world, it is increasingly possible for genuine friendships to exist between men and women. Socially appropriate behavior for women and for men is becoming less rigidly defined.

Bachelor living More and more parents are accepting, and society at large is recognizing, the value to young adults of a period of independent living away from the parental home. This helps some young people to "find themselves." It also tests their readiness to undertake full responsibility for a home and family of their own someday—if indeed that is their goal. Such experiences challenge the self-sufficiency of young adults.

For some, living away from the parental home begins with college. Originally, campus housing had a "home away from home" character. There were "house mothers" and rules laid down *in loco parentis*, that is, in the place of the parents. Some campus housing still maintains this type of atmosphere. Others are like apartment houses.

W̲e are all blind until we see
That in the human plan
Nothing is worth the making,
If it does not make the man.

Why build these cities glorious
If man unbuilded goes?
In vain we build the world,
   unless
The builder also grows.

Man-Making (Edwin Markham)

Whether after high school or after college, an increasing number of young adults live away from their parents' homes when they go to work. Many of these young adults live in large cities. This is possible because of the greater availability of employment, housing, and recreation. In fact, some apartment developments in large cities cater exclusively to "singles" tenants.

Alternative life-styles Some people simply may not marry. Many young adults no longer feel early marriage is a desirable goal. Many take into account the high rate of divorce in teenage marriages. For this reason, they may choose to pursue alternative goals until they feel they are mature enough to marry.

A great number of people will lead personally satisfying lives without ever marrying. For them, remaining single may be a positive choice. Remaining single need not mean that the person does not have a home, is not involved with other people, and does not have a family or circle of friends with whom to share his life. In our society, people can find different ways to meet their needs.

Male-female relationships Moving into the adult world as a self-confident and self-aware male or female takes time and experience. At one time, boys' and girls' relations were clearly directed toward mating and

Some young people search for a life-style simpler than that of their parents. They may choose to live with very few material possessions, in a way that makes as few demands as possible on the environment. They may form an intentional family with others who share their values.

bring people closer together. They create barriers between them.

Your developing personal morality Young adults enjoy a great amount of personal freedom. Along with this freedom comes the responsibility to use it wisely. In no area of personal living does decision making assume more importance than it does in the relationships between young men and women at the launching stage. Such decision making con-

At times, young people want to be away from the rest of society. Their behavior will reflect the respect they have for each other's values and their desire to preserve the love they have for each other.

cerns sex role, the individual's own idea of what it means to be a man or woman in an adult world. It also concerns many areas of interpersonal relationships.

There are many strategies to manage sexual tensions. That of sublimation helps many young adults to redirect their interests and energies while they learn to make mature decisions concerning sexual morality.

The area of sexual ethics is a highly emotional and personal one. It centers on the human being's entire philosophy of life. It forms the central part of every individual's value system and affects his relationships in far-reaching ways. Each individual must see his values and goals clearly. He must ask

TEEN IDOLS

It is not uncommon for teenagers to "fall in love with love." Many have "crushes" on unobtainable members of the opposite sex. These "love objects" may be men or women who have gained distinction in sports, politics, or the arts. Sometimes teenagers choose members of their own peer group to worship from afar. A great deal of fantasy and daydreaming can go on in this kind of experience. A person with an active imagination can fantasize all kinds of possible involvements with the adored person.

All of these emotional experiences are attempts to bring the person out of himself and into a situation where new relationships can be formed. After many years of establishing his or her individuality, the person is now seeking to establish a *duality*, a pairing off with another person who makes him feel more whole and more complete.

whether his behavior will enhance his self-concept and the self-concept of the other person. The person with strong values will not enter casual relationships that will be inconsistent with his values. To do so would hinder the development of a unifying and satisfying outlook on life.

True sexual fulfillment involves the total personalities of the partners. The ultimate satisfaction of sexuality in marriage comes from the fact that two human beings have learned to know each other, to understand each other's wants and needs, to provide each other with trust and security, and to commit themselves to one another's welfare and to the children they may have.

CHARTING THE UNKNOWN

When a ship is launched, it leaves the dock. When a spacecraft is launched, it leaves the launching pad behind it. You, too, as you set out in life, must leave much behind you. Ahead lie what for you are new and uncharted worlds. You may set up a household of your own for a time. You will most likely be increasingly involved in establishing close relationships. Chapter 23 may help you to begin to chart the uncharted. It may help you to clarify your picture of what lies in your near future. Consequently, it may assist you in shaping that future as you carry decision making into your personal life.

THINK BACK

Assuming responsibility for your own life is an important step in maturing.
Discuss: *Should society penalize parents for the actions of their children?*

Readiness to be "launched" depends on the level of maturity you have reached.
Discuss: *Should parents "force" children to become independent of them?*

People should feel free to choose the lifestyle best suited to them as individuals.
Discuss: *Is there an "American way of life"?*

As one's social circle widens, one may have to find different ways to meet psychological and social needs.
Discuss: *Do we "pick and choose" our friends? Are we "picked" and "chosen"?*

Decisions about sexuality and morality become necessary as social relations broaden.
Discuss: *Who should determine the boundaries of moral behavior when dating?*

LOOK AROUND

1. Design "Prepare for Launching" bulletin boards that illustrate various notions of readiness for launching.
2. To what does the phrase *launching your life* refer? For what reasons might some young adults be more ready and willing to enter this stage of growth than others?
3. What does *gaining independence* mean to you? What does it mean to several adults you know? Discuss the similarities and differences in attitudes.
4. What standards of behavior were common during your parents' high school years? What standards prevail today? What influences whether or not standards remain the same or change? What might you expect of your children?
5. Should your school function *in loco parentis*?
6. In your community, is it more desirable to be single or married? Explain your feelings on the issue. What provisions does society make for the single individual?

7. From newspapers, clip articles which reflect current notions of sexuality.
8. Discuss the "double standard" of male-female behavior.

FOLLOW YOUR PATH

PATH ONE: Form a Newspaper

Step 3 Cut pictures from magazines. Prepare a photo essay on various young adult life-styles.

Step 4 Interview a number of teenagers, young adults, and adults. Ask each to give you a short definition of love. Record their answers.

PATH TWO: Plan and Operate a Community Center

Step 4 Evaluate your information. Plan a model community center. Make a list of the services that will be provided. Be sure to provide services for people of all age levels, from children to older people. Describe the location of the center. Describe the facility.

Step 5 Make a list of the equipment that your center will need. Make a list of the jobs that will need to be performed in your center. Make a list of the activities that will go on in the center.

Step 6 Design and sketch the floor plan of your model center. Take into account the services, equipment, and activities that will be housed in the center. Present your plans to the class. Ask for suggestions.

Step 7 Begin the design of a small model for a mural for one of the walls of your community center. The theme of your mural will be "The Developmental Stages of Man" (see Chapter 2). In your design, use photographs of community people of all ages. At the young adult stage, illustrate some of the readiness for launching questions asked in this chapter.

Step 8 Prepare a one-minute commercial for the Path Four soap opera. The point will be to tell the community about your center. Try to include appeals to all age groups.

Step 9 Enact the commercial during a commercial break of the next soap opera.

PATH THREE: Form a Family Court

Step 4 Invent a situation involving a teenager living away from home that can only be solved by the family court. Each person working on this path should play the role of someone involved in the situation. (For example, some of the roles might be the client, a parent, and a social worker.)

Step 5 Have the court stenographer take notes. Role-play the situation. Discuss what happened. How ready is the teenager to be launched?

Step 6 Exchange roles. Role-play the situation for the class. Ask the class to serve as advisors to the judge.

Step 7 Make a list of decisions or options open to the client and the judge. Ask the class to discuss the best options for resolving the situation.

PATH FOUR: Produce a TV Soap Opera

Step 5 Enact your first program. Before you begin, inform your audience about the characters you are playing.

Step 6 Each person should answer the questions in the "Readiness for Launching" section of this chapter as if he were one of the young adults in the soap opera. Discuss your answers among yourselves.

Step 7 What differences are there between the sex-role perceptions of the older characters and those of the younger characters? Might those differences cause conflicts in later episodes? How?

Step 8 What psychological and social changes have each of the young adults in the soap opera been going through?

Step 9 Enact the second episode.

CHAPTER 23

Making Personal
Commitments

The people you choose as friends and those who choose you as their friend have a profound influence on your life. From among your circle of friends, you will select some who will be especially close. There may be one person with whom you are closest of all—someone you love and with whom you choose to share your life. That person might help you to live up to your highest values and reach your highest goals. You may already know the person with whom you will have such an intimate relationship. You may meet that person after you have spent some time away from your family's home. This chapter is about the personal commitments you might make to "someone special."

ENTERING NEW SOCIAL SITUATIONS

Most people feel more alive, energetic, and enthusiastic when their psychological and social needs are "in touch" with other people. Close social contacts reinforce the feelings of safety and security we need to become trusting and trusted human beings. Closeness to others bestows the feelings of love and acceptance that make us feel worthy. Choosing our own friends and loved ones reinforces the feeling of independence. Taking part in activities with people of many types answers our need for stimulation and variety. Sharing experiences with others gives us the feeling that we belong.

With so much at stake, it may be tempting for you to throw yourself into a new situation—whether the armed services, a new school, a job, or a leisure setting. Try to take time to survey the scene. Measure what you find against your personal values and goals.

Many people suffer a kind of temporary "inferiority complex" in new social situations. They may feel that the qualities their old friends recognized in them will not be apparent to new acquaintances.

What is the setup? Who does what? Who is connected to whom? In what way? Who else is also a newcomer to the group? Can you give each other moral support? Who seems to have the know-how to help you get oriented to what is going on? If you take time to ask yourself these questions, you will be in a position to make decisions about what you are going to do and who your friends will be.

You may feel for a time that you are being overlooked. You may feel your good qualities are not being appreciated. If you have a favorable self-concept, you will probably enjoy being left alone to make your own decisions about who you want to share your time with. If you do work you enjoy, belong to clubs that interest you, and pursue activities that help to develop your potential as a person, you will find friends anywhere.

ESTABLISHING A HOUSEHOLD

Many young people who move from their parents' home to work or to go to school will find that, for reasons of convenience, sociability, and economy, they will share living accommodations with other young adults. Young men and women attending schools may live in dormitories with varying degrees of formality in their regulations. Each person will bring to any such living arrangement values and skills learned from the parental family. These values and skills will reflect that person's standards of homemaking, housekeeping, and taste. Each will also have learned ways of handling many physical and psychological needs. These are reflected in attitudes toward other people's habits, ideas, and opinions.

You may soon be living in a barracks, dormitory, apartment, or rooming house. There you might find yourself in close contact with people whose life-styles contrast sharply with your own. If you stay open-minded, this may be an enriching experience.

CASE STUDY: ROSLYN AND TERRI

THE SITUATION The bus would have taken less time, but Roslyn had decided to walk the eleven blocks across town to Terri's apartment. Her friend lived above a delicatessen, and as Roslyn entered the block she got a whiff of the garlic and spice odor of home-prepared pastrami and corned beef. Terri came running from a doorway to greet her. "Hey! I wondered when you'd get here. Come on. I want you to meet Harold."

Roslyn scrambled after Terri and up the five flights of stairs to the warm, cramped apartment shared by Terri and her mother. "Try to ignore the heat," whispered Terri. "The air conditioner broke again. But hey! Harold has something to take our minds off that." She carefully closed the door to the kitchen where her mother was working.

Roslyn had never seen Harold before, but she knew he went to the same school that she and Terri attended. He wasn't exactly someone she'd pick out in a crowd; but according to Terri, he had a lot of friends. He had gotten them tickets for tonight's concert, even though it was supposedly sold out months ago. She expected to see the tickets in Harold's hand. Instead, he opened it to reveal several small pills.

"You have to have these to really feel that concert," he said with a grin.

"Uh, thanks, but I don't feel in the mood tonight, you know?" replied Roslyn.

"We've all had them before," coaxed Terri. "They're like nothing you've tried."

Roslyn was becoming a little uncomfortable because of Terri's insistence; but again she turned down the offer. "Hey! We'd better get going or we'll have to throw someone out of our seats. Come on."

Terri grabbed her arm as Roslyn turned towards the door. "Is everything okay? You won't tell anyone, will you? I mean, we're best friends, aren't we, Ros?"

"Sure, Terri," replied Roslyn. "Look! You do it your way and I'll do it mine."

Harold stuffed the pills back into his jeans pocket. "Come over to my place after the concert. I'll show you some other stuff."

THE INTERVIEW Q: Will you go to Harold's home tonight, Roslyn?
A: I hope not. Maybe I can convince them to go out for an ice cream soda or something.
Q: You think they'll like that idea?
A: I don't know, but I'm going to try it. Harold gets around, though, and he seems like a guy who would get a little extra pushy, once his mind is made up.
Q: Why don't you just say "no thanks" and go home after the concert?
A: I don't want to do anything to hurt my friendship with Terri. We've hung around with each other since grade school.
Q: Wouldn't she understand?
A: Maybe. But Harold might be a little nasty with her. She can't take care of herself very well. She depends on me.
Q: If you go to Harold's, will you accept the stuff he offers?
A: I don't know. It will be a touchy situation. It will be hard to say no without making him frightened or suspicious. And Terri's mother would have a fit if she found out!
Q: What about your own parents?
A: Uh, I don't think about that. Besides, I stay away from the stuff as much as possible. You don't know what you're getting nowadays. I have other things to occupy my time.

REACT What do you think of the friendship between Roslyn and Terri? Should Roslyn keep this from her parents?

Roommates need not share identical values and goals to maintain a harmonious living arrangement, but it is important that their values and goals do not conflict. Prospective roommates should try to ascertain whether they can "live with" the other's interests and friends.

Selecting The "Right" Roommate

If you go into the armed services or away to college, you may not have the opportunity to choose the people with whom you live. You may then do well to make some quick adjustments. Strangers do not stay strangers long in a dormitory or barracks.

You may, however, find yourself in a situation where you can choose your roommate or roommates. Who would you ideally select? Would you pick someone who is a mirror image of yourself? Would you seek out someone with different interests? More than once, a person has picked a roommate who on first acquaintance seemed to have a lot in common with him but who turned out to be quite different. You will remember that one of the strategies of rational decision making is to analyze the choice situation. To do this requires information. Talk with prospective roommates. Find out their feelings about privacy and personal possessions. Do you have similar ideas about orderliness? Do you have similar tastes in furnishings? Do you look for the same things in people?

If you are thinking about sharing living space with a group, keep in mind that the makeup of the group will probably change. This happens as jobs or schools change, marriages occur, and personality conflicts arise. It is not always easy to bring together a compatible group. Holding it together may be even more difficult. The larger the group, the more problems are likely to occur.

Allocating and Accepting Responsibility

What is to be done? Who is to do it? When should it be done? How much will it cost to do it? Establishing a smoothly running household with other people can involve asking and answering all these questions. Those who plan to live together may first wish to reach agreement on the standard of living they hope to achieve. They may wish to allocate financial responsibility for the cost of housing, utilities, furnishings, and food. They may wish to allocate responsibility for such housekeeping tasks as preparing food, cleaning, and straightening living space.

Financial responsibility "Keeping a roof over your head" involves financial planning and money management. If you live in a dormitory room, furnished room, or an apartment, you will have to pay rent on an annual, week-to-week, or month-to-month basis. You may be required to provide *security*, a deposit equal to one or more rent payments, as a guarantee of your financial responsibility. (For a time, your parents may agree to accept financial responsibility for your home away from home.)

There may also be the costs of utilities, furnishings, and food. Clearly defining and allocating various responsibilities to individuals in the household may help reduce the possibility of household conflict.

Housekeeping responsibility Money is not the only resource used in running a house. Time and energy are also used. It is sometimes hard for people from different backgrounds to agree on even minimum standards of housekeeping. Those sharing housing frequently face the problem of cleaning such shared facilities as the bathroom, kitchen, and living room. Some may find it helpful to

Most young adults who share an apartment do not view the situation as permanent. They may prefer to furnish their living quarters without making extensive financial commitments for mutually owned property.

set up a schedule telling who cleans what and when. In some households, responsibilities may be shared.

Facility-sharing responsibility If you have never done it, you may not be prepared for the adjustment you have to make when sharing living space with those outside your family. In some cases, it may be important to arrive at a clear understanding of who owns what. To some people, for example, toothpaste and tissues may be "public property." To others, such possessions may be strictly personal. The roommate who picks up another's toothpaste may be surprised at receiving an angry look. It may also be im-

Living successfully in cramped quarters requires special consideration for others. Planning the use of facilities will help to maintain as much privacy as possible, which in turn will reduce conflict.

portant for everyone to understand in which areas a "hands off" policy applies. To one person, it may be sufficient to knock and then enter a closed room. To another, it may be important to wait outside until invited in.

Arguments may be avoided if everyone concerned agrees on the times for using shared facilities. Young women who have similar work or school hours, for example, may have to come to an agreement with regard to the use of the bathroom. Irritation concerning noise can be avoided if everyone agrees on the time to turn off the TV and the time to wash clothes.

Creating a Positive Atmosphere

What qualities do you think might help to create a positive home atmosphere? Your answer might include willingness to cooper-

ate, ability to communicate, sensitivity to the feelings of others, and coping calmly with conflicts in personal relations. Here are some ways in which roommates reflect these traits. Can you see how learning these traits in your family would make it easier to live with others?

Willingness to cooperate Once decisions have been made concerning financing, housekeeping, and living arrangements, roommates must still cooperate in the execution of these tasks. This involves some flexibility on everyone's part.

Suppose it has been decided that the breakfast dishes are John's responsibility. Every morning he leaves a clean kitchen. One day Bill gets up at noon. He leaves his dishes in the sink, feeling that they are *his* breakfast dishes and therefore John's responsibility. How can this conflict be resolved?

Suppose Marge strings wet laundry across the bathroom as Rosemary is expecting company. "It's *my* turn in the bathroom now!" says Marge. How could these persons cooperate more effectively?

Ability to communicate Communication occurs in many ways and at many levels. Living closely with others requires considerable skill in both verbal and nonverbal communication. Suppose Don looks at Bob's unmade bed and cluttered desk with a frown, saying, "I don't care whether you straighten up or not." Is he communicating honestly?

Suppose Jane says to her roommate Sue, "Why don't you join my date and me?" and Sue accepts. Later Jane berates Sue, saying, "I was only being *polite!*" How well is Jane communicating? If Sue took it for a genuine invitation because she came from a home where people meant what they said, is she right to be annoyed with her roommate?

Sensitivity to other people's feelings You will find that people are sensitive to different things: one person may be able to take teasing or mild criticism; another may brood or sulk when criticized. No one likes to be the butt of another person's humor. Such humor may disguise hostility. The person who is laughing loudly when "the joke's on him" may be boiling with rage and frustration inside. Bragging about achievements or romantic involvements may reveal both insensitivity and immaturity. Actually, a bragger may not really think he is all that good. He may be giving himself the approval and recognition that he feels are being denied him by others.

Resolving and coping with conflict Not everyone has learned to utilize decision making as a means to resolve conflicts. As you know, decision making is a skill that must be learned.

Members of the same household must be aware of the emotional climate created by conflict. A person who comes from a family where an open show of ill will was discouraged may just "turn off" and sulk in silence. Such people usually snap out of their moods if left alone—but unless and until the conflict is openly resolved, the problem is likely to persist. A person who comes from a home where people vented their feelings in a loud fight that sounded worse than it was may use the same technique with a roommate. That may be very hard for someone who is not used to it. If two people coming from such different homes live together, real problems are sure to arise. Unless they can examine the situation openly and objectively at some point, they may need to seek help from a counselor or religious advisor.

There are several ways to share housekeeping. One roommate may take complete responsibility for the household on alternate weeks. Another system is to alternate tasks. Still another is to divide tasks according to those that each likes to do best, or minds doing least.

ESTABLISHING RELATIONSHIPS

You encounter people all the time. Some relationships do not go very deep. They may be pleasant and friendly. Conversation may be made up of small talk or slang that passes for communication. Very little of the true self is revealed. Little importance may be attached to the relationship.

Stable, responsible, and continuing relationships require a greater investment of human resources. Even then, you may conclude that the relationship is best terminated.

Stages of Relationships

You may be satisfied with the limitations of a certain relationship. You may wish it to develop further. In making decisions about initiating, continuing, or terminating relationships, it can be helpful for you to look at the relationship as objectively as you can. As an aid to your doing that, we here consider the possible stages of a relationship. In the early stages, one sees the other person as something "outside" himself. In later stages, the two people become closely iden-

During adolescence, boys and girls reach a new awareness of each other as members of the opposite sex. They want to be noticed by one another. In their efforts to attract attention, they become very conscious of the way they look and behave.

People are frequently attracted to each other for different reasons. As they learn more about each other, their interests may coincide and their relationship grows. When their interests are not compatible, the relationship may be discontinued.

tified with one another. They may come to feel and act as one. This does not necessarily mean losing one's identity entirely. It means having such insight into a partner's needs, values, and goals that your actions and decisions reflect that insight. This feeling for the feelings of another is called *empathy*.

Some people experience these later stages intensely and violently. Other people move calmly and confidently from one stage to the next. Many long-term romances that bloom into marriage have this quality. Some relationships never reach the later stages at all.

This is frequently because one of the partners has moved beyond the level of involvement of which the other is capable at that time. People do not so much tire of a relationship as lose their sense of personal fulfillment in it. They then strive to go on to something that they feel will meet their needs on a higher level. Individual differences in attitude, temperament, and role expectation will influence behavior in all these stages.

The need for recognition is often expressed as a desire to be noticed by members of the opposite sex. Hence, people try to look the

Companionship is in evidence when people are completely at ease with each other. Mutual attraction leads to companionableness as people are assured that their behavior is acceptable to others.

part of attractive and desirable dating partners. They show some interest in appearances, in outward display.

Clothing, grooming, achievements in school, and personal possessions can all be used for this outward purpose.

One-sided attraction A relationship may begin with one person showing an interest in the other—an interest which is not immediately returned. Some people are repeatedly attracted to those who are not attracted to them. Such one-sided relationships are frequently experienced by young adults, who are just learning to recognize the ways in which people signal their interest in each other. A great deal of nonverbal communication goes into such exploration.

At this stage, there is little give and take. However, there may be a casual tolerance of the one who is involved by the one who is not.

Mutual attraction When people find each other attractive, they begin to talk, to joke, to walk together. They begin to exchange some information about themselves. They may discover that they both like skating, hiking, bicycling, or dancing. They may find a common interest in music. They may both dislike their parents' rules or their teachers' discipline. In any case, a spark is lit.

This is a period of mutual discovery. It is during this time that people uncover the qualities that they consider attractive in members of the opposite sex. A boy may admire boys who play football, for example, but take a dim view of a girl who wants to be a quarterback. A girl may like the outdoors, but she may not care to tramp over a golf course or sit still in a swamp, bird watching or duck hunting. During this time, couples test each other out. They are still trying to create a favorable impression.

Companionableness When a couple reaches this stage, they have discovered their mutual interests. They like to spend time talking and doing things together. They admit that they like each other very much. They like what they are finding out about each other. They like the feeling of being able to share their interests, opinions, hopes, and dreams with each other. The more they have in common, or think they have in common, the closer the relationship becomes. They make opportunities to be together. The relationship may be accepted by both as comfortable and unstrained.

Affection   After finding out how much they have in common, a couple begins to experience a new level in their relationship. They—and this comes as a great discovery—find that they have the same feelings for each other. They respond to each other and, as they respond, barriers are broken down. Displays of affection of many kinds are involved at this stage. There is a special wonder and delight for those who experience this stage for the first time.

THE DATING GAME

Dating has become recognized as a way for teenagers and young adults to get to know each other. Dating may follow several patterns, including random dating, group dating, and steady dating. The customs involved in this form of socializing may vary from group to group and from time to time. The basic purpose is the same: an opportunity to get to know a member of the opposite sex and to compare possible marriage partners. In random or casual dating, couples may date several partners for short or long periods of time. Each is free to date as many partners as he chooses. In group dating, which is the initial dating experience for many young couples, a group of boys and girls or young men and women will plan a joint activity. In some group dates, the pairs are specific. In others, there may just be an understanding that some couples are paired off within the group, but others are not bound to a single partner. Some blind dates, in which neither partner has previously met the other, are also arranged in groups. Group dating has the advantage of peer-group support. This helps inexperienced daters to get over many hurdles in making conversation, thinking up activities, or coping with the unexpected. In steady dating, the couple dates each other exclusively. For some, the advantage of this arrangement is the safety and security it offers for a partner on any and all social occasions. Steady dating may reflect dependence on the partner rather than the independence of choice. In early dating experiences, couples often drift into an arrangement out of convenience. Some are pushed into such arrangements by their friends or the feeling that "it's the thing to do." Dating experience can provide the opportunity to learn to adjust to the different needs, interests, wants, and goals that individuals may have. It acts as a preparation for more serious commitments later. It gives young people practice in communicating their thoughts and feelings.

Feelings of affection are usually accompanied by the need to express these feelings, either physically or verbally. Some couples may consider such tenderness to be a very private means of communication. Others are quite comfortable when displaying affection in public.

Some people never reach this stage. This may be because they find it hard to show their true feelings and to run the risk of rejection. Some who have kept their emotional needs pent up for a long time may not know how to express their feelings. Others may go overboard. They may express all their feelings with a frightening intensity.

Love The feeling of love is hard to explain. Consequently, many people ask themselves every day whether what they are experiencing is the "real thing." Here are some of the characteristics that a group of mature teenagers agreed characterized love.

Love is unselfish. It helps to place the other's good above one's own.

Love is productive. It builds one's self-concept so that energy can be channeled into self-actualizing activities.

Love is shared. It is supportive and reassuring, and not demanding. It seeks to build the other person's sense of worth and to strengthen each person's self-concept. It leads people to share their feelings, interests, activities, goals, and resources. It is conveyed in *mutuality*, an ongoing sense of giving to and taking from the other person.

Love is unifying. It helps the individual to "get himself together." It can join two people

392

CASE STUDY: BECKY AND PAUL

THE SITUATION *It was almost time for Paul to arrive home from work. Becky picked up two-year-old Mark and stood by the window. Mark would wave to Daddy when he got out of the car. This was a weekday ritual the three of them had shared since Mark was old enough to recognize his father. Whether Becky was shopping, working around the home, or entertaining guests, she always reserved this special time to await Paul's homecoming.*

Becky had met Paul four years ago when she was just out of high school, working as a secretary at her first job. Paul had "swept her off her feet." She had dated him exclusively from their first date until marriage eight months later. She worked for several months after marriage, but then decided she preferred being a housewife. Paul agreed readily to her wishes, noting that she was much happier when she had more time to devote to her own interests. She soon became restless, however, and felt it a good time to begin thinking of having children. Paul was hesitant at first. He wanted time to get "established" in his job before becoming a father. It depressed Becky to think of waiting. After all, she wasn't getting any younger. She wanted to "grow up with her children," just as her mother had done. Her insistence had changed Paul's thinking. She hugged Mark, pleased with the outcome.

"Hi, honey!" she said as Paul came through the doorway. "You didn't call me at your usual time today. I missed you."

"I couldn't," he said excitedly. "I was talking to the boss about another education program the company is offering. He wanted to know if I'd be interested in signing up for it. There would be a three-week training course on the West Coast and chances for promotion after taking the course. It sounds good. What's the matter? You don't look very excited about it!"

Becky answered slowly. "Three weeks is a long time for you to be away. Is it too far for you to come home on weekends?"

"Of course it is. And too expensive," answered Paul impatiently. "Three weeks will go quickly. I'll call you every night to see how you are. Don't worry, I'll tell you what I'm doing." And then he realized what she was thinking. "You don't want me to go."

Becky shook her head very slowly. "Why should I! I love you. I don't want us to be separated. And the baby will miss you."

"The baby?" asked Paul angrily. "He's too young to know what's going on! Becky, you did the same thing last year when I was offered an opportunity like this. I'll never get anywhere if you don't stop hanging on the way you do. I like my job and want to get ahead in it. Why can't you understand that? You're happy with your job. I want to be happy with mine."

THE INTERVIEW Q: This seems like a good opportunity for Paul to advance his career. Will he take the training?
A: I don't want him to go away. I like him to be here when I need him. There will be other opportunities, maybe closer to home.
Q: Will you prevent him from going?
A: If he has any respect for my wishes and happiness, he will stay here. The company will understand. If they don't, then he should work for someone else. If he goes against my wishes, I'll never forgive him.

REACT *Are Paul and Becky in love? What solutions do you suggest for this problem? Are there many people like Becky and Paul?*

IS IT LOVE OR INFATUATION?

Songs and stories have been written about feelings that seemed like love but that turned out to be "just infatuation." In some of these tales, there seems to have been no way of knowing beforehand whether the feeling was indeed the "real thing." Is the distinction between love and infatuation a meaningful one?

Some writers describe love as arising from a real understanding of the other person. They describe infatuation as incorporating a large amount of fantasy. Someone who is in love understands the existing and potential problems of a relationship. Someone who is infatuated believes that his feeling is strong enough to sweep away all problems.

Do you feel that such infatuation is possible in the fifth stage of the ideal relationship described here? Why?

in a sense of oneness and togetherness unknown in other relationships. Love begets more love. It becomes deeper, richer, and more satisfying with time. Love spills over into other relationships as a creative, energizing, vitalizing force.

Not all people experience love in all these aspects. Furthermore, people demonstrate love differently. Some people show their feelings openly. Others, who may feel just as deeply, are quiet and reserved in the way they express their emotions.

Mutual commitment When two people are in love, it becomes important for them to further develop their relationship, to further develop a mutual commitment and an exchange of trust.

Love is an investment of oneself in the well-being of another. A commitment is mutual when each person expands his self-centered feelings to other-centered feelings. A mutual commitment may be known only to the couple involved; an engagement or a marriage ceremony is only its public announcement.

Is love a good basis for making a mutual commitment? Each person's answer to the question will reflect his own values and goals and those of the social group to which he belongs. Each answer will reflect a strong cultural bias. The "love match" is a strictly Western notion. In many other cultures, love develops after marriage. It does not necessarily exist before the marriage ceremony takes place; the partners may hardly know each other.

Intimacy Commitment opens the door to intimacy. Intimacy is that stage of a relationship when each person becomes totally familiar with the feelings, moods, strengths, and weaknesses of the other. It is a union of body, mind, and spirit. There are many intimate relationships without a sexual component. When people reveal their true selves in an intimate relationship, they are already committed to neither exploiting nor condemning the other. They are committed to understanding and supporting the wants and needs of each other.

Drifting or Deciding

When a person is found *not* to possess the characteristics that were imagined, or not to the degree imagined, disillusion is likely to set in. When unattractive characteristics are revealed as the relationship continues, disappointment ensues. If a conflict in values and goals or a breach of trust occurs, a sense of betrayal may be felt. This moment of truth is hard to face. How it will be handled depends on the personalities and the levels of maturity of the participants. The person with injured feelings may feel anxious and guilty. He may be surprised to find himself capable of harboring such feelings toward another person. He may be embarrassed by them. If, on the other hand, the feeling is that the relationship has reached a stage of commitment, there may be considerable psychological and social pressure to continue the relationship and work things out. Couples may hear the argument that "love conquers all." The real question is whether the relationship has the potential for growth. Otherwise, the people involved may find themselves trying to maintain what is essentially a dead relationship, rather than a growing one. It takes maturity to recognize the difference, and sometimes the proper decision cannot be made because of the intensity of the feelings and the complications of the personal relationships involved.

Some people simply drift along with the tide of their emotions. They may suddenly find themselves in deeper water than they ever intended. Being swept along in this way sooner or later causes many shipwrecked romances. The partners will react to this experience in different ways. One may sink and one may swim. The partners may feel marooned and helpless—unable to pick up the broken pieces of their lives. Nevertheless, breaking up a relationship is sometimes necessary.

CHOICE
AND PERSONAL COMMITMENT

It has been said that the three most important decisions a person will make in his lifetime are the philosophy of life he chooses to live by, the work he chooses to do, and the person he chooses to marry. It is clear that interpersonal relationships require more than drifting. They require decision making. People can learn from their experiences. It is possible that future relationships will lead them further along the road, not leave them in a dead-end relationship that cannot develop or grow. In the next chapter, we will discuss some of the characteristics that have been found to predict success in a marriage.

THINK BACK

Learning to live with others can be the first step in gaining independence from family members.
Discuss: *How can one be independent while living with others?*

Sharing a household requires decision making in both practical and social matters.
Discuss: *What is your reaction to the person who says "It's boring to be practical"?*

Lasting relationships are built on mutual decisions of commitment to each other's welfare.
Discuss: *Does "love conquer all"?*

Understanding the steps of emotional involvement can help you see personal relationships with a clearer eye.
Discuss: *Are the "games people play" fair ones?*

LOOK AROUND

1. Based on suggestions of the authors and classmates, how would you advise a friend about entering a new social situation successfully?
2. Develop a "Living Together and Liking It" newspaper article. In it, give tips for getting along with one or more roommates.

3. Make a list of various responsibilities you feel one must meet when establishing a household. Are most young people able and ready to meet such responsibilities?

4. Illustrate problems regarding cooperation, communication, conflict, and understanding that arise when living with others. How might these problems be resolved?

5. Make a "How Do You Rate?" checklist of characteristics of the ideal dating partner.

6. Analyze the lyrics of currently popular songs that have "love" as their theme. Based on your understanding of chapter information, decide if the lyrics present the most realistic ideas about love and personal relationships.

7. What are the stages leading to intimate involvement with another individual? Are any steps ever skipped? For what reasons might a couple not progress beyond a certain stage?

8. Based on chapter information, explain the quote, "Love is not love which alters when it alteration finds."

FOLLOW YOUR PATH

PATH ONE: Form a Newspaper

Step 5 Using your data from Step 4 and the information on "Stages of Relationships" in this chapter, write an article entitled, "What is Love?"

Step 6 Check out available dwellings in your community that you feel might be suitable for young adults establishing their first household. Check prices. Make floor plans.

Step 7 Write an article based on the information you gathered in Step 6.

PATH TWO: Plan and Operate a Community Center

Step 10 Make up a series of mottos to remind those who will use your community center what they might do to maintain a positive atmosphere.

Step 11 Discuss having a party to help young adults become better acquainted. How will you serve this purpose? What specific measures will you take? How will you arrange the furniture? Will you have music? What kind?

Step 12 Make up a one-minute commercial advertising your party. Consider carefully how you will appeal to young adults.

Step 13 Perform your commercial during a commercial break in the next soap opera.

PATH THREE: Form a Family Court

Step 8 Invent a situation in which a young couple is involved in a crisis of friendship, love, or personal commitment. Create a situation so that the family court is needed to resolve the problem. Each team member should take a role.

Step 9 Enact the situation.

Step 10 Discuss the case. Can you describe the relationship between the couple in terms of the stages of an ideal relationship described in this chapter? Describe what you feel are the good points and bad points of the relationship.

PATH FOUR: Produce a Television Soap Opera

Step 10 Discuss the young couple's relationship in terms of the stages of relationships. At what level are they?

Step 11 Discuss the plot for the next episode, which should center around a discussion of the possibility of marriage between the couple.

Step 12 Enact the next episode.

CHAPTER 24

Modern Marriage

Young adults today have views on marriage that are different from the views of their parents and grandparents. All over the world, changes are taking place in the way people think and feel about the family. Many of these changes are concerned with the role of women in social and family life. These attitudes reflect today's thinking concerning the woman's right to be independent and self-determining. Such basic institutions as marriage and the family cannot be challenged without deep social repercussions affecting men and women of every generation and in every walk of life.

MARRIAGE AND THE FAMILY

Social customs concerning family life and relationships differ in different cultures. In some, a broad association of people related by blood, law, or intention forms a kinship network. In others, families are units of a husband, a wife, and children. (See Chapter 2.) Most societies have some form of marriage—a bond that unites a couple. As a result of this bond, a couple is obliged to care for their children.

Functions of the Family

The family unit provides the framework for a variety of functions. It meets the basic needs of its adult members. It is also responsible for the socialization of children. It is responsible for the development of personality and character. Thus, the family is a group of people in physical, psychological, social, and spiritual interaction.

There have been times when the family alone was responsible for supporting its members and educating its young. Other institutions contribute to these functions today. Families may be helped in their support function by various forms of service institutions. The one thing that is primarily within the family's control is the emotional climate of the home in which its members live. The family helps to shape each member's self-concept by contributing feelings of safety and security, trust, acceptance, and recognition. It is thereby developing each

Nursery schools, kindergartens, and day-care centers are institutions that provide early support for the child-rearing function of the family. They provide social training and experience for children, including those whose mothers do not work outside the home.

member's competence to be able to deal with the kinds of issues and pressures that confront him in the course of modern living.

Structure of the Family

Even the higher animals have been observed to have a rudimentary form of family life. That life is based on the biological relation of the mother to her offspring and the father to his mate. Some animal species mate for life. Clearly, the longer it takes for an infant of any species to become self-reliant, the more important the family unit is to the survival of the species. The human family differs from the families of other species because it has functions beyond physical care. It contributes to the psychological, social, and cultural development of the young. It blends the functions of procreation (childbearing) and socialization (child rearing). As society changes, the function of the family changes with it.

All civilized societies place some restrictions on mating behavior. This is because fleeting or promiscuous mating is socially damaging. It threatens the safety and security of children by failing to consider their long-range needs. In the Western world, *monogamy*, the uniting of one man and one woman in marriage, has been the prevailing form. Other cultures have had variations of group marriage. One of the better known of these variations is called *polygamy*.

Monogamous marriage   The Judeo-Christian tradition favors the monogamous marriage. In the monogamous marriage, the partners are expected to be involved exclusively with each other. The ideal has been a union for life, as suggested by the phrase "Until death do us part." The practice among some people to divorce and remarry has been referred to as *serial monogamy*. In this, the partners dissolve one monogamous relationship to form another.

An extended family has an additional resource for fulfilling the child-rearing function of the family. The child is offered an opportunity to have a close relationship with an adult who is not a parent.

Polygamous marriage In polygamous marriage, one person may have several mates. According to the Islamic faith, for example, a man is permitted to have as many as four wives. In spite of this, many devout followers of Islam today contract marriage with only one person.

The form of group marriage in which one man has several wives is called *polygyny*. It has existed in cultures where men were able to support large households and where women and children were regarded as possessions that conveyed status to the husband and father.

The custom of *polyandry* provided a woman with several husbands. It has been practiced in societies where the ratio of men to women is high and the work of several husbands was needed to provide for a woman and her children.

Plural marriages Some communities have experimented with various forms of plural marriage, in which all members of the community were regarded as a family.

Marriage Models

The relationship of the partners in a marriage is personal and unique. We can never see anyone else's marriage except from the outside. Nevertheless, certain characteristics typify a great many relationships. Some of these are fairly realistic and stand the test of time quite well. Others may be harder for one or both partners to adjust to and maintain.

Romantic models Everyone has some notion of what he considers an "ideal marriage." We have all been influenced in these attitudes by what we have seen in our own families, what we have read, and what we have been shown in films, TV, and advertising. Romantic models focus on "ideal couples" that are "meant for each other." They never fight, they understand each other perfectly, and they never seem to get old. Yet, people who

have remained happily married long enough to celebrate silver and golden wedding anniversaries will tell you that their feelings of love are stronger toward one another in middle and later life than they were in the early years of marriage. Clearly, such ideal marriages have spanned the levels of commitment discussed in the previous chapter. It is odd that most young couples seeking advice on their choice of marriage partners turn to other engaged or newly married couples, rather than to those who have been successfully married for some time.

Traditional models The roles of husbands and wives in traditional marriages center around clearly defined areas of performance and decision making. In the *matriarchal* model, the mother rules the home with an iron hand. She makes all the decisions concerning the children and the home. Her word is law. By contrast, in the *patriarchal* form of traditional marriages, the father is boss. In traditional marriages, each parent generally has only a single role. The father is the breadwinner, the provider. The mother is the homemaker, the housekeeper, and the conserver of resources. When both husband and wife are satisfied with these roles, such marriages can work out to the partners' satisfaction. Their shared values and goals strengthen their relationship. Today, many people are questioning these conventional roles in marriage.

Contemporary models The changing status of women has contributed to modifications of even some of the most traditional marriages. The woman is no longer considered as first her father's and later her husband's property. A married woman can vote, own property, and conclude most business transactions in her own name. In fact, many women, by choice or necessity, may become the family's provider and breadwinner. Many young women today take pride in being prepared to meet any social or economic demand

Society and culture may influence what marriage model a couple will choose. But many cartoons and comic strips, including "Bringing Up Father," point out that family authority patterns define a marital relationship more accurately than does the marriage model.

that relates to the well-being of their families. The *democratic marriage*, or *companionate marriage*, views the couple as partners who share in all aspects of family living, including decision making. They pool their resources and work together toward joint goals. When they have children, the children share in the democratic processes of the home. Another contemporary model is the *friendship*, or *colleague model*. These couples maintain a "his" and "hers" approach to living. They meet and share on some issues, but they may maintain separate resources and pursue individualized as well as joint

In a democratic marriage, the couple share as equal partners in both the decisions and the work. Traditional sex roles are less likely to define the homemaking responsibilities for the couple.

goals. Some such marriages are *dual profession* marriages. In these, each partner pursues highly specialized professional goals (such as medicine or law) either jointly or separately. Many couples without children find this a satisfying model to follow.

Suggested models   Clearly, the last word on marriage has yet to be heard. Dr. Margaret Mead, a noted anthropologist, has no objection to early marriage. She does, however, see a danger in premature parenthood. As the concept of responsible parenthood gains genuine acceptance, Dr. Mead's proposal, discussed below, may gain wider attention among those willing to examine romantic, conventional, and contemporary models. She proposes two distinct types of marriage; each has its own roles and responsibilities.

In the first type, the couple would be bound together in a form of *individual marriage*. This arrangement would last only as long as husband and wife wished to remain together. This form of marriage would give young couples a chance to know one another as people. This would be an acknowledged and socially supported relationship, not a clandestine love affair. If the partners found their values and goals different from what they had believed during their dating days, they could part. If parting seemed advisable, they would do so without guilt or blame, and without having brought children into an ill-fated relationship. This form of "protomarriage" would require a serious commitment on the part of the couple. It would not be entered into lightly, and it would have legal validity. If the marriage were dissolved, there would be no legal or financial ties. The restriction would be that the couple would have no children at this stage.

The second type, *parental marriage*, would follow individual marriage. The purpose of this form would be the founding of a family. A couple embarking on a parental marriage would make a greater commitment. Their concern would be for the welfare of their

CASE STUDY: SONIA AND DARLENE

THE SITUATION *As Sonia and her boyfriend Lou walked along Spruce Street, they were approached by Sonia's best friend, Darlene. "I got the most wonderful Christmas present! Look!" Pulling off her glove, Darlene revealed a sparkling engagement ring.*

"It's beautiful!" exclaimed Sonia. "When did you get it?"

Soon Darlene was relating the whole story of her surprise engagement and how her fiancé had presented her with the ring. "Isn't he fabulous?" she asked. "We're getting married in June. I can hardly wait to begin planning the wedding." She hurried off, promising to call Sonia later that evening.

"Was it really that much of a surprise?" Lou asked after Darlene had left.

"Yes and no," replied Sonia. "They've been going together for a year and Darlene has talked often about wanting to get married. Christmas is the usual time to receive an engagement ring. I think she was expecting one."

The couple walked along quietly for a while. They had been going together since their senior year in high school, several years ago. Neither seemed in a hurry to get married, though they dated no one but each other. In fact, Sonia could not remember discussing the subject of marriage in any conversation with Lou. He had never mentioned the subject to her.

"What's the matter with you?" Lou asked, noticing Sonia's silence. Sonia said nothing and he repeated his question.

"Why didn't you get me an engagement ring this Christmas?" Sonia asked suddenly. Lou didn't know what to say. Her question had caught him off guard. Finally he replied, "I didn't know you wanted one."

THE INTERVIEW *Q: Did you expect a ring for Christmas, Sonia?*
A: No, I guess not. There's no reason to have expected one since we haven't even talked of marrying each other. But for some reason, seeing Darlene's ring upset me.
Q: Are many of your other friends getting engaged this Christmas?
A: Most of my closest friends married soon after high school graduation.

I'm the only single one left from our old crowd. I feel a little left out. I'm not in a hurry to get married but—well, Lou could have surprised me with a ring!
Q: Would you have accepted it?
A: Of course. Well, maybe. Oh, I don't know. I guess I'm jealous of Darlene. But with all my friends married, I do feel pressed to join the crowd. Poor Lou! I surprised him, as well as myself, with my feelings.

REACT *Does society "push" us into marriage? When is a person ready for engagement?*

children. Economic, social, and legal support would be of primary importance.

While such a proposal may strike some as shocking, it is an attempt to help people clarify the two aspects of marriage—the personal and the parental relationships. Those who marry under traditional and contemporary models should keep these distinctions clearly in mind. Many married couples try to plan their families so that they have had a chance to know each other as people before they proceed into parenthood. For those couples who are determined to plunge into a marriage, individual marriage offers a cooling-off period during which they can begin to see each other realistically.

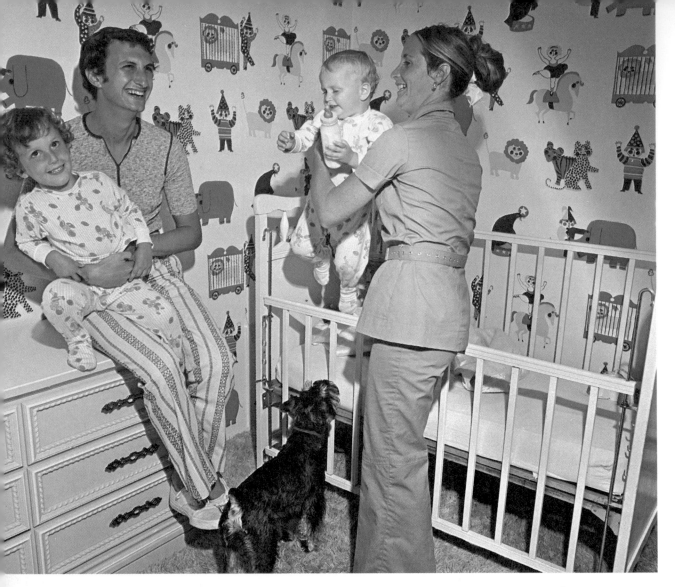

Children change a marriage. What was once a personal relationship becomes a parental one, as well. This new dimension of the marriage may affect the personal relationship beneficially or adversely, depending on how well the couple were adjusted prior to becoming parents.

THE DECISION TO MARRY

Young adults may not consider it "romantic" to look at the decision to marry as objectively as other decisions. However, the ability to recognize cause and effect, to look at the problem realistically, and to be willing to accept ("for better or worse") the outcome of the decision, improves the likelihood of making choices that lead to a successful marriage and a fulfilling family life.

Marriage does not instantly solve individual problems. In fact, it raises problems of its own. The solutions depend on the readiness of those involved to accept responsibility.

At one time, parents were eager to marry off their daughters. They wanted their daughters to be assured, at an early age, of protection and economic security. Today, young couples usually expect a wider range of psychological and social independence.

Limitations on Choice

Every social group limits the choice of marriage partners in some way. In some cultures, partners may be chosen only from within the same group. This restriction is referred to as *endogamy*. Today, it is observed by people who favor marriages among those belonging to the same religion, ethnic or national background, or social class. The practice of marrying outside the social, economic, political, or religious group into which one was born is called *exogamy*. This practice does not seem surprising or outlandish in a society where there are already wide differences among individuals and groups that come in contact with each other every day. In primitive cultures, exogamy has the advantage of enriching the hereditary stock of future generations.

In contemporary society, studies have shown that the greatest chances for success in marriage occur in relationships where husbands and wives share similar values and goals. This is likely to occur when young adults have come from similar, although rarely identical, backgrounds.

Most people meet in a situation that assures a large degree of similarity. To marry, they must first meet; and most young people meet as a result of living in the same neighborhood, attending the same church and schools, sharing mutual friends, or working in the same place. Thus, the first round in mate selection is often a matter of chance —of being in the right place at the right time. Some people have experimented with allowing a computer to play cupid. The long-range success or failure of such arrangements has yet to be scientifically studied. It may be, however, that this very attitude toward mate selection is a sufficient reflection of the values of the individuals involved.

Factors in Mate Selection

Everyone would like a simple answer to the question "Who is right for me?" Most people are right for each other in some ways and wrong for each other in others. Sometimes the differences between a couple in temperament, background, or experience can be an asset. Qualities can be examined from two points of view: similarity and complementarity. *Similarity* suggests that there will be agreement on those things held in common. *Complementarity* suggests that each partner meets some of the other partner's unmet needs. People differ in the degree to which

People have more leisure time than ever before. A couple who share an interest in a sport or hobby can spend this time together happily. They have an added opportunity to make mutual friends.

MOTIVATIONS FOR MARRIAGE

Marrying "for love" (and how many people would be willing to admit that they are not?) may simply be a convenient way to rationalize other reasons. Someone might really be marrying just to have a sexual partner. He might marry to gain the approval of peers or parents or as a sign of rebellion against them. He might marry to escape from loneliness. He might marry for economic gain or for social status. Clearly, people can convince themselves they are in love without being aware of their other motivations for marrying.

they can tolerate ideas, attitudes, and living patterns different from their own. At its best, complementarity brings stimulation and variety into a relationship. At its worst, it generates conflict and deadlocks, rather than decision making. At its best, similarity promotes agreement in decision making. At its worst, it introduces boredom into a relationship. In seeking partners similar to or complementary to themselves, people will be reflecting their self-concept and acting out their role expectations in this close relationship.

Age factors In North America, it is usual for married couples to be close to each other in age. The husband is usually expected to be slightly older than the wife. In young-adult marriages, this tends to equalize the difference in social maturity between males and females, since women mature earlier than men. For couples marrying later in life, this may be a less important factor.

Many early marriages are headed for trouble if the partners are immature. If the marriage has been forced because of premarital pregnancy, a residue of bitterness and resentment at being prematurely involved can cause a breakup.

Background factors People with similar cultural, ethnic, and religious backgrounds marry more often than people whose backgrounds are quite different. Success seems to favor those with similar, if not identical, backgrounds. The couple's values, goals, attitudes, beliefs, and behavior patterns are formed in their own families. Observing the same customs and traditions is a powerful force drawing people together. Habits and behavior patterns are also learned in a cultural setting. We take many of these for granted, and when someone with whom we are closely involved does things differently, there is a strong urge to try to change the person into doing things the "right" way—that is, the way "we" used to do them at home. Failure of the marriage partner to conform to the role expectation learned from the other's observation and experience can leave the person feeling that something is not quite "right" about the partner, and hence the relationship. It is possible, however, for couples from seemingly different backgrounds to develop the same values and goals. It is also possible for them to have just the right "mix" of similarity and complementarity to establish a strong relationship between themselves.

Education and intelligence Education and intelligence are often confused. Many highly intelligent people have little formal education. Many educated people have their knowledge limited to a very narrow sphere of experience and information. For a marriage to generate satisfaction, the couple will have to communicate. Attitudes and opinions will have to be brought into the open. Some may be shared, some may be changed, and some may have to be "tabled" to keep conflict from paralyzing the relationship and shutting down channels of communication. People sometimes have blind spots. People who are similar in intelligence and education are likely to share a wide range of interests and activities. If there is a wide difference, and the couple is comfortable with a complementary relationship in which one is the intellectual leader and the other is the follower, the relationship may proceed smoothly and congenially. If, however, one partner regards mental stimulation and variety as important a factor as physical or emotional compatibility, disappointment in a partner with narrower interest or a lower level of intelligence or education may create problems.

Social and economic status Families take pride in their achievements. They are usually eager for their children to maintain at least the same social level that they have attained. In most Western countries, social status was won by men through achievement and by women through getting married to men of achievement and status. As women gain more opportunities to earn status through achievement, this pattern is steadily changing.

Social and economic status has a strong bearing on many areas of living that affect expectations in marriage. The material comforts that one person dismisses may be

Couples with the same religious background have an additional resource for ensuring a happy marriage. Because they share the same beliefs, spiritual needs can be met without conflict. A common faith creates a strong bond between people.

Values, goals, and personal taste are all involved in establishing a household. A couple with similar economic backgrounds are more likely to agree on what is needed for a home that will satisfy the psychological and social needs of both of them.

important to a partner who has been deprived of these things. Value differences are likely to be quite wide when marriage partners have been reared in homes with vastly different standards and levels of living.

Predicting Marital Success

No one has yet found a method for predicting marital success with certainty. Every marriage is composed of such a variety of interpersonal factors that only time and the parties involved can truly tell whether the marriage is successful. Based on statistics gained from dissolved marriages, how-

ever, we can say that later marriages have a higher predictability of success than teenage marriages. Here are some of the questions you can ask yourself as you consider this important decision. Be aware of how similarity and complementarity are involved in your answers.

Is there mutual understanding of each other's values, goals, and expectations from marriage?

Is there mutual acceptance of each other as a person with some flaws and faults?

Does the relationship reinforce your concept of yourself? Does it make you feel worthwhile and valuable both to yourself and the other person? Does it reinforce the other's self-concept in the same way?

Is the relationship one in which you feel natural and can be yourself, or do you find yourself trying to "make yourself over" into the kind of person you think the other wants?

Is the person someone you would like, admire, and enjoy, even if love were not present?

Is it a relationship that others recognize and approve?

People do not stop growing because they are married. In fact, any marriage in which neither partner is prepared for change is probably headed for trouble. For marriages to succeed, each partner must be responsive to change. Each should be willing to change in response to new wants, needs, values, and goals. Married partners affect one another's plans. At the time of marriage, no one can predict what opportunities will arise, what luck will come their way, or what obstacles will be placed in their paths. Possibilities unfold. Potential must be discovered and developed. Each new experience of the couple changes their response to future experience. All married couples must be prepared to learn as they live together. They must be aware of the changes in each other, and they must respond to change without damaging the basis of their partnership.

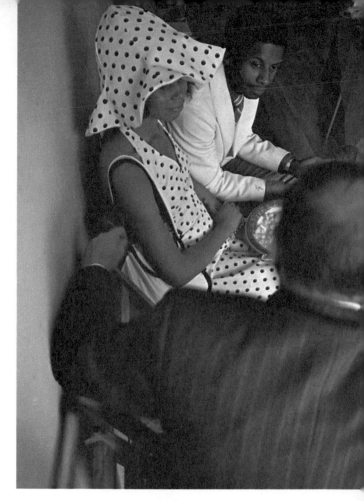

To be supportive of each other, married couples need not agree on everything. But it is important that each partner know that the other trusts him and considers his judgments and opinions worthwhile.

FROM COURTSHIP TO MARRIAGE

Most young couples who marry pass first through periods of courtship and engagement. Partly because of the expectations of society, they react differently during each of these periods, toward each other and toward many of the people they know.

Courtship

Courtship customs vary from culture to culture. In some, there is no direct contact between prospective marriage partners. They size each other up through intermediaries. They may never actually see one another or be alone together until after they are married. Courtship customs in the Western world are in a state of flux. They are changing in response to the changing roles of men and women.

Our culture still expects that the male will be aggressive and that the female will be passive and seductive during courtship. However, there is an increasing tendency for young adults to treat each other as equals and as friends. However it is handled, the period of courtship is a period of selectivity.

Courtship should settle the question of compatibility and begin to set down the ways in which the couple will communicate their feelings and needs to each other. In a successful courtship, couples are honest with themselves and with each other. They do not pretend to hold values and goals different from those they really feel. To

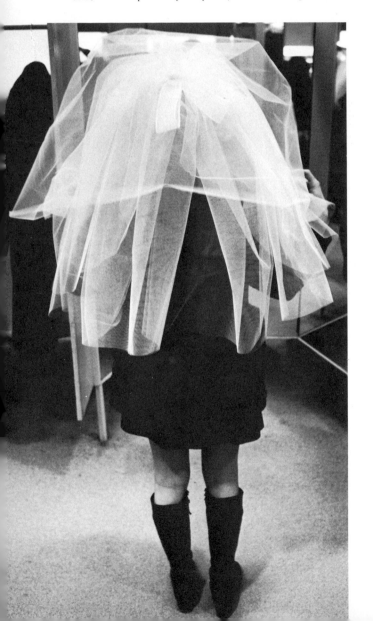

When a couple becomes engaged, they formally declare that they intend to spend their lives together. The engagement period provides time to plan for the wedding and, more importantly, to plan for the marriage.

do so would be both deceitful and hypocritical. Such feelings are impossible to sustain after marriage. If a person has been putting up a "false front" in order to make a good impression, the illusion created will soon crumble after marriage.

Trying to preserve romance with illusion is self-defeating. Yet this is the advice given to many young people in many popular songs, films, magazines, and books. Relationships are not built on appearances, but on authentic feelings shared by a couple. Therefore, the most important goal in courtship is to test the authenticity of one's own feelings and those of the intended partner.

Society, through the ceremonies and rituals associated with engagement and marriage, puts its "stamp of approval" on a match. Sociologist Philip Slater compares this situation with the parent who discovers a child eating candy and says, "I didn't hear you ask for that." At that the child says, "May I?" Then the parent says, "Yes, you may!" In a similar way, approval of a young couple's decision to marry usually comes after the fact.

Engagement

When an engagement is announced, the relationship becomes formalized. It becomes public knowledge—and sometimes to the dismay of the partners, public property as well. What was once an intensely private and personal matter is now subject to pressure and scrutiny by a host of outside people. Family, friends, religious advisors, and associates at school and at work begin to make the couple aware of the fact that their role has changed. Many new personal, legal, and ceremonial responsibilities come to the fore. The relationship comes out of the clouds and into the arena of social decision making. Suddenly, the partners must make plans and reorganize their lives. Not all young couples are equally prepared for the pressures this involves.

CASE STUDY: VERONICA

THE SITUATION *As Veronica walked downstairs to the mailbox, she thought about her friend, Ella. It had been three months since Veronica had been told of Ella's engagement. She knew Ella wanted to be married near Christmas, but she knew nothing of her plans. Oh well! Ella was a very organized person. She was probably getting some of the details concerning announcements and reception arrangements out of the way before deciding who would be in the bridal party.*

Veronica and Ella had been friends since high school and all through nurse's training. Veronica found it easy to be loyal to her friend because she was such an interesting person and the two got along well together. If anyone had asked who Veronica's best friend was, she would have said, without hesitation, "Ella Matthews." Oh sure, they had had their ups and downs, their little disagreements and competitive experiences. But they both seemed to get over the problem spots quickly, and with no noticeable hard feelings remaining in either person.

After graduation, Ella had chosen to work in a private office. Veronica had chosen a hospital in another state. When the two got together at vacation time, it was as though they had seen each other just yesterday.

Now, Veronica unlocked the mailbox and retrieved the long-awaited letter from Ella. Sure enough! It was loaded with wedding plans and ideas. And Ella wanted Veronica to be a bridesmaid with three other friends . . . Wait a minute! A bridesmaid? Who was going to be maid of honor? As she read, Veronica saw that Ella's maid of honor would be her cousin, someone Veronica had never met or heard of. In fact, Veronica didn't even know Ella had a cousin old enough to be considered for either bridesmaid or maid of honor. She suddenly felt deep disappointment. It had never occurred to her that someone else would be asked to hold that honored position in the wedding party. She certainly would have had Ella as her maid of honor. Veronica sat on the steps, trying to think the situation through more carefully.

THE INTERVIEW *Q: Are you excited about Ella's wedding plans?*
A: They sound lovely. But I'm so disappointed that she didn't ask me to be maid of honor.
Q: Why is it so important to you?
A: Because we're friends! I thought we were best friends! A wedding is such a big thing in a girl's life. It is something to share with people who mean a lot to her. No wonder Ella didn't write to me for a long time.
Q: Will you be a bridesmaid?
A: I don't know. Oh, this is so upsetting! I'll have to think about it later.

REACT. *Is a wedding as important an event as Veronica thinks it is? What do you think about Veronica's reaction?*

Some young couples suddenly feel that they have lost control of what is happening to them. For example, they now have to decide who to include in their plans, and why. Sometimes people near and dear to the couple may be slighted unintentionally. Even if the new partners have exchanged ideas about their feelings toward one another, suddenly a whole new area of loves and loyalties is exposed to view. From being exclusively concerned with their own feelings and with one another, they are now faced with the problem of handling other emotional ties. They have to examine old

Weddings are social occasions that relatives and friends identify with and want to take part in. Couples may find conflicts arising when others want to participate in decisions they consider to be their own.

loyalties. They have to see how their new roles affect their relationships with parents, friends, and family members who have been close to them—and for whom their intended marriage partner may feel no "instant liking." If, furthermore, any of the family members have their own reservations concerning the advisability of the union, they may find them hard to conceal. The couple may even have their own doubts; their problems are likely to be intensified as soon as they make their decision to marry.

The more elaborate the wedding plans, the greater the potential for conflict, stress, and tension. Couples who never disagreed about what to do on a Saturday night may disagree on many details.

After The Wedding

Following the wedding ceremony, a young couple may or may not plan a wedding trip, or honeymoon. Some may simply move into their new home—or the home of one or the other partner. The custom of the honeymoon was intended to provide the newlyweds (who in former times were rarely unchaperoned during their courtship) with a "getting acquainted" period before settling down to the day-to-day responsibilities of marriage.

At a time when young couples scarcely had a chance to meet and talk in private, this custom offered a transition between single and married life. Much of this has already taken place in the course of dating and engagement for today's young couple. They may see the honeymoon more as a joint vacation needed by both, after the elaborate planning and strenuous activities of the engagement and wedding.

The honeymoon, if there is one, is a period of continued courtship, sanctioned by mar-

A honeymoon is a period of adjustment before a couple settles down to the responsibilities of married life. Consider the phrase, "The honeymoon is over." Does it mean the "end" or the "beginning"?

412

riage, in which both of the partners gradually come to know and understand each other better and better.

They find they have problems they never anticipated during dating and courtship. They may have problems of physical (including sexual) adjustment. They may have difficulty adjusting to the emotional demands of thinking of "we" instead of "me" all the time. They will be faced with unexpected practical problems that confront people who live together. This may upset their idealized version of what marriage was to be like. If, for example, the young husband comes from a home where someone else picked up his clothes after he took them off, he may expect his bride to become that "someone else." If she, on the other hand, came from a home where everyone looked after his own things, she may find his habits more than annoying.

Sexual expression in marriage involves the total personality. Many behavior patterns, while not sexually related, do relate to the individual's masculine or feminine self-concept. Sexual responsiveness requires patience and understanding. Each partner must have an understanding not only of the differences between the sexes, but of the differences in intensity, mood, and emotional feelings of the individual husband or wife. Such adjustment is most often learned through experience. Few adjustments of any kind are ever instant and spontaneous. Most result from having taken advantage of opportunities to learn about, understand, and communicate with the partner.

THE FUTURE OF THE FAMILY

Decisions made by family members on a day-to-day basis shape the family of the future. The family of the future, stripped of some of its workhorse functions, may well become the center for human development in a mechanized and depersonalized world. From the home and family will radiate the warmth and concern that keep people human. Home will represent the safe harbor from the storms of urban life—a haven where each individual feels that he has value to himself and to others. The society of the future will have need for richer, more creative, more supportive family ties.

THINK BACK

Choices about marriage and family living styles reflect our attempts to adapt to life in our changing society.
Discuss: *Are people today less moral about marriage and family living than people who lived in past years?*

Both the similarities and the differences in background, education, physical features, and status can have an important influence on a couple's chances for success or failure in their marriage.
Discuss: *Can you expect to "change" a person after marriage?*

In "happy" marriages, each partner pays careful attention to understanding, accepting, and satisfying the other's needs.
Discuss: *In a marriage, does one person "give" more than the other?*

Marriage tests your ability to make and carry out practical decisions.
Discuss: *Does this take the "romance" out of love and marriage?*

The wedding ceremony may begin a period of emotional and social adjustment for the couple.
Discuss: *"You never get to know a person until you live with him."*

LOOK AROUND

1. What are the functions of the family discussed in this chapter? Can you think of anything to add to this list?
2. What features characterize monogamous, polygamous, and plural types of marriages? Which do you consider most effective for meeting an individual's needs in society?
3. What is the marriage model suggested by Dr. Margaret Mead? What are some of the pros and cons of her suggestions?
4. What do you think should be discussed and understood by all young people planning to marry?
5. What changes take place between a couple from courtship to the engagement and honeymoon? Ask older family members and friends what they think have been the major changes in family life over the past thirty years. How do you feel about these changes?
6. What are the "advantages" of arranged marriages? Could they work in a changing society like our own? Why?
7. What are some of the reasons why people marry? What do you feel are the best reasons for marrying?
8. What are the cultural restrictions on mate selection in our society?
9. Is the nuclear family suitable for today's world? Discuss.

FOLLOW YOUR PATH

PATH ONE: Form a Newspaper

Step 8 What are the principal causes of serious marital problems today? You may wish to consult books and articles. You may wish to interview marriage counselors or ministers.

Step 9 Write an article summarizing your results.

PATH TWO: Plan and Operate a Community Center

Step 14 A number of young marrieds will probably be using your community center. Plan a program about starting a family. Invite a guest speaker to talk with the class. Ask the class to role-play newly marrieds.

Step 15 Make several posters on the theme of "Will your marriage succeed?"

Step 16 Prepare a questionnaire in which you ask the class to rate—on a scale of one to ten--different marriage models. Write an article summarizing your results. Publish it in the Path One newspaper.

PATH THREE: Form a Family Court

Step 11 Investigate the legal aspects of marriage. Talk to a lawyer, a tax specialist, and a county clerk.

Step 12 Invent a situation in a marriage that requires the services of the family court. (For example, the probate of a will, an adoption, or an annulment.)

Step 13 Role-play the situation for the class. Ask the class to suggest options for the people involved in the situation.

PATH FOUR: Produce a TV Soap Opera

Step 13 For purposes of an informal debate, split up into two groups—exclusive of the two young adults. One group will present arguments in favor of marriage between the young adults. The other group will present arguments against it. The young adults should comment on the arguments. Invite the audience to participate.

Step 14 What kinds of products and services are offered to couples who are "courting," about to be engaged, or about to be married? Select one of these products or services. Prepare a commercial.

Step 15 Perform your commercial.

CHAPTER 25

Planning for Responsible Parenthood

For a long period of human history, the miracle of life—of conception, pregnancy, and childbirth—was shrouded in ignorance, myth, and superstition. Much misinformation concerning these important human experiences still persists. However, more and more young people are growing up with the mystery concerning human reproduction replaced with scientific information. With the information we now have, it is possible for every child born to be a wanted child. It becomes increasingly possible, through our knowledge of the mechanisms of heredity and the desirability of prenatal care, to have every child come into the world a healthy child.

ANALYZING
THE CHOICE SITUATION

In planning for responsible parenthood, first consider who you are. Consider your values and goals as they pertain to children. As far as possible, consider the kind of child that you might bring into the world.

Understanding Your Attitudes

Making rational decisions about having children begins with an understanding of your own attitudes towards children and family size. This involves knowing what children and families mean to you. It involves understanding the economic impact of having children. It involves an awareness of the ecological implications of population growth.

Attitudes toward children Attitudes toward children differ and have differed with individuals, time, and place. In some cultures, children represent proof of masculinity or femininity. Some people think that having children will hold a shaky marriage together. Some want children to carry on a family name or a family business. Most people realize that children have a value in their own right. Such people may have a deep desire to love and care for children of their own.

It has been suggested that love of children is one of the strongest reasons for not having children of your own. There are already many children in the world with no adults to love and care for them. One could give to these children the love and security they need by becoming an adoptive or a foster parent.

Today, social pressure on couples to have children is somewhat diminished. Couples are freer to evaluate their reasons for wanting children. Do they want them as a means to some other goal, or do they really want to create and help mold a new and individual life?

CASE STUDY: GINNY AND MRS. KEMP

THE SITUATION *"Next time we come for a visit, we'll bring the baby bed with us. Then you'll have it on hand when you are ready to use it." Ginny laughed at her mother-in-law's words. The two of them were visiting a furniture store and had just walked through the children's furniture section.*

"Well, you can bring it if you want to, but we don't know when we're going to have children," she said.

Ginny was used to both her own mother and Mrs. Kemp hinting that she and Kevin should think about having children. She usually laughed off their references to babies and motherhood. But she could see that Mrs. Kemp was visibly disturbed. Of her children, Kevin was the only childless one.

"Well, I suppose you young people live like you want to these days. I'm the kind of person who was happiest when surrounded by children," continued Mrs. Kemp. "I wanted a large family. And I enjoyed doing housework and taking care of everyone. It's not a bad life, Ginny. There is much to be gained from seeing your children grow up to be capable adults raising families of their own. It's your life, though. You have to do what you think best."

"That's right," thought Ginny. "And right now it's best for us to continue as we are. Kevin needs time to get himself settled into the kind of life that will make him happiest. And I need time to do the same."

"Well," Ginny said aloud, "neither one of us wants to have children because 'it's the thing to do' or because it's a way of escaping from an unpleasant situation elsewhere. I know women who have had babies because they couldn't face problems at work. I know husbands who were pressured by the company they worked for to become 'family'

men. We don't want to have children until we're good and ready for them."

"What if you're never 'good and ready' for them?" asked Mrs. Kemp. "Life is only so long, you know. You have to make a decision sometime."

Ginny said nothing. She busied herself by looking at the merchandise in front of her.

THE INTERVIEW *Q: You didn't answer Mrs. Kemp's last question. Why?*
A: I was thinking that she'll never understand our ideas about having children. She'll never understand that I am not the kind of person she is.
Q: How will you know when you are ready for children?
A: When Kevin is settled into the kind of life that will make him happiest—and when I have had time to do the same; when we feel we have answers to some of the problems of raising children; when we have enough money and goods to raise them comfortably and keep ourselves comfortable at the same time; when we can be sure they'll get a reasonably good education; when we know better how to teach them to live in the kind of world they'll be faced with, then we'll have children. Who knows? Maybe that will never happen!
Q: Mrs. Kemp raised her sons without much trouble. Is the problem so complicated?
A: Don't be ridiculous! It is a complicated problem! Having children is a big responsibility! If more parents realized it, maybe we wouldn't have the kinds of problems that are facing society today.

REACT *How would you reply to Ginny? Should Ginny explain further her ideas to Mrs. Kemp? Are Ginny and Kevin selfish?*

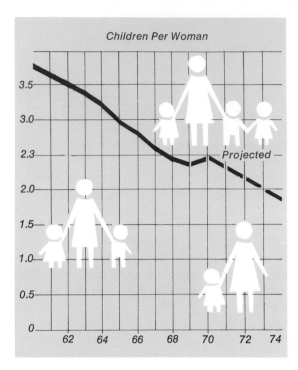

Children Per Woman

3.5
3.0
2.3
2.0
1.5
1.0
0.5
0

62 64 66 68 70 72 74

Projected —

While world population is exploding, this chart shows that the United States population is growing, but at a slower pace. The decline has already made changes in the age profile of this country's population.

Attitudes toward family size At one time, children represented economic assets to the family. They added to the family's potential labor force and potential productivity. At a time when many infants never grew to maturity, large families provided the assurance that some children would survive to adulthood. Improved infant medical care and feeding practices kept more children alive. Families began to feel that they should have only as many children as they could properly take care of.

Children today demand a considerable economic investment on the part of parents. Each child in the family makes demands on a portion of the family's resources. In 1971, the cost to a middle-income family for raising a child to age eighteen, without including college, was estimated by economists at the Institute of Life Insurance in New York at about $25,000. This was for a family in the $7,500 to $10,000 income range. For those in higher income brackets, the costs can be $50,000 to $75,000.

In general, the cost of raising a child to the age of eighteen is three times a family's annual income. Even if the family's income increases over the years, the proportion of income spent on children may remain the same. Each additional child spreads the family's resources a little thinner. For most families, a rational decision to have a child represents a willingness to accept a lower level of living in return for the satisfaction to be gained from parenthood. As most people know, material advantages alone do not build children with positive self-concepts and responsible characters.

Many environmentally minded people argue against having large families. They feel that parents should have only two children—enough to replace themselves.

Understanding Your Inherited Traits

Understanding your choice situation with regard to responsible parenthood involves an awareness of the heredity of you and your partner. It involves being aware of the possible influences of this heredity on the health and well-being of any children you might have. Genetic counselors can be called upon to assist you in understanding the hereditary factors of parenthood.

The mechanics of heredity A person's biological blueprint (see Chapter 2) is contained in most of the cells of his body. It exists in chemical particles called chromosomes. Each chromosome contains smaller particles called genes. Different genes are responsible for passing on different inherited traits from parents to children.

The 46 chromosomes comprise two sets of 23. One set comes from each parent.

418

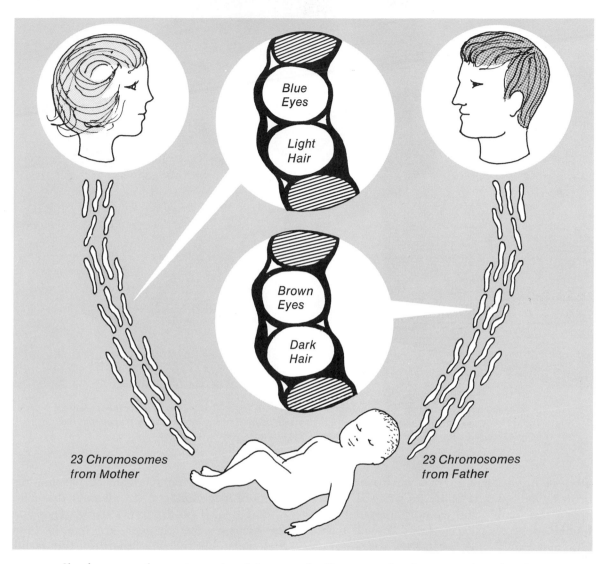

If a chromosome from one parent contains a gene for blue eyes and a chromosome from the other parent contains a gene for brown eyes, the baby will have brown eyes. But the gene for blue eyes is part of the child's genetic makeup. It can be passed on to his children.

Each set normally contains the genes for determining all of an individual's inherited traits. Having sets of chromosomes from each parent, a person has two possible determinants for each inherited trait.

A trait inherited from one parent will often appear in the child while the corresponding trait inherited from the other parent will not. For example, if one parent passes on to the child the genetic material for blue eyes and the other parent gives the child the genetic material for brown, the child will have brown eyes. In this case, brown eyes are the *dominant trait*; blue eyes are the *recessive* trait. This is not to say that a brown-eyed parent and a blue-eyed parent

In the past, adoption agencies concentrated on finding the "right" babies for prospective parents. Today, they try to find the "right" parents for the babies. More emphasis is placed on the couple's reasons for wanting to adopt and on their attitudes toward children.

always have brown-eyed children. The brown-eyed parent may have, and pass on to the child, the genetic material for blue eyes. In this case, the child will have blue eyes.

Birth defects Not all babies are born free of defects. Some defects, such as a club foot, can be corrected after birth. Others, more serious, may handicap a child for the rest of his lifetime. The majority of birth defects are the result of defective chromosomes or genes. Some 1,500 genetically linked birth defects are now known. Many of them are recessive traits. Hence, neither parent may suffer from the mental or physical defect. Neither may be aware of what they might pass on to their children.

To illustrate the chances of passing on a defect to a child, let us consider the case of diabetes. If both parents carry genes for the disease, the chances are one in four that their children will inherit an increased risk for developing the disease. The odds are greater if a parent has the disease.

Genetic counseling Genetic counselors advise prospective parents on the probabilities that children they might have will be born with or free from genetic defects. To do this, they take careful case histories of each of the parents. Among other things, they find out what diseases each has and has had. They also gather information about the past generations of each prospective parent. This helps them to see what defects each partner might have. It is possible for doctors to identify and catalog chromosomes. This also helps the genetic counselor to predict the possibility of birth defects.

ALTERNATIVES TO NATURAL PARENTHOOD

Some people feel compassion for the infants and children of the world who have no real home. Some are committed to doing their share to control the rapid growth in world population. Some couples are biologically unable to have children. Others who can have children may run a high risk of their being born with birth defects. Such people, should they want children, might consider adoptive and foster parenthood.

Adoption

Adoptive parents must sometimes wait longer for their children than biological parents do. They will have had ample opportunity to consider and reconsider their decision. After the child comes into their home, there is an additional waiting period. Some adoptions may be arranged privately through doctors and lawyers and the mothers of available children. This is not a highly recommended practice. Adoptions are more professionally handled through adoption agencies. Agency personnel are trained to select prospective parents carefully. Among other things, they screen prospective adoptive parents for age, health, income, stability, and reasons for wanting to adopt. The agency's goal is to place a child in a home where the child's well-being is assured. They may be able to select children that closely resemble the family into which they are being adopted.

Adoption laws regulate the placement of children through adoption agencies. Such laws and court decisions increasingly place emphasis on the welfare of the child over the "natural rights" of natural parents.

Before the rise of public institutions, religious groups took the primary responsibility for the care and education of homeless children. This 1850 woodcut shows a boy being received at an orphan asylum.

(Natural parents sometimes surrender their children and then attempt to get them back.) The earlier the adoption, the stronger the influence of the adoptive parents on the child's growth and development.

Foster Parenthood

Adoptive parents are the legal parents of a child. They have the same rights as natural parents. Foster parents are responsible to the social agency that placed the child with them. Foster parents are paid to care for children. They are given a sum of money which is intended to compensate the parents for the child's upkeep. Many foster parents use their own funds,

CASE STUDY: BETTY

THE SITUATION *Just as Betty was preparing to bathe the baby, she heard a knock on her front door. Opening it, she was delighted to see Jessica, a close friend she had not seen for several months.*

"I was in the neighborhood and decided to stop by to see you," said Jessie.

"Good," replied Betty. "Come in, take off your coat and come with me to bathe the baby."

"Baby?" answered an astonished Jessie. "I didn't know you had another child! How old is it?"

"Oh, this baby isn't our own," laughed Betty. "Our smallest child is in first grade now and we really couldn't afford to have more children. But I do love babies so! We're foster parents of infants who are waiting to be adopted. Come see Bruce."

Jessie followed her friend into the bedroom. Bruce was a wide-eyed, healthy-looking infant.

"I get them six days after they're born," added Betty. "I've had Bruce longer than any other baby. He's the seventh since June. My ten-year-old daughter loves to help me take care of them." She picked up the baby carefully, placing him in Jessie's arms.

"It was so hard to give the first one up," Betty remembered. "I just love taking care of them, but then I know they'll be going to good homes."

THE INTERVIEW *Q: Do you love these infants as if they were your own?*
A: Yes. I take care of them as though I were their real mother. I get them clothing, take them to the doctor, feed them in the middle of the night—the whole routine.
Q: How do your children and husband feel about your role as foster mother?
A: My husband is very much in favor of the idea. There are so many homeless children who need love and attention! And he treats these little ones as though they're his own. My children were confused at first. They couldn't get used to the idea of babies coming and going. But now they swing right into action when it's time for a feeding or changing. And it makes me feel good to have little ones to care for again.

REACT *Are foster parents as "good" for the child as real parents are? What are advantages and disadvantages of being a foster or adoptive parent?*

NATURAL PARENTHOOD: ACTIVATING THE CHOICE

Today, more and more couples try to plan the birth of a child. They may wish to be assured of a stable marital relationship and reasonable financial security before starting a family. They may wish to have completed their education and gotten a start on their life's work before choosing parenthood.

Once they have chosen to have children, and once the wife becomes pregnant, a whole sequence of growth and development begins. The woman undergoes physiological changes. The baby is born. The relationship between husband and wife changes as they assume the new roles of father and mother. Their changed status brings into play a whole new range of social roles with their own parents, relatives, and friends. As they plan for their baby together, husband and wife will share in making some of the most important decisions of their lives: they begin to think of the developing new life.

Pregnancy and Prenatal Care

Profound physical changes take place in the pregnant woman. Sound sleep, proper diet, and reasonable exercise are essential. Regular visits to a doctor or prenatal clinic can help make this experience the profoundly joyful one it was meant to be.

The signs of pregnancy The first symptom of possible pregnancy is usually a missed menstrual period. For those who may *not* miss a period, there are other symptoms. One of these is "morning sickness," a feeling of nausea on rising. A woman may also have a sense of distension, a bloated feeling, in the lower abdomen. Her breasts may feel sore. Some of these symptoms (except morning sickness) also occur in some women prior to menstruation.

Each woman experiences the symptoms of pregnancy differently. The same woman may have different early symptoms in each pregnancy. Simple laboratory tests performed in a doctor's office or a family planning clinic will be accurate in most cases. A positive diagnosis of pregnancy can usually be made about two weeks after the first missed menstrual period.

Between the sixteenth and the twenty-second week of pregnancy, most mothers feel the "quickening," as the baby within them begins to move. A doctor can hear the baby's heartbeat by placing a stethoscope on the mother's lower abdomen. At this time, growth of the baby is more rapid, and the external signs of pregnancy—enlarged abdomen, adjusted walk, and enlarged breasts—become more noticeable. Maternity clothes may begin to be worn at this time. Such garments should be loose-fitting, thus affording ease of movement. A doctor may recommend special support garments for abdomen and breasts as pregnancy advances.

Couples must make housing decisions when they know they are going to be parents. They will need space and furniture for the new baby. As they rearrange and prepare their living quarters, a couple can share in the anticipation of the baby's arrival.

Regular medical care during pregnancy is essential for the baby and reassuring to the mother. The doctor, monitoring the progress of the pregnancy, can foresee possible problems and help to prevent them.

Prenatal care Everything a mother takes into her body affects her unborn baby. Each woman's doctor will give her specific instructions based on individual circumstances. In general, a doctor will advise a well-balanced diet. He may also suggest that the pregnant woman stay away from cigarettes and stimulants (including coffee and tea) and any drugs that have not been prescribed by him.

Some drugs and some diseases are known to damage the unborn baby at certain stages of development. A pregnant woman should contact her doctor immediately if she feels she may have taken in any damaging substances. She should also be concerned if she has been exposed to such illnesses as German measles. German measles during the early stages of pregnancy is known to damage the developing baby.

At one time, many superstitions ruled the behavior of pregnant women. Women took special care to avoid any situations that were thought to "mark" the child. Doctors discount most general influences from the outside environment. It is known, however, that the internal environment—the mother's womb and the surrounding tissues—affects the health of the unborn baby. Strictly speaking, the mother does not "eat for two." She does, however, provide nutrients and oxygen for the child she is carrying.

Every pregnant woman should be aware of the possibility of some irregularity. Pain, headache, bleeding, backache, swelling of the hands, ankles, legs, or feet should be called to a doctor's attention. Many such symptoms can be avoided by carefully restricting weight gain while supplying sound nutrition. Most doctors suggest a regulated weight gain during pregnancy.

For most women, pregnancy is a normal, healthy condition of life. It should be treated as such by all concerned.

Childbirth

The onset of birth is signalled by *labor pains.* These are caused by muscular contractions which are needed to force the baby through the birth canal. The mother can aid in this process by "bearing down" on the contractions. She can be assisted at the birth by an attending doctor or midwife. In difficult or complicated births, the highest skill of the obstetrician may be needed to preserve the life of both mother and child. At one time, childbirth entailed considerable risks. Today, the risk in normal births is negligible.

A *full term* baby is one that has been carried, on the average, for 280 days. It weighs between 5½ and 8½ pounds. The *premature* baby may be born up to three months short of full term. Any baby weighing less than five pounds is also classified as premature, no matter how long the mother has carried it. Parents of premature babies must take this into account as their babies grow and develop. In a few years, growth and development seem to average out. The parents of such children must take this lag into account when considering "average" ages for sitting, walking, talking, and entering school.

Occasionally, the hormone changes following birth cause unexpected emotional states in the mother. She may find herself feeling depressed, rather than elated, at the birth of her baby. These feelings may make her feel guilty and unhappy. She should confide these feelings to her doctor, who will explain the reasons for them. As hormone balance is restored, the mother's emotional state is likely to improve. Such an experience requires understanding and sympathy on the part of the father. He should not take this mood, over which the new mother may have little or no control, as an indication that his wife will not later respond positively to the role of motherhood.

Sharing the Experience

When conception, pregnancy, and childbirth were shrouded in mystery and superstition, women were often shut away from outside contacts while they were "expecting." Even husbands were excluded from this process, which was considered strictly feminine. Today, many husbands and wives feel that the total physical, mental, emotional, and spiritual intimacy sanctioned by marriage is extended to the period of pregnancy and labor. It has been reported that, in some cases, husbands have even experienced morning sickness.

Sharing with each other In sharing the experience of pregnancy, a husband and wife can deepen and strengthen their relationship. The wife can assure her husband that he is part of her experience. She should assure him that he is being rewarded, not replaced, by the new life within her. The husband can assure his wife that she is genuinely loved. He can demonstrate concern and protectiveness as his wife copes with new and unfamiliar experiences.

Mild, but regular, exercise is an important part of prenatal health care. Keeping the muscles in tone may make delivery easier and will help a mother to regain her figure after the baby is born.

CASE STUDY: BUCK AND JANE

THE SITUATION *Jane stood by the kitchen window, restlessly waiting for her husband Buck's return. She had been to the doctor this afternoon and now knew for sure that she and Buck would have a baby in May. She wondered how her husband would receive the news. The couple had not planned to have children for at least another year. They had recently moved into their house and were spending much energy and time remodeling and decorating every inch of it. As she looked around, Jane thought that there really was not much room for a baby. There was hardly room for the two of them! She knew Buck would be thinking the same thing. Besides, Buck liked her attention all for himself. In a crowd, conversation had to revolve around him. He was upset if someone other than he were in the spotlight. He had to out-joke, out-work, and out-think everyone else. Jane wondered what would happen when he realized how much time and attention would be diverted from him to a new baby.*

As Buck walked across the porch and into the house, she could see he was still thinking about work. She prepared dinner as she listened to his opinions and impressions about events on the job. Finally he asked,

"You went to the doctor today, didn't you? Everything all right?"

Jane answered slowly. "Everything's fine, Buck. We're going to have a baby."

Buck said absolutely nothing, staring at his wife. Then he stood up, and walked out of the house. Two hours later, he was still out.

THE INTERVIEW *Q: What now, Jane?*
A: I guess I'll just stay here and wait until he comes back. I thought he would be upset, but I wasn't sure how he'd react. Now I know.
Q: What do you suppose he'll say?
A: When he comes back, he'll probably be ready to make plans about where to put the baby, how to tell my folks, and what he'll say to his friends. He will probably want to make all the announcements himself, rather than letting me do it.
Q: How do you feel in this situation?
A: I'm a little bothered by his immaturity. I should be used to it by now, though. I knew what he was like before I married him. He'll be all right as soon as he gets used to the idea of a third person in the house. I'll have to humor him for a while.

REACT *What would you do in Jane's situation?*

Expectant parents will have to make decisions concerning hospital arrangements. They will have to estimate the resources available to them for prenatal, delivery, and postnatal care. The hospital may permit the presence of the husband through labor and delivery. Such an experience may bring some couples even closer together. Fathers report a special tenderness after participating in this aspect of parenthood.

Sharing with others How will each of the prospective parents feel about sharing their experience with grandparents, parents, and close friends? All of these people are likely to have some interest in the important event. If one parent comes from a home where a new baby is everybody's business, while the other believes it to be "strictly personal," conflicts may arise. Choosing a name for a new baby has a way of involving old, and sometimes conflicting, loyalties. What is the family's feeling toward the sex of the coming child? What are their feelings about names? Does the father's family want a "Jr." or a number such as "the third" tacked at the end of a boy's name. Does the mother's family want him named after a male relative? Each couple will have to decide the degree of involvement of family and friends.

Formal religious ceremonies surrounding childbirth also involve family members. In Christian families, the choice of godparents involves selecting from among the two parents' friends and relatives.

Resources for New Parents

In almost any community, there are many resources available to those anticipating parenthood. Couples, as well as parents without partners, may need help in learning to adjust to their new roles and responsibilities.

Family resources New parents may find much willing support and assistance within their families. If in-laws live close at hand, they will be adjusting to their new roles as grandparents, often with great pride and pleasure. The new parents' relations with

Some hospitals allow the father, properly gowned and masked, to be present in the delivery room. Many couples feel that this is a very important way to share the experience of pregnancy and birth.

When a couple already has a child, a new pregnancy occasions a very special kind of sharing. If this is done openly and warmly, the child is less likely to feel left out and upset when the new baby is born.

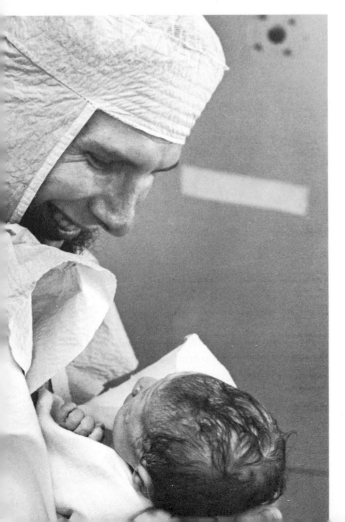

In some religions and cultures, choosing a name for the baby may have deep significance. Other rituals, such as Christian baptism, consecrate a new life. While such rituals are meaningful in themselves, they are also occasions to celebrate the birth of a child.

their own parents and their in-laws will influence the quality of feeling surrounding the event. Family interest in the welfare of the coming child can help reduce the anxieties of prospective parents. Support and encouragement can help make them optimistic about experiences that are to come.

Medical resources Prospective parents will want to find and use the best medical services, either private or public, both before and after the event. The medical specialties include *gynecology* (care of the female reproductive system), *obstetrics* (care of the pregnant woman and delivery of the baby),

and *pediatrics* (care of infants and children). These specialized medical services may be supplemented by the paraprofessional support services of *midwives* (who are trained for routine deliveries in or out of a medical facility). They may also be supplemented by professional obstetric and pediatric nurses. Young parents with resources for private nursing care may decide to engage the services of a pediatric nurse to help the mother make the change from hospital to home.

Community resources Communities will vary in the availability of such resources as family planning centers, prenatal and maternity clinics, well-baby clinics, and day-care centers. Public health nurses, nutritionists, and health aides work with mothers. They bring their clients up-to-date and individualized information concerning infant feeding and child care. Expectant parents should seek out and evaluate the services available to them. Adult education centers may offer courses especially for prospective fathers. Today, many fathers expect to become more closely involved with their children and are interested in learning how to care for small babies. Government agencies at every level offer services to parents and children. Many of their publications provide easy-to-read and ready references for parents.

Religious resources Parents may find the religious group of their choice is helpful in guiding them toward both the physical and spiritual growth and development of their infants and young children. Each religion has its own interpretation of the spiritual meaning of parenthood. All agree on the serious responsibilities it involves. The observation of religious rituals soon after birth are matters for parents to decide. The practice of male circumcision, practiced as a sanitary measure by some, has religious significance for others. The operation, a simple one, is generally performed before the infant boy leaves the hospital. Decisions concerning baptism and christening will be made by some parents.

THE PLEASURES OF PARENTHOOD

The responsibilities of parenthood offer many satisfactions. In parenthood, a husband and wife have the opportunity to share the love they feel for each other. They can gain a sense of their joint identity through their children. Mature adults gain deep satisfaction from sharing and giving to meet the physical, psychological, and spiritual needs of helpless children. Through the guidance provided for children, parents experience the feeling that they have reached a goal and that their values will be carried forward through time.

To meet their responsibilities effectively, parents will need both emotional maturity and economic security. The experience of parenthood offers an opportunity to give and to receive unselfish love. The decision to have a family reflects a couple's basic values concerning human life. It gives them a chance to demonstrate in their day-to-day living the value they place on guiding a human life to its greatest personal, psychological, social, and spiritual potential.

THINK BACK

Decisions about family size must reflect concern for both natural and personal resources.
Discuss: *"It is a natural right for a couple to have as many children as they wish."*

Responsible parenthood involves thinking ahead.
Discuss: *Are most teenagers mature enough to be responsible parents?*

Both parents contribute hereditary characteristics to their children.
Discuss: *Do you believe that each of us has a "twin" located somewhere in this world?*

Family, community, and religious resources are among the aids to family planning and child rearing.
Discuss: *Do they interfere with the rights of the parent?*

Adoption can be a satisfying way of increasing family size.

Discuss: *How might a parent explain adoption to an adopted child?*

LOOK AROUND

1. For what reasons are people concerned with population problems? What are predictions concerning increases in population and corresponding environmental problems?
2. What is your opinion of the various reasons for having children that are stated in the text? Develop a bulletin board illustrating the reason you favor most.
3. How are physical traits transferred from parent to child? What are examples of dominant and recessive traits?
4. What are some reasons why people adopt children or take foster children? Would you consider either alternative? Why?
5. What are some signs of pregnancy?
6. What must a pregnant woman be careful about?
7. Do you see pregnancy and childbirth as experiences to be shared? Are there points beyond which they should not be shared?
8. What agencies for the protection, health, and growth of children exist in your area?

FOLLOW YOUR PATH

PATH ONE: Form a Newspaper

Step 10 Write a review of the Path Four soap opera. How realistic is it? Do you feel the conflicts it presents are relevant to most people? Does the program miss something you would like to see?

Step 11 Write a human interest story about the Path Three family court.

PATH TWO: Plan and Operate a Community Center

Step 17 Interview a number of retired grandmothers and grandfathers in your community. Ask how they would feel about working as babysitters—either for free or for a small sum—at a center such as yours.

Step 18 Model a "Substitute Granny" service based on the suggestions of these grandparents.

Step 19 Make up an advertisement for the "Substitute Granny" program. Place it in the Path One newspaper.

Step 20 Invite a guest speaker to address your community center on the subject of prenatal care.

Step 21 Prepare a bulletin board which shows the steps involved in adopting children. Review at least three current books or articles to check your facts.

PATH THREE: Form a Family Court

Step 14 What problems in an adoption proceeding might be discussed before a family court? You may wish to research your answer by consulting an adoption agency.

Step 15 Enact a session of Family Court. Base the situation on one of the problems you uncovered in Step 14.

Step 16 Ask the class to comment on the session and especially on the judge's decision.

PATH FOUR: Produce a TV Soap Opera

Step 16 Plan an episode in which a family discusses the possibility of foster or adoptive parenthood.

Step 17 and 18 Enact these episodes.

Step 19 Ask the class to discuss the episodes. Have them talk about the relevant values, goals, and resources of each family.

CHAPTER 26

Caring for Infants and Young Children

Children are our most precious human resource. In them lies our hope for the future of mankind, our nation, and our world. At one time, children remained almost exclusively in the care of the family, especially the mother, until they reached school age. A few preschool children in well-to-do homes had nursery school, play school, day camp, or kindergarten experience provided for them. Such learning experiences in early childhood may be of enormous value to the child. Properly planned and supervised child care contributes to the child's overall physical, mental, and social development. Today, children from many economic levels are cared for outside the home by persons outside the family. Nevertheless, the influence of the home has a great impact on the growth and development of the child.

CARING FOR THE BABY

Some babies are more active than others. Some babies have a stronger sucking instinct; they stay at the breast or bottle longer than others. Some respond more readily to environmental factors, such as lights, noise, and handling. Some seem more sociable and cry less when other people are around. From birth, each baby has its own rhythm of eating, sleeping, elimination, and activity. These rhythms may be related to the rhythm of the mother's activities during pregnancy. They are also related to the "biological clock" mentioned earlier. Together, these influence the rate at which a baby develops. They influence the timing of developmental stages and of such activities as lifting arms.

EMPATHY WITH INFANTS

Adults can sense a child's feelings of dependence and vulnerability. They can express this sensitivity with tender, loving care. In this way, they can help the child to feel safe and secure. The child then tries to respond in ways that give the adult pleasure. He learns to enter into their feelings. This is the *empathy* that can develop between adults and children. Empathy is expressed in the quality of parenting—the warmth, interest, and tenderness displayed by mothers and fathers or their substitutes. When parents share their tasks, enjoy their baby, and communicate their enjoyment to the baby, development proceeds smoothly, and the child grows physically, psychologically, socially, and spiritually in an atmosphere of love.

Babies need environmental stimulation to develop normally. They need to be held, cuddled, and talked to. Babies who are ignored do not develop rapidly or fully.

Parents should try to establish a routine. Their baby's individual pattern of needs for food, water, sleep, rest, elimination, and attention should be understood. The baby will help them in this. He will resist being fed when he is not hungry, put to sleep when not tired, and changed when comfortable.

The baby's schedule can be guided to mesh with the activities of other family members. When both parents work, for example, a baby's schedule might be arranged to allow parents and baby to be together at mealtime, bathtime, and bedtime—even if these are not the customary times when other babies are fed, bathed, or put to bed.

A schedule that is established gradually is likely to leave everyone happier and more relaxed than a schedule that is imposed all at once. It takes only a few weeks to set times for meeting the baby's needs.

Infant Feeding

A baby's first feeding is arranged soon after delivery. At that time, he may be put to the mother's breast. This feeding provides no actual nourishment, but a watery fluid called *colostrum*. Colostrum appears to have a mildly laxative effect on the baby. It helps to clear the intestinal tract of wastes.

Feedings occur at three- to four-hour intervals for the first week or so of life. They will last from ten to twenty minutes. However, babies differ in their need and ability to suck, as well as their strength and staying power at breast or bottle. By the time the mother and baby leave the hospital, the mother and doctor will have decided whether the mother will breast- or bottle-feed the baby. Sometimes, a combination of both may be advised. The doctor will suggest a formula that is considered appropriate for the baby's needs. In some rare cases, an inborn genetic

If a baby has learned to enjoy his bath, bath time will not be a chore for his mother. Since babies can drown in only a few inches of water, they should never be left unattended, even for a few seconds.

in the middle of the meal to be sure the air does not take the place of food in the stomach. Finally, he can be bubbled at the end so he will rest comfortably. Each baby will soon establish his own pattern of bubbling. After about three months, the baby will probably have learned to do this by himself. Adults can discontinue this practice, but not the cuddling and closeness the baby looks forward to at mealtime.

Offering solid food The eruption of teeth at around four months signals the baby's readiness for strained solid foods. Some doctors advise cereals mixed with milk sooner. A doctor, public health nurse, or nutritionist can offer reliable suggestions concerning appropriate foods for infants.

Babies have strong reactions to unfamiliar tastes and textures. Small quantities of new foods can be offered to the baby when he is relaxed. It is important for the person offering the food to maintain a relaxed attitude at this time. Any tension caused by the baby's refusal to eat may result in feeding problems later. As their teeth begin to erupt and babies begin gumming their food, they will take pleasure from the opportunity to bite coarse or crisp textured foods, such as toast or wafers. The amounts given should be chewable, so that they are thoroughly moistened when they are swallowed. Small, hard pieces of food such as candy or nuts should be avoided. (They may cause choking or suffocation.)

Food offered to babies should be fairly bland. Food seasoned or salted to an adult's taste may not suit a baby at all. Foods to which artificial flavorings and sweeteners have been added should also be avoided. A baby's body chemistry is still quite precarious. What the baby needs is to receive nutritionally balanced meals. When diets adequate in all nutrients are provided, additional vitamin supplements may not have to be recommended by a doctor. In climates or at seasons when the baby is not exposed to sunlight and fresh air, however, vitamin D may be prescribed. It is better not to give vitamins in any form to a baby without a doctor's advice. Excess vitamins and minerals in an infant's diet can upset normal growth.

By the end of the first year, self-feeding of small morsels of food will probably begin. The baby will also be trying to hold bottles, cups, and spoons for himself. However awkward and untidy these efforts may be, help should be offered only when the baby is

For normal physical and mental development, infants need regular physical contact with other human beings. Lack of such stimulation can result in impaired development, called "failure to thrive." Feeding time is one of the many opportunities for parents to cuddle the baby.

error may require a highly specialized formula because the baby cannot digest ordinary milk, food, or formula. One such error is called *phenylketonuria* (PKU). If undetected early in infancy, it will result in irreversible brain damage. Many states now require that newborn infants be tested for PKU. If it is detected, the baby can be put on a special diet to avoid impairment.

Most babies eat when they are hungry and turn from nourishment when they do not need food. Therefore, a relaxed attitude toward the baby at feeding time will allow the infant to set the pace. The habit of over-

eating learned by babies may be extremely hard to break later. Overeating is the fairly universal cause of excess weight, which can be a serious health problem.

Eventually, the baby will be taken off bottle or breast and given solid food.

Breast or bottle Food should not be offered to keep a baby quiet when he is whimpering to have other needs met. He may be wet, uncomfortable, cold, hot, thirsty, or lonesome.

Just as important as the food a baby receives is the cuddling and cradling that occurs either at the breast or when the

CASE STUDY: ANNA AND HER FAMILY

THE SITUATION *Christmas was the time of year for the Breck family's reunion. How special this particular year was going to be! Neither Mrs. Breck nor Uncle Charles had seen Anna's new baby boy yet. Both had been busily preparing for the baby's arrival home for at least two months. Charles repainted the crib that had once been Anna's. He even bought a new mattress for it. He built a rocking horse and put on the finishing coat of paint just before the baby's arrival. Mrs. Breck had arranged a vacation from work for the three days Anna would be home; and she had spent much time "sanitizing" the rooms in which the baby would spend his time.*

On the evening of Anna's homecoming, Mrs. Breck and Uncle Charles had taken charge of Anna and her son. After a long day of traveling, Anna was relieved to let someone else look after the baby for a while. But when her family continued to give her advice on baby care the next day, she became a little disturbed. She said nothing, thinking that they would "get over it" once they had gotten used to the baby. After all, this was Anna's first child. It would take time for them to see her in her new role as mother.

Now, as Anna sat on the floor holding the baby in her lap, she heard her mother say, "You shouldn't sit there, dear. This house is too drafty. The baby may catch a cold."

Trying to calm her feeling of resentment at her mother's interference, Anna replied, "We're all right. He has nice warm clothing."

Uncle Charles immediately added, "Put him in his bed now, Anna. It's time for his nap."

THE INTERVIEW *Q: Why are you angry with your family?*
A: Because they insist on telling me how to care for my own child. I wish they'd just leave us alone. If there's something I want to know about his care, I ask my doctor. So far, I've had no trouble taking care of him. And I expect to be quite capable of taking care of any problems that might develop in the future.
Q: Maybe you hurt your mother's and uncle's feelings.
A: Maybe I did. But I'm not a child anymore. It's about time they realize that. We're all part of the same family, but I'm the one responsible for my son's health and safety. I'm his mother and I don't want to have other people telling me how to raise him.

REACT *Should care of a new baby be the concern of all family members? What do you think is the best approach Anna could take to this problem?*

---

bottle is given. Babies respond to protective love with a growing sense of trust.

The choice about **breast feeding** a baby is a highly personal one. For those mothers who are interested and able to do so, the experience can benefit both mother and child.

Sucking stimulates the flow of a mother's milk within three to five days. Until the mother begins to produce milk, therefore, the baby will receive little actual nourishment. All newborn babies lose some of their birth weight in the first few days of life. Since both mother and baby are tired from the effort involved in childbirth, this loss is not usually important for full-term babies. The sucking action of the baby stimulates the mother's uterus to contract and return to its previous state.

The advantages of breast milk include certain "custom made" factors that are not found in formula or ordinary milk. Mother's milk contains substances that provide the baby with immunity from certain illness in the first weeks or months of life. This is germ-free and likely to meet the individual needs better than a formula.

To be sure, breast feeding may keep the mother from other tasks, require her presence at home, and may cause temporary weight gain. If the mother is in good health and well nourished, she is usually able to provide her baby with an ample supply of milk. If not, she can supplement breast feedings with bottle feedings.

Two alternatives are available for **bottle feeding:** a formula prepared at home and a commercial formula, sometimes sold in disposable containers for ease and sanitation.

Homemade formulas may be based on whole, dry, or powdered milk. Babies who are allergic to milk may have milk substitutes of various kinds in their formula. All formulas should be prepared in accordance with instructions from a doctor or a nutritionist specializing in infant feeding.

Since milk attracts disease-carrying microorganisms, homemade formulas must be sterilized. This may be done after the formula has been placed in bottles. Baby bottles and other equipment may be sterilized separately. Cleanliness and good sanitation are necessary in all phases of formula preparation.

It may take several experiments with nipple holes of different sizes to provide the baby with a satisfying flow of milk and sufficient opportunity to suck. The mother should follow her doctor's recommendation concerning the temperature at which milk is to be given. Warming the bottle approximates the temperature of breast milk, but some babies show no ill effects when given a bottle straight from the refrigerator.

Air swallowed during feeding can cause stomach discomfort. Thus, burping or bubbling, which brings up the air, is needed to

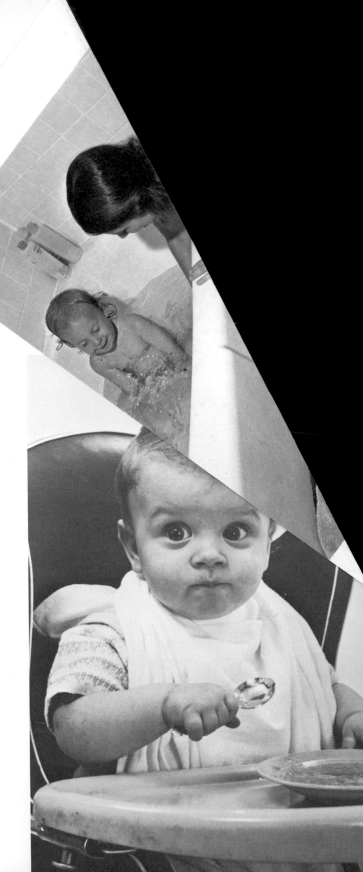

tired or is being frustrated in his efforts by lack of muscular coordination.

Weaning A baby who has received great comfort, security, and gratification at breast or bottle since birth must gradually grow accustomed to taking milk and other liquids from a cup, glass, or spoon. Unless accomplished calmly, firmly, and gradually, weaning may cause tension. Weaning ordinarily begins anywhere between eight and nine months, when the baby's first teeth have come through. Attitudes toward weaning should be relaxed and unforced. If the baby resists, efforts may be discontinued.

Keeping The Baby Clean

As soon as the navel and (for a boy) the circumcision have healed, the new baby can be safely immersed in water. Until then, cleansing with oil followed by a warm sponge bath is recommended. A bassinette (a tub and table combined for bathing and dressing) is helpful at first. Elaborate special equipment, however, is not really necessary. A washbasin, large plastic dishpan, or kitchen sink with towel placed at the edge near the baby's head are also practical. When the baby can sit up with little support (at seven or eight months), he may be ready for bathing in the family tub. If the baby is ill or fidgety, a sponge bath may be substituted for the tub bath. By the time he is a year old, support of the head and back of the neck should no longer be necessary. The baby can be bathed in shallow water. Never leave an infant or young child alone in a bathtub. Babies can drown in a few inches of water.

After eating, burping, or spilling milk or food, a baby's face and hands should be gently cleansed with a warm cloth. Keeping him clean without irritating him helps to establish the habit of cleanliness before and after meals. If baths are given too quickly and roughly or soap is allowed to get into eyes and nose, the baby may become frightened

of his bath. The baby needs to have his feeling of trust and security reinforced. He needs reassurance. He gets this from being handled with special tenderness and understanding. He needs quiet talk to distract him from his fearful and apprehensive attitude. Bathtime should be fun for all.

Drying, Diapering, and Dressing

Drying, diapering, and dressing a baby are usually easier on a flat-topped, soft-covered surface. Such an arrangement also affords an opportunity for communication through touching, talking, and smiling. Babies are most comfortable in loose, light, clean clothes that allow freedom of movement. In warm weather, the less clothing the better.

Clothes that do not have to be pulled over a baby's head make it easier for the mother to dress the baby. When a child is learning to dress himself, clothes with simple front fasteners are helpful.

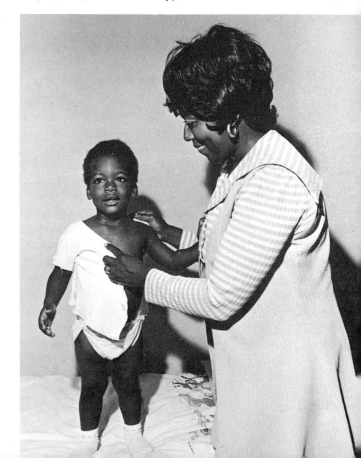

As they develop, children need freedom to exercise creativity and imagination. This does not mean they should be absolutely unrestricted; but if too many activities are "off limits" because they are messy or troublesome, a child's curiosity may be dulled.

Chafing, irritation, and rashes result when babies are overdressed. Babies are often overdressed to please their parents or relatives. Dressing a baby for looks at the expense of comfort can cause tension.

Diapers may be made of cloth or cloth substitutes. Double diapers are advised at night. Babies whose diapers are changed as needed soon appreciate the pleasant feeling associated with being clean and dry. This helps to motivate their behavior when the time for toilet training arrives.

Putting the Baby to Sleep

Bedtime problems, like other problems with infants, can usually be avoided with calm, competent handling. If an adult under-stands that even a baby has to be relaxed to fall asleep, he will help the baby to relax. A baby that has his basic needs met is usually relaxed and happy. If he has been fed, played with, talked to, and bathed, he will probably begin to sleep at fairly regular times. The sound of a voice or a few firm pats can help a tense or active baby calm down.

The baby needs a clean, quiet, flat surface on which to sleep. He needs the protection of a crib when he is too small to control his movements and is likely to fall out of a bed. A baby does not need a pillow. He needs to have his nose left free to breathe. Plastic pillow protectors and excessive bedding may cause suffocation. Babies seem to have preferred positions for sleeping. Some doctors advise turning the head from

For normal physical and mental development, infants need regular physical contact with other human beings. Lack of such stimulation can result in impaired development, called "failure to thrive." Feeding time is one of the many opportunities for parents to cuddle the baby.

error may require a highly specialized formula because the baby cannot digest ordinary milk, food, or formula. One such error is called *phenylketonuria* (PKU). If undetected early in infancy, it will result in irreversible brain damage. Many states now require that newborn infants be tested for PKU. If it is detected, the baby can be put on a special diet to avoid impairment.

Most babies eat when they are hungry and turn from nourishment when they do not need food. Therefore, a relaxed attitude toward the baby at feeding time will allow the infant to set the pace. The habit of over-eating learned by babies may be extremely hard to break later. Overeating is the fairly universal cause of excess weight, which can be a serious health problem.

Eventually, the baby will be taken off bottle or breast and given solid food.

Breast or bottle Food should not be offered to keep a baby quiet when he is whimpering to have other needs met. He may be wet, uncomfortable, cold, hot, thirsty, or lonesome.

Just as important as the food a baby receives is the cuddling and cradling that occurs either at the breast or when the

CASE STUDY: ANNA AND HER FAMILY

THE SITUATION Christmas was the time of year for the Breck family's reunion. How special this particular year was going to be! Neither Mrs. Breck nor Uncle Charles had seen Anna's new baby boy yet. Both had been busily preparing for the baby's arrival home for at least two months. Charles repainted the crib that had once been Anna's. He even bought a new mattress for it. He built a rocking horse and put on the finishing coat of paint just before the baby's arrival. Mrs. Breck had arranged a vacation from work for the three days Anna would be home; and she had spent much time "sanitizing" the rooms in which the baby would spend his time.

On the evening of Anna's homecoming, Mrs. Breck and Uncle Charles had taken charge of Anna and her son. After a long day of traveling, Anna was relieved to let someone else look after the baby for a while. But when her family continued to give her advice on baby care the next day, she became a little disturbed. She said nothing, thinking that they would "get over it" once they had gotten used to the baby. After all, this was Anna's first child. It would take time for them to see her in her new role as mother.

Now, as Anna sat on the floor holding the baby in her lap, she heard her mother say, "You shouldn't sit there, dear. This house is too drafty. The baby may catch a cold."

Trying to calm her feeling of resentment at her mother's interference, Anna replied, "We're all right. He has nice warm clothing."

Uncle Charles immediately added, "Put him in his bed now, Anna. It's time for his nap."

THE INTERVIEW Q: Why are you angry with your family?
A: Because they insist on telling me how to care for my own child. I wish they'd just leave us alone. If there's something I want to know about his care, I ask my doctor. So far, I've had no trouble taking care of him. And I expect to be quite capable of taking care of any problems that might develop in the future.
Q: Maybe you hurt your mother's and uncle's feelings.
A: Maybe I did. But I'm not a child anymore. It's about time they realize that. We're all part of the same family, but I'm the one responsible for my son's health and safety. I'm his mother and I don't want to have other people telling me how to raise him.

REACT Should care of a new baby be the concern of all family members? What do you think is the best approach Anna could take to this problem?

---

bottle is given. Babies respond to protective love with a growing sense of trust.

The choice about **breast feeding** a baby is a highly personal one. For those mothers who are interested and able to do so, the experience can benefit both mother and child.

Sucking stimulates the flow of a mother's milk within three to five days. Until the mother begins to produce milk, therefore, the baby will receive little actual nourishment. All newborn babies lose some of their birth weight in the first few days of life. Since both mother and baby are tired from the effort involved in childbirth, this loss is not usually important for full-term babies. The sucking action of the baby stimulates the mother's uterus to contract and return to its previous state.

The advantages of breast milk include certain "custom made" factors that are not found in formula or ordinary milk. Mother's milk contains substances that provide the baby with immunity from certain illnesses in the first weeks or months of life. The milk is germ-free and likely to meet the baby's individual needs better than a formula.

To be sure, breast feeding may keep the mother from other tasks, requires her presence at home, and may result in a temporary weight gain. If the mother is in good health and well nourished, she should be able to provide her baby with an adequate supply of milk. If not, she can supplement breast feedings with bottle feedings.

Two alternatives are available for **bottle feeding:** a formula prepared at home and a commercial formula, sometimes sold in disposable containers for ease and sanitation.

Homemade formulas may be based on whole, dry, or powdered milk. Babies who are allergic to milk may have milk substitutes of various kinds in their formula. All formulas should be prepared in accordance with instructions from a doctor or a nutritionist specializing in infant feeding.

Since milk attracts disease-carrying microorganisms, homemade formulas must be sterilized. This may be done after the formula has been placed in bottles. Baby bottles and other equipment may be sterilized separately. Cleanliness and good sanitation are necessary in all phases of formula preparation.

It may take several experiments with nipple holes of different sizes to provide the baby with a satisfying flow of milk and sufficient opportunity to suck. The mother should follow her doctor's recommendation concerning the temperature at which milk is to be given. Warming the bottle approximates the temperature of breast milk, but some babies show no ill effects when given a bottle straight from the refrigerator.

Air swallowed during feeding can cause stomach discomfort. Thus, burping or bubbling, which brings up the air, is needed to avoid pain. Some babies burp promptly. Others may not bring up the air for as long as fifteen minutes. Sometimes a small amount of milk is brought up with the air, so a moist cloth should be kept handy.

To release the air, the baby can be placed over the shoulder and gently patted on the back. He can also be placed on the lap, bent from the waist (supporting the head from the front), and patted. He may be bubbled shortly after the beginning of feeding, when crying and "eager eating" are likely to bring in large quantities of air. He can then be bubbled

Babies who are learning to feed themselves need plenty of time and a relaxed atmosphere in which to experiment with a cup and spoon. Mothers who are too eager to help may delay the baby's accomplishment.

If a baby has learned to enjoy his bath, bath time will not be a chore for his mother. Since babies can drown in only a few inches of water, they should never be left unattended, even for a few seconds.

Offering solid food The eruption of teeth at around four months signals the baby's readiness for strained solid foods. Some doctors advise cereals mixed with milk sooner. A doctor, public health nurse, or nutritionist can offer reliable suggestions concerning appropriate foods for infants.

Babies have strong reactions to unfamiliar tastes and textures. Small quantities of new foods can be offered to the baby when he is relaxed. It is important for the person offering the food to maintain a relaxed attitude at this time. Any tension caused by the baby's refusal to eat may result in feeding problems later. As their teeth begin to erupt and babies begin gumming their food, they will take pleasure from the opportunity to bite coarse or crisp textured foods, such as toast or wafers. The amounts given should be chewable, so that they are thoroughly moistened when they are swallowed. Small, hard pieces of food such as candy or nuts should be avoided. (They may cause choking or suffocation.)

Food offered to babies should be fairly bland. Food seasoned or salted to an adult's taste may not suit a baby at all. Foods to which artificial flavorings and sweeteners have been added should also be avoided. A baby's body chemistry is still quite precarious. What the baby needs is to receive nutritionally balanced meals. When diets adequate in all nutrients are provided, additional vitamin supplements may not have to be recommended by a doctor. In climates or at seasons when the baby is not exposed to sunlight and fresh air, however, vitamin D may be prescribed. It is better not to give vitamins in any form to a baby without a doctor's advice. Excess vitamins and minerals in an infant's diet can upset normal growth.

By the end of the first year, self-feeding of small morsels of food will probably begin. The baby will also be trying to hold bottles, cups, and spoons for himself. However awkward and untidy these efforts may be, help should be offered only when the baby is

in the middle of the meal to be sure the air does not take the place of food in the stomach. Finally, he can be bubbled at the end so he will rest comfortably. Each baby will soon establish his own pattern of bubbling. After about three months, the baby will probably have learned to do this by himself. Adults can discontinue this practice, but not the cuddling and closeness the baby looks forward to at mealtime.

tired or is being frustrated in his efforts by lack of muscular coordination.

Weaning A baby who has received great comfort, security, and gratification at breast or bottle since birth must gradually grow accustomed to taking milk and other liquids from a cup, glass, or spoon. Unless accomplished calmly, firmly, and gradually, weaning may cause tension. Weaning ordinarily begins anywhere between eight and nine months, when the baby's first teeth have come through. Attitudes toward weaning should be relaxed and unforced. If the baby resists, efforts may be discontinued.

Keeping The Baby Clean

As soon as the navel and (for a boy) the circumcision have healed, the new baby can be safely immersed in water. Until then, cleansing with oil followed by a warm sponge bath is recommended. A bassinette (a tub and table combined for bathing and dressing) is helpful at first. Elaborate special equipment, however, is not really necessary. A washbasin, large plastic dishpan, or kitchen sink with towel placed at the edge near the baby's head are also practical. When the baby can sit up with little support (at seven or eight months), he may be ready for bathing in the family tub. If the baby is ill or fidgety, a sponge bath may be substituted for the tub bath. By the time he is a year old, support of the head and back of the neck should no longer be necessary. The baby can be bathed in shallow water. Never leave an infant or young child alone in a bathtub. Babies can drown in a few inches of water.

After eating, burping, or spilling milk or food, a baby's face and hands should be gently cleansed with a warm cloth. Keeping him clean without irritating him helps to establish the habit of cleanliness before and after meals. If baths are given too quickly and roughly or soap is allowed to get into eyes and nose, the baby may become frightened of his bath. The baby needs to have his feeling of trust and security reinforced. He needs reassurance. He gets this from being handled with special tenderness and understanding. He needs quiet talk to distract him from his fearful and apprehensive attitude. Bathtime should be fun for all.

Drying, Diapering, and Dressing

Drying, diapering, and dressing a baby are usually easier on a flat-topped, soft-covered surface. Such an arrangement also affords an opportunity for communication through touching, talking, and smiling. Babies are most comfortable in loose, light, clean clothes that allow freedom of movement. In warm weather, the less clothing the better.

Clothes that do not have to be pulled over a baby's head make it easier for the mother to dress the baby. When a child is learning to dress himself, clothes with simple front fasteners are helpful.

As they develop, children need freedom to exercise creativity and imagination. This does not mean they should be absolutely unrestricted; but if too many activities are "off limits" because they are messy or troublesome, a child's curiosity may be dulled.

Chafing, irritation, and rashes result when babies are overdressed. Babies are often overdressed to please their parents or relatives. Dressing a baby for looks at the expense of comfort can cause tension.

Diapers may be made of cloth or cloth substitutes. Double diapers are advised at night. Babies whose diapers are changed as needed soon appreciate the pleasant feeling associated with being clean and dry. This helps to motivate their behavior when the time for toilet training arrives.

Putting the Baby to Sleep

Bedtime problems, like other problems with infants, can usually be avoided with calm, competent handling. If an adult under-stands that even a baby has to be relaxed to fall asleep, he will help the baby to relax. A baby that has his basic needs met is usually relaxed and happy. If he has been fed, played with, talked to, and bathed, he will probably begin to sleep at fairly regular times. The sound of a voice or a few firm pats can help a tense or active baby calm down.

The baby needs a clean, quiet, flat surface on which to sleep. He needs the protection of a crib when he is too small to control his movements and is likely to fall out of a bed. A baby does not need a pillow. He needs to have his nose left free to breathe. Plastic pillow protectors and excessive bedding may cause suffocation. Babies seem to have preferred positions for sleeping. Some doctors advise turning the head from one side to another because the bones of the head are still soft.

Most importantly, the baby needs coverings that give him enough freedom but are not easy to dislodge. No loose pins or other small objects should be left in the baby's bed. A short period of irritable crying may simply indicate that the baby is overtired. If all his needs have been taken care of, he will probably fall asleep fairly soon after being placed calmly in bed.

HELPING YOUNG CHILDREN TO GROW

A child's job is to learn about himself, about others, and about the world around him. He accomplishes much of this learning as he plays. It is important that adults provide an atmosphere in which purposeful play can take place. Such an environment is a safe environment. It is an environment in which the child is exposed to a variety of people and things. A principal responsibility of parents is to provide a home environment in which children can learn.

Creating an Environment for Child Development

Adults can help guide children in the accomplishment of developmental tasks appropriate for their stage of development. They should not push or force children to undertake tasks for which they are not ready. An environment for growth offers opportunities for progress without pressure. It offers encouragement without making children fearful of failure or of disappointing adult expectations. All children learn. Their achievements deserve to be recognized.

Providing a Safe Environment

As soon as children toddle, they move around poking and pulling, examining

When buying toys for children, check to see that parts small enough to be swallowed are not removable and that nontoxic paint is used. Even some soft toys have sharp, and dangerous, wire frames inside.

curiously everything they can. At this time, children are unaware of dangers in the environment. In terms of the child's healthy development, it is better to adapt the environment to the child, by keeping unsafe things out of his way. Saying no all the time may blunt the child's curiosity. Supervision is also important. An older person should always keep an eye on an active child.

Until children are aware of the danger of heights and can negotiate stairs with ease, stairways and windows should be blocked. Furniture should be stable and sturdy. Small children often seem fascinated by fire. Playing with matches, stoves, and cigarette lighters behind their parents' backs or in their absence causes many deaths every

CASE STUDY: JUDY AND MICHAEL

THE SITUATION *"Michael, move out of the way. Can't you see you're going to trip me?"* As usual, Jackie heard her neighbor Judy before she actually saw her. As she rounded the corner of the building, she almost ran into two-year-old Michael as he peddled along in his go-car. *"Look out, Michael!"* yelled Judy. *"I told you to watch yourself. Now get over here before I really get mad."*

"Every day it's the same thing," thought Jackie.

The screaming started at eight o'clock in the morning. Not a day went by in which Michael was not reprimanded or threatened by his mother. And when Dad came home in the evening, his voice replaced Judy's. *"Michael needs to be put in his place,"* they explained.

Today, Michael had tears in his eyes. Jackie stopped in front of him. *"Big tears, Michael?"* she asked. *"Are you having a rough day?"*

"He should have it so bad!" said Judy as she hurriedly wiped the tears from his eyes. *"These kids! I don't know what I'm going to do with them. They drive me crazy all day long."*

"Why don't you get a job and hire a baby-sitter?" Jackie asked suddenly. *"Then you wouldn't be bothered by your kids. There must be lots of older people around who would like to take care of children."*

"You try to tell my husband that," replied Judy. *"He doesn't permit me to work."* He says I have to stay home until Michael goes to school, and then I can look for a job. I don't think I'll last that long. Look out, Michael! You're getting that jelly sandwich all over your shirt. Can't you do anything right?"*

The longer she stayed with her, the more upset Jackie became by Judy's treatment of Michael. It wasn't right! There was no reason for an adult woman to spend her day yelling at her children. When she saw Michael flinch as his mother approached him, Judy wondered how long Michael would last in the atmosphere created by Judy and her husband. He was going to give people a lot of trouble some day. She left the pair, unable to witness further Judy's treatment of her son.

THE INTERVIEW Q: Why don't you tell Judy that her behavior bothers you and that you are concerned?

A: It just doesn't seem to be any of my business. But I feel so sorry for Michael! Doesn't she realize that he's only two years old?

Q: What upsets you the most?

A: Judy's not fit to be a mother! Did you see the way Michael flinched away from her when she came toward him? He acts as though he expects to get smacked or yelled at when she's around. A child growing up in a home atmosphere like that is going to have a rough time when he's older. He won't know how to act around other people. Judy is going to make him a nervous wreck before he's five years old.

Q: Why did you suggest the job?

A: To get her out of the house and away from Michael! For her own good as well as for his. Really! They would both be very much better off.

REACT What would you do in Jackie's situation? How might Judy's children feel around her? Are people "fit" and "unfit" to be parents?

year. Electrical appliances, equipment, and outlets intrigue young children. Appliances should be off unless an adult is close by. Appliance cords and electric outlets invite disaster. Cords should be put out of reach. Outlets should be hidden behind heavy furniture, or covered with tape or plastic caps.

As long as children put everything into their mouths, they must be protected from all forms of potential poison. Bathroom medicines and drugs should be kept locked up or at least out of reach. Furthermore, medicine should never be disguised as candy, or children will find it and eat it as if it were. Kitchen cleaning products should also be kept out of reach. Aerosol cans should be kept away from children. Keep the number of the local poison control center.

Understanding the Goals of Play

Play is the business of the child. It is a serious enterprise through which the child grows and develops physically, psychologically, socially, and spiritually. Through play, the child learns about himself and his world. He can increase his strength, gain independence, and bring simple experiences into more complex frameworks of meaning.

Carefully selected and supervised play situations can offer the child opportunities to learn without penalizing him for his relative helplessness and inexperience. Play can also provide an introduction to decision making. It does this when the child has some freedom in choosing his activities. It does this when the child is left free to solve the problems involved in certain types of play.

Different types of play have different values for the child. None are time-wasters.

Developing physically When a child runs, skips, jumps, and balances, he is using up much of his abundant energy. He is strengthening his muscles, increasing his lung capacity and endurance, and improving his coordination. Playing outdoors also exposes a child to the sunshine and fresh air his body needs to stay healthy. Active play allows a child to test his physical potential for sports and muscular work. Playing with toys and games strengthens small muscles and improves coordination.

Mastering skills Written symbols surround children today. Alphabet and number games and songs interest children in "unlocking" or "decoding" the meaning behind letters and figures. The sooner a child masters the skills of reading and writing, the sooner he will be able to learn more complex things. Learning can be fun when it seems like play.

Parents can begin to teach a child respect for drugs by helping him understand that drugs are meant for very special purposes. They should avoid the association of fun or pleasure with taking medicine.

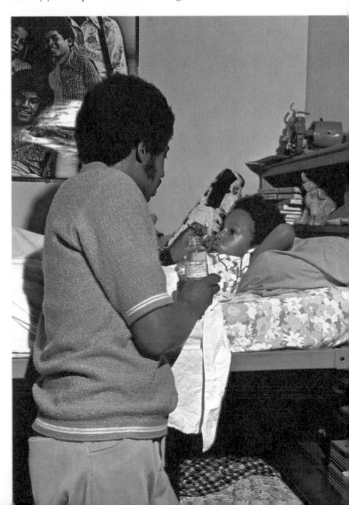

Most children can play happily with no other companion than their imagination. But playing with others their own age offers an opportunity for children to learn communication and other social skills.

Controlling the environment A child is fascinated at being able to control parts of the environment. He handles things to see how they work. He is delighted when his handling produces an effect. Young children like to bang on a can with a spoon to test the outcome of their activity—often to the distress of nearby adults. As they grow older, children become interested in more involved forms of manipulative play. They like to build with blocks, work with clay, and splash paints. As they learn to control such things, they learn to express themselves through their play. Eventually, they learn complex ways to manipulate things like tools, equipment, and machines.

While they are learning to manipulate things, they must also be learning that they cannot manipulate people in the same way. The quality of empathy, mentioned earlier, is important in helping children understand the difference between objects and people. Children must learn to distinguish between the insensitive and sensitive elements of the environment. People should not be maneuvered to suit their purposes.

Making sense of the environment Through play, the child learns to make sense of his environment. Before he can do this, he must explore his physical boundaries. He looks at his hands. He feels his limbs and hair. He pokes at his nose and ears. He investigates his genitals. Once a child understands how he is made up, his curiosity usually moves outward to the external environment.

A child's interest in exploring the environment is boundless. The environment that is rich in things to see, taste, touch, smell, and listen to will stimulate him.

Games and toys based on cause and effect relationships and those that present problem-solving situations can help a child to learn to make sense of his environment. Almost all good games have an instructive element. Such games leave something for the child to discover; and such discovery can be great fun for the child. Some children are fascinated by putting the pieces of a puzzle together to form a recognizable image.

Interacting with others An important form of play for children involves imitation of adult models and life situations. Imitative play, such as "playing house," can give children a chance to express their understanding of adult roles and responsibilities.

Supervised play teaches children to take turns, follow instructions, and cooperate with others. It helps them to take their place in groups outside the family. Play can help children to learn to express even their fear and anger in socially acceptable ways.

Stimulating imagination To stimulate a child's imagination is to stimulate him to grow in a most important way. Stories, songs, dolls, and other toys are springboards in the use of the imagination. Creativity depends a great deal on a child's sensory awareness. Opportunities to touch, feel, and taste are all important in imaginative play.

A NOTE ON THE EXCEPTIONAL CHILD

Not all children fall within the range of "normal" or "average." We have spoken of individual differences and accepted the idea that human beings are far from identical. Some differences are inherited; others result from illness or injury. Some problems may result from unfortunate emotional experiences in early childhood.

The Handicapped Child

The handicapped child may have problems in meeting the physical, mental, or emotional demands made on him each day. The extent of the handicap determines the kind of special treatment needed to help a child to live a full and productive life. When infants do not respond normally to the environment, problems with the senses of sight, speech,

Children realize very early that they share the world with many, many living things. As soon as he is able, a child wants to touch and explore the things he sees. This fascination with nature explains why bird nests, cocoons, and the like are "classic" childhood treasures.

It is important that a child play outdoors. Many activities that require a child to expend physical energy or some that encourage his independence are not suitable for indoor play.

Children like to imitate adult models. Knowing this, adults should be careful to see that children do not harm themselves or others as they try to play with real tools and utensils.

All people need to achieve and be recognized. The Special Olympics, sponsored by the Joseph P. Kennedy, Jr. Foundation, gives mentally retarded children the joy of being able to compete.

children can benefit from low-key learning situations that reward their efforts.

The Gifted Child

The child with exceptional gifts may have "handicaps" of an unsuspected kind. At an age when understanding is important, he may feel misunderstood. At an age when peer-group acceptance is paramount, he may be shunned as being "different." Teachers often leave a gifted child to himself, feeling that their attention should be focused on the child with learning difficulties. They believe that the gifted child will, after all, learn on his own. This may create in the gifted child a feeling of rejection. He may become an under-achiever. He may become rebellious. Sometimes a gifted child is made to feel that *only* his gifts give him value in other people's eyes. Such a child may develop a one-sided personality. Like anyone else, the gifted child must be accepted as a total person.

GROWING CHILDREN AND THEIR "NEIGHBORS"

Parents are not the only ones who help to shape children's personalities. All the people who come into contact with children can be involved in this process. All can listen to children and answer their questions. It is simple for anyone to show appreciation of children's handiwork or to tell them stories. We can all play a part in helping those of the coming generation to grow.

or hearing may exist. Special medical attention and teaching methods and apparatus may compensate for some handicaps.

The mentally handicapped or retarded child also needs special attention to help him reach his potential. He is more helpless than the average child. He needs more patience and more understanding. In some cases, retardation is so severe that the individual cannot be educated. Most retarded

444

THINK BACK

The care given to a baby should satisfy his physical and emotional needs.

Discuss: *Is a mother more capable than a father of caring for their child?*

A parent's attitudes toward his child greatly influence the child's behavior.

Discuss: *"Do as I say, not as I do."*

A child's play offers many opportunities for growth and development.

Discuss: *Do adults "play" like children?*

LOOK AROUND

1. Compare breast and bottle feeding.
2. What are advantages and disadvantages of getting a baby "all dressed up"?
3. What is empathy? How do we become empathetic? How is empathy shown between a child and an adult?
4. What information should junior high school babysitters have?
5. Name ways that children play. What are the values of each?
6. List agencies in your community that are involved in child care.
7. What are some games which help a child to interact with others?
8. What are some children's games which stimulate imaginative growth?

FOLLOW YOUR PATH

PATH ONE: Form a Newspaper

Step 12 Speak with your classmates from the Path Two community center. Gather as much information as you can about their facilities and write an article.

Step 13 Write an article on "Bathing the Baby." Include information about various bassinettes and bassinette substitutes. Price these articles in various stores.

PATH TWO: Plan and Operate a Community Center

Step 22 Prepare a commercial for the TV soap opera in Path Four. The point will be to convince parents that your center provides a safe environment for children.

Step 23 Go back to your model for a mural. Fill in the rest of the background. Behind the adults, show some of the resources helpful for prospective and new parents. Behind the infants and children, show some of the resources that can contribute a safe environment in which they can develop.

PATH THREE: Form a Family Court

Step 17 Visit the Path Two center. Examine their floor plans and list of activities.

Step 18 Visit at least three child care facilities in your community.

Step 19 Prepare a report on Step 18.

Step 20 Does the court believe that the Path Two community center provides adequate facilities to supply the child care services it wishes to provide? If not, what improvements would you recommend?

PATH FOUR: Produce a TV Soap Opera

Step 20 Visit with your classmates from the Path Two community center. Find out about their programs. Examine their floor plans. Ask any questions you might have.

Step 21 Plan an episode in which you discuss the possibility of doing volunteer work for the Path Two community center.

Step 22 Enact the episode.

CHAPTER 27

Careers In Human Services

In earlier career chapters, it was possible to speak of a food *industry*, a clothing *industry*, and a housing *industry*. There is no human-services industry to speak of, yet of the many occupational fields from which you might choose, the field of human services offers a special kind of satisfaction and reward—that which comes from working with and doing things directly for people. Careers in human services require of the worker at every level, both competency and concern for others. The special quality that sets these careers apart is that of human empathy —the ability to "feel" for people at every age and in every circumstance of life.

THE RANGE OF CAREERS IN HUMAN SERVICES

Careers in human services have increased almost 10 percent over the last decade and will continue to increase in the years to come. Modern living causes stresses in human relationships that were unknown a century ago. These stresses affect both individuals and families. The widened scope of life and career opportunities for women in recent years has created an overwhelming demand for competent, reliable, and concerned child-care services. The extended human life that science has made possible has increased the need for care, attention, and concern for older people.

Caring For the Family

The increased mobility of families has removed some of the comfort and in-home support that families of earlier times took for granted. Families today are separated by great distances. Public and private agencies have moved to fill the gaps created by our mobility. Scores of persons in every city and town are serving individuals and families in various ways.

How have family agencies in your community touched you and your family? Do you belong to a church? Are there service agencies for families in trouble, such as a family crisis intervention center? Does your community have adequate recreation facilities for young and old? Does it have a mental health clinic, a public health department, or a Red Cross chapter? Does your community operate a senior citizens' center or a child-care center?

Caring For the Sick

Increased concern for the physical and mental well-being of our people places a heavy burden on existing medical personnel and facilities. Trained personnel are needed to perform the myriad of services for outpatient care. Outpatient care is offered for those who are not sick enough to be hospitalized, but who need supervision of medical or health problems.

Halfway houses, such as those now in existence for convalescent patients from mental institutions, are in great demand. Former prison inmates, drug addicts, and alcoholics can benefit from their services.

Retirement facilities, communities for senior citizens, and homes for the elderly are creating a need for paraprofessional

CHARITABLE ORGANIZATIONS

The Red Cross and the Salvation Army are two charitable organizations that employ professional directors and coordinators. Within these organizations, fund raising is systematized to support the many services provided.

The primary concern of the Red Cross is with disaster: floods, fires, wars, disease, and epidemics. Services of professionals, aides, and volunteers are needed. The Red Cross is international in scope and is often the only service available for communication with war prisoners.

The Salvation Army has a religious orientation and provides care to the "outcasts" or "dropouts" of society in missions where food, shelter, and clothing are provided free to any or all in need. Organized charity and support are the primary services. Training is available through the organization. Aides, volunteers, and community members are needed to help in the many services that this organization provides.

health staffs to provide a wide variety of services.

Home health aides or nurse's aides are needed for at-home care of family members. Any homemaker who has children and a home to maintain and who is bedridden is in need of visiting homemaker assistance.

Caring For the Aged

The gift of longer life creates an entire field of needs and specialized human services. Facilities for the semiconvalescent have increased tremendously in the last decade.

Providing transportation, providing beauty-salon and barbering services, preparing meals, and offering recreational activities all help the elderly to feel happy and pleased with the gift of longer life. Such work is a challenge and offers great rewards.

Young people can gain deep satisfaction helping older people. Their vitality can serve as a tonic for the elderly.

Caring For Children

Sociologists suggest that the time may come within our country when the care of children will be largely in the hands of specially trained professionals and paraprofessionals. Parents will care for their children only at certain times. Who will these specialists be? Among them will be directors of child-care centers, teachers, classroom assistants and aides, nutritionists—trained people of many kinds. Such programs will also require an entire realm of support staff. Among these will be secretaries, food-service personnel, and maintenance crews.

Have you ever done babysitting? Have you ever worked as a recreational aide at a playground? Have you ever been employed as a mother's helper? If so, you have already had experience in human service.

Traditionally, women have been considered the main force in child care. However, this idea is changing.

A society built around the nuclear family has little room for its elderly citizens. As the number of elderly people increases, care of the aged will become a very important area for careers in human services.

449

A career in child care offers an opportunity to contribute to the development of many human beings. With more and more mothers working outside the home, a large part of the socialization process takes place in schools, day-care centers, and recreation programs.

LADDERS AND LATTICES

Here we consider only a few of the careers in human services. This will give you an idea of what is involved in some of the wide variety of jobs that exist in this field.

Entry-level Jobs

Entry-level jobs in human services require no special training. Generally, the experiences obtained in one's own home and community are adequate background. This is certainly true of the careers considered here: those of child-care attendants and household workers.

Private household workers Private household workers are called by a number of different names, depending on the kind of work they do. *Maids* and *housekeepers* perform the widest variety of tasks. They take

responsibility for cleaning, washing, and straightening up a household. They may also buy, cook, serve food, and watch the children. The difference between the two is that housekeepers have more responsibility. They actually take charge of running the home. The *day worker* is one who works on a daily or hourly basis. This job offers some advantages to those who may want part-time work.

Launderers, laundresses, and *cooks* perform only their specific tasks. Unlike other household workers, launderers and laundresses may work from their own homes.

Child-care attendants The principal qualification for becoming a child-care attendant is a desire to work with children. Child-care attendants work in institutions. They provide such functions as waking children in the morning, helping them throughout the day, and seeing that they rest securely at night. Child-care attendants supervise and lead children's recreational activities. The functions of child-care attendants range from giving comfort and taking disciplinary action to sewing on buttons. Some child-care attendants supervise housekeeping activities in particular sections of institutions.

Careers Requiring Special Skills

Especially in the health professions, there are a variety of careers requiring some special training, but not necessarily a college degree. These include x-ray technicians and the two careers considered here: dental hygienists and licensed practical nurses.

Dental hygienists Most dental hygienists work in private dental offices under the supervision of dentists. They clean patients' teeth. In the process of doing this, some may locate cavities and mark them on a chart for the dentists to inspect more closely. Dental hygienists may take and develop x-rays. They are responsible for sterilizing instruments and for mixing filling compounds. They may instruct patients about proper tooth brushing techniques and improved eating habits.

A pleasant personality is an important asset for a dental hygienist. Clean personal habits and fair manual dexterity are necessary to do this job.

To practice in most states, dental hygienists must pass a written examination and obtain a license. In most cases, to be eligible for this test, one must have completed a two-year course following high school. Some colleges include dental hygienic training in a four-year bachelor's degree program. This is an excellent career for those preferring part-time work.

Paraprofessional teachers relieve the teacher of administrative tasks, so that he or she has more time to devote to the students. They may also supervise meals and recreation, or work with groups of children while the teacher gives attention to individual students.

THE SITUATION *Georgia left the high school counselor's office, heartened by her interview with Mrs. Bowman. She had been discussing her work in the special household training program that she attended during regular school hours. Part of the program centered on actual work experience in private homes as a household aide. Students put to use information they had learned concerning cleaning a home, caring for children, catering parties, answering telephones — whatever a homemaker needed help with. Administrators of the vocational home economics program were careful to match student qualifications with particular jobs. The cooperation between homemakers and the school had been good so far.*

When Georgia had first heard of the training program, she had very little interest in knowing details of the curriculum. As a high school junior, she was having a difficult time at home and at school. Her father was unable to work as a result of a back injury. Money problems depressed the normally good spirits of family members. Georgia had tried to get a job, but her father insisted she complete high school. Concern with family problems led to lack of concentration on schoolwork. During the first marking period, Georgia got the worst grades she had ever gotten. She was called into the guidance office by Mrs. Bowman, her counselor. Mrs. Bowman introduced her to the work-study program. Within two weeks, she was enrolled.

THE INTERVIEW *Q: What were your first impressions of the program?*
A: I wasn't interested in cleaning somebody else's house. I have enough to do in my own.
Q: What changed your mind?
A: I thought about what Mrs. Bowman said about earning money. And I thought about the way it was part of the school program instead of something extra I'd have to do. I talked to kids who took the course. They liked it, and they don't feel ashamed about working in other people's houses. The wages I get are set in advance — not just what somebody feels like giving me.

The people we work for are real nice people and they like us — at least the people I work for like me. Mrs. Bowman is always ready to talk to us and help us.
Q: Why would some people feel ashamed about being household aides?
A: Because they think scrubbing floors and taking orders from people are low jobs. But they aren't. They pay money. Some of these people I work for have the dirtiest houses I've ever seen. There's a lot to know about organizing and planning when you run a house, and I'm learning it better than the people I work for. If I didn't do a better job than they do, they wouldn't have me.

REACT *Should people take care of their own household duties or hire others to help them? What are some problems that might occur in this type of work?*

Licensed practical nurses Most licensed practical nurses work in hospitals and nursing homes. Some work in private homes. They work under the supervision of medical doctors and registered nurses. (Registered nurses have more extensive and specialized training.)

Licensed practical nurses bathe patients. They change bandages. Under supervision, they can give medicine. They take temperatures and blood pressures. They may assist doctors and registered nurses in a variety of other tasks — the delivery of babies, for example. Licensed practical nurses working in homes may prepare meals. A large part of their job is in keeping up patients' morale. They may instruct family members about care of the patient.

To become a licensed practical nurse, one must pass a licensing examination. In most states, this must be preceded by at least two years of high school and a training program of one year. Many of those involved in such training programs receive financial assistance from the Federal government.

Management Careers

Management careers in many areas are in some respects interchangeable. Once one has acquired the needed skills in dealing with people and with budgets, and once one has learned how to make effective decisions, even when under pressure, one has a chance to move into a number of management careers. Here we consider two management careers in human services that are quite specialized. Most hospital administrators

This student nurse is training to become an RN, or registered nurse. Registered nurses require more training and education than practical nurses, and their responsibilities are greater. Registered nurses, like doctors, may specialize in one area of medical care.

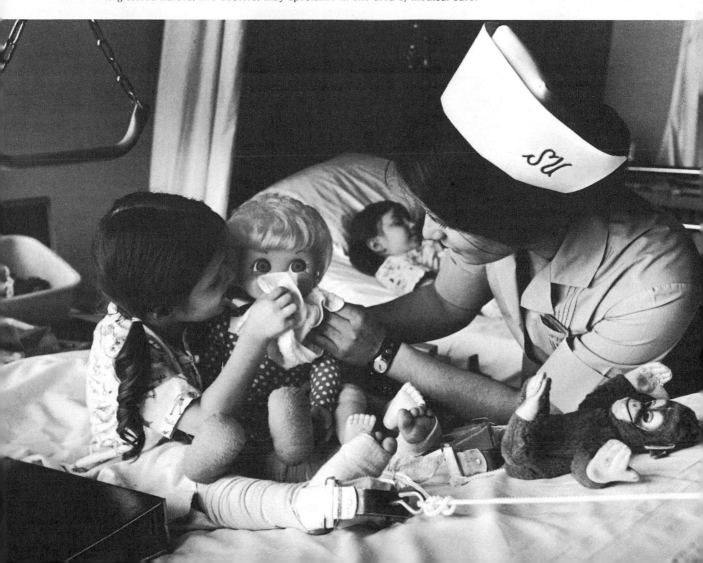

have specialized degrees, often in the field of public health. Day-care center directors manage, among other things, the daily affairs of small children.

Hospital administrators The management of hospital affairs is entrusted to hospital administrators. Small hospitals may have only one hospital administrator. Larger hospitals may have a number on staff.

Hospital administrators need skill in dealing with people. They are responsible for hiring personnel. They work with heads of various departments—nursing departments, for example—in setting up training programs. They bear general responsibility for representing their hospital to the public in fund-raising and building campaigns.

Hospital administrators also need the ability to organize and make plans. They plan and implement the hospital's budget. They supervise the purchasing of supplies and authorize the lease or purchase of equipment. They are responsible for seeing that equipment is properly used and maintained. Most hospital administrators have a master's degree in hospital administration.

Day-care directors Day-care centers may be operated by public or private agencies. They require licensing in most communities. Cost for child care in some facilities may be on a sliding scale, depending on the parents' ability to pay. Some may be organized on a cooperative basis, with parents donating hourly services in return for hourly child

In ministering to the spiritual needs of people, the clergy perform a valuable human service. Beyond conducting religious services, they give hope, comfort, and guidance to the lonely or distressed. They may also function as educators or administrators.

CASE STUDY: MRS. WRIGHT AND JUDGE REED

THE SITUATION *"That Judge Reed certainly was convincing! Why, the way he tells it, we'd have all our family problems cleared up in no time if we'd just put some of his ideas to work. Still, 'Volunteer for Victory' has some good things about it. There were lots of kids who needed someone to talk to."*

With that thought in mind, Mrs. Wright committed herself to working in Judge Reed's group of "Volunteer for Victory" citizens who would become responsible, on a one-to-one basis, for young people on probation. Nothing like this had been tried in the city yet, though other urban areas were examining the idea. It was a big enough step to volunteer for anything at all these days! People just seemed to want to stick to their own lives. And to volunteer to be responsible for the life of someone outside your own family! Well! That was risky business.

But Mrs. Wright didn't plan to have total responsibility for a youngster's life. The way she figured it, a person had to learn to be responsible for his own life. She intended to try to help "her child" see how it could be done. It wasn't something that would happen overnight, she admitted. She had raised four children of her own and knew what a job of "teaching" it took. She'd made her share of mistakes on her own kids. Some they laughed over. Others were still a little too new to joke about, but she expected they would laugh about those, too, after a while. And there was no guarantee that she'd be successful with kids who weren't her own.

Judge Reed had outlined a well-organized program. There were training sessions planned so volunteers could talk over their problems and try to figure ways of solving them. There were suggestions about the kinds of activities kids and their volunteer friends could do together. There were meet-ings planned with teachers and parents who could help Mrs. Wright and the other volunteers learn more about the youngsters they were trying to help. Maybe the program would work. Mrs. Wright would give it a try.

THE INTERVIEW *Q: Starting on your second family, Mrs. Wright?*
A: It looks that way, doesn't it? Here I am, retired, comfortable, free to do as I wish. You'd think I would have had enough of kids' problems the past thirty years. But life goes on. Someone always needs attention.
Q: What help can you give a youngster who is in trouble with the law at such a young age?
A: I wonder the same thing, to tell you the truth. But I think it depends on the person. There are some kids who are "hardcore" criminals even before they're fourteen, I'm sure. The way they've lived their lives might make them too difficult for anyone to influence. Those kids can't think any other way than bad. They're old before their time. But there are other kinds of children who need a break. They need someone to give them confidence, to help them think, and to provide a foundation. Maybe I can get along with someone in this group.
Q: Might the boy or girl in the program resent you?
A: That's a possibility. I have to be very careful not to lecture or to become a rigid teacher. We just have to live a normal life, getting to know and trust each other and getting to like one another. It might take more than anyone imagines. I just might fail.

REACT *What suggestions can you offer Mrs. Wright? What is the best kind of help to give to others? What kinds of problems might need to be overcome by all the people in this program?*

The Red Cross provides a variety of human services that range from running blood banks to operating service centers in disaster areas. Although it is staffed mainly by volunteers, there are paid, full-time personnel who organize and administer the various programs.

care. Day-care centers are licensed on the basis of their meeting certain health and safety standards.

Day-care centers usually operate from early in the morning until late in the evening. Some are open twenty-four hours a day.

Directors of a day-care center may supervise the work of teachers, assistant teachers, and aides. They may arrange to use the services of medical doctors, nurses, and nutritionists. At times, they may have to arrange for hospital care.

An advanced degree in social work or early childhood education, home economics, or a related field helps to prepare for this work.

Professionals

Doctors, clergymen, marriage counselors, recreation workers, home economists, and social workers are just a few of the many professionals working in human services.

Doctors Training for the medical profession begins with three or four years of undergraduate school with some specialization in science. This is followed by medical school (usually for another four years) and a year of internship. Residency for one or two years is required before a physician finally enters the specialized practice of medicine.

Medical specialists who treat and care for women prior to, during, and shortly after the birth of a baby are called *obstetricians*. Obstetricians carefully check the progress of pregnancy at regular intervals. They plan diets and exercises for the patient. They also deliver the baby. The services of obstetricians are in continuing demand. These specialists either operate their own offices with staff privileges at a local hospital or are permanently on a hospital or institutional staff.

Physicians who specialize in the care of children are called *pediatricians.* With modern concepts of postnatal care, their services are in great demand. Many are in private practice. They employ receptionists and nurses in their own specially equipped offices. In addition, private practitioners usually belong to and work on a hospital staff. Some pediatricians—including child psychiatrists—work exclusively through public agencies, hospital staffs, or medical health program plans.

Geriatricians specialize in care of the elderly. Their field needs many more trained specialists. The majority of geriatricians work through hospitals, institutions, or public health agencies; a few are on research teams with behavioral scientists.

Among medical doctors, only brain surgeons receive more extensive training than *psychiatrists,* who treat patients with emotional and mental problems. Psychiatrists can devote their treatment time to private practices and hospital staffs or industrial consultant facilities. Some consult with large corporations on questions regarding their employees. Many psychiatrists teach, write, and do research. As is the case with all specialists, psychiatrists study and learn all of their professional lives.

Since the 1940s, the trend of the medical profession towards specialization has created a scarcity of *family physicians.* The need is so great that some towns offer to provide a doctor with a home, car, clinic, and guaranteed income. Many such towns are still unable to locate a physician.

The family physician knows the parents, grandparents, children, and neighbors of a patient. He is concerned with the total well-being of the family unit. Medical schools now offer specialization in family medicine and encourage students to choose this field.

Marriage counselors Marriage counselors have usually had training in such social sciences as psychology and sociology. They also have considerable experience in field work with marriage counselors who are already practicing. Licensing is required in a few states. Professional associations have specific degree requirements which someone must meet if he is desirous of qualifying for membership.

Marriage counselors in private practice may have clients referred to them by lawyers, judges, psychiatrists, or family courts. Some marriage counselors are salaried staff members of mental health clinics and public service agencies, not to mention family courts.

Marriage counselors meet individually with family members as well as with the entire family. They also work with premarital couples and church groups. Sometimes they work with cases of desertion, child abuse, or potential suicide.

IN CONCLUSION: A HOPE

The limits set on careers in human service in this chapter are arbitrary. We could easily have considered farmers: they do us a service in supplying us with food. Similar services are provided to us by textile dyers and dress designers and by furniture upholsterers and bricklayers. What about toy designers and book publishers? Perhaps it could fairly be said that the only activities that are not human services are those that somehow deplete the resources of our environment or do harm to other human beings. Of course, we all engage in human service from time to time, often in the process of being helpful. The authors would like to think of *Personal Perspectives* as a human service. They hope it has helped you, in some way, to clarify your values as you plan your life.

457

THINK BACK

Careers in human services offer opportunities to work with people of all ages.
Discuss: *What kind of job is available for the person who declares he "dislikes people"?*

Improving the quality of individual and family life is a sound basis for working in human services.
Discuss: *Should a person avoid becoming personally involved in his work?*

Job possibilities exist for a wide range of skills, training, and educational background.
Discuss: *What help could you offer the person who feels he "can't do anything very well"?*

Work in human services can originate at home, in public agencies, or in private agencies.
Discuss: *How effective is a "bureaucratic" agency in helping its clients?*

LOOK AROUND

1. Develop a poster showing some of the jobs serving people at different ages.
2. How can your knowledge of developing satisfactory relationships with others be applied in a job situation?
3. Might people who have difficulty in relating with others work successfully in a human services career? Read the "Coping Strategies" section of Chapter 1 again before answering.
4. Consult your local telephone directory. Catalog the public and private agencies offering work in human services in your county. What kinds of jobs do you think are available within each agency?
5. Develop a "We Need You!" bulletin board that highlights opportunities for volunteer work with people in and around your community.
6. Very often, when people are turned down for or fired from a job, they are not given the real reason why. What do you think some of these real reasons are? Why do you think this is so?
7. Why do employers ask for personal references on a job application? What can an employer expect to learn from a reference about a potential employee?

FOLLOW YOUR PATH

PATH ONE: Form a Newspaper

Step 14 Make a chart showing all the different kinds of jobs with which you had some contact in following this path.
Step 15 Might you be interested in a career related to your activities on this path? Write a short theme about this. For further information, consult your guidance counselor.

PATH TWO: Plan and Operate a Community Center

Steps 24 and 25 Same as Steps 14 and 15 of Path One.

PATH THREE: Form a Family Court

Steps 21 and 22 Same as Steps 14 and 15 of Path One.

PATH FOUR: Produce a TV Soap Opera

Steps 23 and 24 Same as Steps 14 and 15 of Path One.

Index

Management
energy 74, 76, 77; money 78, 79, 370, 371; resource 67; time 74, 76, 77
"Man-Making" (Edwin Markham) 372
Marriage
and choices of alternative life-styles 373; career 93–95; housing location 307–309; mate-selection factors 406–408
individual 402; and communication in 406–407; courtship 409; engagement 410–412; sexual expression in 413; task sharing 148–149; weddings 412
models: contemporary, romantic, traditional 400–403
types: monogamous 399; parental 402–403; plural 400; polygamous 400
Maslow, Abraham 14, 15
Materials. *See also* Housing, Clothing
building 268–270: regional 286–287, 288; traditional construction 292–294
clothing 199–210; bonded, woven, knit fabrics 206–208; finishes 209–210; man-made fibers of acetate, acrylic, nylon, polyester, rayon 203–205; natural fibers of cotton, flax, silk, wool 200–202
Material Values 36–37
and clothing 192–194; consumer choices 87; *drive for status 36;* employment 370; food choices 109; goals and standards 40–42, 52; judgement 38; measured by money 70; and worth in job market 370
Maturity
in adults 23–25; children 22; parenthood 429; social life 375
and decision making 49, 57, 65; developmental stages 21–25; environment and heredity 26; individual differences 25;
physical 21, 25, 59, 201
psychological 20–21, 25–26, 59, 429
Mead, Dr. Margaret 402
Meals 135–149
buying food 152, 155–159; cooking 155–156, 158, 160; cultural patterns 111; equipment 143–144, 317, 342; formal and informal occasions 138–139; kitchen facilities 315–317; nutritional needs *(food selection guide) 130,* 142; planning for 136–142; resources and recipes 142–143, 147; table settings 136, 138, 140
Measurement
of foods 158, 162–164; and use of energy, money, time 68–69
standards of 42
Meat-group Foods 130
buying 155–160; standards of quality 155
types: meat 155, 156, 158; eggs 159; fish 159–160; poultry 158
as source of: cholesterol 122; minerals 125, 130; proteins 121, 130; vitamins 126, 129, 130
Milk-group Foods 130–132
buying 160–162
types: cheese 162; milk 160–161
as source of: cholesterol 122; minerals, 125–130; proteins 121–130; vitamins 126, 128, 129–130

Minerals 123–126
macronutrients 123–125; micronutrients 125–126; in rice and cereal 163
Moral Values 38
and consumer behavior 85; and goals and standards 42–43, 48, 52, 64, 85; independence 368, 371–372; personal morality 36, 375, 378–379
Mortgages. *See* Housing, Laws

Needs 6–15
meeting: in career choice 92; clothing 7, 181, 184, 186–188, 197; with coping strategies 15; as consumer 84, 87; family 398–399; and independence 368; intelligence 30; marriage 405–406; maturity 20; parenthood 429; in social life 13, 55, 375–377, 382
overarching needs 14, 276
physical needs 6–7: and children 421, 429; for food 104, 106–107, 119, 136; housing 273; society 13
psychological needs 7–10: for food 104, 136; love 7, 392–394; personal identity 8, 392; recognition 389; safety and security 7; stimulation and variety 10
social needs 10–14: to achieve 13; for approval 13; to belong 10–13; for food 104–108, 136; friends 375–378; housing 275, 310; interpersonal relationships 377; recognition 13; self-fulfillment 14; status 407–408
spiritual needs 14: and housing 276, 311; self-fulfillment 14
Nourishment. *See* Food, Nutrition
"Nowhere Man" (Lennon and McCartney) 42
Nutrition, Nutrients
food: groups 130–133; infant formulas 435; labeling 164; meat 155; menu planning 140, 142, 149; *selection guide to balanced diet 130*
nutrients: carbohydrates, fats and oils, minerals, proteins, vitamins 120–133; macronutrients, micronutrients 123–126; water 120
personal nutrition: appearance 116; digestion 120; education in 113, human ecology 104; prenatal care 424; psychological needs 107

Occupations. *See* Careers
Orpen, Sir William, "Leading the Life in the West" 368

Parenthood. *See also* Family
and adoption 416–421; *illustration 420;* childbirth; cost of raising children 418; foster parents 416, 421; heredity 418–421; pregnancy 423–424; planning for 415–422; rewards of 429
Peer Group
and clothing 188, 288; need to belong 13, 15
Personality, Personal Identity
affected by: clothing 186–187, 189, 193–194, 219–220, 222–223; grooming 185, 195; environment 30; housing 275; human resources 43; individual differences 30; life-style 222; nutrition 116; personal commitments 381; play 442

Credits

Acknowledgment is gratefully made to the following publishers, artists, museums, galleries, collectors, libraries, photo collections, and companies for their gracious and generous assistance in making possible the reproduction of the art and documentary material for this text.

Key for positions: T (top), C (center), R (right), L (left), B (bottom), and any combination of these, such as TC (top center).

Page 59: from "A Shropshire Lad," authorized edition, from *The Collected Poems of A. E. Housman.* Copyright 1939, 1940, © 1959 by Holt, Rinehart and Winston, Inc. Copyright © 1967, 1968 by Robert E. Symons. Reprinted by permission of Holt, Rinehart and Winston, Inc.

Page 271: reprinted from *Autobiography,* by Frank Lloyd Wright, revised edition, copyright © 1943, by permission of Mrs. Frank Lloyd Wright.

Page 42: from "Nowhere Man," by Lennon and McCartney, copyright © 1965, Northern Songs, Limited, used by permission, all rights reserved.

Page 106: from "Prayer for Children," by Francis Cardinal Spellman, copyright © 1944, reprinted by permission of Terence Cardinal Cooke and The New York Foundling Hospital.

Page 30: reprinted from "The Rich Boy," by F. Scott Fitzgerald, *The Fitzgerald Reader,* copyright © 1963, Charles Scribner's Sons, New York. Reprinted by permission of Charles Scribner's Sons.

Page 275: from "The Two Houses," by Thomas Hardy, from *Collected Poems,* copyright © 1925, The Macmillan Company, New York. Reprinted by permission of The Macmillan Company, the Trustees of the Hardy Estate, Macmillan London and Basingstoke, and The Macmillan Company of Canada, Limited.

Page 93: from "Two Tramps in Mud Time," from *The Poetry of Robert Frost,* edited by Edward Connery Lathem. Copyright 1936 by Robert Frost. Copyright © 1964 by Lesley Frost Ballantine. Copyright © 1969 by Holt, Rinehart and Winston, Inc. Reprinted by permission of Holt, Rinehart and Winston, Inc.

Alpha Photo Associates, Inc.: Max Eckert 320, Koepper 297, Zimmerman 326; American Institute of Baking: 174; American Olean Tile Company: 321 (R); The American Red Cross: 456 (L&R); ARA Services, Inc.: 170; *Architecture: Drafting and Design* by D. E. Hepler and P. I. Wallach, © 1971, McGraw-Hill, Inc.: 314; Armstrong Cork Company: 318; Avon Products, Inc.: 196 (T&B): Austrian National Tourist Office: 135; The Baltimore Museum of Art: "Woman With Mango," 1892, by Paul Gaugin, Cone Collection, 185; Shalmon Bernstein: 78, 111, 167, 172 (L), 247, 307, 309, 311, 337, 345, 346, 351, 356, 357, 377, 385, 387, 389, 390, 392, 402, 408, 409, 410; The Bettmann Archive, Inc.: 32 (T&B), 287 (TL), 421; Black Star: Bob Fitch 373, Dr. M. P. Kahl 189 (T), Fred Kaplan 231, Dan Landi 187 (TR), John Launois 332, Sandra Petellin Miller 443, Charles Moore 340, Ted Spiegel 454; Brown Brothers: 192 (TL); Cityarts Workshop, Inc.: 48; Clairol, Inc.: 260; Robert E. Coates: 164; Karen Collidge: 121; Comark Plastics: 333; Cone Mills Marketing Company: 200 (L&R), 225 (TR); Creighton-Brandfonbrener: 141 (L&R); Crompton–Richmond Company, Inc.: 208 (L&R); Culinary Institute of America: 172 (R); Culver Pictures, Inc.: 85, 202 (T); Rick Davis: 12 (TL); DeWys, Inc.: Joyce Brusse 361; DPI, Inc.: Horst Schafer 188, Jon Sinish 339; DuPont Company: 199, 203, 204 (TL), 205, 222 (TR), 225 (TL, BL, BR); Editorial Photocolor Archives, Inc.: 7, 8, 46 (TR), 53, 67, 72, 73, 80, 107, 109, 114 (TL), 125, 151, 194, 240, 285 (R), 286, 287 (B), 331, 458, Marion Bernstein 106, 399, Daniel S. Brody 415, E. V. Harris 169, Ellen Levine 23, David Robinson 21 (L), Andrew Sacks 51; Eleanor Lambert, Inc.: 253; Estee Lauder, Inc.: 196 (C); *Family Circle:* March 1972, 316, February 1972, 324; Fashion Institute of Technology: 251; Laurence Fink: 258; FMC Corp.: 202 (B); FPG: George Schwartz 39; Joshua Friewald: 292; General Foods Kitchens: 126, 142; Gerber Products Company: 110 (T), 433, 435; Grant Heilman: 6; Mark Hispard, *Modern Bride Magazine:* 209 (L); Honeywell, Inc.: 76; Jeannette Ingold: 96; Institute of Rehabilitation Medicine, NYU Medical Center: 273; Italian Government Travel Office: 285 (L); Japan Air Lines: 12 (TR); The Joseph P. Kennedy, Jr. Foundation: 445 (B); Kaiser Aluminum: 344; © King Features Syndicate: 401; Kohler Company: 321 (L); The Kraft Kitchens: 161 (L&R); Lane Bryant, Inc.: 191 (L); Lennox China: 140; Levi Strauss & Company 227 (L&R); Levitt & Sons, photo by Cyril Morris: 358; Magnum Photos, Inc.: Micha Bar-Am 19, Wayne Miller 388, © Marc Riboud 381; Massey Jr. College: 245 (L&R); Helen Mather: 445 (T); The Maytag Company: 354; McCall's Patterns: 257; Norman McGrath: 300 (L&R), 325; The Metropolitan Museum of Art, New York: Bruegel, Pieter, the Elder: "The Harvesters," detail: lower left, figures in field, Rogers Fund, 1919: 105; Sterne, Maurice: "The Winding Path," bequest of Samuel A. Lewisohn, 1951: 269; Orpen, Sir William: "Leading the Life in the West," Gift of George F. Baker, 1914: 369; Milton Bradley Company: 439; Mobile Homes Manufacturers Assn.: 293; Monkmeyer: Phil Carol 5, Sam Falk 21 (R), Nancy Hays 55, Hugh Rogers 35, 69; Monsanto Textiles Company: 204 (BL&R); Cyril Morris: 407; The Museum of Modern Art Film Stills Archive: 215;

Nancy Palmer Photo Agency: Ron Sherman 453; NASA: 83; National Broiler Council: 159; National Homes Corp.: 283, 295; National Livestock & Meat Board: 156 (B); National Marine Fisheries Service: 160; New Jersey Bell Telephone: 37; The N.Y.C. Board of Education: 451; The New York *Daily News*: 244; New York Hospital–Cornell Medical Center: 177; The New York Public Library Picture Collection: 229 (R), 272; *The New York Times*: 191 (R), 334; Norwegian National Travel Office: 405; Oneida, Ltd.: 137; Owens-Corning Fiberglas: 301, 327, 328; Pix, Inc.: Vytas Valaitis 46 (TL); Photo Researchers, Inc.: Van Bucher 280, Arvil K. Daniels 313, Lynn K. Daniels 276, Margaret Durrance 420, Larry Mulvehill 412 (B); Photo Trends: John Linkletter 84; Rapho-Guillmette: Christa Armstrong 94 (L), Marc & Evelyn Bernheim 12 (B), Hella Hammid 457, Inger McCabe 427 (L), Bob Smith 46 (B); Reynolds Metals Company: 148; Dennis Rizzuto: 219, 256; Shoji Sadao: 348; The Salvation Army: 447; Walter Schwarz: 308; Sears Roebuck and Company: 88, 206, 232; Seldin Development & Management Company: 296; Servicemaster Industries, Inc.: 353 (L&R); Shostal Associates: Sid Avery 378, Ed Cooper 288, G. Kubica 108, S. Labrot ii–iii, F. Olson 123; Simplicity Pattern Company: 216 (L&C); Simplicity Pattern Company and *Good Housekeeping Needlecraft*: 216 (R); Ezra Stoller © ESTO: 289; Synoptic Systems Corporation: 236; Suzanne Szasz: 427 (R); Frank Tartaglia: 438; 3M Company: 209 (R); Trans World Airlines, Inc.: 229 (L); Paul Tucker: 16, 110 (B), 119, 370; UNICEF: 122; United Press International: 43, 86, 94 (R); United States Department of Agriculture: 113, 155, 156 (T), 207 (L) (C) (R); Peter Vadnai: xiv–1, 3, 45, 57, 58, 100–101, 103, 116, 128, 129, 144 (TL), 153 (T), 176, 178, 180–181, 183, 235, 238, 241, 243, 248, 254, 264–265, 267, 364–365, 367, 398, 404, 416, 423, 424, 425, 428, 431, 436, 437, 441, 442, 444, 449, 450; V-Dia-Scala: 14; Vera Industries: 261; The Wallcovering Industry Bureau: 323; Wide World Photos: 270, 397; Window Shade Manufacturers Assn.: 278; The Wool Bureau, Inc.: 201 (L&R); Donald Yeager: 124.

Artists

Victoria deLarrea: v, vii–ix, xii–xiii, 24, 41, 61, 62, 63, 97, 131, 195, 212–213, 221, 303, 304, 384

Lee Lorenz: 4, 10, 36, 56, 64, 77, 87, 114, 138, 144, 147, 153, 187, 189, 192, 222, 224, 237, 242, 277, 302, 341, 372, 375, 382, 386, 412

Santo Scarzafava: 15, 27, 29, 68, 92, 157, 193, 211, 315, 336, 418 (adapted by permission of The New York *Daily News*), 419

5 6 7 8 9 10 VHVH 82 81 80 79 78 77 76